ENEMYSHIP

RHETORIC AND PUBLIC AFFAIRS SERIES

- *Eisenhower's War of Words: Rhetoric and Leadership*, Martin J. Medhurst, editor
- *The Nuclear Freeze Campaign: Rhetoric and Foreign Policy in the Telepolitical Age*, J. Michael Hogan
- *Mansfield and Vietnam: A Study in Rhetorical Adaptation*, Gregory A. Olson
- *Truman and the Hiroshima Cult*, Robert P. Newman
- *Post-Realism: The Rhetorical Turn in International Relations*, Francis A. Beer and Robert Hariman, editors
- *Rhetoric and Political Culture in Nineteenth-Century America*, Thomas W. Benson, editor
- *Frederick Douglass: Freedom's Voice, 1818–1845*, Gregory P. Lampe
- *Angelina Grimké: Rhetoric, Identity, and the Radical Imagination*, Stephen Howard Browne
- *Strategic Deception: Rhetoric, Science, and Politics in Missile Defense Advocacy*, Gordon R. Mitchell
- *Rostow, Kennedy, and the Rhetoric of Foreign Aid*, Kimber Charles Pearce
- *Visions of Poverty: Welfare Policy and Political Imagination*, Robert Asen
- *General Eisenhower: Ideology and Discourse*, Ira Chernus
- *The Reconstruction Desegregation Debate: The Politics of Equality and the Rhetoric of Place, 1870–1875*, Kirt H. Wilson
- *Shared Land/Conflicting Identity: Trajectories of Israeli and Palestinian Symbol Use*, Robert C. Rowland and David A. Frank
- *Darwinism, Design, and Public Education*, John Angus Campbell and Stephen C. Meyer, editors
- *Religious Expression and the American Constitution*, Franklyn S. Haiman
- *Christianity and the Mass Media in America: Toward a Democratic Accommodation*, Quentin J. Schultze

- *Bending Spines: The Propagandas of Nazi Germany and the German Democratic Republic*, Randall L. Bytwerk
- *Malcolm X: Inventing Radical Judgment*, Robert E. Terrill
- *Metaphorical World Politics*, Francis A. Beer and Christ'l De Landtsheer, editors
- *The Lyceum and Public Culture in the Nineteenth-Century United States*, Angela G. Ray
- *The Political Style of Conspiracy: Chase, Sumner, and Lincoln*, Michael William Pfau
- *The Character of Justice: Rhetoric, Law, and Politics in the Supreme Court Confirmation Process*, Trevor Parry-Giles
- *Rhetorical Vectors of Memory in National and International Holocaust Trials*, Marouf A. Hasian Jr.
- *Judging the Supreme Court: Constructions of Motives in Bush v. Gore*, Clarke Rountree
- *Everyday Subversion: From Joking to Revolting in the German Democratic Republic*, Kerry Kathleen Riley
- *In the Wake of Violence: Image and Social Reform*, Cheryl R. Jorgensen-Earp
- *Rhetoric and Democracy: Pedagogical and Political Practices*, Todd F. McDorman and David M. Timmerman, editors
- *Invoking the Invisible Hand: Social Security and the Privatization Debates*, Robert Asen
- *With Faith in the Works of Words: The Beginnings of Reconciliation in South Africa, 1985–1995*, Erik Doxtader
- *Public Address and Moral Judgment: Critical Studies in Ethical Tensions*, Shawn J. Parry-Giles and Trevor Parry-Giles, editors
- *Executing Democracy: Capital Punishment and the Making of America, 1683–1807*, Stephen John Hartnett

ENEMYSHIP

DEMOCRACY AND COUNTER-REVOLUTION
IN THE EARLY REPUBLIC

Jeremy Engels

MICHIGAN STATE UNIVERSITY PRESS • *East Lansing*

Michigan State University Press
East Lansing, Michigan 48823-5245

Printed and bound in the United States of America.

19 18 17 16 15 14 13 12 11 10   1 2 3 4 5 6 7 8 9 10

LIBRARY OF CONGRESS CATALOGING-IN-PUBLICATION DATA
Engels, Jeremy.
Enemyship : democracy and counter-revolution in the early republic / Jeremy Engels.
p. cm.—(Rhetoric and public affairs series)
Includes bibliographical references and index.
ISBN 978-0-87013-980-2 (cloth : alk. paper) 1. United States—Politics and government—1783–1809. 2. United States—History—Revolution, 1775–1783—Social aspects. 3. Political culture—United States—History—18th century. 4. Enemies—Political aspects—United States—History. 5. Democracy—United States—History—18th century. 6. Nationalism—United States—History—18th century. 7. Rhetoric—Political aspects—United States—History—18th century. 8. Political socialization—United States—History—18th century. I. Title.
E302.1.E54 2010
973.3'1—dc22
2010003508

Cover design by Heather Truelove
Book design and typography by Charlie Sharp, Sharp Des!gns, Lansing, Michigan

Visit Michigan State University Press on the World Wide Web at *www.msupress.msu.edu*

The American war is over; but this is far from being the case with the American revolution. On the contrary, nothing but the first act of the great drama is closed. It remains yet to establish and perfect our new forms of government; and to prepare the principles, morals, and manners of our citizens, for these forms of government.

BENJAMIN RUSH, "Address to the People of the United States," 1787

Contents

Acknowledgments

A s solitary and, frankly, lonely as the work of an academic can be and often is, good scholarship is the product of many conversations and interactions. Several people had a direct role in making this book happen. Stephen Hartnett, Cara Finnegan, Ned O'Gorman, Fred Hoxie, and David Zarefsky read this manuscript back in 2006 when it was a quickly written—perhaps *too* quickly written—dissertation that I needed to finish so I could start my job at Penn State. Their patience through the process, as well as the many hours each of them spent taking ideas and improving my writing, made me a better scholar and this book a better book. I hope that they find this final version of *Enemyship* unrecognizable and that it puts the memory of that harried dissertation out of their minds. Marty Medhurst has been my editor for this project and for several essays in *R&PA*. Supportive and kind, yet challenging and blunt, I could not ask for a better editor or advocate. Had Marty not exercised his editorial hand—and had the excellent reviewers for Michigan State University Press not had their say—this would have been a very different book, probably unreadable, too theoretical to the point of being historically anachronistic, and certainly not as interesting. My dear friends Greg Goodale, Mike Tumolo, Donovan Conley, and Ryan Blum read the manuscript at multiple stages of development. For that I am grateful, though I am even more grateful for their friendship. A big thanks goes out to my rhetoric colleagues at Penn State for welcoming me into the community. I'd especially like to thank Mike Hogan for being such a good friend and mentor—our afternoons sitting outside at Otto's have been some of my happiest in Happy Valley. Many others deserve thanks in one way or another, for reading parts of the manuscript, for commenting on presentations where I discussed ideas central to the book, for chatting about rhetoric and history more generally, and, quite simply, for inspiring my work: Bob Ivie, Dave Tell, John Murphy, Jim Jasinski, Lester Olson, Chuck Morris, Tom Conley, Brad Vivian, Jenny Biedendorf, Nate Stormer, Josh Gunn, Chris Lundberg, Kendall Phillips, Mitch Reyes, Mike Butterworth, Beth Innocenti, Jen Mercieca, Ray McKerrow, Dan Larson, Vince Pham, Anna Nielson, Troy Cooper, Kassie Lamp, Robin Jensen, Jiyeon Kang, Rich Besel, Darren Mulloy, James Hay, Matti Bunzl, Rachel DeLue, Max Edelson, Dana Nelson, Chris Castiglia, Sophia Mc-Clennen, Mike Elavsky, John Christman, David Roediger, Sara Ann Mehltretter, Eric Fuchs, John Lucaites, Aric Putnam, Pat Gehrke, Nathan Crick, Bob Hariman, Pete Simonson, Robin Rowland, and Bob Antonio. Much of what is good about this book is due to their insights, though the faults are, sadly, all of my own. Were it not for the inspiration provided by Andrew Davis, Kay Davis, and Greg Shepherd, I'm not sure I would be an academic—to Andrew, Kay, and Greg, my academic family, you have all my love. Last, but not least, a big thanks to my family. My parents-in-law, Jim and MaryLou Sunderland, and my sis, Katie Sunderland, have welcomed me into their family as though I was one of their own—thanks for always being so amazing to me, for putting up with my bad skiing, and for letting me win at Scrabble that one time. My parents, David and Cathy Engels, sacrificed so much to ensure that I had a good education and to make sure that I was happy. I literally owe you everything. My brother,

Nate Engels, will always be a rock-star in my book. And, finally, I cannot thank my dearest love Anna enough. There are no words for what you mean to me, and I study words. Thanks for always being there, in Kansas, in Illinois, in Pennsylvania, and wherever is next.

ENEMYSHIP

The Second American Revolution

The date was April 13, 1943—the 200th anniversary of Thomas Jefferson's birth. The place was Washington, DC. The occasion was the dedication of the Thomas Jefferson Memorial. "Today in the midst of a great war for freedom we dedicate a shrine to freedom," President Franklin Delano Roosevelt proclaimed, using Jefferson's memory to bridge the chasm between the American Revolution and World War II. In the midst of this grueling conflict, President Roosevelt suggested that Americans were dying in Europe for the same reason that they died during the Revolutionary War: to fight tyranny in all its forms. The president observed that "Thomas Jefferson believed, as we believe, in man. He believed, as we believe, that men are capable of their own government and that no king, no tyrant, no dictator can govern for them as wisely as they can for themselves."[1] Jefferson had, in short, what John Dewey called the "democratic faith": an unwavering belief in the moral composition of everyday people and the merit of self-government.[2] Building to an eloquent climax, President Roosevelt simultaneously praised Jefferson and honored Americans fighting in Europe, Africa, and Asia by invoking a theme that would resonate with Americans both past and present: no king, no tyrant, no monarch—be he named King George or Adolf Hitler—would ever determine America's destiny or deny the United States' proud tradition of self-government.

The centerpiece of the Jefferson Memorial is the larger-than-life, 10,000-pound, nineteen-foot-tall bronze statue of the third president that was installed in 1947. Looming just as large are Jefferson's words as etched into the memorial's Georgian white marble walls. "The words which we have chosen for this memorial speak Jefferson's noblest and most urgent meaning," President Roosevelt insisted.[3] But who is really speaking through the memorial? Is it Jefferson? Or someone else? While the sentences inside the Jefferson Memorial bear Jefferson's name, it is not at all clear that the historical Jefferson would have liked the words he was made to speak by the twentieth-century designers of his memorial, for the Jefferson Memorial presents a carefully edited, overly facile, and ultimately antiseptic Jefferson for public consumption. The memorial's Jefferson is a staunch foe of slavery, even though the historic Jefferson held more complex opinions on the subject.[4] Equally vexing, the memorial removes the crux of the Declaration of Independence, its justification for revolution. Finally, the memorial distorts Jefferson's doctrine of perpetual revolution as enumerated in one of his most famous letters. As such, the memorial completely misses one of Jefferson's most important contributions to American politics: his solution to the problematic legacy of revolution in the United States.

I begin with the Jefferson Memorial because it acts as a gateway into an argument that Americans have been having, with varying degrees of intensity, since the founding of our nation. The argument has to do with the loftiest subjects—with government, sovereignty, and power—but at bottom it is a rumpus about revolution and the place of democracy in our political landscape. Today, with Fourth of July fireworks and in little-kid plays, we celebrate the fact that the United States was born from a revolution against a greedy king and his petty bureaucrats. We tend to forget about the problems that revolution created once Great Britain was defeated. The conventional wisdom makes it seem as though the United States sprung forth from revolution like Athena from Zeus's head, fully formed and ready to scrap. As such, the period of intense post-Revolutionary conflict over the meaning of revolution and the future of a nation is lost, remembered only by conscientious historians and curious genealogists.

This book is about what happened, during the latter years of the Revolutionary War and in the immediate post-Revolutionary period, when the rhetorics and energies of revolution began to seem problematic to many wealthy and powerful Americans. In the 1780s and 1790s, the leaders of revolution began to worry that common folks, emboldened by talk of the power of the people and promises of democracy, would never submit to elite control over the economy and the levers of power. They worried, in short, that the rhetorics attacking British authority would undermine American authority as well. I begin with Jefferson to create perspective by incongruity, for he saw this problem differently than almost all of his fellow nation-builders. For him, the issue was how to perpetuate the spirit of revolution in post-Revolutionary times. For others, the issue was how to restrain the spirit of revolution in the difficult days of national formation. This was primarily a rhetorical problem, and it necessitated a rhetorical solution. To mitigate the dangers of revolution, the founders of the United States deployed what I call the rhetorics of "enemyship," while adapting these rhetorical strategies to the unique challenges of building a nation. As they did so, the founders set a precedent for how to govern that continues to resonate, even today.

When they took up arms against England in 1776, the revolutionaries faced a vexing rhetorical problem. According to the dictates of natural law, declaring war was lawful only when it was "necessary." It was therefore imperative that the Revolutionary War be portrayed as "natural." The challenge was to demonstrate that the American Revolution was an unavoidable revolution, not a disobedient rebellion, for revolution connoted a natural cycle akin to the revolution of the heavens, whereas rebellion was unlawful, wicked, and worthy of the swift retort of the king's army.[5] The need to portray independence as revolution and not rebellion explains the Declaration of Independence's list of twenty-eight grievances against King George III, designed to frame England's rule over the colonies as tyrannical and illegitimate, and the king as an enemy with whom there could be no concord. By giving causes for revolution and making it appear that revolution was natural, necessary, and enacted on behalf of "the people," the colonists' violence could be justified in the terms of natural law.

As the primary drafter of the Declaration, Jefferson's rhetorical maneuvers were based on an astute reading of available rhetorical traditions. In fact, England offered the colonies a long revolutionary precedent to draw upon. To justify the Glorious Revolution of 1688, John Locke claimed that the end of government was "the good of mankind," and that citizens were justified in revolting if their rulers "grow exorbitant in the use of their power, and employ it for the destruction, and not the preservation of the properties of their people."[6] The Declaration was clearly influenced by Locke's rationale for revolution, as it argued for the right to overthrow a nonrepresentative, tyrannical government:

> We hold these truths to be self-evident: That all men are created equal; that they are endowed by their Creator with certain unalienable rights; that among these are life, liberty, and the pursuit of happiness; that, to secure these rights, governments are instituted among men, deriving their just powers from the consent of the governed; that whenever any form of government becomes destructive of these ends, it is the right of the people to alter or to abolish it, and to institute new government, laying its foundation on such principles, and organizing its powers in such form, as to them shall seem most likely to effect their safety and happiness.

While this passage is rightly remembered as a remarkable (though limited) declaration of rights, it also sanctioned revolution. If a government abused the inalienable rights of life, liberty, and the pursuit of happiness, then it became the inalienable right of citizens to overthrow that government.

From a distance, the British philosopher Jeremy Bentham looked on aghast at this startling document. In his *Short Review of the Declaration*, published in 1776, Bentham expressed concern that the Declaration of Independence's state-toppling, monarch-defiling, over-the-top rhetorical delirium undid the foundations of government. He labeled the revolutionaries "fanatics" who "have put the axe to the root of all Government."

Their crime was producing an enduring defense of revolution that would rattle governments for ages to come. If this group of people could come together and "justify rebellion," why couldn't anyone draw up a list of grievances and revolt? Bentham believed that the Americans arrogantly and stupidly paved the way for bedlam. If the colonists could reject British government, Bentham reasoned, then any government could be discarded at any time, and "there never was, never can be, established, any government upon earth."[7]

The fact that Bentham's *Short Review of the Declaration* was anti-American propaganda did not make it wrong. In fact, it accurately forecast a pressing challenge of the postwar years: as politicians turned their minds toward the task of nation-building, the Declaration's timeless justification for state-toppling violence lived on in public memory, where it continued to sanction revolution in a nation in which mob violence, or "mobocracy" (as democracy was known to skeptics), was an accepted fact of social life.[8] This included burning effigies, tarring and feathering, and the infamous "Hillsborough Paintings," where hated officials were smeared with human feces.[9] Mob violence was the engine for social and political change in the 1760s and 1770s, and a way for poor and often disenfranchised citizens to make the fiction of popular sovereignty real. Though protests were highly ritualized and mobs rarely killed people, such tactics nevertheless threatened the emerging post-Revolutionary order.

Just as the Declaration of Independence drew on historical precedent and rhetorical tradition to justify change, so too would later generations of Americans mine their nation's early history and use the Declaration in the same manner. For example, take David Walker's courageous abolitionist tract, *Appeal to the Coloured Citizens of the World* (1829), which quoted the Declaration of Independence's words about equality and revolution and then pleaded, "See your Declaration Americans!! Do you understand your own language?" Walker admonished Americans for not following though on their own words, and, perhaps most dangerously, quoted the Declaration's justification of revolution to threaten his white readers. "Now, Americans! I ask you candidly, was your sufferings under Great Britain, one hundredth part as cruel and tyranical as you have rendered ours under you? Some of you, no doubt, believe that we will never throw off your murderous government and 'provide new guards for our future security.' If Satan has made you believe it, will he not deceive you?"[10] Here, Walker hinted at an enduring line of argument that would vex governing authorities for much of the eighteenth and nineteenth centuries: revolution, he claimed, was a legitimate option if "the people" (which for him included slaves and free black men) concluded that their rights were abused by government, and if they could rhetorically justify their actions to a "candid world." Walker stared down his readers by turning one of the nation's founding documents against slave owners and everyone else who was complicit in the political economy of slavery. As Walker threatened to instigate another revolution, he revealed a persistent danger to stability and order built right into the DNA of the United States.

The rhetorical power of the Declaration of Independence continued to inspire resistance to government well beyond the Revolutionary War.[11] It is therefore noteworthy that the Jefferson Memorial rewrites history to counter the original spirit and purpose of the Declaration of Independence by removing the justification for revolutionary violence from the shrine, displaying instead a strategically expurgated version of the Declaration that reads:

> We hold these truths to be self-evident that all men are created equal, that they are endowed by their Creator with certain unalienable rights, among these are life, liberty, and the pursuit of happiness, that to secure these rights governments are instituted among men. We . . . solemnly publish and declare, that these colonies are and of right ought to be free and independent states . . . And for the support of this declaration, with a firm reliance on the protection of divine providence, we mutually pledge our lives, our fortunes, and our sacred honour.

Notice that the phrases that justified revolution in 1776 are erased from the memorial. Although two edits from the Declaration's final paragraph are marked by ellipses (. . .), the words that sanctioned violence against an abusive government are expunged without record. This strategic misrepresentation significantly alters the meaning of the Declaration of Independence as it lives in public memory: whereas the original Declaration justified revolution against Britain and against "any form of government" that abused the rights of "the people," implying that the Declaration was a timeless document aimed at present and future oppression, the memorial twists the Declaration and makes it appear that it created "free and independent states" to which citizens would pledge their lives, fortunes, and sacred honors. The Jefferson Memorial transforms the Declaration of Independence from a government-destroying document into a nation-building one. Whereas Jefferson had defended the ability of "the people" to take matters into their own hands and topple abusive governments, and whereas most citizens in the 1770s accepted the legality of mobs and other forms of popular protest, the Jefferson Memorial erases both privileges from public memory.

In a 1973 issue of the *William and Mary Quarterly*, historian Frank Whitson Fetter wrote a stinging rebuke to the stupid tourists who had failed to notice that the Declaration of Independence had been altered by the designers of the Jefferson Memorial. Fetter wondered "why, in the thirty years in which the panel in the nation's capital has been seen by hundreds of thousands of persons—a number of whom undoubtedly had a Ph.D. in history or political science—no one appears to have called attention publicly to the mistakes on the panel." He explained Americans' myopia as a byproduct of tourism and television, for Americans had lost their ability to be critical. Moreover, he noted, "Youngsters, and even Ph.D.'s in American history, do not visit the Jefferson Memorial in the frame of mind with which they would examine the Jefferson archives. They are there to sense the grandeur of the Memorial and look at the vista of Washington." Fetter's main point is on target: though public memorials are reconstructions of history, they are presented as fact (not as fictions) and experienced as tourist attractions (not as attempts to persuade). The Declaration of Independence is a document that questions authority and sanctions revolution. By calling on visitors to passively accept the world as it is presented to them, the Jefferson Memorial itself embodies the antithesis of revolution.[12]

Fetter was right in spirit, but wrong on one crucial detail. He explained the memorial's changes of the Declaration as "mistakes on the panel." These were not mistakes. Nor was the Declaration chopped for aesthetic reasons. On the contrary, the careful editing of Jefferson's words in the 1940s was part of a cultural attempt, begun by politicians in the 1770s, to alter the radical collective consciousness of the United States by

carefully editing the Declaration of Independence and taming revolutionary democracy in order to build a nation. This becomes clear on a second
panel, which, like the Declaration, was edited to expunge revolutionary
possibilities and rhetorical contradictions from America's past.

The words on this panel are taken from one of Jefferson's most famous letters, written in 1816 to Samuel Kercheval. The panel reads:

> I am certainly not an advocate for frequent changes in laws and con-
> stitutions. But laws and institutions must go hand in hand with the
> progress of the human mind. As that becomes more developed, more
> enlightened, as new discoveries are made, new truths discovered and
> manners and opinions change, with the change of circumstances, in-
> stitutions must advance also to keep pace with the times. We might as
> well require a man to wear still the coat which fitted him when a boy
> as civilized society to remain ever under the regimen of their barbarous
> ancestors.[13]

The metaphor of the ill-fitting coat is one of Jefferson's most famous
statements, and this passage argues, as Jefferson did all of his life, that
government should advance along with its people. Here, the memorial
makes Jefferson a rhetorical precursor to, and a perfect spokesman for,
Roosevelt's progressive New Deal policies.

There is much from this letter that is excluded, however, making the
Jefferson Memorial's representation of it deeply problematic. By removing the context for Jefferson's statement that he was "not an advocate for
frequent changes in laws and constitutions," the memorial distorts Jefferson's main point about laws and constitutions. In this letter, Jefferson
responded to Kercheval's suggestion that the Virginia Constitution should
be revised, by arguing that periodic changes in constitutions were necessary in order to prevent further revolutionary bloodshed in the United
States. He told Kercheval that though "some men look at constitutions
with sanctimonious reverence, and deem them like the arc of the covenant, too sacred to be touched," nevertheless constitutions must keep
up with progress; therefore, "let us provide in our constitution for its revision at stated periods," which he determined (using the French naturalist
Buffon's mortality tables) to be every nineteen or twenty years. Periodic

revisions of the Constitution would act as a release for the pent-up frustrations that erupted in popular movements against the government, such as Shays's Rebellion and the Whiskey Rebellion, and would ensure that the commitment of citizens to their government was constantly renewed. Far from arguing for the sanctity of constitutions, Jefferson warned that if his plan was not followed, the bottling up of democratic discontent would eventually cause the nation to self-destruct. "If this avenue be shut to the call of sufferance," he concluded, "it will make itself heard through that of force, and we shall go on, as other nations are doing, in the endless circle of oppression, rebellion, reformation; and oppression, rebellion, reformation again; and so on forever." To end this "circle," Jefferson proposed channeling revolution into periodic revisions of the Constitution, and breaking up the nation into autonomous units of local self-governance.[14]

With the events of Shays's Rebellion not far from his mind, Jefferson made a similar proposal in 1789 to his friend James Madison, suggesting that "no society can make a perpetual constitution, or even a perpetual law. The earth belongs always to the living generation." Institutionalizing revolution in periodic revisions of the Constitution would provide citizens with a more constructive outlet for their democratic needs than a bloody revolution, he maintained, effectively rendering the need for citizens to invoke the state-toppling rhetoric of the Declaration of Independence nugatory. Jefferson was confident that his plan would "exclude, at the threshold of our new government the contagious and ruinous errors of this quarter of the globe, which have armed despots with means not sanctioned by nature for binding in chains their fellow-men." By removing the chance that despots could chain their subjects, and by building revolution into the system through periodic renewals of the laws and the Constitution, Jefferson believed that he solved the enduring problem of revolution that he himself had helped to cause.[15]

By transforming all laws, including the Constitution, into short-term rewritable contracts, Jefferson argued that the explosive spirit of revolution could be channeled into the creation of laws. Jefferson's plan for perpetual revolution was never implemented, however, and even his protégé rejected it as recklessly idealistic. Madison explained that Jefferson's plan was "not in *all* respects compatible with the course of human affairs." Madison couched his most devastating objection in the form of a

question: "Would not a Government so often revised become too mutable
to retain those prejudices in its favor which antiquity inspires, and which
are perhaps a salutary aid to the most rational Government in the most
enlightened age?" Of course it would, Madison argued, and he therefore concluded that periodic revisions of the Constitution would lead to
"anarchy." Madison highlighted the problems of Jefferson's ideas, which
would, he argued, destroy any possibility for lasting government and political stability. Other solutions to the dilemmas of American nationalism
were needed, Madison counseled Jefferson.[16]

When born, we are thrown into a world built upon traditions we did
not begin, and alive with conversations we did not initiate. Past rhetorical
productions consequently provide the foundation for present exigencies.
Though some tried, in the years following the Revolutionary War it was
impossible to do what the Jefferson Memorial did in the 1940s and simply
erase the problematic passages of the Declaration of Independence once
they had served their purpose. The revolutionaries invented arguments
justifying revolution that were wildly effective at spurring a colonial uprising against British authority. However, these arguments threatened political stability once independence was achieved. Given its revolutionary
past, the United States is founded on a series of dilemmas. To grow a nation born on the battlefield to maturity, politicians had to repress the very
revolution that brought their nation into being—for the Revolutionary
War taught resistance, but the Constitution demanded consent. Because
of their revolutionary heritage, Americans wanting to create a government
had to renege on, or at the very least rewrite, their history.

Jefferson was unique among the founders because he called for more,
and not less, democracy as a solution to the United States' problematic
relationship to revolution. Not surprisingly, given the boldness of his
democratic pronouncements in an age that feared democracy, Jefferson
has been hailed by democratic theorists as a visionary and an inspiration: from John Dewey to Hannah Arendt to more contemporary writers
including Richard Rorty, Benjamin Barber, and Richard Matthews, Jefferson is something of a hero. Dewey labeled Jefferson "our first great
democrat," and he justified a long exegesis of Jefferson's thought in one
of his final and most important works, *Freedom and Culture* (1939), because "he was the first modern to state in human terms the principles of

democracy."[17] Thanks to the work of philosophers including Dewey and Arendt, and rhetorical scholars including my colleague Stephen Howard Browne, we have a rich understanding of the Jeffersonian tradition and all that it entails.[18] This tradition is premised on almost total confidence in the individual's judgment and moral sense. Indeed, Jefferson instructed Kercheval: "I am not among those who fear the people. They, and not the rich, are our dependence for continued freedom."[19] The Jeffersonian tradition then calls on citizens, through the local community politics of the ward republics and through civic dialogue on a more national scale, to render their collective judgments on issues that affect them. Jefferson's solution to the problematic legacy of revolution was to educate, and then trust, citizens to judge for themselves what form of government was best. As he revealed during Shays's Rebellion, "I am persuaded myself that the good sense of the people will always be found to be the best army. They may be led astray for a moment, but will soon correct themselves. The people are the only censors of their governors: and even their errors will tend to keep these to the true principles of their institution."[20] In the Jeffersonian vision of American democracy, the people are the ultimate corrective to greedy bureaucrats and petty tyrants.

While Jefferson's writings offer a continued source of inspiration for democratic theorists, his solution to the dilemmas of American nationalism was not adopted by the elites who wrote the Constitution. Dewey himself noted that there was an alternative tradition in American politics, a foil to Jeffersonian democracy that he associated with Alexander Hamilton. "As long as there are different parties in the United States, there will be dispute as to the soundness of the respective political philosophies associated with the names of Hamilton and Jefferson," Dewey observed, reflecting on "our great fortune in having two extraordinarily able men formulate the fundamental principles upon which men divide."[21] Dewey was speaking, here, not only of economics—about Jefferson's bucolic pastoralism vs. Hamilton's industrial finance capitalism, which is how the difference between Jefferson and Hamilton is customarily troped. Dewey was also thinking of temperament, for Jefferson shared his democratic faith while Hamilton did not. This led these two founders to wildly divergent positions on the legacy of revolution. Jefferson hoped to prolong revolution; Hamilton hoped to stop it, once and for all.

Jefferson and Hamilton disagreed on the "fundamental principles" of politics, and their disagreement spawned wildly divergent rhetorical traditions. Jefferson spoke in hyperbolic terms about the virtue of the people, and excused violent uprisings because "the tree of liberty must be refreshed from time to time with the blood of patriots & tyrants."[22] Hamilton demeaned democratic governance as inherently and dangerously unstable and spoke sternly about the danger of the people erupting in acts of explosive violence. Jefferson's rhetorics of democratic faith became popular in the twentieth century, but they, like Jefferson's fame itself, were late in the coming.[23] In the early Republic, the rhetorics of democratic fear were dominant.

The democratic ideals that inspired many colonists to fight British tyranny—ideals that, at least initially, much of the gentry shared—became abhorrent to elites in the volatile postwar years, when democracy became a synonym for anarchy in public discourse. In Federalist 10, Madison argued that "democracies have ever been spectacles of turbulence and contention," and he concluded matter-of-factly that good politicians turned away from democracies because they "have, in general, been as short in their lives, as they have been violent in their deaths."[24] Adams wrote similarly, "Democracy never lasts long. It soon wastes, exhausts, and murders itself. There never was a democracy yet that did not commit suicide."[25] Madison, Adams, and other political leaders slandered democracy because they feared that weak-willed citizens could be manipulated by smooth-talking demagogues into unspeakable acts of destruction.[26]

Elbridge Gerry, one of Boston's leading sons and a signer of the Declaration of Independence, said as much. "The evils we experience flow from the excess of democracy. The people do not want virtue; but are the dupes of pretended patriots," he concluded, for "the people are uninformed, and would be misled by a few designing men."[27] Believing that a skilled orator could manipulate citizens and take control of the state by exploiting the weakness of individual judgment, Madison and Adams advocated for the less-democratic Constitution. Gerry, on the other hand, did not initially support the Constitution, because it failed to include a Bill of Rights. Though he was one of three delegates to the 1787 Convention who refused to sign the Constitution, he and his fellow dissidents shared the Federalists' view that democracy was a central cause of America's political and economic problems. Thus, while Gerry lamented the post-Revolutionary "excess of democracy," George Mason chastised the thirteen state governments for being "too democratic" (though he did express his fear that elites would "incautiously run into the opposite extreme," and called on his fellows to respect the "rights" of all Americans), and Mason's fellow Virginian Edmund Randolph observed that "the evils under which the U.S. laboured" were caused by "the turbulence and follies of democracy."[28]

Fearing the people, Hamilton and other counter-revolutionaries developed several rhetorical strategies for taming democracy and thereby negotiating the United States' problematic relationship to revolution. This book is about those counter-revolutionary strategies—which can, I argue, be grouped under the term "enemyship." Enemyship signifies the many ways that political actors name the enemy in order to achieve desirable rhetorical effects, which, in the early Republic, included unity, hierarchy, and deference. Unlike friendship, whose bonds are forged by mutual affection, enemyship is a bond of mutual antagonism for an enemy, resulting in a solidarity of fear, a community of spite, a kinship in arms, and a brotherhood of hatred. In the early Republic, counter-revolutionaries employed the rhetoric of enemyship to great effect, naming enemies to distract rowdy Americans from their political and economic grievances and to encourage allegiance to the Constitution by trading obedience for protection. Elites managed democracy by cultivating fears—some real, some imagined.

As we will see, Hamilton represented one face of enemyship as a counter-revolutionary strategy in the early Republic. Hugh Henry Brackenridge represented a second. And George Washington, Noah Webster, Benjamin Rush, and John Quincy Adams a third. All hoped that talk of the enemy would transform the many, and the democratic sentiments they espoused, into something easier to control. All made enemyship, in its many modalities, central to their counter-revolutionary efforts in the 1780s and 1790s. We should study these figures because their rhetoric was brilliantly adapted to the demands of the post-Revolutionary moment. We should study these figures because their rhetoric has proven historically resilient. We should study these figures, in short, because their rhetorical achievements continue to influence how citizens govern and are governed, even today.

Counter-Revolution

I am hardly the first to notice that there was a counter-revolution in the 1780s aimed at tempering the democratic impulses of revolution. Gordon Wood advanced this thesis in his 1969 masterpiece *The Creation of the American Republic.*[29] In turn, historians in recent years have extended Wood's work and greatly enriched our understanding of the complicated foundations of the United States. The Revolutionary War drew on a rich tradition of transatlantic political activism that brought together men and women of different races committed to winning a democratic victory against monarchy, Peter Linebaugh and Marcus Rediker observe. "The motley crew had helped to make the revolution, but the vanguard struck back in the 1770s and 1780s, against mobs, slaves, and sailors, in what must be considered an American Thermidor," they write, comparing the period following the American Revolution to the period of repression during the French Revolution after Robespierre was guillotined and the Reign of Terror ended.[30] Elites in America did strike back by criminalizing democratic mobilization and turning the state's monopoly of violence against rowdy citizens.

Terry Bouton tells a similar story. He argues that the Revolutionary War was guided by the democratic assumptions "that government needed to extend political access, protect freedom by promoting wealth equality among white men, and arm citizens with a wide range of political weapons to defend their rights." While the gentry initially championed these ideals, in the years following 1776, elites undertook a "stunning about-face" as they went from championing popular government to demeaning it. "The turnaround was so radical," Bouton asserts, "that the elite enacted postwar policies that were nearly identical to the ones Britain had put in place during the 1760s and 1770s, which at the time the gentry had decried as 'tyranny' and 'oppression.'" Fed up with popular demands and terrified by the rowdy spirit of revolution, whatever else divided them, the well-educated, generally wealthy men who participated in the Constitutional

Convention were bound by the desire to shackle democracy and regain control over the economy. For the founders, "the objective was a government that was less responsive to ordinary Americans and more compliant to the will of moneyed men—something the founders believed that no state government had done effectively during the 1780s."[31]

Today, more than two hundred years later, it is easy to speak of the Declaration of Independence and the Constitution in the same breath, as the two pillars of American identity in the founding period. But the Declaration and the Constitution were different documents produced during different rhetorical situations aimed at achieving different ends. The Declaration justified revolution; the Constitution attempted to contain it. Of course, it would be incorrect to argue—in spite of the founders' own caustic rhetoric—that the Constitution was intended to destroy democracy altogether. While the founders denounced democracy in the strongest of terms, they continued to assert that all political power was derived from the people, and that a government without popular consent was an illegitimate government. Once the Bill of Rights was included, the Constitution became a document capable of protecting the interests of wealthy gentlemen and common folks alike. The founders' goal was not to obliterate democracy and divorce the people from government, but instead to tame, control, and discipline democracy, channeling the popular spirit of revolution into a constitutional framework that would provide for more elite control over the economy and the levers of power.

While it was addressed to a "candid world," the primary audience of the Declaration of Independence was Americans.[32] When printed on July 4, Congress directed that copies "be sent to the several assemblies, conventions and committees, or councils of safety, and to the several commanding officers of the continental troops; that it be proclaimed in each of the United States, and at the head of the army."[33] The Declaration was also intended to be read aloud—to be "proclaimed"—throughout the states, in churches, public gatherings, town halls, and taverns.[34] The authors of the Declaration hoped that their rhetoric would inspire Americans to act differently. For the longest time, they had bowed to their monarchal father. The Declaration sanctioned growing disobedience by telling Americans that it was okay to rise up and strike a mortal blow to kingly authority. Jefferson's words had an immediate effect, as

newly independent citizens up and down the seaboard celebrated independence by burning effigies of the king and destroying his coat of arms.[35]
The Constitution was the Declaration of Independence for the Second
American Revolution: a political counter-revolution that reorganized the
democratic mindset and paved the way for a nation to grow to maturity
in the 1780s and 1790s. It, too, was addressed to Americans. It, too, was
intended to inspire Americans to act differently. While the Declaration
called on Americans to rise up against the king and "provide new guards
for their future security," the Constitution announced that it was just
such a guard, and that Americans now had a duty to obey the government
that protected them from danger.

The Constitution was written in a unique rhetorical style that hid its
furtive, elite origins. The rhetorical structure of the Constitution—with
its opening "We, the People"—made it seem as though Americans had
written it and were speaking to themselves through its words. This rhetorical style was central to the Constitution's legitimacy. "In the preamble
the reading citizen interpellates himself—even herself—into the juridical
order precisely at its foundation," Michael Warner argues, and "in this
sovereign interpellation the people are always coming across themselves
in the act of consenting to their own coercion."[36] While the rhetorical
structure of the preamble made it appear as though the people had
consented to the Constitution, nevertheless in the early Republic the
Constitution did not inspire the sanctimonious reverence it does today.
Many Americans did indeed embrace the Constitution for its promises of
safety and financial stability. "The only question," Noah Webster wrote, "is
whether it is necessary to unite, and provide for our *common defense and
general welfare*. For this question being once decided in the affirmative,
leaves no room to controvert the propriety of constituting a power over
the whole United States, adequate to these general purposes."[37] Many
others feared the Constitution and the federal bureaucracy it created.
For the anti-federalist polemicist Brutus, "the power in the federal legislative, to raise and support armies at pleasure, as well in peace as in
war, and their controul over the militia, tend, not only to a consolidation
of the government, but the destruction of liberty." This author chided
Americans not just with their slavery to government, but with the slavery
of their children and also their children's children, writing, "If you adopt

it, this only remaining assylum for liberty will be shut up, and posterity will execrate your memory."[38] Though one commentator dismissed Brutus's concerns as a "baseless assemblage of gloomy thoughts," others took them more seriously because they harbored similar fears.[39]

How did the founders of the United States convince skeptical Americans to abandon their first Declaration of Independence in favor of a second, the Constitution, which inaugurated a very different type of revolution—a counter-revolution in the structure of government and in the conduct of citizens? Building on the path-breaking scholarship already mentioned, in this book I investigate how the Second American Revolution was waged and won by considering the *rhetorical* strategies elites developed in the 1780s and 1790s for persuading citizens to talk, think, and act differently than they did during the Revolutionary War. Specifically, I will focus on the rhetoric of enemyship.

The art of naming and denouncing enemies has been central to the practice of rhetoric from its beginnings in Ancient Greece. Famously, Aristotle cleaved rhetoric into deliberative, forensic, and epideictic genres.[40] His division was premised on a distinction between the types of judgment produced by these forms of rhetoric: forensic rhetoric concerned judgments about true or false and guilty or innocent in the past; epideictic rhetoric concerned judgments about what or who was praiseworthy or blameworthy in the present; and deliberative rhetoric concerned judgments about what course of action was expedient or inexpedient in the future. Aristotle then suggested that deliberative rhetoric was properly political while epideictic rhetoric was merely ceremonial. Centuries later, Quintilian complained in his *Institutio Oratoria* that in this tradition, invective was reduced from "the principal side of oratory" and not given its due as a central form of rhetorical expression.[41] In the Roman Republic of Cicero and Quintilian, however, the lines between praise, blame, and deliberation began to break down—if they existed at all.[42] By the eighteenth and nineteenth centuries, most Americans who studied rhetoric would have recognized the art of praise and blame as valid in deliberative settings where rhetors considered what course of action was expedient.[43]

John Witherspoon, the prominent theologian, rhetorical theorist, and president of Princeton from 1768–1794, blurred the lines between political and ceremonial rhetoric in his lectures on invective, suggesting that the epideictic rhetorics were valid forms of speech in deliberative assemblies where questions of policy were decided. "The chief passions eloquence is intended to work upon are, rage, terror, pity, and perhaps desire in general," he expounded, teaching his students that political debate involved rational argumentation and logical deduction, but also emotional, and at times violent, appeals to the passions. He continued to explode the fiction of purely rational deliberation—a fiction that many philosophers of the Enlightenment championed—with the following wisdom: "A speaker in political or deliberative assemblies may be said to have it in view to excite the passion of rage: he may naturally desire to incense his hearers against their enemies, foreign and domestic, representing the first as terrible and dangerous, to excite aversion and hatred, and the other as weak or worthless, to excite contempt."[44] Witherspoon understood the constitutive role of the enemy in politics, which was, as he taught, primarily antagonistic.

The lines between deliberative and epideictic rhetoric blurred in the early Republic, meaning that tactics typically associated with more ceremonial rhetoric—for instance, the passionate denunciation of enemies—were characteristic of rhetoric in more deliberative settings. The rhetorical culture of the early Republic blended reason and passion, the rhetoric of the head and the heart.[45] The rhetorical maneuver by which rhetors escalated a present danger, either real or imagined, into a future crisis that demanded immediate action was a common form of political speech during, and following, the Revolutionary War. In fact, one of the most striking things about this period was how many enemies were named—including, to list just a few, Indians, poor farmers, French Jacobins, closet monarchists, New England banking interests, male effeminacy, Catholics, Muslims, Jews, outspoken women, rebellious Haitians, the Society of the Cincinnati, Masons, the Irish, the Spanish, runaway slaves, and slave owners.[46] As they burned witches; as they fought, killed, and colonized Indians; as they enslaved Africans; as they battled with the French during the Seven Years War; and as they worked through their feelings of attachment and hostility toward Great Britain before and after the Revolutionary War, early Americans became particularly fluent in the art of naming enemies.

The rhetorics of enemyship, in turn, became important in the post-Revolutionary years as a strategy for taming revolutionary democracy.

By tying together the elite fear of democracy with the naming of enemies, I am venturing into territory charted and explored by Robert L. Ivie, whose work probes the United States' paradoxical relationship to war. He asks: how can a nation, outwardly committed to peace, have such a warlike history? Writers from Alexis de Tocqueville to Michael Hardt and Antonio Negri have argued persuasively that war destroys democracy.[47] Consequently, shouldn't a nation that values democracy be peaceful? Yes, Ivie answers, concluding that the United States must not value democracy as much as our leaders' rhetoric suggests. On the contrary—American elites have feared democracy from the beginning. This fear, which Ivie provocatively labels "demophobia," has fueled a long history of wars meant to secure the borders of the demos and eliminate the foreign influences that might prey on democratic weakness. "The United States is a violent nation motivated by a tragic sense of fear, a country tyrannized by an exaggerated image of the danger endemic to domestic politics and international affairs," he writes, concluding that "An image of the savagery of the Other and corresponding fragility of civilized institutions of freedom, democracy, reason, law, and order has been America's traditional motive for war and ideological incentive for imposing its version of democracy on an unwilling world."[48] Because America's terrible love of war is a coping mechanism for democratic fear, Americans need to develop new and more humane ways of relating to the "other" than those currently practiced—or else we will never break free from the corrosive political cycle of uneasy peace and looming war that has characterized much of U.S. history.

American warfare—and American constructions of the "savage" enemy—are violent and destructive expressions of our nation's deep and abiding fear of democracy. The vector of rhetorical energy runs outward, as America's fears of itself are projected onto a world that must be subdued so that we, ultimately, can tame ourselves. The opposite is also true. Indeed, the construction of an enemy external to the nation reflects back upon, and ultimately alters, the composition of democracy at home. This is the aspect of enemyship I am most interested in: its dialectical side, as the rhetorical construction of the enemy makes demands on the demos, bringing about a change in behavior. In this book I explore how the act of naming the enemy was used to manage democratic fears in the early

Republic—not just by projecting those fears outward onto an enemy who had to be eliminated, but also by cultivating fear of the enemy and then making this emotion the premise of an argument for a fundamental change in democratic behavior. These are the two sides of enemyship— the cycle of projection, victimage, and sacrifice that Ivie charts, and the dialectical act of democratic transformation that I map in this book. In the early Republic, Americans named enemies not just to make the world safe for democracy but also to discipline democracy at home. Here, then, we can see enemyship as a technique of governing: the art of naming enemies as a means of controlling and containing the will of the people on which the right of revolution against the king had been premised.

How the Founders Disciplined Democracy: Book Overview

During the American Revolution, unity was premised as much on the danger of an external enemy as it was on shared ideals such as life, liberty, and the pursuit of happiness. In the first installment of *The American Crisis*, published in December 1776, Thomas Paine observed that "Mutual fear is the principal link in the chain of mutual love."[49] Later, looking back on the Revolutionary War, John Jay reported in Federalist 2 that Americans became a "united people," "a band of brethren," when "fighting side by side" against "common enemies."[50] For John Quincy Adams, colonial union was "formed by the coalescence of a common enmity," and for George Clinton, during the war Americans were "cemented by the ties of common danger and the imperious motives of self preservation."[51] Thomas Jefferson made a similar observation in his *Autobiography*.[52] For these Americans, colonial unity was the product of mutual fear, common enmity, and shared danger, as threatened hostilities facilitated relationships between colonists under siege. If America's enemies were so frightening, why didn't colonists run and hide? How was talk of danger translated into coordinated action rather than the alternative, stultifying, mass panic? To better understand how Americans became a "united people" committed to fighting for their independence during the Revolutionary War, in the first chapter, I offer a detailed rhetorical analysis of *Common Sense*—focusing specifically on how Paine transformed "enemyship" from an undesirable state of affairs into a motivational strategy for bringing Americans to battle.

When the Continental Congress met in July 1775, it extended an Olive Branch Petition offering friendship and reconciliation to the king, and it issued the Declaration of the Causes and the Necessity of Taking up Arms, which justified armed resistance to British aggression, but not independence from the British Empire. These actions were intended to mend fences, not burn bridges. Paine later recalled that "Independence was a doctrine scarce and rare, even towards the conclusion of the year 1775; all our politics had been founded on the hope of expectation of making the matter up."[53] Jefferson observed similarly: "It is well known, that in July 1775, a separation from Great-Britain and the establishment of Republican government had never yet entered into any person's mind."[54] When published in January 1776, *Common Sense* shot through the colonies with unimaginable speed and unprecedented influence—historians have estimated that there were between 75,000 and 120,000 and perhaps as many as 500,000 copies in circulation at the end of the year.[55] While a large part of this success can be attributed to the pamphlet's spot-on serendipitous timing, Paine inspired conflict by arguing that the king was a tyrannical despot, that the colonial relationship with Great Britain was broken beyond repair, and hence that revolution was the only logical option for Americans who wanted to protect their families from the avaricious reach of monarchal power.

In *Common Sense*, Paine articulated a case for independence that transformed the British into enemies, denied that communication was possible with them, and then escalated the crisis with rhetorics of fear, danger, and imminent attack. Using *Common Sense* as a heuristic, I outline the rhetorical norms of enemyship. Enemyship in early America fused three interlocking rhetorical maneuvers: naming, estrangement, and escalation.

1. *Naming.* Enemyship involves naming someone to play the role of enemy. This enemy is stripped of its positive characteristics while the negative is amplified. In this way, the individuality of enemies is erased; one Tory or "Indian" or Shaysite is just as bad as another. Once the enemy is named, this image is calcified by frequent repetition.

Enemyship produces rhetorics of impersonalization that reduce humans to caricatures, altering reality by changing the orientation of self toward other.[56]

2. *Estrangement.* Naming the enemy is not enough to create enemyship. The relationship between self and other, us and them, must be *figured* (i.e., defined rhetorically) in a way that erases the possibility for communication and facilitates the perception that the relationship is broken beyond repair. Enemies are enemies not only because they are "bad" or "evil" but because we cannot coexist peacefully or negotiate with them. Enemyship negates the rationality of enemies and denies that conflicts can be managed through diplomacy; in short, it figures the relationship with the enemy as an antagonism that must end in violence.

3. *Escalation.* Once an enemy is named, and the possibility of peaceful coexistence and meaningful dialogue is denied, the groundwork for enemyship is established. Finally, the crisis is escalated. Escalation works largely through tropes of imminence and inevitability as rhetors make it appear that the coming crisis is unavoidable, thus forcing the audience to alter their behaviors accordingly. To motivate, rhetors deploy the discourses of fear, paranoia, and anxiety to focus their audience's thoughts on how best to defend themselves and their families from the enemy, and how best to exact hurt on the enemy if the chance arises.

Using these three moves, Paine denied the possibility of peaceful coexistence with a rhetorically constructed enemy and then made it appear that an attack on America was imminent. In this way, enemyship made the rhetorical management of fear the essence of politics.

Common Sense was one of the most influential rhetorical performances in American history, and in this tract, Paine taught a new generation of Americans the rhetorical norms of enemyship. What was perhaps most useful for America's founders, however, was a lesson that Paine did not intend to teach. Paine's hope was that the battle for independence would create a crucial precondition for a lasting colonial friendship. Nevertheless, the structure of Paine's enemyship placed certain insatiable demands on the community he imagined. Paine's rhetoric demanded a unanimity of sentiment that was not, nor could ever be, achieved. In later editions of the work, he therefore ripped into dissenters, including Philadelphia's Quakers, with an acid pen. While Paine preached a democratic message of equality, self-reliance, friendship, and peace, his rhetoric—which cleaved the world into friends and enemies, Americans and British, patriots and the king's minions—undermined the democratic premises driving the argument of *Common Sense* by turning citizens both towards and against their neighbors. *Common Sense* thus demonstrated the possibilities, and the limitations, of enemyship. Though Paine's rhetoric complicated his hope for democratic friendship, this rhetoric was extremely useful for the founders who hoped to do intentionally what Paine did inadvertently: to upend democracy.

Building outward from the politics of enemyship in *Common Sense*, I tell the story of how enemyship became a form of common sense in the United States. In 1813, with their friendship rekindled and feeling a bit nostalgic, Thomas Jefferson and John Adams exchanged letters reflecting upon the tumultuous early years of the United States. They both recognized that they had lived through an unprecedented age of revolution; not surprisingly, given their clashing philosophical positions, they disagreed about how best to interpret history. Jefferson praised the popular participation engendered by the Revolutionary War and lauded revolution, yet Adams equated revolution with terrorism, deriding Jefferson's praise of democracy and attacking "the Terrorism of Chaises Rebellion in Massachusetts," "the Terrorism of Gallatins Insurrection in Pensilvania," and "the Terrorism of Fries's, most outrageous Riot and Rescue."[57] The three events about which he spoke were Shays's Rebellion in Massachusetts in 1786–1787 (chapter 2), the Whiskey Rebellion in Pennsylvania in 1794 (chapter 3), and Fries's Rebellion in Pennsylvania in 1799 (chapter 4). By focusing on these events, I investigate uprisings that emboldened some Americans (like Jefferson) and terrified others (like Adams)—because these uprisings, as expressions of the democratic energies that propelled the Revolutionary War, demonstrate how the legacy of revolution created problems in the new nation. In these events, we see a generation of Americans struggling to have their voices heard and their demands met. We also see the founders of the United States working out how best to tame democracy and nurture a sense of national American identity that was orderly and deferential. In these events, we see power in the act of composing itself.

Chapter 2 begins with the profound post-Revolutionary letdown. Following the Revolutionary War, the newly independent states fell deep into an economic recession that was so severe historians now believe it was equivalent to—and perhaps even worse than—the Great Depression. Elites responded to the post-Revolutionary financial crisis by advancing what Bouton calls the "gospel of moneyed men." In the years following the Revolutionary War, "much of the gentry also replaced its support for wealth equality with a new belief that the only way to make America great was to put most of the money and land in the hands of the wealthy." Wealthy Americans came to believe, in short, that "America would only stand alongside the nations of Europe when government dedicated itself to putting wealth into the hands of the affluent."[58] In the 1780s, acting on the advice of the deeply influential Robert Morris and his disciple Alexander Hamilton, the state governments alongside Congress instituted policies aimed at achieving the upward concentration of wealth. Morris actively encouraged wealthy Americans to speculate in war bonds, and his plan for this unprecedented monetary redistribution included the creation of private banks with private currencies backed by public funds, taxes collected in hard money, and a new system of tax collection that ensured that poor debtors weren't let off the hook. This system, in which the gentry placed its hopes for financial salvation, was a profound reversal of revolutionary dreams of equality. It did not sit well with poor Revolutionary War veterans, who fought for a brighter future but who struggled even to pay the taxes levied on their swindled wealth.

Seeking debt and tax relief, in the middle 1780s farmers up and down the seaboard rose up, demonstrating that revolution was not dead and that citizens had no problem using coordinated violence to achieve what they took to be the democratic promises of the Revolutionary War. In 1786, backcountry Massachusetts farmers, fed up with government policies favoring aristocratic elites, marched on courts to bar the entry of judges and juries. Thus enacting a long-standing democratic tradition known to colonists as a "Regulation," the farmers' movement became known as Shays's Rebellion. Erupting in the turbulent days following the Revolutionary War, yet predating the formation of the national Constitution,

Shays's Rebellion was understood as a crucial postwar crisis of order. In turn, the government's response to Shays's Rebellion—which included labeling protestors "rebels" and countering their actions with an army of 4,400 soldiers—was understood as a pivotal postwar attempt to deploy state violence to manage popular dissent.[59] Shays's Rebellion hence produced deeply problematic yet lasting rhetorical conventions for justifying the compromised forms of republicanism that marked the early Republic.

The Regulators believed they were acting on the Revolutionary War's precedent of rising up against unresponsive, unrepresentative, and tyrannical government, and their rhetoric "resounded with themes and images that had mobilized colonial resistance to the British only a decade earlier."[60] In the short term their uprising was a success, as Governor James Bowdoin was swept from office and his successor, John Hancock, granted most of their demands. In the long term it was a failure, however, as politicians—aghast at how easily citizens manipulated the state governments into financial relief—seized on uprisings like Shays's Rebellion as a justification for drafting a new Constitution that was much less responsive to popular pressure.

To win ratification of a document derided by anti-federalists as contrary to the aims of the Revolutionary War, federalists marshaled a vast array of arguments, claiming that the Constitution would lower taxes, fix the economy, and better protect citizens than the Articles of Confederation.[61] Federalists also implied that Shays's Rebellion was emblematic of a deeper democratic disease—a disease Dr. Rush labeled *"anarchia."*[62] While coercion ultimately led to the downfall of the Massachusetts government, during the ratification debates federalists named everyday people—and democracy itself—the enemy of the wealthy and the powerful. They then escalated this demophobia by tying it to the legacy of the Levellers and making wealthy Americans fear for their property and investments. In the context of the ratification debates, then, the coercive response to Shays's Rebellion made perfect sense—for if the people really were as greedy, stupid, and gullible as Hamilton, Madison, and other federalists made them out to be, then violence was an essential bulwark against popular anarchy.[63]

In chapter 3, we will see that the dynamics of the Whiskey Rebellion played out differently. During 1787, Governor Bowdoin could not persuade the state legislature to fund an army to take on the Regulators—so the counter-revolutionary forces were privately funded by wealthy Bostonians fearful for their property.[64] The Constitution, however, gave the new federal government the power to suppress domestic dissent—a power that it almost immediately put to use. On August 7, 1794, President George Washington invoked the Militia Law of 1792 and led nearly 13,000 militiamen, light cavalry, and cannon into western Pennsylvania to stifle the uprising and arrest the rebels. Though this massive military force soon restored order, the lesson that President Washington drew from the Whiskey Rebellion was not about the efficacy of coercion. Instead, Washington praised the virtue of those Americans he labeled "the army of the Constitution," citizens who were willing to fight and even die to defend the Constitution from its enemies. For Washington, the Republic's salvation was found not just in the state's monopoly on violence, but in the people's willingness to serve. The crucial point, here, was when activated by dangers to their lives and their property—and the Whiskey Rebellion was framed as such a danger—then the people could become *centinels* (to use a common eighteenth-century term) watching not just over government but also over each other. During the Whiskey Rebellion, Federalists had great success in consolidating an orderly, virtuous, law-abiding American identity in opposition to the discord of riot and revolution.

As the government called forth citizen-soldiers and deployed military force against the "rebels" in Pennsylvania, a fortuitous war waged in the Ohio Valley opened up new possibilities for governing elites. For much of 1792, 1793, and 1794, General Anthony Wayne had been drilling an army aimed at reversing U.S. military defeats in 1790 and 1791—an army that would secure American claims to the Ohio Valley as spelled out in the Northwest Ordinance of 1787. Wayne's army defeated a confederacy of Indian nations in the Battle of Fallen Timbers on August 20, 1794—and news of this victory broke just before Washington's army marched into the rebel areas. Here, displacement and the joys of empire matched coercion as counter-revolutionary strategies for managing democracy. The resolution of the Whiskey Rebellion was tied to victory in the Ohio Valley, for by opening the Northwest Territory to expansion, and by naming "the Indian" an enemy, it was possible to distract angry frontiersmen from their economic grievances and persuade them that it was to their advantage to abide by the nation's laws.

In chapter 4, we will see that enemyship again acted as an instrument of distraction in 1798, as tensions with France boiled over into the so-called Quasi-War. As the XYZ papers circulated in the American press, enraged patriots from around the country re-formed the Army of the Constitution and publicly avowed their support for government. Thus, the citizens of Albany, New York, announced: "We therefore solemnly pledge ourselves, in the most unequivocal manner, to sustain, with energy, the constituted authorities of our country, against all the machinations of its enemies, whether foreign or domestic."[65] Federalists capitalized on such sentiments and cemented them in public consciousness by stressing a new code of conduct: the contract of blood. Though the Federalist Party would soon be relegated to obscurity, Federalists furthered the Second American Revolution by engendering a shift in historical consciousness that encouraged citizens to focus on the debts they owed to revolutionary martyrs. Americans could only repay these debts, it was said, by acting virtuously and defending the Constitution from its many enemies. Federalists thus made the rhetoric of enemyship productive of national identity and republican government by transforming the social contract into a contract of blood.

Deploying the language of blood sacrifice, Federalists argued that Americans had an obligation to defend their children and uphold the legacy of their dead mothers and fathers by protecting the Constitution from its enemies. But agitations were necessary to call the Army of the Constitution to order. Federalist leaders therefore talked about small-scale tax protests in eastern Pennsylvania in early 1799 as though they were even more severe than Shays's Rebellion or the Whiskey Rebellion. Fries's Rebellion, as it became known, was framed as the opening shot of a new revolution that would topple the existing property order and reduce the Republic to dust—a revolution, it was said, supported, and perhaps even instigated, by foreign enemies. Fries's Rebellion was indeed a challenge to government. However, as the troops sent to Pennsylvania to suppress the protests soon realized, it was not a foreign-backed attempt to topple the Constitution. Nevertheless, President Adams responded to the crisis as elites had been responding to such crises for the past decade, by crushing protests with military force.

And then the president changed course. Rather than seeing John Fries, a poor auctioneer, executed for treason, President Adams pardoned him, hence redeeming himself and also the republican promise of American politics: for while he would soon lose the presidential election to Jefferson, Adams demonstrated that there was another way of governing, another way of treating dissenting voices—not as enemies to be crushed, but as fellow citizens with a right to voice their opinions (even if they turned out to be wrong). Later in life, Adams did not differentiate between Shays's Rebellion, the Whiskey Rebellion, and Fries's Rebellion. All, for him, were equivalent to "terrorism." He refused to embrace the strategy of governing that he modeled at the end of his presidential term, when he championed education and dialogue over coercion and force as the proper means of dealing with dissent. It would be left for Jefferson to represent this alternative strategy of governing in public memory.

While Adams turned away, however briefly, from the coercive and manipulative strategies of enemyship, the precedent was set. Having proved successful in response to one crisis, the rhetorical strategies used to resolve conflicts in the past become resources available for governing future conflicts, eventually becoming norms that continue to guide discussion, debate, and decision making. Thus, elites learned a triptych of strategies for managing democracy in the early Republic: first, they could turn the people into enemies, rally the wealthy and powerful against them, and then unleash the state's monopoly of violence to crush them; second, they could engage in a politics of distraction and displacement by which citizen anger was redirected outward at the enemy; and third, they could engage in a politics of fear that reiterated the need for obedience, hierarchy, and authority against democratic demands for equality. These were the three faces of enemyship as a counter-revolutionary strategy in the early Republic: enemyship as the means to justify coercion, which worked directly on the minds and bodies of citizens; enemyship as a tool of distraction, which did not require anything more of citizens than to indulge their violent fantasies and imperial greed; and enemyship as an instrument of discipline, which called on citizens to act differently—to trade obedience to the Constitution for protection from danger.

In these three strategies, we see progressively more effective techniques for managing the democratic aspirations nurtured during the Revolutionary War. Naming the people enemies and crushing them with military force could be effective in the short term, but long term this strategy did more harm than good. Turning the state's monopoly of violence against its own citizens was tricky business, for coercion always threatened a potential legitimation crisis for those who deployed it.[66] Ultimately, power could not be won by violence.[67] As Webster rightly noted in an essay on the Constitution, "the supreme power in America cannot enforce unjust laws by the sword; because the whole body of the people are armed, and constitute a force superior to any band of regular troops that can be, on any pretence, raised in the United States."[68]

The naming of enemies to distract citizens from their grievances proved effective during the Whiskey Rebellion and the XYZ Affair, and has been a popular strategy of governance since the early Republic. During moments of domestic tension, politicians have long understood the utility of distracting citizens with talk of the enemy. The hang-up with this strategy was that it required a boundless horizon into which conflicts could be displaced. The mythic "West" served this purpose magnificently for much of the nineteenth century, but when the horizon closed—as it did during the debates over the expansion of slavery that led to the Civil War—then displacement faltered. Perhaps this is why the American Empire has proven so historically resilient and creative in seeking out new territories to colonize and peoples to turn into enemies.

The final strategy, naming enemies in order to turn citizens into patriot-soldiers, was a useful counterpart to displacement in the early Republic. This strategy was flawed because it could lead to wars like the War of 1812, which was framed as a necessary exercise for hardening citizens grown soft during days of commercial luxury and peace.[69] Theorists have long noted that war can be beneficial for the state. Even Tocqueville, who argued that war was the surest means of destroying freedom in a democratic nation, felt compelled to offer a clarification in *Democracy in America*, insisting that "I do not wish to speak ill of war; war almost always enlarges the thought of a people and elevates its heart."[70] Political theorists in the eighteenth and nineteenth centuries understood that war could be a profitable enterprise for the state, but as politicians repeatedly discovered, war itself could not be controlled by the state—this was one of the lessons of the United States' failed invasion of the Canadian Provinces in 1812. Nevertheless, the naming of enemies in order to transform citizens into an Army of the Constitution was the cornerstone of the Second American Revolution, for in such moments of crisis, politicians could deploy the rhetoric of the contract of blood and thereby redirect the democratic energies of citizens toward pursuits and activities that could bolster the government and the union.

The Constitution was framed by proponents as a remedy to the democratic excesses of the Revolutionary War, as symbolized by events like Shays's Rebellion. Yet the Constitution by itself did not solve the problems of revolution and democracy. It might have interpellated citizens on a symbolic level, but the Constitution had to be implemented and citizens taught what it meant to live in post-Revolutionary times. To reform the behavior of citizens, the founders deployed the rhetoric of enemyship. Ironically, then, I argue in the conclusion that the desire to transform citizens from revolutionary democrats into deferential citizens ultimately led the founders back to the philosophy of Thomas Hobbes— the preeminent political theorist of monarchal government—and his effort to tie together protection and obedience. Though the Revolutionary War was waged against monarchy, in the early Republic the founders learned the utility of thinking like kings. Once Hobbes's philosophy was adapted to the demands of American nationalism through the contract of blood, it became one of the most lasting contributions of the founders to the philosophies and rhetorics of governing.

While the road from revolution to consent was uneven—full of zigzags, bumps, false starts, and dead ends—the founders had success during the early Republic in negotiating the dilemmas of American nationalism, and in disciplining democracy. They did this in large part by naming enemies and then persuading citizens that the enemies they feared were in fact national enemies—demonstrating the necessity of government by arguing that it protected Americans from danger. When the enemy threatened the lives and property of citizens, it became more difficult for citizens to complain about the evils of the Constitution, because the government was protecting them from death. In such moments, revolutionary sentiments became illogical—for, it was said, to instigate another revolution was to invite the enemy to strike, making revolution tantamount to a death sentence. In the early Republic, protection from death became a basis of the obligation to obey authority. Indeed, it was much easier for citizens uneasy with federalism, centralization, modernity, and bureaucracy to get behind the federal government if their support meant security, stability, and order. This was the genius of enemyship: it did not make citizens powerless, but instead coordinated power in a way that encouraged citizens to feel that they had to back the authorities or die.

The founders of the United States learned that talking about the threats to personal liberty, private property, and national security posed by the nation's enemies tended to have three provisional effects. First, such talk cultivated a national identity where there was none, defining what it meant to be an "American" by positing an enemy that was barbarian, savage, crazy, disobedient, and uncivilized. Enemyship produced identity through antithesis.[71] Second, such talk persuaded Americans, who were deeply divided on issues including religion, language, ethnicity, slavery, taxation, industrialization, urbanization, and the franchise, to come together into a national community. Enemyship did not preclude dissent, but it did produce fragile working coalitions by finessing citizens' psychological attachments to—and investments in—war. Third, such talk distracted Americans, redirecting their anger away from the government and toward a collective scapegoat. Enemyship thus acted as a safety valve for citizen resentment. In the period following the Revolutionary War, enemyship had several desirable political effects, including the production of a national identity, socioeconomic stability, and more obedient citizens. Enemyship facilitated the development of group identities as Americans became a people in opposition to a collective enemy; they also facilitated the creation of legitimate governing bodies.

There are many excellent studies of the melodramas, the military and diplomatic triumphs, the misfires, the backroom deals, the political intrigue, the unlikely friendships, the philosophical contradictions, and the shocking failures that the founding period of the United States comprised. My contribution is to read this early and formative moment as a revolution in the art of governing. By naming enemies, the first generation of American politicians found it easier to govern the Americans who, just years earlier, fought British authority for freedom, autonomy, and democracy. By naming enemies, the founders of the United States managed revolution and, for a time, disciplined democracy.

CHAPTER ONE

How Enemyship Became Common Sense

I t is one of the most famous lines in American history: echoed in mov-
ies; recited by schoolchildren. On March 23, 1775, Patrick Henry told
his audience at St. John's Church in Richmond, Virginia, to "Give me
liberty or give me death." Like many episodes in American mythology, this
defining moment might not have happened. The text of Henry's speech
did not survive, and Americans, at the very least, learned about Henry's
words only in the early nineteenth century.¹ Apocryphal or not, Henry's
words color how we remember the Revolutionary War: as an idealistic act
of daring will. In turn, Henry's words encapsulate something essential
about what it means to be an American—or at least about how Americans
like to think of themselves. American history is the history of the uncon-
ditional "can-do," of stepping up, of *carpe diem*, of betting big against
long odds and taking down the house. The biggest gamble was the first,
a revolution against the mighty British for the highest stakes: liberty or
death. The story of the American Revolution as Americans learned it in

the nineteenth century, and as we learn it today, is a story of the happy
marriage of transcendental ideals with the steely determination to confront tyranny no matter the cost. With pluck and grit, Americans willed
themselves to victory, nationhood, and liberty.

The primary author of the Declaration of Independence, Thomas
Jefferson, remembered things somewhat differently. The Revolutionary
War was of course about ideals, including life, liberty, and the pursuit
of happiness. But alongside those ideals was a powerful emotion spurring Americans on to battle: fear. In his 1821 *Autobiography*, Jefferson
recalled that the working union forged during the American Revolution
was premised not so much on alluring promises of liberty, but instead
on the colonies' shared recognition of the dangers posed by Great Britain. "During the war of Independence," he noted, "while the pressure
of an external enemy hooped us together, and their enterprises kept us
necessarily on the alert, the spirit of the people, excited by danger, was a
supplement to the Confederation, and urged them to zealous exertions,
whether claimed by that instrument, or not." Things quickly fell apart,
however, for "when peace and safety were restored, and every man became engaged in useful and profitable occupation, less attention was paid
to the calls of Congress."[2] According to Jefferson, an "external enemy"
"hooped" Americans together, and therefore the colonial war effort—and
the rudimentary forms of federated colonial government—were possible
only because of colonists' shared fears of mutual enemies. For the third
president of the United States, Americans became Americans when
"excited by danger." Once "peace and safety were restored," Americans
stopped being Americans and became New Yorkers and Virginians again.

Putting the shared fears of Americans at center stage allows us to see
the Revolutionary War from a slightly different angle: not just as an economic, political, or ideological conflict, but as a rhetorical one in which
proponents of revolution struggled to bring their reluctant fellows along
with them, and then, once the war had begun, to keep morale high and
the guns shooting. In turn, by focusing on this pivotal moment, we can
probe rhetorical forms and patterns of persuasion that have long been
central to the American experience, in war and peace.

To better understand how Americans were "hooped" together in 1776,
in this chapter I offer a detailed rhetorical analysis of Thomas Paine's

Common Sense. In the able judgment of Bernard Bailyn, Paine's work was "the most brilliant pamphlet written during the American Revolution, and one of the most brilliant pamphlets ever written in the English language."[3] Paine's genius was found both in style and form. Paine understood that if he did not write in a style accessible to everyday people, then he would not reach them—and thus *Common Sense* was noteworthy for its rough but shimmering prose. *Common Sense* was also noteworthy for its rhetorical structure, which, following Paine, I label "enemyship." Paine's enemyship wove together divergent fears and heightened them to a degree that demanded action. In turn, we should study the structure of persuasive tracts like *Common Sense* because arrangement is central to the practice of rhetoric. Many Americans who read *Common Sense* copied Paine's language. Some even acted out the more dramatic scenes of the tract. Less noticed is that Americans also copied the structure of Paine's masterpiece, arranging their arguments for various ends as Paine arranged his. This is what enemyship is: rhetorical architecture. *Common Sense* was a blueprint of sorts for moving people to action. In the coming decades, the structure of Paine's argument was emulated by activists and politicians. Some used enemyship for revolutionary ends, others to tame revolution. As it was deployed and redeployed, adapted and revised, enemyship became instantiated in the public culture of the United States. In the early Republic, to be "excited by danger" became central to what it meant to be an "American."

The Illusion of Security

For someone who did so much good, Paine's tale is one of tragic neglect. "To trace the curve of Paine's reputation," it has been observed, "is to learn something about hero-worship in reverse."[4] Paine immigrated to America in 1774 and became a leading voice of independence with *Common Sense*, which was the most important pamphlet published during the American Revolution and is today recognized as one of the most influential publications in American history.[5] Following the Revolutionary War, Paine returned to Europe to agitate for change. His *Rights of Man* was outlawed in Britain, and hostile reaction to its publication in

1791 forced Paine to flee to Paris, where he served in the National Convention. A change of government found Paine imprisoned on Christmas Eve, 1793. The U.S. minister to France, Gouverneur Morris, let him rot in his cell, where he languished for nearly a year—narrowly escaping the guillotine on at least one occasion—until the new American minister James Monroe secured his release. Paine's support of the French Revolution, his scathing indictment of organized religion in *The Age of Reason* (1794), and harangues like the *Letter to George Washington* (1796), which denounced the great American leader as a hypocrite, turned popular opinion in the United States against him. At President Thomas Jefferson's invitation, Paine returned to the United States in 1802, only to be savaged by the Federalist press. Philadelphia's *Port Folio* labeled Paine "a drunken atheist, and the scavenger of faction," and Boston's *Mercury and New-England Palladium* denounced him as a "lying, drunken, brutal infidel, who rejoiced in the opportunity of basking and wallowing in the confusion, devastation, bloodshed, rapine, and murder, in which his soul delights."[6] While many Americans saw Paine as a staunch patriot during the Revolutionary War, in his later years he was viewed by these same people as the Antichrist.

Though Americans came to feel distaste for Paine's later politics, the shine of *Common Sense* has never dulled. This pamphlet resonated with Americans then, and continues to resonate with them now, because it offered an idealistic vision of human equality; because it expressed nothing but searing contempt for all forms of social, political, and economic inequality; and because it legitimated American conceptions of popular sovereignty, democratic government, and the power of common people. Democratic writers in the early Republic made it a habit to sign their editorials "Common Sense." Its trenchant egalitarianism was also why it frightened elites. Paine and other democratic writers found traction by smoothing out society's bumps. As such, his ideas shocked many leaders who believed that revolutionary thought was best kept to elites. John Adams denounced *Common Sense* as "so democratical, without any restraint or even an Attempt at any Equilibrium or Counterpoise, that it must produce confusion and every Evil Work," and he later dubbed the tumultuous decades of the 1780s and 1790s, in which political elites in the United States and France struggled to suppress democratic energies, "the Age of Folly, Vice, Frenzy, Fury, Brutality, Daemons, Buonaparte, Tom Paine."[7]

Common Sense was one of the earliest and most persuasive cases for popular government in American history. Paine wrote in a style that was accessible to all, and he argued that all men were created equal, that equality was the natural state of humankind, that human labor was innately dignified, and that humans were meant to govern themselves. Having settled in Philadelphia, the City of Brotherly Love and the home of the most politically conscious working classes in America, Paine observed the proletarian list of revolution first-hand. He was a tireless supporter of the working man and a vocal critic of slavery. In a 1775 essay published under the pseudonym "Justice and Humanity," he questioned the good faith of his fellows, arguing that it was neither just nor consistent to fight a revolution without abolishing slavery.[8] Above all else, Paine praised freedom, autonomy, and self-government.

Paine was a rare rhetorical talent, a master wordsmith of the first degree. The persuasiveness of *Common Sense* was found not just in its claims, but in how those claims were made. Paine used language to reorient Americans' relationship with the mother country in a way that created the impression that war was inevitable—and it did this with an unrivaled populist eloquence. Most of the arguments in *Common Sense* were not new. But novelty was not the only mark of genius; the best buildings were often built from ancient materials. In the traditional rhetorical theory of Aristotle, Cicero, and Quintilian, the art of rhetoric consisted of five canons: invention, arrangement (or disposition), elocution, delivery, and memory. Paine's genius was found not in the invention of new arguments, but in their arrangement and stunning presentation. At a moment in which political discourse was formal to the point of being paralyzing, *Common Sense* employed a blunt democratic argot.[9] To reach a wider audience, Paine eschewed legal metaphors and the lexical bling-bling of inkhorn terms. In their place, he deployed taunts, bawdy jabs, and the type of earthy metaphors common to farmers' almanacs: the cant, in short, most Americans could understand.

Common Sense was organized in five parts: a brief introduction set forth the purpose of the work, the first section deconstructed the English constitution, the second section mocked monarchy and kingly rule, the third section narrated a case for American independence, and the fourth section discussed America's readiness to win the war. As Stephen Lucas notes in his masterful investigation of revolutionary rhetoric, *Portents of Rebellion*, the pamphlet was organized for maximum motivational effect, for it began by stating a problem (English oppression of America), it then offered a solution to that problem (independence), and it closed on an optimistic note, by reassuring Americans that they could win a war against the formidable British forces.[10] As he composed *Common Sense* in Philadelphia's coffeehouses and taverns, Paine found fuel in the heady idealism of the pre-Revolutionary moment. *Common Sense* was written before Americans were forced to confront "the times that try men's souls," to use his timeless phrasing from *The American Crisis*.[11] It was therefore a profoundly hopeful pamphlet. According to Paine, Americans could start over—and as they transcended the narrow limits of monarchy and forgot the horrors of the 1770s, they would rewrite the history books and inspire people all over the world to rise up for their freedom.

Aristotle once argued that it was not hard to praise Athenians among Athenians, a basic rhetorical principle that Paine understood and exploited in *Common Sense*. In the course of the original pamphlet's forty-six pages, Paine appealed to Americans' feelings of global importance, to their exceptionalism, and to the millennial view of progress, espoused by some Americans, that suggested they would realize a New Canaan, God's kingdom on earth. Paine defined the American Revolution not only as an American revolution but a world revolution, announcing: "The cause of America is in a great measure the cause of all mankind." Positioning America at the heart of a global conflict between freedom and tyranny, Paine imagined his new home as an asylum for the oppressed. "Every spot of the old world is over-run with oppression," he contended, and "Freedom hath been hunted round the globe. Asia, and Africa, have long expelled her.—Europe regards her like a stranger, and England hath given her warning to depart. O! receive the fugitive, and prepare in time an asylum for mankind." America could be such an asylum because it was not bound by the sins of Old World feuding and feudalism; for Paine, Americans were the divinely ordained vessels of worldly freedom and the saviors of the world's oppressed.[12]

According to Paine, "a long habit of not thinking a thing *wrong*, gives it a superficial appearance of being *right*," and thus he suggested that the Revolutionary War was intended to get Americans to "see with other eyes," to "hear with other ears," and to "think with other thoughts, than those we formerly used."[13] To the extent that revolution was about a change in perception and vision, it was also about rhetoric, for documents like *Common Sense* brought about the change in principle, opinion, sentiment, and affection by redefining the relationship between Americans and Britons in a way that promoted independence and justified war. Though *Common Sense* was a hopeful pamphlet, to understand its motivational appeal we must also recognize that Paine's hopeful message was accompanied by fearful rhetorics that named King George III America's enemy. In fact, the idealism of *Common Sense* achieved clarity in fear, for Paine warned Americans that their hopes and dreams were threatened by ruffians, magnifying what was good about America through the lens of grotesque difference.

Paine's argument for war was grounded in social-contract theory.[14] His reading of the social contract had a decidedly pro-people, anti-government cast, more Rousseau than Hobbes.[15] Society, which Paine defined as a group of citizens living and working together on issues of common concern, was beneficial; yet government, which arose to protect the "freedom and security" of people when societies grew too large to be managed without artificial rules and regulations, was restrictive and easily corrupted—as evidenced by the rule of King George III. For Paine, the point of government was protection. "*Wherefore*, security being the true design and end of government, it unanswerably follows that whatever *form* thereof appears most likely to ensure it to us, with the least expense and greatest benefit, is preferable to all others," he wrote.[16] This statement was central to the argument of *Common Sense*, for it provided Paine with a hook to justify independence to a skeptical audience. If protection was the end of government, then Americans could judge the British monarchy by the quality of the protection it provided. If the king's umbrella provided cover from the storm, he should be praised. But if the umbrella leaked, or even worse if the king himself was the cause of the tempest, then he should be deposed. Paine defended independence by reframing the way his audience thought about politics. While public debate up to that point had focused predominantly on economic and ideological issues including freedom, equality, self-government, trade, and taxation, Paine transformed it into a conversation about security and safety.

By the time that *Common Sense* hit the bookshelves in January 1776, Americans were on edge. Boston had been devastated by the British siege, and following the battles of Lexington and Concord, the American press sizzled with tales of dead patriots mercilessly shot down by the king's regulars. In July 1775, the Continental Congress sent an Olive Branch Petition to the king. It was answered with an unforgiving speech on August 23 accusing the colonies of "traitorously preparing, ordering, and levying war against Great Britain," and pledging the king's determination to do everything in his power to put down the rebellion. Then, in an October 26 address before Parliament, the king again denounced the colonists—and his speech reached Philadelphia on January 8, just two days before the publication of *Common Sense*.[17] In these speeches, the king declared Americans out of his protection, which according to Paine meant that Americans were no longer bound to obey him. And then there were the events in the South.

On Thursday, December 14, 1775, the *Pennsylvania Evening Post* published a brief anecdote on page 4, next to shipping news, announcements of apartments for rent and homes for sale, and personal ads. Though its placement was innocuous enough, and though it would have been easy to skip over this short article of seventy-five words, it packed a fiery wallop disproportionate to its brevity because it confirmed the worst fears of slave owners. Supposedly, a black man in Philadelphia refused to step into the muddy street to allow a "gentlewoman" to pass on the narrow sidewalk. This man's defiance was jarring, in part, because hierarchies of social convention held the colonies together; and yet he refused to bow when society demanded that he bow—hence waging a little rebellion against deference that shocked slave owners and polite white society more generally. Accordingly, the anonymous black man's "rude behavior" drew a sharp retort from the white woman. What he said in response was even more troubling than his flagrant rejection of social convention: "Stay, you d——d [damned] white bitch, till Lord Dunmore and his black regiment come, and then we will see who is to take the wall."[18] These words touched a nerve, conjuring up nightmares of rough justice. Slave owners saw the seeds of a potential slave rebellion in the words of this defiant man.

"Tis surprising to see how rapidly a panic will sometimes run through a country," Paine observed.[19] This was certainly the case here, for slave owners were already on edge. Following a humiliating British victory over colonists at Kemp's Landing near Norfolk, the royal governor of Virginia, Lord Dunmore, issued a proclamation on November 7, 1775, freeing slaves who joined the British ranks. Hundreds and perhaps thousands of slaves heeded Dunmore's call in Virginia, Maryland, and South Carolina. Dunmore quickly armed these slaves and formed "Lord Dunmore's Ethiopian Regiment," which pillaged the Chesapeake and participated in several early battles for the king. Dunmore threatened to begin a civil war and engulf the colonies in anarchy by encouraging slaves to fight for their freedom. For slave owners, Dunmore's proclamation was pure madness. With over 430,000 in the southern colonies and another 50,000 in the north, slaves formed a formidable bloc of potential revolutionaries in an increasingly fragile society. At this moment, the norms of social behavior upholding the slave-owning hierarchy were close to unraveling, and the brutal science of intimidation through which slaves were coerced into submission was faltering. Though the story in the *Pennsylvania Evening Post* was most likely apocryphal, the fears it expressed were real; it was therefore less of an anecdote and more of an allegory about the savagery of the British, the coming barbarism of slaves, and the urgency of the moment.[20]

In the winter of 1775–1776, slave owners waited anxiously to defend their homes from retributive slaughter. The tension caused them to lash out, publicly executing and then literally tearing to pieces many of the unfortunate slaves who escaped bondage but were later captured. The fear of a British-backed slave uprising, and the shared violence it would bring, produced a union in sentiment and deed among slave owners that many colonists thought sufficiently noteworthy to mention in their correspondence. Writing from Virginia, Richard Henry Lee reported that "Lord Dunmores unparalleled conduct in Virginia has, a few Scotch excepted, united every Man in that large Colony." Similarly, Edward Rutledge wrote from South Carolina that Dunmore's proclamation would "more effectively . . . work an eternal separation between Great Britain and the Colonies,—than any other expedient, which could possibly have been thought of."[21] These writers suggested that Lord Dunmore's War had two exemplary effects on the southern colonies: first, the threat of war with the British and their slaves helped colonists form a close-knit community to defend their homes and families; and second, Dunmore's actions pushed southern colonists over the edge of revolution, helping them realize that independence from Great Britain was their best chance for survival. In one of the great backfires of American history, Dunmore brought the American Revolution to the southern colonies.

It was into this context that Paine preached a message about broken promises and failed protection. Paine asked his audience: are you safer as colonists of the British Empire than you would be as citizens of independent nations? The commonsensical answer was yes, of course; but even to ponder this question was to create space for change. Paine understood that safety is a material state: the absence of danger. But he also understood that judging safety is one of the most perplexing problems of human existence, for out of unawareness, naiveté, or trained incapacity humans frequently walk right into dangerous situations. At the same time, humans often avoid situations because of perceived threats that do not exist. Safety is not simply a material state, then. Safety is also a feeling that can be divorced from the presence of material conditions and real dangers. Humans can be perfectly safe but still feel threatened. Questions of safety and danger are not empirical but emotional, and thus feelings of security and insecurity can be manipulated with scary stories and frightening prophecies of what is to come. For skilled advocates like Paine, the need to be safe is one of the available means of persuasion that can be tapped to move people to action.

As tempers began to rise in the early 1770s, the question of safety was one of the issues that kept independence off the table, for it was widely assumed that British protection of the American colonies was vital to their well-being. Great Britain was the world's foremost military power, after all, and it was believed that there were enemies all around, poised to attack Americans the moment British protection was removed. Some Tories argued that reconciliation with Great Britain was absolutely vital because the mother country protected Americans from their enemies.

They hoped that by openly pledging their fealty and denouncing rebellion, the king would again offer his protection. Paine offered three counterarguments to this position. First, he claimed that Great Britain's protection did not arise from benevolent motives, but instead was designed for "the sake of trade and dominion."[22] This arrangement was deeply problematic, for Britain's protection would not last beyond her economic and political interests. If these interests changed, Americans would be hung out to dry. Paine thus faulted Great Britain's protection as fickle. Second, he argued that Americans no longer needed Great Britain's protection. This was not an unfounded boast. In fact, the Seven Years War suggested that this statement might be true—for colonial Americans bore the brunt of Great Britain's conflict with France from 1756 to 1763 in North America, proving to some that Americans could protect themselves.[23] Paine thus faulted Great Britain's protection as redundant.

Third, and most importantly, he estimated that Great Britain's protection cost more than it was worth. In one of the most clever and confusing sentences in *Common Sense*, Paine reasoned: "We have boasted the protection of Great Britain, without considering, that her motive was *interest* not *attachment*; that she did not protect us from *our enemies* on *our account*, but from *her enemies* on *her own account*, from those who had no quarrel with us on any *other account*, and who will always be our enemies on the *same account*."[24] Good fathers protected their children; they did not endanger them. Yet Great Britain protected Americans not from America's enemies but from Great Britain's enemies, who were America's enemies only because America was Great Britain's colony. Paradoxically, then, Paine maintained that Great Britain might protect America from her enemies, but if Great Britain's protection was removed, then America's need for protection would also be removed.

Moreover, Paine argued that "whenever a war breaks out between England and any foreign power, the trade of America goes to ruin, *because of her connection with Britain*."[25] Paine was both right and wrong, for while British wars cost Americans markets for their goods, American shipping depended upon the protection of the British Navy to escort their goods to market. Americans learned this lesson in the 1780s when, lacking a navy, they were helpless to prevent the so-called "Barbary Pirates" from ravaging their Mediterranean trade.[26] The transatlantic economy of shipping and trade was infinitely more complicated than Paine made it seem; it took Adam Smith over 1,300 pages to tackle the subject in the original three-volume Dublin edition of *The Wealth of Nations*, published the same year as *Common Sense*. Yet by making it simple, Paine made it persuasive. According to Paine, American trade suffered because of British protection, and thus he deduced it would prosper when that protection was removed.[27] Paine thus faulted Great Britain's protection as pernicious.

Paine found no words to describe the degraded state of Americans in the 1770s. He therefore coined the term "enemyship" to describe the relationship between the American colonies and Great Britain:

> It hath lately been asserted in parliament, that the colonies have no relation to each other but through the parent country, *i.e.* that Pennsylvania and the Jerseys, and so on for the rest, are sister colonies by the way of England; this is certainly a very round-about way of proving relationship, but it is the nearest and only true way of proving enemyship, if I may so call it. France and Spain never were, nor perhaps ever will be our enemies as *Americans*, but as our being the *subjects of Great Britain*.[28]

For Paine, enemyship signified the relationship between a group of people, states, or, here, colonies whose bond was cemented not by love but enmity.[29] In this case, Paine argued that American colonists existed in a state of enemyship vis-à-vis France and Spain because of Britain, and he posited the immediate goal of transcending enemyship and achieving friendship with the European powers whose assistance could decisively shift the war. Because it was their connection to Britain that made the colonies enemies to many European nations, Paine insisted that the only path to global friendship was to cast off the British yoke. In *Common Sense*, Paine imagined a world without enemies, where Americans were the friends of the world. This was the enticing dream he held out to Americans if they would only be brave enough to dance with death.

Paine knew something about dancing with death. His life was full of close calls, and he was fortunate to live as long as he did. The irascible fellow almost died before he could irritate anyone, from an illness he contracted on the arduous 3,000-mile journey from London to Philadelphia in 1774. Had he died then, the American lexicon would have suffered, for Paine was a master neologician. Had he died then, we might not have the word "enemyship"—for, according to the Oxford English Dictionary, it was a term that Paine invented in *Common Sense.* Paine did not invent the idea of enemyship; this existed long before his humble birth in Thetford, England. Yet Paine gave the concept a name, bringing it into public view and opening it to critical inspection. While Paine's masterpiece has been read by thousands of scholars and by all serious students of the Revolutionary War, every scholar that I know of who has written about *Common Sense* skips right over the passage in which Paine introduces the term "enemyship," and never looks back. One might interpret this silence as a sign that enemyship is deemed intellectually or politically unimportant. This would be a mistake, for to study Paine's use of the term "enemyship" is to engage a critical moment in the development of American political and rhetorical traditions.

In fact, the genius of *Common Sense* was Paine's ability to transform enemyship from a description of an undesirable state of affairs into a rhetorical principle for encouraging collective colonial action on the question of independence. By substituting the term "enemyship" for the term "relationship," Paine observed a bond between the colonies that could be exploited to further the revolutionary effort: namely, the colonies' mutual antagonism with Great Britain. As he developed his argument for independence, Paine made *Common Sense* a model of the rhetoric of enemyship. His argument unfolded in three moves. First, Paine named the enemy. Second, Paine denied the possibility of communication with the enemy. And third, Paine escalated the crisis "from argument to arms" (in his words) with disquieting rhetorics of anger, self-righteousness, and revenge.[30]

The Rhetorical Norms of Enemyship

Well into 1776, most Americans were lukewarm about revolution, and many still held out hope for reconciliation.[31] Most agreed with Benjamin Franklin, who as late as 1773 argued in London's *Public Advertiser* that "it was always the Boast of the Americans, that they could claim

their Original from the Kingdom of Great Britain."[32] The British Empire
was widely admired in the world for advancing liberty, securing law, and
augmenting the "interests and benefits" of its citizens.[33] Further, familial
metaphors dominated the political thought of the eighteenth century:
King George III was the father, the colonists his children.[34] To question
the king was to question the core of colonial being, so few questioned
the king. Rather than abandon their worldview, colonists told themselves
that it was Parliament, not the king, who had it in for them. Even as the
British retaliated for the Boston Tea Party by closing Boston harbor and
quarantining troops there, Bostonians displaced their pent-up frustrations onto scapegoats like Massachusetts' hated royal governor Thomas
Hutchinson rather than take the decisive, precipitous step of doubting
the king's motives.[35]

The better we know our enemies, the harder it is to fight, and thus
one of Paine's foremost tasks in *Common Sense* was to make the British
foreign, different, mysterious, unknowable, repulsive. Historians have offered many compelling reasons for the deterioration of colonial relations
and the rise of the revolutionary movement, including economic disagreement and conflict over how the empire should be run.[36] While Paine made
economics and empire central issues in *Common Sense*, he also appealed
to America's affinity for republicanism, and the endemic American fear of
conspiracy to drive home the necessity of independence.[37] Paine argued
that Americans and Britons held different and incompatible ideals of government, and that Americans would never be happy, free, or safe as long
as the British imposed their style of government on America.

The English were proud monarchists. Separated by an ocean, and left
to their own designs for much of the seventeenth and eighteenth centuries, Americans developed more representative forms of government.
Philosophers during the Enlightenment argued that there were distinct
and perhaps inalienable differences between monarchy and republicanism, and Paine invoked one of the most significant in *Common Sense*,
observing that while American power was derived from the people, the
British model invested power in the king. Paine defined monarchal government as an intolerable evil built upon the ruins of natural equality.
Monarchy, he concluded, was an "exceedingly ridiculous" system that
violated the social contract. To back this claim, Paine produced a long

and damning list: monarchy nurtured inequality and led to war; it was savage and heathen; it was contrary to Scripture and divine intention. Monarchy, he asserted forcefully, "was the most prosperous invention the Devil ever set on foot for the promotion of idolatry." To amplify this point, Paine crafted a subversive genealogy of the English crown that, while it did not lead back to the Deceiver himself, did find the path to monarchy littered with deception, lies, and false promises.[38]

One of the most popular tropes in political discourse in the eighteenth century was "the state of nature." This prominent rhetorical device was employed by Enlightenment philosophers to ground their observations in the natural, irrefutable laws of the Newtonian world. Thomas Hobbes used the horrors of the state of nature to justify the Crown. Paine did the opposite. Reaching back into the dawn of civilization, Paine reasoned that the first monarch was probably "the principle ruffian of some restless gang, whose savage manners or pre-eminence in subtlety obtained him the title of chief among plunderers," and thus monarchy for Paine was little more than the institutionalization of thuggery. Wrapped in the trappings of courtly glamour, Paine imagined the throne as a bully pulpit for cheating common people of their lives, liberties, and property. While the English traced the origins and legitimacy of monarchy back to a mythic Anglo-Saxon past, Paine mocked such legends. The founder of British monarchy, William the Conqueror, was in Paine's irreverent reading no hero. "A French bastard landing with an armed banditti, and establishing himself king of England against the consent of the natives," Paine indicated, "is in plain terms a very paltry rascally original." According to Paine, because King George III's lineage could be traced back to a French bastard, he too was a bastard, a rascal, and a usurper. And thus Paine mocked the king with a range of charges: he censured him as an "ass," a "worm," and a "crowned ruffian"; he compared him to a pimp; and, invoking America's latent anti-Catholicism, he labeled monarchy "the Popery of government."[39]

One of the king's most lurid abuses of power was his complete usurpation of the right to make war and peace—which, Paine countered, properly belonged to the people who had to do the fighting, not the people who would reap the glory from their sacrifice. While Hobbes positioned monarchy as an antidote to war, Paine argued that monarchy was in fact anathema to peace. In representative governments, war required the assent of citizens. Yet in England, all it took was the king's word to make war. The king could declare war on a whim. He could send his legions into battle simply because he liked the look of blood on steel, and Americans were sick and tired of being dragged into the king's wars. What Americans wanted more than anything else, Paine asserted, was peace. The king was an enemy because of arbitrary power and feudal inheritance, as manifested in the prosecution of unpopular wars and America's enemyship with Europe.

In place of monarchal power, Paine advocated for a democratic republic of self-rule. Paine framed republicanism as an antidote to the tyrannies of monarchy and the horrors of despotism. He wanted transparency and accountability in order to ensure that power was responsive to the people's needs. In turn, by ousting the monarchs from America, Paine argued that the future could be peaceful and friendly. "*Our plan is peace for ever*," he announced.[40] Yet with Britain as "our master," he reported, "we became enemies to the greatest part of Europe, and they to us: and the consequence was war inevitable. By being our own masters, independent of any foreign one, we have Europe for our friends, and the prospect of an endless peace among ourselves."[41] By achieving self-rule, independence was the surest path to peace.

For Paine, monarchy was absurd, and anyone who submitted to it must have been duped. Thus, he concluded that monarchy was premised on a centuries-long conspiracy of deception. For Paine, the pro-monarchy case was like "some superstitious tale, conveniently timed, Mahomet like, to cram hereditary right down the throats of the vulgar."[42] In eighteenth-century Anglo-American discourse, the founder of Islam, Mohammed, was often called "Mahomet," and thus in this passage of *Common Sense*, Paine invoked the specter of Islam to smear the British monarchy. The British were not the rightful rulers of America. Rather, they were no better than Muslims, who in the eighteenth century were unfairly characterized as inhuman butchers, bent on worldly domination and happy to use any means to achieve it.[43]

A popular Anglo-American "biography" of Mohammed titled *The Life of Mahomet* defined Islam as a religion of "sophistry" and labeled its dogmas "a bundle of contradictions" and "a motley jumble of inconsistencies."[44]

Similarly, an article in Boston's *Massachusetts Magazine* labeled Islam a religion of sophistry and compared Mohammed to "the daemon of Socrates."[45] In Plato's *Gorgias*, the character Socrates lambasted rhetoric because it "pays no regard to the welfare of its object, but catches fools with the bait of ephemeral pleasure and tricks them into holding it in the highest esteem."[46] Though Plato used a fictional Socrates to defame rhetoric—it is likely that the real historical Socrates had more respect for this art—Plato's Socrates was nevertheless a master of *rhetrickery*, the practice of wordplay and sophisms, trapping his interlocutors with twisted logic into undesired conclusions.[47] For this editorialist, the sophistic Socrates returned as a false prophet who represented the threat of Islamic contagion in the Western world.

By invoking Mohammed and Islam, Paine created an atmosphere of tension in *Common Sense*. Through the popular genre of captivity tales, which publicized the gruesome fates that met the unfortunate Christians who wandered into Muslim lands, and of the poor weak souls who were corrupted by the imposture and "turned Turk," Americans learned that reason would have no place in their dealings with Muslims.[48] "To reason with [Mohammed] would be an absolute waste of time," it was said.[49] Once reason goes out the window, so too does any possibility of getting along. Without persuasion, there is only coercion. The irrational, sophistic king was therefore no friend of America. Printing the words in capitals for emphasis, Paine concluded that "HE MAY ACCOMPLISH BY CRAFT AND SUBTLETY, IN THE LONG RUN, WHAT HE CANNOT DO BY FORCE AND VIOLENCE IN THE SHORT RUN. Reconciliation and ruin are nearly related."[50] In this sentence, Paine labeled the king an enemy not just for things he had done but also for things he might do, for things going on behind the scenes, for similarities to idolatrous religions hidden just below the surface, and for subtle actions that many failed to recognize as evil. For Paine, the king might look like a friend; he might even talk like a friend. But Americans had to wake up and see that he was really plotting their destruction. Though Americans had, for the longest time, loved their monarchal father, Paine insisted that he was untrustworthy: a liar, a sophist, and a deceiver.

Paine had been in America for little more than a year, but he was an astute observer of both local traditions and the mindset of a people.

Conspiracy theories were common in pre-Revolutionary America, and Paine capitalized on this fact in *Common Sense* in order to turn the king, the British Parliament, and the British people into enemies.[51] There was a plot afoot, he told his readers, vocalizing what many of them had come to believe in the 1770s. King George III was an "open enemy" of the colonies and "an inveterate enemy of liberty" because he had hatched a malevolent plan to take Americans' money, steal their freedoms, and usurp their liberties.[52] The evidence for this conspiracy included the Stamp Act (1765); the Townshend Duties (1768); the Tea Act (1773), which led to the Boston Tea Party; the Intolerable Acts (1774); and the murders at Lexington, Concord, and Bunker Hill. Paine urged his readers to see events like these as expressions of a monarch's design on American lives. The British were coming.

Though Paine successfully labeled the king an enemy, this alone was not enough to get the muskets firing. Americans attacked some of their enemies and demanded compliance or assimilation from others; some they left alone and others still they negotiated with. War with enemies was not preordained; there were other paths. To ensure that Americans chose the path of war over peace, Paine denied that they could coexist with the British enemy, because, he said, there could be no dialogue with the king.

The art of politics was then, and remains today, in large part about drawing lines of communicative possibility, of who Americans would and would not talk with. Prior to the telegraph, the word "communication" connoted travel, and thus Americans communicated across colonial boundaries on horse and foot. In the burgeoning public sphere, ideas were disseminated in newspapers. There were séances with the dead. And elites communicated with their pens in committees of correspondence and the republic of letters.[53] While communication in the eighteenth century was multimodal, the personal relationship was central to how communication was conceived. Americans tended to judge the quality of communication on grounds of character or *ethos*. In this "culture of performance," public speaking was conceptualized as "an occasion for the public revelation of the private self," and the speaker or writer was judged successful to the extent that he or she exhibited private virtues associated with moral-sense philosophy: "prudence, temperance, self-control, honesty, and . . . sincerity."⁵⁴ Shifting from a Ciceronian rhetoric of *controversia* to a more evangelical model of "heartfelt persuasion," Americans at this time conceptualized persuasion as "a matter of the heart as much as of the mind."⁵⁵ This meant that persuasion required sympathy and identification between speaker and audience, lest an orator's words fall on deaf ears and uncaring hearts.

In *The Theory of Moral Sentiments* (1759), one of the Enlightenment's most profound meditations on psychology and moral philosophy, Adam Smith claimed that communication could only occur between individuals who knew and trusted one another. For him, communication was premised on a "harmony of minds." "The great pleasure of conversation and society," he wrote, "arises from a certain correspondence of sentiments and opinions, from a certain harmony of minds, which like so many musical instruments coincide and keep time with one another."⁵⁶ For Smith, modern, liberal, commercial societies sat on the bedrock of a communication revolution that included the proliferation of viable communication networks including roads, canals, and the mail, and also the generation of shared assumptions about the world and interpersonal trust between interlocutors. Without this basic harmony of minds, there could be no communal life. Pondering similar issues, David Hume surmised that distance was a limit condition for communication, communion, and community. "We sympathize more with persons contiguous to us, than with persons remote from us: With our acquaintance, than with strangers: With our countrymen, than with foreigners," he concluded.⁵⁷ For Hume, sympathy decreased as physical and psychological distance increased, and with sympathy went communication.

Paine turned the philosophical insights of Smith and Hume into active rhetorical principles. Concerns with distance, both physical and psychological, were central to *Common Sense*. Paine denied the possibility of communication with the king because of the thousands of miles separating Great Britain from America. While eighteenth-century Americans were immersed in a transatlantic economy of circulating goods and ideas, this increasingly globalized world was not like our own, which thrives on speed. This world was slow. Paine knew the 3,000-mile journey between London and Philadelphia well, for it had nearly killed him. The journey Paine made to America was an equal-opportunity killer, dispatching people and messages alike. Following the Seven Years War, Great Britain guaranteed the monthly delivery of mail to three destinations in the New World: New York, Charlestown, and the West Indies. Still, words printed in London could take five to six weeks to arrive in North America, and then even longer to be disseminated there—which entailed an inconvenient delay of news, proclamations, laws, ordinances, and orders.[58] To the extent that effective communication required a timely response, this delay distanced the colonies from Great Britain and made it impossible to effectively communicate. "To be always running three or four thousand miles with a tale or a petition, waiting four or five months for an answer, which when obtained requires five or six more to explain it in, will in a few years be looked upon as folly and childishness," suggested Paine. "There was a time when it was proper, and there is a proper time for it to cease."[59]

The ocean created distance in one sense; Great Britain's actions created it in another, more profound sense. An interpretation of the events of April 19, 1775, was absolutely vital to Paine's enemyship. Attempting to ensure that British troops did not seize munitions hidden by the Massachusetts militia, on that day colonists skirmished with British regulars at Lexington and Concord in the first battles of the Revolutionary War. The colonial militiamen killed at Lexington were technically criminals, for they were engaged in armed resistance to British law. Nevertheless, Whig leaders wishing to foment a wider uprising named the British tyrannical aggressors who, without justification, massacred innocent colonists. After the shots were fired at Lexington and Concord, Whig leaders put a well-oiled propaganda machine into motion, circulating their account of Lexington widely.[60] In major colonial and British newspapers; in a broadside, *Bloody Butchery of the British Troops*; and in a book, *A Narrative of the Excursion and Ravages of the King's Troops*, advocates of independence labeled the king's troops murderers of innocent men, hence denying the possibility of a peaceful reconciliation between the colonies and the mother country. Pro-revolutionary leaders attempted to prove the justness of independence by convincing colonists that their relationship with the mother country was broken beyond repair.

Events like Lexington and Concord facilitated the metamorphosis of the king from a colonial father who could do no wrong into a public enemy. Paine professed his belief that these battles, when coupled with the king's enduring hostility as symbolized by his angry denunciations of the colonies, made conflict inevitable. "No man was a warmer wisher for reconciliation than myself, before the fatal nineteenth of April 1775," he confessed, but following that "fatal" day, "I rejected the hardened, sullen tempered Pharaoh of—for ever; and disdain the wretch, that with the pretended title of FATHER OF HIS PEOPLE can unfeelingly hear of their slaughter, and composedly sleep with their blood upon his soul." Now, he concluded simply, "the period for debate is closed. Arms, as the last resource, decide the contest; the appeal was the choice of the king, and the continent hath accepted his challenge." Communication, and by extension reconciliation, was no longer possible with the false father and the Britons who bowed to him. The time for prayers, petitions, and diplomacy was past. "Wherefore since nothing but blows will do, for God's sake, let us come to a final separation, and not leave the next generation to be cutting throats, under the violated unmeaning names of parent and child." By naming an enemy and making communication seem impossible, Paine attempted to dissuade Americans from communicating with their British brethren. If Americans communicated with their enemies, they might have found that they were really friends. To move colonists toward independence, Paine worked to ensure that this did not happen.[61]

Having named an enemy and made it appear that there was no chance of friendship or reconciliation with that enemy, Paine attempted to move Americans to immediate action by making the British danger appear present and real. He attempted, in short, to make Americans feel that they had no other choice but to fight. The desired effect of Paine's rhetoric was to induce a state of acute psychological distress: by deploying conspiratorial language to foster panic, Paine attempted to consume his audience with thoughts of self-defense so that they believed that independence was their only option for safety and peace. Capitalizing on events like the British occupation of Boston, the deaths at Lexington and Concord, and the crisis surrounding Lord Dunmore, Paine transformed the small-scale fighting that occurred in 1775 into a looming crisis—the imminent, full-scale British invasion of America. In *Common Sense*, Paine attempted to convince colonists that resistance was their only option, with the hope that Americans would respond to grievances with collective violence rather than the comity of reconciliation.

A revolution would require the successful cooperation of strangers. Paine learned upon his arrival in 1774, however, that local concerns came first for Americans. The thirteen colonies were deeply divided on substantive issues, including religion, language, ethnicity, slavery, taxation, industrialization, urbanization, and the franchise. These divisions acted as a prominent barrier to Paine's message of colonial union, as did the unequal distribution of hardship throughout the colonies. Many eighteenth-century moral philosophers assumed that humans were fundamentally self-interested, and therefore that personal pains and stomachaches would cause more discomfort than the deaths of strangers.[62] The selfishness of modern liberalism vexed revolutionaries like Paine. The social fact was that many colonists did not understand colonists in distant towns to be their fellows, divided as they were by gaps in affection.

Though the British perpetuated several "atrocities" in the 1770s, few colonists felt these hardships. In the eighteenth century, grievances generally were local. Such events in and of themselves did not further the revolutionary movement. Indeed, one of the primary rhetorical challenges Paine confronted in this task was the inability of colonists to identify with their fellow subjects. By spreading the misery around, *Common Sense* inspired those who were not directly affected by the events in New England to empathize with the woes of their fellow colonists. He overcame isolation by producing a bond of shared fears, mutual threats, and communal losses. "But let our imaginations transport us for a few moments to Boston," Paine reported, and "that seat of wretchedness will teach us wisdom, and instruct us for ever to renounce a power in whom we can have no trust."[63] There was wisdom in shared wretchedness, for it allowed a disparate people to imagine a more national community. Paine redefined colonial relations as bonds of shared oppression.

After detailing the woeful conditions of the Bostonians, Paine fired off a series of questions meant to inspire his readers to support their fellow sufferers: "Hath your house been burnt? Hath your property been destroyed before your face? Are your wife and children destitute of a bed to lie on, or bread to live on? Have you lost a parent or a child by their hands, and yourself the ruined and wretched survivor?"[64] To ensure that fear engendered defense and not paralysis, Paine deployed *cataplexis*, or the rhetoric of threats, and focused it on the topic of families. By talking about parents and children, husbands and wives, Paine appealed to the emotions of his audience: for who would not do anything to protect their family from harm? The underlying threat of *Common Sense* was intended to hit Americans where it hurt the most. The home was supposed to be a castle, but Paine cautioned that its ramparts were weak. Paine warned that if the British were not defeated, all colonists would soon have their houses burnt, their property destroyed, their families abused and murdered, and their lives ruined. Destitute, they would all be one.

Proponents made war appear glamorous, honorable, and manly—and peace weak, cowardly, and effeminate. Yet when Paine asked a rag-tag bunch of colonial farmers and militiamen to take on the most powerful military in the world, he understood that choosing life over death was not cowardly. In fact, for those with any sense, the rational response to the call of battle was to run and hide. However worthy the cause might have been, a colonial civil war was certain to be brutal and perhaps even worse than the Seven Years War. Families on all sides would be torn in two. Children would be ruthlessly slaughtered. Crops and fortunes would be ruined. Who would not want to avoid such carnage? Paine and others who wanted a war for independence understood that it was not natural to kill or cowardly to avoid carnage. The obstacles Paine confronted in *Common Sense* were human: the frailty of our bodies, the love of our families, and the banal routines of daily life, all of which define the orbits of our universe and keep us at home.

Today, we remember the Revolutionary War for its ideals, including freedom, liberty, equality, happiness, and sacrifice. Clearly, Paine had the highest hopes for independence. These high hopes in fact drove his rhetoric of enemyship. While the enemy stood in the way of an ideal American future, at the same time the enemy was also necessary to spur Americans on to achieve this future. Paine's vision of the future achieved clarity in contradistinction to ruin. While ideals including freedom, equality, self-government, and republicanism were central to Paine's argument, the rhetorical situation required something more. There were things worth fighting for, and a group of slaves or prisoners might reasonably die for their freedom, but life in the 1770s was not that hard for most Americans. The so-called Intolerable Acts hit merchants hardest; most Americans (outside of Boston) never felt their effects. To argue that Americans should fight for freedom was a tough sell, because Americans were freer than almost all other peoples in the world—freer, certainly, than the slaves many owned. Freedom and other ideals were inspirational in retrospect. But the American Revolution required warm bodies to wield guns and kill redcoats, and *Common Sense* therefore folded idealism into an argument that engendered fear and encouraged paranoia. In 1775, Paine argued that Americans should unite in defense of their ideals.[65] In 1776, he argued instead that Americans should unite in defense of their lives.

Paine interpreted the battles at Lexington and Concord, and also the king's angry words, as attacks on the colonies' rights and privileges. And, he put his audience on notice, the worst was yet to come. Americans were obligated to fight because the attacks would not cease. The Bostonians were first; everyone else was next. Paine thus positioned the Revolutionary War as a defensive war against imperial aggression. "Beneath the shade of our own vines we are attacked; in our own houses, and on our own lands, is the violence committed against us," he argued. "We view our enemies in the characters of Highwaymen and Housebreakers, and having no defence for ourselves in the civil law, are obliged to punish them by the military one, and apply the sword, in the very case, where you have before now, applied the halter."[66] This argument was doubly clever, for it masked the lawlessness of the colonists' actions at Lexington and Concord by making the British aggressors, and applied a motivational logic of innocent self-defense to argue for war. Just-war theorists argued that if any war was justifiable, it was a war for self-defense. By arguing that the British had attacked America, Paine legitimated what many in North America and Europe believed to be an illegitimate rebellion against the Crown. At the same time, by arguing that the British had attacked America, by warning that the worst was yet to come, and by threatening that all would be lost if Americans did not unite in self-defense, Paine tried to force Americans to act.

Transforming fear, anxiety, and worry into action was tricky business. Hegel argued in *The Phenomenology of Spirit* that fear caused people to freeze, not fight, hence breeding immobilization, inaction, and bondage.[67] Foreshadowing Hegel's illuminating analysis of the stultifying effects of fear, Paine observed that fear was actually one of the major obstacles to revolution because it prevented those with something to lose from fighting. In fact, he acknowledged that it was hard to persuade rich people to fight because they had so much to lose. "The more men have to lose, the less willing they are to venture. The rich are in general slaves to fear, and submit to courtly power with the trembling duplicity of a spaniel," he deduced.[68] But without the capital, encouragement, and influence of the wealthy, there could be no revolution. Fear has many modalities, and when it came to motivation, persuasion, and political argumentation in the Revolutionary era, there seemed to be a hierarchy of fears. A kill-or-be-killed moment was easy to figure out. It was a moment beyond politics. When an enemy tries to kill you, Paine argues, you react. There is no other recourse: you kill him first. Americans could not flee, and if they froze, they would be mercilessly killed. The only option was to fight.

Paine was born to a Quaker father, and in his revolutionary writings he wrestled publicly with his pacifist heritage. Though the founder of Quakerism, George Fox, did not object to his followers taking up arms in the period of persecution leading up to the 1660 Restoration in England, hence suggesting that violence was tolerable if used in self-defense, the Quaker church in America came to see pacifism as an integral and inescapable plank of their faith.[69] While many Quakers had withdrawn from political life in Pennsylvania in the late 1760s, the profound Quaker influence on Philadelphia politics was one of the primary impediments to independence—not because all Quakers sympathized with the British (though many did), but because the Quaker peace witness categorically forbade the use of violence, even for self-defense. Quakerism represented the limits of Paine's rhetoric, for with their New Testament doctrine of turning the other cheek, Pennsylvania's Quakers denied Paine the hatred and fear of the enemy he needed for war.

In 1775, Paine published an essay in the *Pennsylvania Magazine* announcing his philosophical agreement with pacifism, noting, "I would gladly agree with all the world to lay aside the use of arms, and settle matters by negotiation; but unless the whole will, the matter ends, and I take up my musket and thank heaven he put it in my power." Pacifism was fine in principle, Paine suggested, but its theoretical beauty was contradicted by the nefariousness of the British enemy and the need to take up arms in self-defense. "Whoever considers the unprincipled enemy we have to cope with, will not hesitate to declare that nothing but arms or miracles

can reduce them to reason and moderation," Paine advised, and then he
turned this insight against Quakers, who had "lost sight of the limits of
humanity."⁷⁰ The Quakers' pacifism shut down Paine's enemyship from
the onset, for it refused to cleave the world into friends and enemies,
and to recognize that humanity might have limits. Furthermore, it stifled
Paine's argument by denying the legitimacy of self-defense. If there were
no enemies, then the arguments of *Common Sense* were nonsensical.

Paine's rhetoric faltered to the extent that Americans denied the logic
of self-defense. If they would not defend themselves, then the character
of the enemy, or the audacity of his design, did not matter. The doctrine
of self-defense was so important to Paine's argument that he closed *Common Sense* with a lengthy, blistering attack on Quakers and other pacifists.
The pre-Revolutionary moment was characterized by a fluctuating economy of friendship as Americans expanded and contracted their circles of
friends and enemies. Yet the trend was toward the suppression of dissenting voices; those who opposed independence became enemies.⁷¹ Paine
therefore mocked his opponents as hypocrites. He charged them with
preaching fantastical doctrines that made no sense, that were contrary to
Scripture, and that they themselves would quickly abandon in a moment
of crisis. Paine issued the following threat to such characters: "If ye really
preach from conscience," he told America's pacifists, "convince the world
thereof, by proclaiming your doctrine to our enemies, for *they likewise
bear* ARMS." "Give us proof of your sincerity by publishing it at St. James's,
to the commanders in chief at Boston, to the Admirals and Captains who
are piratically ravaging our coasts, and to all the murdering miscreants,"
he objected, taunting pacifists with a brutal world of redcoats and pirates
who would happily slaughter their families if given the chance. Paine
railed against Quakers because his rhetoric was dependent upon the belief that the real war was at hand and that violence was consequently an
(unfortunate) necessity of self-defense. There were things worth fighting
for, and if there ever was a just war, Paine said, this was it.⁷²

While Pennsylvania's Quakers continued to preach their consciences
and shun military service during the Revolutionary War, Paine's message reoriented the relationship between the American colonies and the
mother country in a way that facilitated conflict. *Common Sense* was a text
of foreboding, of the coming attack. Its goal was to push colonists' backs

against a wall. Though Paine was insistent that colonists were helpless to prevent the hammer from falling, *Common Sense* was nevertheless an empowering text in one sense: for it called on Americans to band together and defend themselves. Paine thus turned fear, paranoia, and anxiety into a colonial community focused on defense.

The Consequences of Enemyship

Paine's goal in *Common Sense* was to encourage Americans to fight for their independence. But to win a war against the mighty British Empire, with its disciplined lines and formidable masts, Americans had to come together like never before. Seeing how shared dangers brought Americans closer together in 1774–1775, in the aftermath of the siege of Boston, the battles of Lexington and Concord, and Lord Dunmore's War, Paine believed that Americans could become friends by emphasizing their shared animosity against England. Thus, while denouncing how England put America in a state of enemyship with the rest of Europe, Paine proceeded in *Common Sense* to put Americans in a state of enemyship with England by transforming the king, his minions, and even innocent British citizens into national enemies to be detested, feared, and defeated in battle. He did this by naming an enemy—the thieving, murderous, sophistic king; by denying that communication, diplomacy, and hence reconciliation were possible with that enemy; and then by escalating the crisis so that it seemed that Americans could not avoid the battle. They would have to fight.

While Paine practiced enemyship in *Common Sense*, he nevertheless recognized that enemyship was not a good thing—for in a state of enemyship, Americans were not friends but comrades in arms. Paine hoped that the Revolutionary War would create a lasting foundation for future greatness, and the relationship between friends would be stronger than the relationship between comrades. Friends cooperated because of mutual affection; comrades cooperated because they had to or else. Because comrades did not have a foundation in mutual affection, enemyship was more fragile—and indeed more volatile—than friendship. Enemyship was no substitute for friendship, and in *Common Sense*, Paine claimed

that he believed Americans would quickly transcend a state of enemyship and achieve something closer to genuine friendship with their fellow
citizens: "The intimacy which is contracted in infancy, and the friendship
which is formed in misfortune, are, of all others, the most lasting and un-
alterable."73 But enemyship was not easily transcended. In fact, the decision to name the enemy fundamentally altered Paine's democratic vision
by pushing it toward anger, hostility, suspicion, and revenge. *Common
Sense* illuminated the consequences of premising political communities
on shared fears of an enemy. Though Paine began his pamphlet with the
highest hopes, rather than friends talking, laughing, and debating, *Common Sense* quickly devolved into a scene of friends hitting, kicking, and
screaming: at the enemy, and at each other.

During the Revolutionary War, Americans were fighting for more than
their safety: they were fighting for a better tomorrow, a postmonarchal
future in which the voices of citizens mattered. In place of monarchal
tyranny, Paine called for a representative democracy with small voting
districts, annual elections, and a rotating president between each of the
thirteen states. This simple system, he announced, would form the basis
of a peaceful republic of laws. "The nearer any government approaches to
a republic the less business there is for a king," he observed. In America,
there would be no king because "in America, THE LAW IS KING."74 To win
this future, however, Americans would first have to embrace the politics
of enemyship and engage in the act of "drawing a line," finding unity
through the performance of division:

> WHEREFORE, instead of gazing at each other with suspicious or doubtful
> curiosity, let each of us, hold out to his neighbour the hearty hand of
> friendship, and unite in drawing a line, which, like an act of oblivion,
> shall bury in forgetfulness every former dissension. Let the names
> of Whig and Tory be extinct; and let none other be heard among us,
> than those of *a good citizen, an open and resolute friend, and a virtuous
> supporter of the* RIGHTS *of* MANKIND *and of the* FREE AND INDEPENDENT
> STATES OF AMERICA.75

Fretting that Americans were reluctant to extend their hands to help their
neighbors, in *Common Sense* Paine asked Americans: why can't we all

be friends? This passage suggested that American friendship would be premised on two bonds: a shared commitment to "the rights of mankind," and unified opposition to a shared enemy. Though Americans weren't yet friends, if they could only unite in drawing a line, then a key precondition for friendship—a common goal—would be in place. In opposition to the enemy, no longer would colonists be divided into Whigs and Tories; they would simply be Americans.

Paine discovered enemyship in the political situation of the colonies, but through the constitutive power of rhetoric to alter the relationship between self and other, he adopted it as a primary rhetorical technique for destroying colonial dependence, justifying independence, and moving Americans to revolutionary action. In turn, Paine's democracy was founded on the self-righteous enmity of comrades under attack. For him, then, enemyship created the conditions of possibility for friendship and democracy, as colonists buried their former disputes and disagreements in oblivion and shook hands as brothers in arms.

While this assumption drove the rhetoric of *Common Sense*, it was perhaps misguided. While an enemy can call the demos to attention, acting as a spur to deliberation and possibly shared action, rhetorical scholars have long noted that it is difficult to deliberate during times of war, when the enemy threatens.[76] Good decisions take time and require a quiet space for rumination. What democratic theorists call the "enlightened understanding" necessary for deliberation needs a slowing down, a willingness to forestall judgment and honestly consider the issues.[77] Enemyship might bring a democratic people together to deliberate, yet the fear of the enemy constricts the breathing room needed to consider and discuss the issues in the way that democracy demands. Fear, in fact, fundamentally alters the landscape of deliberation and democracy.

Moreover, popular governments require compromise and goodwill. While antagonism is perhaps inescapable in the political realm, citizens in a democracy must treat their adversaries as mistaken, not evil, for it is hard to work with fellow citizens who are labeled evil. Paine's *Common Sense* suggests that enemyship is a deeply problematic rhetoric for cultivating popular government, because it is a type of rhetoric that quickly monopolizes the discursive field, narrowing the realm of acceptable choices and subject positions that political actors can occupy.

Paine's enemyship placed certain insatiable demands on the community constituted inside the line, in particular by calling for the suspension of "every former dissention" and hence a unanimity of sentiment that was impossible to achieve. If one marker of a good government was how well it dealt with disagreement and dissent—a criterion elaborated in *Common Sense* in Paine's attacks on monarchal oppression of American voices—then Paine's enemyship corrupted democracy by turning it towards the creation and preservation of dangerously unstable homogeneities of friend and enemy, Whig and Tory, revolutionary and criminal. His enemyship fabricated solidarity by accentuating the similarity of citizens, meaning that it was hostile towards political, cultural, racial, and religious difference as represented in dissenting figures like the Quakers. If Paine's picture of the British was accurate, then Americans had to mobilize for defense; there was no time for objection or counterargument. In this state of enemyship, those who dissented became enemies.

By bringing Americans together and forging them into a people, enemyship created the conditions of possibility for the Revolutionary War. With his rhetoric, Paine created an American public. It was impossible, however, to achieve the perfectly bifurcated world of friends and enemies that Paine's rhetoric sought. As the crisis was escalated and Americans began to fear for their well-being and that of their families, the stark boundaries between inside and outside broke down in the paranoia of a state of emergency. Consequently, it became increasingly unclear who was and who was not an enemy—revealing how unstable, albeit powerful, a discourse enemyship was. Even in the early months of 1776, Paine's cut-and-dried ontology of friends and enemies collapsed. Eloquent Tories spoke out against the war, outwardly true-blue merchants profited from colonial hardship, and Philadelphia's Quakers answered *Common Sense* with a pacifist ethic that forbade violence. Paine's enemyship, however, could not tolerate even a single voice of dissent. The state of enemyship demanded unity in the face of danger. Thus, in the later editions of *Common Sense*, Paine dealt with dissenters, including Tories and pacifists, by ripping into them with righteous fury.

The textual shift between the first and second editions of *Common Sense* illuminates how enemyship can shape democratic discourse in undemocratic ways, for in the pamphlet's later editions, Paine turned his formidable pen against Americans who disagreed with his arguments. The first edition of *Common Sense* was published on January 10, 1776, by Robert Bell; the second, enlarged edition on February 14, 1776, by William and Thomas Bradford, which was also translated into German for Pennsylvania's large German-speaking population.[78] The later editions contained an appendix in which Paine employed his rhetoric of enemyship as a weapon to silence his critics. Here, Paine cajoled doubters and threatened them with the worst of fates if they did not come around to his view of war and the king. The dissenter, Paine argued, was an "apostate" to be damned; he was also less than human, to be marked "as one, who hath, not only given up the proper dignity of a man, but sunk himself beneath the rank of animals, and contemptibly crawls through the world like a worm." For Paine, "there is no punishment which that man will not deserve" who opposes independence. Those who blocked the independence movement were as bad as the British, and hence subject to all the cruel punishments humans had devised to torment their foes.[79]

In his discussion of Lexington and Concord, Paine wrote somewhat disingenuously that "I mean not to exhibit horror for the purpose of provoking revenge, but to awaken us from fatal and unmanly slumbers, that we may pursue determinately some fixed object."[80] This disclaimer was astute, for while revenge was an integral part of colonial life, both on the colonial frontier where "subsistence activities and border warfare governed the rhythms of daily life," and also in elite cultures that embraced dueling as the preferred channel for rectifying insult, revenge was portrayed as immoral in most public and philosophical discourse at the time.[81] Nevertheless, Paine recognized the utility of revenge for motivating his audience during wartime. "Men read by way of revenge," he observed.[82] By arguing repeatedly that Americans were attacked without provocation, he justified American violence as self-defense while egging Americans on to destroy the ravishers of their land.

To be gripped by the desire for revenge is to be awakened from a slumber—it is to be psychologically stimulated and primed for decisive action. Paraphrasing Milton, Paine claimed that Americans suffered "wounds of deadly hate" in the 1770s, and *Common Sense* proceeded from the assumption that these wounds were to be both lamented and nurtured—for if Americans could be made to desire revenge, they might act in concert to kill their enemies.[83] Thus, Paine channeled the angry passions of the 1770s into coordinated behavior directed at "some fixed object"—namely, *retribution*, which seeks to restore the proper balance between right and wrong with a cathartic act of vengeance that destroys the enemy and, in the process, rights a perceived wrong. Paine understood that if he could inspire Americans to seek retribution for British atrocities like Lexington and Concord, this would advance the cause of independence, even though many who would fight were inspired not by ideals but instead by their angry passions.

Revenge is one of the primary motivations for war, and as such, calls for revenge figure prominently in war rhetoric. Revenge can also be a primary motivator for the formation, and sustenance, of political communities. In the context of Paine's enemyship, however, the desire for revenge was transferred from righting British wrongs to punishing dissenting colonial voices. If the primary bond that Americans shared was their enmity toward the king, then to balk at conflict was to prove oneself no American; it was to side with the enemy. In this environment of enemyship, dissent became shameful, even treasonous, and revenge acceptable, even praiseworthy. Echoing Jesus' words in Luke 23:34 when he was crucified, Paine taunted Tories and pacifists: "Ye that oppose independence now, ye know not what ye do."[84] He continued to compare dissent to the most heinous rebellion available, proclaiming that "He that would promote discord, under a government so equally formed as this, would join Lucifer in his revolt."[85] For the Christians reading or listening to *Common Sense* as it was read aloud in churches, public gatherings, town halls, and taverns, these examples were serious business, for they likened dissent to Lucifer's rebellion against God, and dissenters to those who crucified Christ. Paine was not a religious man. In fact, he has been convincingly labeled the first great American atheist.[86] It was troubling, then, that Paine's most provocative use of religious language, allusions, and metaphors arose when he pondered divine retribution for his opponents. For this staunch defender of the separation of church and state, while Americans should banish religion to the private sphere, they were nevertheless free to employ the language of religion to justify pursuing and punishing their enemies with divine fervor.

In turn, Paine warned that there would be no forgetting past insults. Here, Paine contradicted his suggestion that American friendship was premised on an act of oblivion as participants buried in forgetfulness past disputes. To scare moderates and punish dissenters, Paine was adamant that independent Americans would never forget yesterday's wrongs. "There are injuries which nature cannot forgive," he opined. "As well can the lover forgive the ravisher of his mistress, as the continent can forgive the murders of Britain."[87] Like the betrayed spouse in a Shakespearean tragedy or the sentimental fiction of the day, Paine's America was filled with resentful hatred for its enemies. Accordingly, Paine's America spent much of its time and energy plotting to get even.

While humans can change the world through their rhetorical choices, they are also shaped by those choices. How we talk influences how we know and experience the world. Paine imagined a world without enemies—in which Americans were friends of Europe and the world, a world of peace and happiness for all. Yet insofar as *Common Sense* called a democratic people into existence, it suggested that this people would be violent, vengeful, intolerant, and hateful—toward the enemy, and toward each other. If this was friendship, it was not particularly friendly. Yet this was not friendship; this was enemyship. As Americans named the enemy in the post-Revolutionary years, they were forced, time and time again, to deal with the consequences of a persuasive discourse that quickly monopolized the discursive field, but that could never quite monopolize the social world by mirroring in reality what was so clear in the realm of symbols. While those engaged in the rhetorical politics of enemyship attempted to create a perfect antithesis of friend and enemy, they never could. But this did not stop politicians in the post-Revolutionary years from naming enemies. Enemyship was too useful. And thus the founders of the United States embraced many of the unintended consequences of enemyship in *Common Sense* and made them productive in the post-Revolutionary years, naming the enemy to cultivate a sense of national identity and nurture obedience to authority.

CHAPTER TWO

The Dilemmas
of American Nationalism

Victory in the Revolutionary War was greeted with jubilation and a big sigh of relief. But Americans who lived through the war won something they had not bargained for, for victory required cooperation across far-flung communities and between people who had little in common besides their foes. The colonists who tangled with the British received more than military training. As they shared fears and prosecuted a war, they got the experience of working together toward a common cause: in short, the experience of being a people. The rhetoric fueling revolution helped colonists imagine a national community that blurred the lines between here and there, my backyard and yours, Massachusetts and Virginia, New York and Georgia. "You know (for some of you are men of abilities and reading) or ought to know" Noah Webster observed, "a principle of *fear*, in times of war, operates more powerfully in binding together the States which have a common interest, than all the parchment contracts on earth."[1] After years of trying to forge a more unified

67

national community in the 1760s and 1770s, Americans came together in 1776 to confront a common enemy. This national community, however, was unstable—and while victory meant independence, the cessation of hostilities with Britain also resulted in a sociological step backward as Americans returned home to their families, their kinship in arms expired.

During the war, citizens cooperated to survive. Once independence was won and peace restored, however, the American community fractured as citizens once again put local interests before national concerns. The immediate postwar years were characterized by weakness, division, and a public debate over who was really in charge. The Revolutionary War drew lines between Americans and Englishmen. This relatively broad and ambiguous concept of an "American" worked during the war. When it was time to build a government and determine who would rule, however, the gentry believed that it was necessary to draw a second, internal distinction between the people and those who would govern them. While they happily shared the costs of battle with the lower classes and democratic masses, educated elites demanded deference from common folks and did not plan on sharing the reins of government with them once the war was won.[2]

The transition from revolution to independence was a rocky one, for while elites demanded deference, the Revolutionary War nursed in the masses a feeling of political entitlement, an insistence on popular sovereignty, and a profound belief in political and material equality. With a motley crew of sailors, slaves, free blacks, artisans, merchants, farmers, and elites shooting, hollering, and dying together to achieve independence, the Revolutionary War exhibited strong democratic tendencies.[3] As one of the Revolutionary War's first historians, Mercy Otis Warren, observed in her 1805 *History of the Rise, Progress, and Termination of the American Revolution*, the Revolutionary War represented "one of the most extraordinary eras in the history of man" because it resulted in an "experiment of levelling all ranks, and destroying all subordination."[4] The Revolutionary War was indeed a democratic "experiment," for the popular politics, widespread cooperation, and potent rhetorics of revolutionary documents, including *Common Sense* and the Declaration of Independence, made it possible to ponder more democratic governments.

Though Thomas Paine did not use the word "democracy," in *Common*

Sense he expressed faith in the ability of common folks to make a meaning-ful contribution to public affairs, and he imagined a postwar America that was a more democratic place in which citizens assumed the reins of gov-ernment. As *Common Sense* threw down the gauntlet against monarchy, it also praised popular government. Obliterating the hereditary distinc-tions of monarchy was the goal of the Revolutionary War; to ensure that monarchy would never rear its ugly head in America again, Paine called on his readers to metaphorically smash the king's crown and distribute the pieces among themselves, "whose right it is."[5] Paine conceptualized the American Revolution as a symbolic act of decapitation in the name of democracy, and all across the colonies, Americans enacted his words.

By July 1776, colonists had come to see the destruction of their father, the king, as inevitable—meaning that the Revolutionary War exhibited characteristics of both an oedipal conflict and a coming-of-age rite.[6] In the aftermath of the signing of the Declaration of Independence, the symbolic patricide committed in *Common Sense* was matched by physical acts of violence against representations of the king. The shift from loyalty to rebellion took over a decade, but once it occurred, "Americans turned on George III with a fury as remarkable as the loyalty that preceded it."[7] King George III was symbolically murdered in all thirteen colonies. In Baltimore, colonists threw his effigy into a fire. In New York City, the Sons of Liberty ripped down a gilded equestrian statue of the king and destroyed it. The king's crest of arms was destroyed in all the colonies, and in at least one city (Worcester, Massachusetts), the arms were broken into pieces and carried off by the townsfolk in a literal reenactment of Paine's charge. In Savannah, a large crowd staged a mock funeral for the dead potentate.[8] At Huntington, Long Island, colonists fashioned an effigy of the king from the materials of a liberty tree that had been dedicated to him, blackened its face, dressed it in feathers, wrapped it in the Union Jack, and then hung, burned, and exploded it.[9] Independence thus came with a joyous bang as Americans turned their colonial father into an enemy, destroyed the symbol of his power, and incorporated that power into themselves.

Imagining the American Revolution as a democratic revolution that would finally, once and for all, put the nail in the coffin of arbitrary power, and that would usher in an era of freedom and equality, many participants expected that democratic ideals would form the foundation of the newly independent nation. In a series of articles appearing in the *New-York Journal* in May and June, 1776, the author "Spartanus" imagined that post-Revolutionary America would embrace democracy, because a democratic state, he or she argued, would deliver up the benefits that he believed persuaded humans to form societies in the first place. Premising his case on a lengthy disquisition on the social contract, Spartanus situated democracy as the government most capable of satisfying the natural human yearning for equality.[10] The anonymous author of the 1776 pamphlet *The People the Best Governors: Or a Plan of Government Founded on the Just Principles of Natural Freedom* similarly defended democracy by arguing that it would fulfill God's will. "*GOD gave mankind freedom by nature, made every man equal to his neighbour, and has virtually enjoined them, to govern themselves by their own laws,*" this author wrote. "*The people best know their own wants and necessities, and therefore, are best able to rule themselves.*"[11] In the heady early days of the Revolution, this author, and many others, leaped beyond the present to a future election of government. Arguing that self-government was the only possible foundation for a strong and lasting nation, the author of *The People the Best Governors* offered several radical suggestions for nation-builders, calling for an equitable division of property, and annual elections of representatives answering directly to their constituents. This writer hoped to make government responsive to the popular will, and not the other way around.

Though the United States would not exist without the sacrifices of poor farmers and merchants who fought for a more democratic world, there was a pronounced backlash against the democratic spirit after the Treaty of Paris. In the years following the Revolutionary War, elites called on common citizens to undergo a fundamental reorganization of the revolutionary mindset. No longer would citizens have the extralegal right to harass the government and void laws they disliked through mob rioting and coordinated violence. Now, citizens had the duty to defer to decisions made by their representatives and upheld by the courts; this was the essence of republican government. "Free governments, like all others," Philadelphia's *Gazette of the United States* explained during the Whiskey Rebellion in 1794, "must have a certain degree of subordination—and the very idea of submission, in matters of a civil nature, implies a yielding up, or surrendering the wills and judgments of the few to that of the many. It is certainly the duty of a good citizen to do so, however disagreeable the task may be."[12] Freedom in the United States did not mean revolution or unrestrained agency, the *Gazette* objected. Instead, it meant acting within the framework of rules established for the good of all.

James Madison framed government as an unfortunate evil in Federalist 51. "But what is government itself, but the greatest of all reflections on human nature? If men were angels, no government would be necessary," he concluded. The "great difficulty" in building a government was "you must first enable the government to control the governed; and in the next place oblige it to control itself."[13] Checks and balances were essential, Madison maintained, but even before that, the government had to gain control over the hearts and minds of citizens. Telling citizens that they had power only on their election days, as it was sometimes said, was one thing. Persuading them of this fact was another, for the memory of revolution nursed a feeling of political entitlement, engendered an insistence on popular sovereignty, created an expectation that government would work for equality, and taught colonists that coordinated violence was effective in securing their goals [jails] when government became disrespectful of them.

The Revolutionary War brought independence to the former colonies, but the challenges of nation-building did not end there. In the years following the Treaty of Paris, American politicians had to somehow tame the rhetorics and politics of revolution. This crisis was not unique to the United States; all postrevolutionary governments face this problem—for the revolutionary spirit works against the institutionalized stability that governments seek to achieve.[14] The problem specific to the United States concerned how politicians attempted to institutionalize revolution during and immediately following the war: they established representative forms of popular government. Far from achieving stability, these governments disappointed both citizens, who desired more democracy, and their representatives, who desired less. Here, the evolution of Paine's rhetoric is particularly revealing. Just as Paine was symbolic of the revolutionary spirit in the 1770s, so too was he indicative of the disappointment many felt about revolutionary settlement in the 1780s.

When he first arrived in Philadelphia, Paine fanned the fires of revolt by preaching the glories of democracy and self-rule. Following the successful completion of the Revolutionary War, however, he modified his position. Just ten years after crafting the rhetorical bombs of *Common Sense*, Paine penned an attack on popular protest titled *Dissertations on Government* (1786). Writing in the wake of widespread protests in Philadelphia against the state's financial polices, Paine attacked the "delusion" that led to complaints, and argued that protesters should judge "the naked truth of things" with "a cooler spirit" of rationality. Paine implied that overheated protestors behaved irrationally and improperly. He further contended that if they cooled off, they would quickly realize that as citizens of Pennsylvania, they existed within the structures of a representative government, and hence that they no longer possessed a right to insurrection or revolution. He concluded that unlike monarchies, which were unrepresentative and therefore unlawful, "the republican form and principle leaves no room for insurrection, because it provides and establishes a rightful means in its stead." Because citizens elected their representatives, they had no right to invoke the democratic precedents of the Declaration of Independence and the Revolutionary War to challenge the authority of government.[15]

Paine's rhetoric reveals the uniqueness of the post-Revolutionary crisis in the United States. During the Revolutionary War, Paine championed democratic government—and he continued to champion it for the rest of his life. Though Madison went to great lengths to distinguish democracy from republicanism in Federalist 10, for Paine and many other eighteenth-century political thinkers there was little difference between the two. Both were popular governments, and a republican system could made democracy feasible in a large territory. Yet representative democracies are always characterized by a potential slippage, or what philosophers call a "disjunctive synthesis."[16] Systems of representation, which work through the rhetorical maneuver of *synecdoche*—or a part for whole substitution—simultaneously connect citizens to the government while divorcing them from it.[17]

The more representative and hierarchical form that American democracy took in the postwar years created tension between citizens and their representatives. Representative democracy connected Americans to their leaders in a way that made dissent seem unconscionable—thus

Paine's anger at Pennsylvania protestors. At the same time, representative democracy created a wide enough gap between Americans and government that citizens could feel that they were not represented, and that their leaders were acting contrary to their interests. In such situations, it seemed to common folks that they were trapped by the social contract. As they petitioned for redress only to be rebuffed by governing elites, citizens were forced to undertake more drastic measures to achieve their aims. These measures, in turn, came to seem more and more inappropriate to governing elites, setting in motion a deadly spiral that left protestors and government soldiers dead, and that eventually led elites to write and champion the Constitution.

The crisis in post-Revolutionary America was apparent in Massachusetts, where people on both sides died in the battle over financial policy and the norms of government. Shays's Rebellion was one of the most severe protests of the 1780s and also one of the most significant. Were it not for Shays's Rebellion, George Washington might not have attended the Constitutional Convention—for it was news from Massachusetts that caused him to return to public life and accept the invitation to the convention he had earlier declined.[18] Had Washington not attended and lent his gravitas to the constitutional process, who knows what the United States would look like today. Shays's Rebellion was not the only reason that elites desired a new constitution, nor was it the only reason that Americans chose to ratify it. However, Shays's Rebellion was a persistent topos in public discussion about the Constitution—a topos that encouraged Americans to talk, and perhaps even to think differently, about democracy, "the people," and government. In turn, how Shays's Rebellion was deployed in public discourse moved Americans into a new age of governing.

Shays's Rebellion and the Crisis of Post-Revolutionary Democracy

On July 8, 1786, the Massachusetts legislature closed without addressing repeated pleas from citizens in the western part of the state for hard money, a simplified court system, and a more centrally located state capital. The disappointment these citizens subsequently expressed was indicative of the frustrations many citizens felt in the post-Revolutionary years. Fed up with government policies favoring aristocratic elites, and believing that the government did not represent them, backcountry farmers took up arms and marched on courts to bar the entry of judges and juries, effectively shutting down the machinery of justice. "Regulation," as these actions were known, dated back to the 1680s in England, and was practiced by colonial farmers in South Carolina during 1768–1769, and North Carolina during the 1770s.[19]

During August and September, Regulators closed courts from Northampton to Worcester, and they justified their actions as a continuation of the Revolutionary War. One participant explained these closings by proudly announcing that he was a veteran of the revolution, and "as liberty is the prize that I so early stepped forth in the defence of the country to gain, and so cheerfully fought for, so liberty is the prize I still have in view, and in this glorious cause I am determined to stand with firmness and resolution."[20] The most dramatic closing occurred on August 29, 1786, when nearly 1,500 citizens marched on the Northampton courthouse in Western Massachusetts. On January 25, 1787, in the blustery cold and deep snow, hundreds of backcountry Massachusetts farmers marched on the federal arsenal at Springfield in an attempt to seize the arms there. This drastic escalation of their protest strategies resulted, according to one historian, in "the American Revolution's final battle."[21]

Shays's Rebellion arose from the Regulators' demands for financial rectitude. Massachusetts frontiersmen were largely subsistence farmers, producing enough to feed their families, and then a little extra to trade to shopkeepers for subsidiary goods such as sugar, lace, or rum. These shopkeepers, in turn, profited from the farmers' goods by trading them in Boston, where, in an increasingly globalized market, urban merchants sold them overseas. In this proto-capitalist world, local and global economies clashed. Local trade was based on bartering and non-cash payment, and participants in the local economies of western Massachusetts tolerated extended debts, while creditors rarely charged interest on small debts. The machinery of long-distance trade was created, in contrast, for the collection of debts. Farmers traditionally paid their debts in goods, but changes in the global economy put pressure on local economies, resulting in "mounting rural indebtedness and pressure to pay it off."[22] When distant merchants refused to extend debts but instead called them in, rural patterns of exchange broke down, and backcountry citizens were plunged into a deep economic meltdown. While Massachusetts farmers weathered several poor harvests in the 1780s, shopkeepers refused to barter with them, courts would not listen to their complaints, and the government, located days away in Boston, rebuffed their pleas for assistance. These changes to their economic universe produced a rupture, as modernity disrupted local customs and resulted in crushing economic change.

The tumults leading to Shays's Rebellion were also related to Massachusetts' counter-revolutionary history. Massachusetts' Constitution, ratified in 1780, reneged on the revolutionary promises of democracy and self-rule by creating strict property requirements for suffrage and political office, hence prohibiting most citizens from participating in government. This representative government was one of the least responsive to popular pressure established in the Revolutionary era. It also empowered a strong executive to oversee the two-house legislature, making the Massachusetts government look suspiciously like a monarchy to many citizens.[23] Though the ever-popular John Hancock was the state's first governor, he withdrew from his post in 1785 due to an illness, paving the way for a wealthy aristocrat, James Bowdoin. As a major landlord with holdings in Boston and Maine (then a Massachusetts province), and a large wholesaler who had helped fund the Massachusetts First National Bank, Bowdoin's main administrative concerns followed logically from the gospel of moneyed men: he attempted to protect property rights, collect taxes, and fuel currency speculation. After being elected the state's governor, Bowdoin worked to ensure that he and other already wealthy currency speculators would profit at the expense of underrepresented farmers and Revolutionary War veterans.

Shays's Rebellion was provoked by the tragic postwar history of many veterans and the pecuniary foresight of speculators like Bowdoin. After the Revolutionary War, Massachusetts was shackled with substantial war debts, and therefore could not fund at full value the security notes issued to soldiers as payment during the war. As Massachusetts' currency depreciated, many veterans needed hard money to live, and out of desperation sold their notes to currency speculators at depressed values. Though some states funded these notes at sunken values to become creditworthy following the war, Massachusetts was heavily influenced by several wealthy speculators who had purchased the veterans' notes at depressed values, and therefore it funded the notes at original value. The Massachusetts speculators' influence was great: thirty-five men held over 40 percent of the state debt, and all of them either served in the legislature or had family who did. No other state equaled this protection of speculators' interests. This merger of state power and private profit hurt backcountry farmers: unable to pay the debts they accumulated while fighting for their country during the Revolution, and forgotten once their duty was done, veterans sold the war bonds they received as compensation to creditors paying less than a quarter of their value. Then Massachusetts funded the notes at full price, creating luxurious profits for speculators. Even worse, when Massachusetts couldn't immediately fund the creditors, it taxed the same veterans to pay the fortunate men who held their swindled notes.[24]

The heavy taxes payable in gold and silver imposed by the Massachusetts government further exacerbated the hardship—and rage—of frontiersmen and women. In order to repay the debts it incurred during the Revolutionary War and the funds it owed the federal government under the Articles of Confederation, Bowdoin's government implemented an aggressive taxation policy that far outdistanced other states. Had citizens paid their taxes in 1786, these taxes would have consumed 8 to 11 percent of their income, up from less than 2 percent in the prewar years.[25] Though these taxes were harsher than in most other states, Massachusetts was not the only state to heavily tax its citizens, and consequently not the only state rocked by popular resistance to financial policies. Protestors in Pennsylvania, South Carolina, and Rhode Island successfully compelled their governments to provide financial relief, and both New Hampshire and Massachusetts itself witnessed widespread riots in the years leading up to Shays's Rebellion.[26]

Shays's Rebellion was no anomaly. However, the circumstances in Massachusetts were especially dire because the Massachusetts government did not initially yield to protestors like other governments, but instead ramped up its financial machine to collect outstanding taxes and punish debtors. Confronted by an unyielding government that refused to respond to citizens' pleas for redress, but instead "devours their inhab-itents," as citizens in one Massachusetts town complained, the conditions for a widespread uprising against the state were realized in the summer of 1786.[27] Even Hamilton admitted that "If SHAYS had not been a *desperate debtor*, it is much to be doubted whether Massachusetts would have been plunged into a civil war."[28]

This whole business left backcountry veterans sour. They were furi-ous at the elite Bostonians who reaped profits by swindling them, and then had the gall to tax them to pay the interest on their stolen fortunes. Berkshire judge William Whiting observed: "How shocking to humanity must be the idea that the poor soldier who has for many years through dangers hardship hunger and nakedness wrought out the salvation of his country must now be compelled to pay his proportion of the interest." He continued, "It would certainly have been much better for him to have re-ceived no wages at all."[29] Whiting would later be arrested and imprisoned for uttering such sentiments.[30] An anti-Bowdoin editorial titled "Plain Truth" echoed Whiting's disbelief, arguing that the situation would not "have occasioned such 'HIDEOUS ROARINGS,' had it not contained such *'damning proofs'* of rectitude, as to make those who have amassed an im-mense hoard of Publick Securities for *a mere song*, TREMBLE for their cheap-bought wealth."[31] For these Massachusetts citizens and many others who rose up to regulate the government, Bowdoin's government demonstrated a shocking deafness to the plight of poor citizens. As such, they concluded that the government's policies were determined by profit, not concern for the public welfare. And as they learned from the Declara-tion of Independence, *Common Sense*, and countless other revolutionary tracts, this was precisely the type of government that could be disobeyed and perhaps even toppled.

In response to the uprising, the Massachusetts government called on the state's militia units, which consisted of over 90,000 men who were bound by law to answer the state's charge.[32] Few did. As the state soon realized, militia members—especially in the western part of the state—tended to sympathize more with the Regulators than with the govern-ment. Angry that other states had better luck calling forth militias to suppress protests, and fearing that a revolution was brewing in the west, many elites called on the state to up the ante and engage in impressive

displays of state violence. The Revolutionary War hero Samuel Adams
called for executions. "In monarchies," he announced, "the crime of treason and rebellion may admit of being pardoned or lightly punished; but
the man who dares to rebel against the laws of a republic ought to suffer
death."[33] Reverend Jeremy Belknap, the pastor of a prominent Boston
church, was equally hostile. He chided the Massachusetts government:
"They ought to *declare*, what everybody knows to be a fact, that a rebellion exists, and then to 'let loose the dogs of war,' who, from the animation
they have already discovered, will soon seize and worry those ravening
wolves."[34] Belknap made no appeal to republican principles or natural
law; he called on the state to unleash the dogs of war on enemies who
were less than human—according to him, the Regulators were wolves
deserving of death. William Shepard, the general from Westfield who led
the government's response to the Regulator push to seize the Springfield
Arsenal, similarly endorsed the violent path. In a December 1786 letter
to Massachusetts governor James Bowdoin, Shepard employed vengeful
rhetoric as a response to the Regulators. He knew of calls for leniency, yet
advocated military force instead: "It appears unseasonable and ill timed to
either procrastinate or introduce lenient measures untill the government
have given proofs of their force and ability, otherwise clemency appears to
proceed from inability or pusillanimity, and comes with an ill grace."[35] "Ill
grace" here was weakness, and it won no battles for Shepard.

Believing that Adams was right, and that criminals in a republic
should be put to death, and also believing that an impressive display of
strength was the proper response to popular violence, the state responded
swiftly and sternly. In September 1786, the Massachusetts government
passed several acts to quiet the court-storming rebels, even going so far
as to suspend the writ of habeas corpus. On October 20, the federal government authorized nearly 2,000 troops to fight the Regulators. On November 10, the Massachusetts government passed an act giving Bowdoin
the power to arrest anyone suspected of being a Regulator. On January
4, 1787, after the Massachusetts government refused to pay, Governor
Bowdoin called on rich Bostonians to fund an army of 4,400 soldiers,
which on January 25, in blistering cold and deep snow, defended the
federal arsenal at Springfield by killing four Regulators. After this battle,
the Regulators scattered. Many were pursued and captured by General

Benjamin Lincoln, who led the government's response to the Regulation, on February 3–4; all others were barred from voting in subsequent elections by the February 16 Disqualification Act. One final skirmish was fought at Sheffield on February 27, in which four rebels and one government soldier were killed—thus bringing the Regulation to a halt.

In 1786–1787, the Massachusetts government was forced to confront the dilemmas of American nationalism head-on as it attempted to tame the lingering spirit of revolution that emboldened citizens to close courts, tar and feather tax collectors, storm arsenals, and otherwise resist the directives of authority. It did this through the application of military force. The government's violence was rhetorical in nature, for it was intended to persuade the Regulators to lay down their arms. But even more than that, it was directed toward altering their subjectivities. In a February 18, 1787, letter to Governor Bowdoin, Shepard celebrated the "rout" of the Regulators in the battle of Springfield. However, he noted that the remaining rebels were "devising every method to embarrass, to intimidate, to revive the dying spirit of rebellion, and to continue to injure the State as far as is in their power from revenge, from despair and from malevolence." Even though the government had won the arsenal, Shepard argued that it would be a mistake to discontinue the state's violence. "Removing too soon that force by which alone they have been quelled, before the idea of their inferiority has become familiar and established in their minds, might be productive of pernicious consequences," he counseled. To really defeat the Regulation, a mental state of "inferiority" had to be established in the rebels' minds. Thus, Shepard counseled that the Massachusetts government should do all it could "to rivet in their minds a compleat conviction of the force of government and the necessity of an entire submission to the laws."[36] There was a psychological component to Shepard's call for violence, for he requested that the government rivet a "conviction" onto the rebels' minds. Not content to use words to persuade the malcontents, Shepard wanted Bowdoin to use violence to alter the rebel psyche, hence moving rhetoric towards force and words towards weapons.

To explain Shepard's metaphor, it is necessary to consider advances in eighteenth-century philosophy, because the "riveting" metaphor arose as the psychological episteme of the eighteenth century shifted.[37] One driving force of this shift was John Locke, whose psychology of the *tabula rasa*

altered the way Anglo-Americans thought about the mind and about language. Published in 1690, Locke's *Essay Concerning Human Understanding* offered a theory of the mind as "white paper." Rejecting Descartes's
a priori ideas, he wrote, "Let us suppose the mind to be, as we say, white
paper, void of all characters, without any ideas:—How comes it to be
furnished? . . . To this I answer, in one word, from EXPERIENCE." Because
the mind was passive, simple ideas could come from experience only.
Similarly, complex ideas such as space and time, and convictions such as
justice and freedom were derived from experience. As Locke wrote, "The
simple ideas we have, are such as experience teaches them us; but if,
beyond that, we endeavour by words to make them clearer in the mind,
we shall succeed no better than if we went about to clear up the darkness
of a blind man's mind by talking; and to discourse into him the ideas of
light and colours." Because all ideas were based on experience, Locke
mistrusted rhetoric, labeling orators "perfect cheats" and arguing that "all
the artificial and figurative application of words eloquence hath invented,
are for nothing else but to insinuate wrong ideas." Indeed, Locke claimed
that because rhetoric was not based on experience, it confused the mind.[38]

Anticipating Locke's argument that the mind was white paper, but
differing from Locke by arguing that speech could introduce ideas directly
into a listener's mind, French logician Bernard Lamy offered a bellicose
theory of rhetoric in *The Art of Speaking* (1675) that was foundational to
the counter-revolutionary tradition in the early Republic. Lamy's manual
compared persuasion to war, and the orator to the soldier. "An Orator is
to imitate a Souldier fighting with his enemy," he taught. "The Souldier is
not satisfied with drawing his Sword, he strikes, and watches to take the
first advantage that is given: He moves up and down to avoid the insults
of his Enemy, and in a word assumes all the postures that Nature and
practice have taught him for invasion or defense." The goal of persuasion
was to "bend and incline [the audience] to what side he pleases," and one
method of doing this is the artful employment of figures, which "imprint
strongly" on a subject's mind. Lamy listed repetition as the most important figure, because "when we are in Combat with our Enemy, we think it
not enough to give him one wound and no more; we multiply our blows,
for fear one should not do the business: So in Speaking, if we think our
first words not well understood, we repeat them, or explain them another

way."[39] Believing as Locke did in the *tabula rasa*, but arguing that words could impress ideas upon the mind in a way that Locke did not believe possible, repetition was a powerful figure, because the more often a word was repeated, the deeper the impression on the mind, and hence the greater the likelihood of producing a desired action in the subject.

Shepard's letter brought together the state's need for powerful language to quell the rebellion with the state's need to use violence to alter the Regulators' minds. For many rhetorical theorists of this era, rhetoric involved penetrating another's mind to produce a behavior. "Now the nature of eloquence is to make *good* and *evil*, *profitable* and *unprofitable*, *honest* and *dishonest*, appear to be more or less than indeed they are; and to make that seem *just* which is *unjust*, according as it shall best suit with his end that speaketh: for this is to persuade," Thomas Hobbes proclaimed, counseling that when it came to persuasion, "opinions are delivered not by right reason, but by a certain violence of mind."[40] This violence of mind was implied in Shepard's words. Notice that Shepard did not argue that the government's sole task was to force the Regulators to submit to their laws; rather, Shepard called for the government to rivet a "conviction" onto the rebels' minds and hence to produce cooperative subjects. Figuratively, then, riveting was a way of short-circuiting Locke's psychology by impressing a conviction directly onto a subject's mind. We can interpret riveting, and the government's strategy, as akin to the rhetorical repetition Lamy championed. To create a conviction in the Regulators' minds, the state needed to mobilize all the available persuasives in its arsenal to assault the Regulators from multiple angles. As Lamy wrote, the Orator-Soldier "keeps his Enemy in breath; the strokes that he makes at him continually, the assaults that he makes at him on all sides, the different ways of his attacks and retreats, keeps him constantly waking."[41] At the same time, however, the state was also required to address the citizens of Massachusetts who did not participate in Shays's Rebellion. The tightrope the state had to walk, then, was how to deploy sufficient ammunition to create mental convictions without attacking the civil liberties of the state's citizens, because to succeed at the former was potentially to fail at the latter.

In the end, riveting became problematic because the rhetorical resources the government deployed to alter the Regulators' minds impinged

upon the civil liberties of all citizens. Emblematic of Bowdoin's tyranny
was a February 23, 1787, act requiring all men licensed to sell liquor in the
commonwealth—including the tavern owners who had harbored meet-
ings of Regulators in August 1786—to take an oath of allegiance to the
administration, lest they be stripped of their licenses. The act's purpose
was to solidify allegiance to the commonwealth. It read: "And it is further
Resolved, That no person shall be licenced by virtue of the forgoing resolve
. . . until he . . . shall take and subscribe the following oath." The oath,
which represented a not-so-subtle attempt to gain allies in repressing the
Regulators, read: "*I A.B. do swear, that I will bear true faith and allegiance
to the Commonwealth of Massachusetts, and that I will to the utmost of my
power, defend the Constitution and Government thereof, against traitor-
ous conspiracies, and all hostile and violent attempts whatsoever.*"[42] Here,
Bowdoin's bifurcating logic became clear: either Massachusetts citizens
were with or against the government. This disjunction provided no space
for dissent, and this act was typical of the government's rhetoric. Tavern
owners and Massachusetts citizens were presented with a stark alternative: they could accept the government's version of the Regulation, or
they could go to jail. As the government depicted Massachusetts citizens,
they had only bad agency; they were portrayed as subjects in need of the
government's protection because they could not protect themselves, and
also as potential criminals who might mimic the Regulators by also taking
up arms against the government.[43] The government hence delegated to
itself the power to jail all the state's subjects.

The government's attempt at riveting backfired due to accumulated
attacks on the rights of Massachusetts citizens. The November 10, 1786,
act suspending the writ of habeas corpus gave Bowdoin nearly dictatorial
control over Massachusetts citizens:

> *Be it therefore enacted* . . . That the Governour, with the advice of the
> Council, be, and he hereby is, authorized and empowered, by warrant,
> under the seal of the commonwealth, by him subscribed, and directed
> to any sheriff, deputy-sheriff, or constable, or any other person, by
> name, to command, and cause to be apprehended, and committed in
> any jail, or any other safe place, within the commonwealth, any person
> or persons whatsoever, whom the Governour and Council shall deem

the safety of the commonwealth requires should be restrained of their
personal liberty, or whose enlargement is dangerous thereto; any law,
usage or custom to the contrary notwithstanding.[44]

In spite of received laws or custom, Bowdoin could now jail his enemies
and compel government officials to aid in repression, and he immediately
put these scary, King George III–like powers to use by apprehending
five rebels: Oliver Parker, Benjamin Page, Nathan Smith, John Kelsey,
and Job Shattuck. This act demonstrated Bowdoin's terrible power, for
Shattuck had long been a thorn in the state's side, and on the night of
November 30, government troops arrested Shattuck, Parker, and Page in
Groton; injured John Hapsgood, a man not named on their warrant; and
were rumored to have "put out the eye of a woman, and stabbed and cut
of the breast of another, and mangled an infant in the cradle."[45] These
actions were denounced as "dangerous, if not absolutely destructive to
Republican government," and as such they damaged the government's
ethos, because it was difficult to persuade law-abiding citizens of the
necessity of state violence when it was used for apparently self-serving
ends that hurt innocent women and children.[46]

Fearing the precedent it would set, many observers counseled against
the decision to violently suppress Massachusetts citizens; yet this was
precisely what Bowdoin did.[47] The Massachusetts government responded
to an ironic rhetorical situation in a logical but nevertheless problematic
manner. During the Revolutionary War, colonists had the task of por-
traying popular violence against England as natural. Now, former revolutionaries turned Massachusetts politicians had to justify using violence
against former allies as, once again, natural. To establish its authority
to govern, the Massachusetts government was forced to criminalize
the methods that led to its own independence from Great Britain. The
government thus assumed a rhetorical stance analogous to the British
government in the 1770s: it portrayed Daniel Shays as the archetype of
anarchy; it painted the violence of "rebels" as an "unnatural" challenge to
government; and it labeled the Regulation a "wicked Rebellion." During
the crisis, Bowdoin's rhetoric echoed the rhetoric of King George III.[48]
As he employed coercion and refused to address grievances, Bowdoin
managed dissent like the king.

Following Bowdoin's orders, state agents convicted scores for treason and sentenced eighteen Regulators to death. Though such actions were designed to contain the misbehavior of citizens and create a coalition of strong-handed elites to govern, many Massachusetts citizens came to believe that the state's policies threatened the gains of the Revolutionary War far more than the Regulators' violence. To take just one example, the Reverend Bezaleel Howard, the pastor of Springfield's Congregationalist parish, reported that Bowdoin's policies pushed Massachusetts society close to anarchy:

> Jealously raging in Every bosom, Envy and malice in Every heart, pride and ostentatious partiality, tyriny and oppresion raging among the magistracy, plainly Discouvering the Byass and Inclination of their mind and the Wickedness of their hearts. Now they had power to punish in what manner they pleas'd and . . . Such a state of anarchy and Confusion, Dispotism and Tyranny succeeded the Disperson of Shays troops. Nothing Could be more Injurious to the Liberty and privileges of a peopal than the Conduct of the Justices and the military men. To be a soldier was sufficient to Invest him with power to drag whomsoever they would from their beds at midnight and commit them to Gaol untill a partiall Examination could be had and, if Innocent, Dismis'd without any recompense for the cruil Behaviour of the Soldiery, some committed to Gaol till Bonds were procur'd for their appearance at the next Supreme Court, but many upon taking the oath, Delivering up their arms, and paying, then went Home.[49]

Howard was no supporter of the Regulators' methods. In the midst of the great crime wave that shook the United States from the middle 1780s into the 1790s, and one of many Americans who turned against the techniques of Regulation after 1776, Howard noted, "Thire things Evidently Call for amendment and redress, but Guns and Bayonets and Hostile appearances was far from being the proper way to accomplish the design."[50] In an age of unsettling crime, the guns and bayonets of protestors were a threat to order. But for Howard, the guns and bayonets of the government were far worse.

Howard related a picture of civic hell. Innocent citizens were ripped from their beds at night and thrown in jail; those proven innocent were not compensated for their suffering. The government's reaction to domestic protests revealed that it, even more than the Regulators, was the enemy of good people: it had wickedness in its heart. Howard portrayed political oppression that, ten years earlier, sparked the American Revolution. In fact, stories of soldiers dragging citizens from their sleeping beds proved to many citizens that Bowdoin's government, like the king's, was founded on malice, tyranny, and oppression. The government's policies endangered the rights of all Massachusetts citizens. Lawfulness and rationality were abandoned. "The Gun and Bayonet was now the only standard of authority," the reverend observed.[51] In a state that still remembered what it was like to mobilize for a war on despotism, Bowdoin's actions were unconscionable. Accordingly, law-abiding citizens rejected the state's government and voted for new representation.

Political participation in Massachusetts swelled to new levels in the April 1787 state elections. Even though hundreds of citizens were disqualified from voting because of their rebellious activities, others turned out en masse to express their deep dissatisfaction with Bowdoin. With promises of tax relief and accommodating policies, a healthy and resurgent Hancock handily defeated Bowdoin by a four-to-one margin.[52] While the Regulators were accused of violating republican norms, Massachusetts citizens concluded that the governor was worse. Then as now, a government protecting its own interests above the public good deserved to be removed. The lopsided election produced a 74 percent turnover in the House of Representatives, giving citizens hope for a fresh start. At least in the short-term, Shays's Rebellion was a success. However, the hopes of the Regulators were soon to be dashed, for following their electoral victory, there was a movement to make use of the uprising to rewrite the structure of the federal government in ways that Shays and his men would have found unimaginable. Portrayed in public discourse as a national calamity, Shays's Rebellion was also an opportunity for the founders of the United States to remake the structure of government so that it was less responsive to popular pressure for political and financial reform. By doing so, they hoped to eliminate the possibility of another revolution.

Life, Liberty, and Property

During the middle years of the 1780s, leading politicians came to believe that the Articles of Confederation were an unsatisfactory foundation for the nation. From 1783 to 1787, Congress was bullied by the states and did not have sufficient powers to do its job. The states, in turn, were bullied by common folks demanding tax relief and economic reform. The nation was stretched by an economic recession. Common folks who felt bullied by government rose up in a series of popular uprisings that shook government to its very core. In September 1786, delegates gathered at the Annapolis Convention to discuss the weaknesses of the Articles, recommending that another convention convene in Philadelphia in May 1787. Though the delegates to the Philadelphia Convention were not instructed to reform America's social contract, they seized the moment and remade the structure of America's government by creating the Constitution.

The summer of 1787 was electrifying, and events like Shays's Rebellion helped to whip elites into a political fervor.[53] Many leaders left the Annapolis Convention persuaded that the Articles were flawed, but content to try gradual reform. Shays's Rebellion convinced them that immediate change was needed. It was now or never, they believed, for soon the state would be destroyed by rogue democrats and other lunatics who longed to level property and power. "That most of us carried into the Convention a profound impression produced by the experienced inadequacy of the old Confederation," Madison recalled, "is certain." Shays's Rebellion had disturbed elites, making them fearful that the entire foundation would soon crumble, the victim of runaway democracy. Madison opined: "Nor was The recent & alarming insurrection headed by Shays, in Massachusetts without a very sensible effect on the pub: mind. Such indeed was the aspect of things, that in the eyes of all the best friends of liberty a crisis had arrived which was to decide whether the Amn. experiment was to be a blessing to the world, or to blast for ever the hopes which the republican cause had enspired."[54] Though Shays's Rebellion satisfied immediate demands, in the long run it failed, for this event convinced elites to create a new system of government with the power to put down another Daniel Shays if he arose.

When Shays's Rebellion occurred, Thomas Jefferson was in Paris doing diplomatic work. Hearing rumors from John Jay and others that something grave was happening in Massachusetts, he wrote to his friend John Adams for news. Adams told Jefferson not to worry. As early as November 1786, Adams had concluded that Shays's Rebellion was actually good news, for it provided elites with the opportunity to create a working coalition for reforming the federal charter to make it stronger. Daniel Shays was precisely the enemy needed to bring a number of states together into a family. Adams was confident that the Regulation would backfire, resulting in support for a stronger government that could in turn coerce the enemies of just laws. "Dont be alarmed at the late Turbulence in New England," he wrote. "The Massachusetts Assembly had, in its Zeal to get the better of their Debt, laid on a Tax, rather heavier than the People could bear; but all will be well, and this Commotion will terminate in additional Strength to Government."[55] Adams was prophetic, because Shays's Rebellion gave politicians a rationale for reforming the Articles of Confederation and increasing the "Strength to Government." In fact, those who were eager to consolidate power in a more centralized government used Shays's Rebellion as rhetorical ammunition to advance their cause. Shays's Rebellion helped to justify the ratification of the Constitution by convincing elites from the thirteen states that a revision of America's government was necessary, and then bringing them together to revise the social contract.

News of Shays's Rebellion prompted some of Jefferson's most famous musings on government and "the people." Hearing of the Regulation from Adams, he was not worried. He was emboldened. Prone to hyperbole when he was moved, Jefferson defended not just the aims but also the methods of the Regulators. He, at least, was not frightened by democratic violence. In a February 1787 letter to Abigail Adams, he defended the uprising as necessary for America's civic health: "The spirit of resistance to government is so valuable on certain occasions, that I wish it to be always kept alive. It will often be exercised when wrong, but better so than not to be exercised at all. I like a little rebellion now and then. It is like a storm in the Atmosphere."[56] In the 1780s, violent rebellions were as natural as storms for Jefferson. Later that year, Jefferson elaborated on his thoughts, arguing that violence would be beneficial for American politics:

We have had 13. states independent 11. years. There has been one rebellion. That comes to one rebellion in a century & a half for each state.
What country before ever existed a century & half without a rebellion?
& what country can preserve it's liberties if their rulers are not warned
from time to time that their people preserve the spirit of resistance? Let
them take arms. The remedy is to set them right as to facts, pardon &
pacify them. What signify a few lives lost in a century or two? The tree
of liberty must be refreshed from time to time with the blood of patriots
& tyrants. It is it's natural manure.[57]

Here, Jefferson painted violence as a necessary component of enacting
democracy in America.

Jefferson's preoccupation with Shays's Rebellion was related to his
obsession with a philosophical puzzle of the postwar years: how to make
the democratic aspects of the Revolutionary War permanent while still
creating a lasting government. Believing that the future of government
was dependent upon the people's frenetic energy, he pondered how best
to keep citizens energized in periods of peace. One of Jefferson's more
ambitious proposals was a system of perpetual revolution, under which
all laws were voided and rewritten every nineteen years (when a new
generation came to political power) because, he claimed, "no society can
make a perpetual constitution, or even a perpetual law. The earth belongs
always to the living generation."[58] In his most diplomatic tone, Jefferson's
correspondent James Madison explained that his plan was "not in *all* respects compatible with the course of human affairs."[59] In the absence of
an institutionalized system of revolution, Jefferson looked for shocks to
the system that proved the people to be alive. Because it challenged the
rigid, resurgent conservatism of the post-Revolutionary years, he praised
Shays's Rebellion as evidence of the robust constitution of citizens.

Jefferson's opinions on Shays's Rebellion diverged profoundly from
the spirit of the times, which tended toward stripping power from citizens and consolidating it in the state.[60] As one observer noted, "In these
circumstances, the Few were all alive for the support of the government, and all those who would not be continually crying, 'Government,
Government,' or who dared to say a word against their measures, were
called Shaysites and rebels and threatened with prosecutions, etc."[61] In

the aftermath of Shays's Rebellion, there was a narrowing of the political vocabulary that closed democratic possibilities. For many, the options were either "government" or "anarchy," which meant that there was no room left for either democracy or revolution in the United States. In *The History of the Insurrections*, published in Boston in 1788 as the first and most influential history of Shays's Rebellion, George Richards Minot observed that the Revolutionary War had created a "thirst for freedom" that was not easily quenched. For him, this thirst would either "decline to an unqualified opposition to authority," which was *anarchy*, or "rise into a disdainful resentment against the enemies of just laws," which was *obedience*. This categorical proposition left no wiggle room for democratic mobilization; protestors were "the real enemies of liberty."[62] Minot's *History of the Insurrections* prefigured the stark binaries that were typical of public discourse following Shays's Rebellion. In fact, Minot's opinions that common citizens could not be trusted, that democracy was untenable, and that a new, less-democratic form of government was essential, were shared by the framers of our government.

The Constitution was framed by many of its proponents as the remedy to Shays's Rebellion and as a necessary step to protect the gains of the Revolutionary War. Historians have debated whether the Constitution was really the culmination or the rejection of the Revolutionary War, and they have also debated why federalists won.[63] The contest was close, after all—1,071 votes were cast in favor of the Constitution, 577 against it by the delegates to the state ratifying conventions.[64] While federalists emerged victorious for many reasons, one of their most prolific rhetorical strategies was naming an enemy, Daniel Shays, who represented the dangers of post-Revolutionary democracy and who consequently sat at the nexus of divergent but potent fears. In the topos of Shays, federalists articulated the fears associated with the terrifying possibility of another revolution that would target their rule, with dread of democratic bodies lusting after private property. Here, then, was the root of demophobia in the early Republic: the fear that democracy would lead to equality and the ultimate leveling of unequal property relations.

The possibility of another revolution was seemingly foretold by the Declaration of Independence. One key to tempering this document with a strong federal Constitution was found in what Jefferson left out.

Jefferson's famous phrase "life, liberty, and the pursuit of happiness" was actually a revision of the more common eighteenth-century phrase "life, liberty, and property." By substituting "the pursuit of happiness" for "property," Jefferson gave the Declaration a rhetorical resonance it might not otherwise have had—he certainly captured the imagination of subsequent generations. Attempting to cope with the Declaration's legacy for inspiring democratic resistance to government, during the ratification debates the founders did something simple but ingenious: they put "property" back into the formula. While the founders still encouraged Americans to think of their happiness, at the same time they told Americans to think of their property and what might happen to it if rogues like Daniel Shays had their way. The founders understood and exploited the fact that in the commercially minded early Republic, the most frightening enemies were often those who targeted Americans' pocketbooks.

Rumors about Daniel Shays spread far beyond Massachusetts. George Washington responded to a frightening report about the Regulation from his friend, the Revolutionary War hero and Virginia delegate to the Continental Congress, Henry "Light Horse Harry" Lee, by writing, "The picture which you have drawn, & the acts which are published, of the commotions & temper of numerous bodies in the Eastern States, are equally to be lamented and deprecated." For Washington, Shays's Rebellion validated British claims that the Americans could not govern themselves, exhibiting "a melancholy proof of what our trans atlantic foe have predicted; and of another thing perhaps, which is still more to be regretted, and is yet more unaccountable; that mankind left to themselves are unfit for their own government."[65] Shays's Rebellion forced Washington to draw a difficult conclusion for a nation steeped in the promises of democracy: democratic states were violently, and perhaps inherently, unstable. Lee urged Washington and other members of the gentry to use Shays's Rebellion to advance the cause of government. Having read Lee's report, Washington came away determined to do just that: to draw strong arguments from the uprising for a new Constitution.

Curiously, Washington ended this letter, containing consequential political judgments from the pen of a future president, with the following personal message: "The China came to hand without much damage; and I thank you for your attention in procuring & forwarding of it to me."[66]

Washington here demonstrated his wealth, because few Americans at the time could afford china, which was a symbol of status; thus, the future President's comment on china ended a letter in which political lessons and indications of wealth were mixed.[67] Indeed, Washington's counter-revolutionary letter disparaged the ability of poor farmers like Daniel Shays to participate in politics. Though Washington was a southern gentleman, and Bostonians like Bowdoin were northeastern speculators and mercantilists, both were angry that the Regulators refused to defer to their political authority. There was, as Jefferson acknowledged, a "natural aristocracy" based on "virtue and talents" in post-Revolutionary America that was distinct from "artificial" English aristocracies based on "wealth and birth."[68] Though Jefferson attacked artificial aristocracies, natural aristocrats, like artificial aristocrats before them, generally thought wealth and power were best concentrated among an educated elite who demanded deference from citizens who had not climbed the social ladder. Washington's letter, colored by patrician disdain for the political aspirations of common folk, portrayed a wealthy, natural aristocrat denouncing revolution in order to protect his and his fellow gentlemen's china from popular uprisings like Shays's Rebellion.

Understanding the gravity of the decision before them, both federalists and anti-federalists expressed their hope that the ratification debate would be a cool, deliberate, rational affair. At the beginning of *The Federalist*, Hamilton invited Americans "to deliberate" about the Constitution, and he was echoed by anti-federalists, including Pennsylvania's Centinel, who announced that "if ever free and unbiased discussion was proper or necessary, it is on such an occasion."[69] What Hamilton and Centinel meant by "deliberation" and "discussion" was a rational conversation between educated discussants whose opinions would be formed only after they carefully considered the facts and consulted the long-term public interest. What they wanted was a "modern" political conversation in the sense described by philosopher Jürgen Habermas. According to Habermas, the rationalization of a public sphere, the beginnings of which he locates in eighteenth-century French coffeehouses and salons, is a central feature of the evolution of modern societies.[70] Habermas argues that there is an inherent *telos* toward mutual understanding in all human speech acts; and thus insofar as modern societies are founded on symbolic activity, they are also dependent upon "the unconstrained, unifying, consensus-bridging force of argumentation."[71] While Habermas insists that all communicative acts entail certain normative commitments, nevertheless for the public sphere to function as Habermas desires, it must be constituted with certain ground rules—in short, there must be a "mutually recognized normative background" in place.[72] This public sphere is a place of impersonal reason where participants speak truthfully, correctly, and with goodwill, and thus the public sphere is purged of passion, division, and persuasion.[73] Habermas posits rule-guided public argumentation as the vehicle for consubstantiality, identification, cooperation, and social cohesion more generally.

At the beginning of the ratification debates, both federalists and anti-federalists hoped to create the transcendental conditions for the possibilities of social harmony through rational public discussion. Hamilton knew that ratification was going to be a fight, but he saw the seeds of a new social order in the back and forth of proponents and opponents using reason to arrive at mutual understanding. It is easy to be persuaded by this communicative idealism. Public life would be smoother if discussion was rationalized—if we reasoned from behind a veil of ignorance, or if we followed rules of transparency and truthfulness—but as Kenneth Burke argues, "Language is but a set of labels, signs for helping us find our way about. Indeed, they can even be so useful that they help us to invent ingenious ways of threatening to destroy ourselves."[74] While Burke finds the drive toward mutual understanding (which he called "identification") in language, he also cautions his readers to "never deny the presence of strife, enmity, faction as a characteristic motive of rhetorical expression." He therefore concludes that "rhetoric is *par excellence* the region of the Scramble, of insult and injury, bickering, squabbling, malice and the lie."[75] The ratification debates unfolded in this broad panorama of discursive possibility, in a world of conversation after Babel, spotlighting the range of the available means of persuasion for political discussion.

As James Jasinski has demonstrated, federalists and anti-federalists brought wildly different standards of judgment to the ratification debate—and these differing standards produced divergent rhetorical trajectories for participants.[76] While federalists and anti-federalists relied on contrasting argumentative strategies, both sides nevertheless found fear-appeals useful in attempting to achieve their respective ends. Far from the cool and deliberate affair that many Americans wanted, the ratification debate was characterized by passion, speculation, hyperbole, and pronouncements of certain doom; to win the day, anti-federalists deployed "*nonsense* and *alarm*," and "thundered against [the Constitution] in every shape of *metaphoric terror*," noted one outraged observer, and federalists, it was said, were committed to "alarming the fears of the people with dangers which did not exist."[77] The ratification debate occurred in an environment of fear and metaphoric terror in the public sphere. When it came to the ability to manipulate emotions and make Americans fear, however, Hamilton understood that federalists began from a position of strength. Hamilton knew that anti-federalists could talk all day long about a *potential* conspiracy against American liberties, but federalists had proof of *real* dangers to the lives and estates of wealthy Americans in Shays's Rebellion.

In September 1787—after the Constitutional Convention, but before the ratification debates were in full swing—Hamilton described the material circumstances that would help and hurt the cause of ratification. In the pro column, he put "the good will of most men of property in the several states who wish a government of the union able to protect them against domestic violence and the depredations which the democratic spirit is apt to make on property," and "a strong belief in the people at large of the insufficiency of the present confederation to preserve the existence of the Union and of the necessity of the union to their safety and prosperity."[78] To the extent that rhetoric is about capitalizing on the persuasive resources at hand, Hamilton forecast one of the dominant rhetorical strategies the federalists would employ to achieve ratification: they would demonstrate that the Constitution was necessary to protect the lives of common citizens and the property of the wealthy by amplifying the threats to both.

The Constitution would provide safety, Hamilton argued, and thus to achieve ratification it would be necessary to prey on Americans' fears. In turn, Shays's Rebellion made frightening wealthy elites all the easier because it symbolized a threat to property rights. The Federal Farmer observed that in public discourse, Daniel Shays was transformed into a threat to property rights—the people known as "Shayites" or "levellers," it was said, were "little insurgents, men in debt, who want no law, and who want a share of the property of others."[79] Thus, the well-to-do, who made up a majority of the delegates to the special ratification conventions in each state, were made to fear the lusting jealousy of democratic bodies for their wealth and property.

Shays's Rebellion terrified elites because it represented a challenge to the gospel of moneyed men and the emerging system of privilege that equated political power with the right to own private property. Anti-Shaysite, pro-Constitution rhetorics fueled concerns that protestors were levelling rogues who planned to kill wealthy citizens and steal their stuff. According to the Connecticut Wit David Humphreys, "there is a licencious spirit prevailing among many of the people; a levelling principle; a desire of change; & a wish to annihilate all debts public & private."[80] Humphreys stated his desire to uphold the unequal property relations produced by the Revolutionary War. He did this, however, by escalating the Regulators' relatively limited goals of Regulation into the abolishment of debt and the seizure of property. Such hyperbole was representative of the ways that Shays's Rebellion was deployed in public discourse, for unlike the later European revolutions of 1789 and 1848, the Regulators in Massachusetts did not follow a "levelling principle." Rather than a revolution redacting all debts and redistributing property, the Regulators desired lower taxes, more rural autonomy, and for distant merchants to honor their local commercial practices. They did not protest the idea of government, but instead the policies of the Massachusetts governments that exacerbated financial inequalities. Their complaints were logical goals in line with what they took to be the promises of the Revolutionary War. Federalists, however, deployed the rhetoric of "levelling" to associate the Regulators with the Levellers, an English religious sect in the 1640s and participants in the English Civil War who were widely derided as lunatics and criminals for their too-democratic beliefs.[81] By overstating the Regulators' goals, politicians chastised them as the desperate pleas of stupid criminals deserving of punishment (which they would provide).

In eighteenth-century discourse, mob violence was associated with poor people; hence, allusions to poverty conjured up fears of popular anarchy, of common folks tearing the social contract to pieces. Charging the Regulators with theft became a popular trope in the pro-government, anti-Regulator rhetoric because political power and private property were linked in the new nation. By arguing that the Regulators desired to seize power, it was implied that they also desired to steal property, and this put them outside the bounds of liberalism, which treated private property as sacrosanct. Locke argued that protecting property was "the great and *chief end* therefore of men uniting into commonwealths, and putting themselves under government."[82] While these sentiments were debatable, defining government as an entity for preserving property assisted the development of capitalism, which depended on inequality and exploitation. In fact, modernity shifted definitions of crime from attacks on bodies to theft of goods; and modern nations sanctioned, and police enforced, a progressive distinction between crimes traditionally condemned (crimes against bodies) and crimes that threatened the new proto-capitalist order (crimes against property). This transition meant that "justice" was defined in ways that supported economic development and favored the emerging class of educated property holders. Once an accepted part of premodern communities, modern criminals were prosecuted and jailed as a way of demonstrating that crimes against property would not be tolerated. The discourse of property rights was enforced in the late eighteenth century by the first police forces, which were created to prevent theft and enforce wage-labor.[83] Police bullied hostile workers into accepting the exploitative system of wage-labor, and in this way state-sanctioned violence enforced modern property rights. In the United States, the system of property rights favored those who already owned property and possessed enough capital to gain more at the expense of peasant farmers like Shays, thereby making him and his fellow protestors likely targets for policing.

Wealthy Americans might not be able to agree on much, but they could agree on the need to protect their property—be it a humble Cape Cod, a New York mansion, or a Georgia plantation—from their enemies. By escalating the Regulators' aims from Regulation to levelling and revolution, and by transforming them into petty, jealous criminals, federalists hoped to unify elites in opposition to the enemies who coveted their property. The democratic potential of the demos had become the enemy that allowed many property-owning elites—who disagreed on many issues, none bigger than slavery—to come together to back a strong federal Constitution. Though the American gentry's enemy was once the British,

Shays's Rebellion made it seem that the enemy was now common folks espousing democratic sentiments, internal enemies who were revolutionaries, anarchists, and levellers.

Paine reported in *Common Sense* that it was difficult to get wealthy citizens with the most to lose to support a war.[84] Yet proponents of the Constitution did not need to get wealthy citizens to support a war; they only needed their votes, and this was achieved by providing them with an enemy against whom they could collectively rally. About Shays, the essayist Philadelphus argued that while "some may perhaps alledge this in his favor, that he is fighting for his liberty, and that of his fellow citizens," nevertheless "those who really feel an honorable sense of that liberty so dearly bought, and wish to see it preserved to their posterity to time immemorial, must undoubtedly, not only blame, but condemn him for his conduct on this occasion." Shays and his men no longer deserved the title of Americans; they were enemies who could absorb the anger of threatened elites, thus acting (in the words of this essayist) "as objects of vindictive justice."[85] Shays became a scapegoat who, when symbolically sacrificed, could absorb all of the tension and division between Americans under the Articles of Confederation. The emerging consensus in 1787 was that Shays deserved condemnation because he acted in ways unbecoming of an American citizen and thereby endangered the entire order of things, from the system of representation to property rights to political order itself. To blame Shays was simultaneously to praise order, a liberal system of property rights, a less-responsive republican form of government, and hence the Constitution.

Daniel Shays, in turn, provided the Constitution's defenders with a convenient trope to smear their opponents. Provocatively, one writer suggested that how Americans talked about Shays's Rebellion was "a *Shibboleth*, by which you may ascertain what spirit they are of."[86] Shays's Rebellion quickly became a touchstone for divining the American-ness of citizens—and federalists therefore did their best to couple anti-federalism with "Shayism," discrediting their opponents as closet anarchists. A South Carolina paper "reported" that anti-federalists toasted Daniel Shays at a meeting, and another essayist in Philadelphia signed his or her essay, which encouraged anti-federalists to contest ratification, "DANIEL SHAYS."[87] New York City's *Daily Advertiser* reported that "almost every man of information" supported the Constitution, while its opponents consisted of "a few weak people and the friends of Shays."[88] These papers implied that anti-federalists were sympathetic to Shays's Rebellion and that Daniel Shays was himself an anti-federalist. According to an article in Boston's *Massachusetts Gazette*, "the Federalists should be distinguished hereafter by the name of WASHINGTONIANS, and the Antifederalists, by the name of SHAYITES, in every part of the United States."[89] Papers from South Carolina to Massachusetts suggested that to dissent was to spit on order, to advocate anarchy, and to rebel against the patriotism of '76. Anti-federalists were pro-Shays, anti-Washington, and anti-American.

The Divergent Rhetorical Legacies of Ratification

In the debate over the United States Constitution, historian Woody Holton finds one of the supreme ironies of U.S. history. The parts of the Constitution that most Americans value above all else, the protections enumerated in the Bill of Rights, were not included in the document's original draft. Hamilton, for one, denounced bills of rights as "dangerous."[90] We only have these rights today because the Constitution's opponents—who believed that the document was a perversion of the spirit of the Revolutionary War and who, consequently, fought tooth and nail against its ratification—convinced politicians like Madison that a Bill of Rights was essential to America's civic health. "It is a remarkable but rarely noted irony," Holton writes, "that Americans owe their most cherished rights—among them freedom of speech and religion, the right to trial by jury, and protection against self-incrimination and illegal search and seizure—not to the authors of the Constitution but to its inveterate enemies." "It is richly ironic," he continues, "that what has arguably become history's greatest experiment in shielding the powerless began as a slur on the capacities of ordinary citizens."[91]

While the record of the Constitutional Congress is filled with statements stressing that all political power was ultimately derived from "the people," to justify the Constitution federalists slandered the civic abilities of common people. The judgment that citizens had wrecked the economy with their selfish demands was just that, a judgment. But it has become something of a truth in historical writings about the early Republic. Thus, Holton laments the fact that historians continue in "mistaking the Federalists' biased assessment of the crisis that led to the Constitution for reality," reinforcing the federalists' judgment that the people could not govern themselves, and that common folks would destroy the economy if given the chance. The legacy of ratification is consequently pride coupled with trepidation: "Today Americans exude immense pride in their democratic republic. But beneath that surface lurk nagging feelings, not only that you can't fight city hall but that you shouldn't, since we all know what happens when ordinary folk get their hands on the levers of power."[92]

The legacy of the ratification debate is deeply conflicted. On the one hand, had it not been for popular dissent, then there would be no Bill of Rights securing the right to democratic dissent. On the other hand, the ratification debate narrowed political vocabularies by making democratic dissent seem increasingly troublesome in a dangerous world. When discussing Shays's Rebellion, federalists' rhetorics tended to focus on potentials rather than realities, transforming debate into speculation as the crisis in government was escalated with slippery-slope pronouncements of impending doom. These rhetorics, in turn, had a two-fold effect: they made democracy seem increasingly like insanity while justifying a beefed-up security state to contain the madness. And here was the irony. In the 1770s, the British use of state violence and standing armies against Americans helped to fuel colonial resentment of the king and thus acted as a necessary condition for the revolutionary movement. In the middle 1780s, state violence was central to the government's bungled response to Shays's Rebellion, and its misuse contributed to the downfall of Bowdoin's administration in Massachusetts. State violence, in short, encouraged Americans to topple two previous governments: one with their own violence, the other at the polls. The way that events like Shays's Rebellion were described in public discourse, however, made a turn away from state violence seem like folly. While few of the founders sang the praises of standing armies, nevertheless one legacy of the ratification debate was the apparent necessity of coercion as a bedrock of government.

Federalists worked diligently to frame Shays's Rebellion as a danger to all Americans, no matter if they lived in Massachusetts, nearby New York, or distant Virginia. This was done, in part, by deploying the rhetorics of madness—which implied that protestors were little more than a crazy mob, and demands for equality and financial remuneration little more than delusional chatter. Philadelphia's Benjamin Rush, the preeminent psychologist in the early Republic, positioned Shays as "a solitary example of political insanity and wickedness."[93] For Rush, Shays was not the product of an unjust economic and political structure; he was pure, delirious, crazed evil. The Regulators were called "crazy" and just about every synonym for crazy in public and private discourse.[94] Knox told Washington that Shays's Rebellion was "a formidable rebellion against reason, the principles of all government, and the very name of liberty."[95] Isaiah Thomas, the publisher of the *Worcester Magazine*, positioned an emotional and patriotic letter from rebel leader Adam Wheeler above the prescription for curing a rabid dog's bite.[96] The simple flow of the page meant that after reading Wheeler's letter, the reader then learned how to recognize, and potentially cure, a rabid animal. Though we have no way of knowing for sure, the positioning of Wheeler's letter above an article about a rabid dog was probably not arbitrary, but instead a clever editorial trick that created the impression that the Regulators, like rabid animals, were crazy. By spatially linking the articles, Thomas slurred the Regulators' sanity—and even more, their humanity. In the seventeenth and eighteenth centuries, rhetorics of madness and insanity were deployed to define the norms of proper "civilized" behavior, and thus Shays acted as a political no-no for Americans learning how to behave in the postwar world.[97] Furthermore, the rhetorics of madness helped escalate the crisis into a danger shared by all the states, for the metaphors used to frame public discussion about Shays's Rebellion suggested that it was contagious.

For many, the lesson of Shays's Rebellion was that the civic judgment of common folks could not be trusted—for they were made crazy by the rhetorics associated with the American Revolution that stressed the virtues of democracy and the power of the people. "The minds of the citizens of the United States were wholly unprepared for their new situation" following independence, Rush concluded after reading about Shays's Rebellion. To explain why the post-Revolutionary moment tended toward social anomie, Rush turned to the language of medicine, diagnosing the democratic "insanity" of Shays and other populist insurgents as "*anarchia*." For Rush, Shays's Rebellion was emblematic of the continuing

problems posed by revolution in the postwar years. Revolution had become lodged in the bodies and minds of citizens, where it was not easily
erased. He explained, "The excess of the passion for liberty, inflamed
by the successful issue of the war, produced, in many people, opinions
and conduct which would not be removed by reason nor restrained by
government."[98] For Rush and other elites, the Revolutionary War had
gone horribly wrong, and the *anarchia* of post-Revolutionary democracy
threatened to hasten the inevitable decline of the nation.

Shays's Rebellion was labeled a storm by one writer, and a "contagion" of "riotous disposition"—in short, a disease—by its first historian.[99]
Hamilton compared it to a "wild fire," tapping into a grave fear at the time
shared by common folks and their rich brethren alike—for most houses
in the early Republic were made of wood, and a well-placed arson could
destroy an entire city.[100] The metaphors of storm, disease, and fire implied
that the energies of rebellion could easily spread from state to state, and
these metaphors were designed to put all Americans, no matter how far
from the action, in danger. Massachusetts' Fisher Ames captured the contagion thusly: "The combustibles are collected; the mind is prepared; the
smallest spark may again produce an explosion."[101] At the Massachusetts
Ratifying Convention in 1788, Ames repeated his concern, arguing that
Shays's Rebellion was emblematic of the dangers of democracy and concluding, "A democracy is a volcano, which conceals the fiery materials of
its own destruction. These will produce an eruption, and carry desolation
in their way."[102] Understanding that America's problematic relationship to
revolution fostered widespread fears that Shays's Rebellion would spark
another revolutionary war, federalists wisely exploited these beliefs and
called for elites across the nation to band together in opposition to the
dangerous masses and their democratic beliefs.

Clearly, Shays's Rebellion represented a danger to government. That
the Regulators would march on the Springfield Arsenal was galling; had
they won the arsenal, they would have been better armed than the state
of Massachusetts. But their conduct at the arsenal suggested that, even
when amassed in numbers for battle, the Regulators were not revolutionaries, but were, in fact, reluctant to harm other citizens. Erected in 1778,
the Springfield Arsenal held 7,000 muskets with bayonets, 1,300 barrels of
powder, and enough shot and shell for a large army, making it a formidable

cache of weapons and home of the repressive violence on which modern states are founded. When the Regulators marched on the federal arsenal at Springfield, they were outgunned by William Shepard's troops. Though the Regulators had twice the number of combatants, Shepard had artillery, and the Regulators were loath to skirmish with weapons.[103] Shepard's troops fired twice, hitting only sky, tree, and snow; on the third volley, however, they killed Ezekiel Root, Ariel Webster, Jabez Spicer, and John Hunter, prompting a chorus of indignant voices charging Shepard's troops with "murder."[104] That the Regulators viewed the government's fusillade as murder indicates a moral and social judgment. For them, there were clear boundaries of legitimate Regulation, and killing people fell outside these bounds. Shays himself reiterated this point, claiming that the Regulators were "unwilling to stain the land, which we in the late war purchased at so dear a rate, with the blood of our brethren and neighbours."[105] This rhetorical clue suggests that although the Regulators were perpetrating what looked like a military revolution, their actions were in fact symbolic acts of self-governance—hence the Regulators' horror at military "murder."

While the Regulators expressed horror at the government's "murder," in popular discourse Daniel Shays was portrayed as a "general" (though he had been a captain during the Revolutionary War with five years service, and was referred to in Regulator discourse as "Captain Shays") and a potential military dictator. The Regulators, it was said, were potential revolutionaries and killers of Americans; in short, the well-armed enemies of life, liberty, and property. Building on these themes, in his devastating Federalist 21, Hamilton piled rhetorical questions one on top of another to create a slippery-slope effect that escalated the threat Shays's Rebellion posed to Americans if they did not cast their vote in support of ratification. "A successful faction may erect a tyranny on the ruins of order and law," he wrote, and "The tempestuous situation from which Massachusetts has scarcely emerged evinces that dangers of this kind are not merely speculative. Who can determine what might have been the issue of her late convulsions if the malcontents had been headed by a Caesar or by a Cromwell? Who can predict what effect a despotism established in Massachusetts would have upon the liberties of New Hampshire or Rhode Island, of Connecticut or New York?"[106] Hamilton's thoughts in Federalist 21 were slightly paradoxical, for the federalist case against Daniel Shays required him to be both a grave threat and an incompetent fool. To justify the Constitution, Shays's Rebellion was portrayed as the most serious of crises. Still, it was successfully suppressed by the Massachusetts government, a fact quickly downplayed during the ratification debates because it demonstrated that the state governments could adequately manage uprisings and defend citizens from domestic dangers. Hamilton and others hoping to frighten Americans therefore had to focus on the potential of Shays's Rebellion rather than the reality. Accordingly, Hamilton queried his readers: What if Shays had been a gifted leader intent on orchestrating another revolution? What if he had possessed talent and influence? What if he had been a George Washington with bad manners? The worst could have happened. All that prevented it, Hamilton implied, was dumb luck. And who wanted to entrust the safety of their lives and estates to luck, to the rollercoaster of *fortuna*?

Many of the founders of the United States believed that the people were weak and would be easily misled by a skilled demagogue. Washington called the people "the grazing multitude," and they were "the common Herd of Mankind" for Adams.[107] These comparisons to cows reveal one of the founders' greatest fears: herd behavior. Believing that the people were easy prey for smooth talkers, Hamilton and others posited a rhetorical domino effect as one state after another fell to rampaging democrats. The ramparts were weak, he announced, and if one was breached the rest would soon fall. The only thing that saved the United States from pandemonium was the complete and utter commonness of Daniel Shays. Though some painted him as an aspiring despot, Hamilton and others knew better. According to the pro-Constitution essayist "A Landholder": "Had Shays, the malecontent of Massachusetts, been a man of genius, fortune and address, he might have conquered that state, and by the aid of a little sedition in the other states, and an army proud by victory, become the monarch and tyrant of America." *This* Shays was not a genius, this writer observed, but the *next* Shays might be, and thus he or she feared that "accident or design will in all probability raise up some future Shays to be the tyrant of your children."[108]

In June 1788, Henry Lee—who had earlier urged Washington and other elites to use Shays's Rebellion to justify a stronger federal government—also talked of danger at the Virginia Ratifying Convention. "Had

Shays been possessed of abilities, he might have established that favorite system of the Gentleman—*King, Lords and Commons*. Nothing was wanting to bring about a revolution, but a great man to head the insurgents; but fortunately he was a worthless Captain," he proclaimed. Had Shays taken the Springfield Arsenal, Lee reasoned, he would have established a monarchy in the United States—an absurd claim given the Regulators' democratic aims. Nevertheless, Lee understood how easily divergent fears are concatenated, and he therefore linked Shays with the king. Shays failed because "he wanted design and knowledge," Lee reported. He then asked his audience: "Will you trust to the want of design and knowledge?"[109] Both "A Landholder" and Lee used the same grammatical structure, a periodic sentence constructed in the conditional tense, to create a striking rhetorical effect. Both sentences were composed in a way that linked the possibility of a future potentiality backwards to a series of completed actions that could have resulted in a particularly horrific result. This rebellion was successfully suppressed, but these authors wanted to use it to justify a stronger federal government; thus, they projected a future threat by offering an alternative reading of the past. These authors belittled Daniel Shays because he was no longer a real person or a real danger; he was a representation of a possible conspiracy, a lurking danger, a coming attack. The enemy was not just Shays; he was a buffoon. The enemy was also the potential for disorder that Shays represented: the enemy was democracy.

This was a point made in *The Anarchiad*, an epic poem published serially in Connecticut newspapers in 1786 and 1787 by the Connecticut Wits: David Humphreys, Joel Barlow, John Trumbull, and Lemuel Hopkins. These poets made a terrifying prediction: Shays's Rebellion was not the end but the beginning, the prologue to a coming campaign that would hasten the end of government and perhaps the end of the world. "Behold the reign of anarchy, begun," they warned, as "maddening mobs assume their rusty guns."[110] While the maddening mobs engaged in riotous violence were terrifying, the real danger was not Daniel Shays or crazy debtors or zombie plebs, but the spirit of democracy itself:

> *Nor less abhor'd, the certain woe that waits*
> *The giddy rage of democratic States,*

Whose pop'lar breath, high blown in restless tide,
No laws can temper, and no reason guide:
An equal sway, their mind indignant spurns,
To wanton change, the bliss of freedom turns;
Led by wild demagogues, the factious crowd,
Mean, fierce, imperious, insolent and loud,
Nor fame, nor wealth, nor power, nor system draws—
They see no object, and perceive no cause;
But feel, by turns, in one disastrous hour,
Th' extremes of license, and th' extremes of power.[111]

This might not have been good poetry, but the Connecticut Wits got their point across with the hazy imagery of biblical prophets. Shays's Rebellion was to be feared because it was an expression of democracy in all its wantonness, insolence, and licentiousness. For them, democracy was not a form of government, but a disease characterized by "giddy rage." Democracy pushed citizens beyond law and reason. Democracy upended the natural social hierarchy by encouraging commoners to lust for power. Democracy made the body politic a sitting duck for eloquent demagogues. Accordingly, democracy was the enemy Americans had to defeat in the post-Revolutionary years.

Echoing the Connecticut Wits, Hamilton prophesied that events like Shays's Rebellion—and there would be more in the absence of a repressive power—would destroy the fragile post-Revolutionary union, if not the United States itself. The slippery-slope logic of his questions in Federalist 21 escalated the crisis beyond the boundaries of Massachusetts. Moreover, Hamilton's logic attempted to convince Americans that they had no other choice. Among the available means of escalating the danger of the enemy was the rhetorical strategy of forecasting a future catastrophe if something was not done about the enemy right then. As an argumentative strategy, federalist enemyship packed a double wallop, for federalists attempted to force a decision immediately, thereby overriding the calm consideration of security issues, while simultaneously coloring the decision with feelings of fear, anxiety, distress, and menace. Having named the enemy, rhetors in the ratification debates amplified a present danger into something much worse. If Americans did not act with all possible haste and ratify the Constitution immediately, Hamilton admonished, then the enemy—Daniel Shays, i.e., democracy—would only become stronger, and the attack would be that much worse.

While the Massachusetts government succeeded in containing Shays's Rebellion in early 1787, coercion ultimately backfired as citizens turned the government out in the election that fall. This might have caused politicians to question the efficacy of coercion, and, indeed, few politicians actively defended standing armies during the Constitutional Convention. Anti-federalists, in turn, were especially persuasive when they warned that the Constitution's provision for a standing army during peacetime was really a proscription for despotism. Following Whig attacks on standing armies in England, and Revolutionary War rhetorics that tarnished standing armies as the disreputable tools of lordly despots, many anti-federalists argued that standing armies were incompatible with republican government. For Centinel, the standing army created by the Constitution "shall be embodied to rivet the chains of slavery on a deluded nation."[112] Centinel used the term "rivet" much less metaphorically than General Shepard, as a synonym for "weld"; he feared that the new government would shackle Americans and bind their free movement with military force. Pennsylvania anti-federalists criticized the Constitution by expounding that a standing army "would be inconsistent with every idea of liberty; for the same force that may be employed to compel obedience to good laws, might and probably would be used to wrest from the people their constitutional liberties."[113] According to these anti-federalists, Americans should rebuke the Constitution because it portended a dark future of the military repression of democratic dissent.

The ratification debate, however, heightened demophobia to such a degree that it made coercion appear an acceptable and logical response to democratic dissent. For Philadelphus, who talked about turning Shays into an object of vindictive justice, Shays's Rebellion proved the utility of state violence—not only as an instrument of repression, but as a tool of reform. This writer argued that internal conflicts within the nation arose because common folks confused liberty with anarchy, and in the process lost sight of the bounds of civil decorum. "To some people liberty and licentiousness appear to be synonymous terms; but in my opinion, when liberty borders on licentiousness, it is then wholly lost, and the

perpetrators ought most undoubtedly to be brought to condign punishment," he or she argued. Punishment, in turn, would stake the boundaries
of polite society by demarcating what types of behaviors were appropriate
and inappropriate. State violence, in short, would teach citizens how to
act in post-Revolutionary times. As such, punishment was the key to the
nation's future.

While federalists talked about the Constitution as an agent of protection, Philadelphus was realistic about how much the government could
do to protect Americans. "Are there in reality any walls too high to be
scaled by a valiant enemy? And of what use are ramparts against intestine
divisions seconded by foreign powers?" In spite of the federalist refrain
that the Constitution would protect Americans, bulwarks and ramparts
were of little use against a determined enemy. Of much better use was
the symbolic projection of unity to the world: for a united people were
much more difficult to subdue. Thus, Philadelphus called for domestic
punishment to frighten Americans into line and hence to bring them
together—countering domestic faction with an image of strength and
unanimity that would ensure that no foreign enemy would ever attack the
young nation. Thus, when this writer called for "unanimity, sobriety, and
justice" and "a steady observance of civil policy" at home, he also voiced
his support for the state to turn violence into civic pedagogy.[114]

Hamilton, too, found hope in the state's capacity to punish rebellious citizens like Daniel Shays. As he would argue repeatedly during the
1790s, especially when he successfully advocated coercive responses to
the Whiskey Rebellion in 1794 and Fries's Rebellion in 1799, standing
armies were an essential tool of modern governance. Hamilton based this
argument on two premises. First, he argued in Federalist 8 and Federalist
24 that the old civic republican ideal of a domestic militia was no longer realistic in a proto-capitalist world. Indeed, as the type of capitalism
unleashed in Great Britain in the eighteenth century and described by
Adam Smith in The Wealth of Nations swept the globe, it produced a new
type of subject who was greedy, avaricious, and always looking to make a
buck: a subject, in short, who was too busy to serve in the militia. It was
better to leave protection up to the professionals. Hamilton hence rooted
his support for standing armies in a sensitive attunement to changing
economic conditions.

Equally important, Hamilton argued that standing armies were necessary to control the mob: to shackle rowdy citizens who, at any time, could explode into revolution. Drawing on his experience living during the tumultuous years of the middle 1780s, in Federalist 28, Hamilton came to the opinion that civic discord was not an aberration, but an unfortunate element of the social fabric. He observed that "seditions and insurrections are, unhappily, maladies as inseparable from the body politic, as tumours and eruptions from the natural body." Moreover, he noted that "the idea of governing at all times by the simple force of law, (which we have been told is the only admissible principle of republican government) has no place but in the reverie of those political doctors, whose sagacity disdains the admonitions of experimental instruction." The American experiment taught that the force of law was not enough. Government required another, equally robust means of governing. For Hamilton this was military force. Just as healthy bodies required doctors at the ready when something went wrong, so too the state necessitated a standing army prepared for a quick response to the "contagion." "An insurrection, whatever may be its immediate cause, eventually endangers all government," he concluded, closing the space for any popular uprising, no matter how local, by suggesting that the inevitable result of any democratic mobilization was anarchy. Understanding that his logic backed him up against the deep distrust many Americans felt for standing armies, he conceded that the state's power to coerce citizens might be abused. But, he asked, "who would not prefer that possibility, to the unceasing agitations, and frequent revolutions, which are the continual scourges of petty republics?"[115]

While Hamilton's rationalization of standing armies did not yet achieve the sophistication of Philadelphus's, the 1780s proved to him and many others that coercion was a necessary tool of governing. Still, he recognized that his arguments for military force would not be popular with Americans. He even admitted that fears of a standing army were too ingrained to be touched by the pen. The "apprehension" against standing armies, Hamilton conceded, was beyond persuasion, and "may be considered as a disease, for which there can be found no cure in the resources of argument and reasoning."[116] Americans would always fear standing armies, and they would always guard their liberties jealously. So,

Hamilton and others began to think about ways to govern that might get around Americans' apprehension that the new federal government might suppress them as the king had done in the 1770s. They began to think, in short, about how to redefine the meaning of power for a new age.

Power in Post-Revolutionary Times

The founders recognized that achieving the transition from the Declaration of Independence, which justified revolution, to the Constitution, which sought to suppress it, would not be easy. Here, the testimony of Benjamin Lincoln is particularly revealing. Lincoln was the Massachusetts general who led the military response to Shays's Rebellion. He therefore understood, first hand, how jealously citizens guarded what they took to be the democratic legacy of the Revolutionary War, and their corresponding skepticism about state power and centralized government. In February 1788, while the fate of ratification was uncertain, but looking forward to the period when a new and much stronger national government would assume power, Lincoln astutely outlined the problems endemic to the early Republic in a letter to George Washington. The Revolutionary War had been a blessing and a curse, for while it brought independence, it also turned the world upside down by inspiring "the many" (as the masses were often known) to actively participate in politics and government. Now, he averred, the Revolution entered a second phase during which the American gentry had to take back much of the political power common folks won during the war.

This phase of the Revolution was no less important than the first, and no less challenging. Thus, Lincoln cautioned Washington not to expect that "those men who were so lately intoxicated with large draughts of liberty and who were thirsting for more would in so short a time submit to a constitution, which would further take up the reins of government, which in their opinion were too strait before."[117] Lincoln informed Washington that Americans were "intoxicated with large draughts of liberty," comparing liberty to a type of alcohol that impaired the judgment of common folks, and revolutionary violence to a drunken rage that was beyond control. During his terms as the first President of the United States,

Washington and others in his administration came to believe that Lincoln was right, and that citizens were indeed drunk on the Revolutionary War's promises of liberty, equality, and democracy. For Lincoln, Washington, and other counter-revolutionaries trying to move citizens toward sobriety, a central task of government was teaching Americans how to cope with the long and painful hangover from a revolutionary binge.

Benjamin Rush understood, perhaps better than anyone else, how the counter-revolution would proceed. In the years following the Revolutionary War, Rush brought his obsessions with medicine and nosology to the problem of how best to create social order.[118] Popular uprisings following the war proved that before elites could gain power over citizens, they would first have to redefine the meaning of the American Revolution. In a speech reprinted in Philadelphia's *American Museum* during Shays's Rebellion, he corrected the "common" misperception that confounded "the terms of the American revolution with those of the late American war." For Rush, the American War and the American Revolution were distinct events: "The American war is over; but this is far from being the case with the American revolution. On the contrary, nothing but the first act of the great drama is closed. It remains yet to establish and perfect our new forms of government; and to prepare the principles, morals, and manners of our citizens, for these forms of government." Distinguishing between a disruptive "war" that toppled a colonial power and a "revolution" that altered the behaviors of the masses, Rush defined the real American Revolution as an ongoing experiment in moral and political education that would prepare citizens to be governed. Rush was right to recognize that revolution stirred the collective consciousness and that, as a consequence, most citizens were not ready to exchange autonomy for long-term stability. For Rush, nation-building therefore meant correcting the too-democratic spirit of the Revolutionary War. Here, Rush spoke for the founders of the United States in calling for a Second American Revolution. Only by reforming the attitude and manners of citizens, he argued, could politicians gain power over citizens and establish a lasting foundation for government.[119]

Power had long been thought of as the capacity to wield violence, and therefore one popular solution to the problem of stabilizing the new order of things was coercion—which aimed at using the state's mighty military power to crush crime and force citizens to behave. Proponents of coercion advocated a strong army to crack dissenters' heads, thereby upholding a deferential hierarchy by forcing the masses into line. But coercion did not solve the dilemmas of American nationalism. There were tremendous problems associated with naming citizens enemies and turning state violence against them. Furthermore, while the Constitution created the infrastructure for domestic repression, the founders could not frighten Americans into obeying the law.[120] When America's elites established a new government, they cleared the first hurdle toward creating a lasting nation. The second hurdle, however, was even taller: for the new government had to gain *power* over its subjects, and this required more than the tools of domestic repression—it required a revolution in the hearts and minds of citizens.

In the late eighteenth century, the meaning of power was changing. Power had traditionally meant the ability to force subjects to act, i.e., coercion. The Enlightenment changed how humans thought about power: power now meant not just *coercion* but also *discipline.* As the framers of the United States Constitution met in Philadelphia's Constitution Hall during the electrifying summer of 1787, the meaning of the word "discipline" was evolving. In the seventeenth and early eighteenth centuries, discipline meant "of the Lash" as schoolteachers punished their students, inflicting pain to alter their behaviors. In the late eighteenth century, discipline now meant something closer to indoctrination, and the target of disciplinarians was no longer just the body but also the pupil's soul. The goal of a disciplinary education was not to punish subjects but to create them; it did this not by telling citizens "no," do not do that, but rather by telling them "yes," do that, only in a certain way.[121] Along with these shifting notions of discipline, the physical geography of schools changed. Schoolrooms became ever more like prisons and monasteries as teachers carefully regimented the days of students and made their bodies malleable for shaping by the state.[122] In the eighteenth century, education was about internalization, cultivation, molding, and hailing, making it similar to military training.

The founders of the United States possessed a dual conception of power: they understood that power worked not only on citizens but also through them. Their goal was to establish a system of government that could coerce citizens if necessary, but that would simultaneously alter how they behaved so that coercion was no longer necessary. As we will see, the founders tied the two levels of power, the structure of government and the production of correct behavior, together with the rhetoric of enemyship. In fact, one reason why the Constitution called and Americans answered was because the founders convinced Americans that they shared national enemies—just as they did during the Revolutionary War.

CHAPTER THREE

The Army of the Constitution

O n December 12, 1787, Pennsylvania became the second state to ratify the federal Constitution. In celebration, local federalists planned a parade in Carlisle on December 26. They were met with the shouts, taunts, and blows of determined anti-federalists, who stole a cannon intended to mark the occasion with bombast. The next day, anti-federalists continued to protest, whipping and then executing effigies of prominent Pennsylvania federalists. When several of the rioters were arrested, representatives from local militia units marched to the Carlisle jail to free them. Parading in Carlisle was hence turned upside down as anti-federalists seized the same city streets that federalists claimed as their own. The Carlisle riots provided federalists with evidence that popular government was indeed *anarchia* and that anti-federalists were really Shaysites. These riots demonstrated that some Americans rejected the new Constitution and would continue to fight it. The anti-federalist critic Centinel praised the rioters, arguing that "the great body of the people are awakened to a due sense of their danger, and are determined to assert their liberty, if necessary by the sword" against "a junto composed of the lordly and high minded gentry." The people's enemies were "harpies of power" who acted as though "they had already triumphed over the liberties of the people, that the chains were rivetted and tyranny established."[1] To resist these would-be dictators, Centinel called on people all over the United States to rise up.

The Regulation in Massachusetts helped to convince many elite Americans who were already pondering greater centralization to abandon the Articles of Confederation and write a new Constitution for the United States. Elites in Pennsylvania responded to events like this in the same way that elites from across the country responded to Shays's Rebellion: by rewriting its constitution. Pennsylvania's 1776 constitution established a unicameral legislature, a weak executive, and widespread suffrage. Furthermore, it was a democratic document founded on the principle that government served the people. It claimed (echoing the Declaration of Independence) that citizens could "take such measures as to them may appear necessary" if the government became abusive, and delegated to citizens the right to nullify unpopular legislation.[2] Pennsylvania's 1790 Constitution took away these rights while establishing a government more friendly to political elites. The new constitution did not stop popular violence, however, and protests like those in Carlisle grew more widespread in the 1790s, culminating in the summer of 1794 with a violent uprising now known as the Whiskey Rebellion. When citizens burned a tax collector's house to the ground and staged a military demonstration near Pittsburgh, they posed a direct challenge to the federal government's authority to tax citizens—and, more seriously, to govern at all.

Like all happenings in the early Republic, the events of the 1790s were read in the long shadow of the Revolutionary War. Acting as a common past and a precondition for nationalism, the American Revolution was one way that rhetors defined the boundaries of American identity.[3] How citizens related to the American Revolution was a litmus test—a shibboleth—but the meaning of the revolution itself was unstable. By arguing that the Whiskey Rebellion was the logical result of the Revolutionary War, the pastor of West Springfield's Congregational Church, Joseph Lathrop, captured the dangers of the moment in a 1794 Fourth of

July Address titled *The Happiness of a Free Government, and the Means of Preserving It.* Though this temperately toned speech was delivered in Massachusetts, it nevertheless emphasized the themes that made post-war protests in Pennsylvania and other states dangerous. Writing from the cradle of Shays's Rebellion, Lathrop argued that the happiness of a free government was determined by "the people," who had the right to preserve their rights by any means necessary:

> To frame and reform their own government, and to choose and change their own governors, is the natural right of mankind; but a right which few nations have the happiness to enjoy, or the boldness to claim. These American states are now in the full possession and free exercise of this right; and may they ever have the wisdom to retain it. We were once happy in a connection with Britain. The time came, when we found we could be happy in this connection no longer. We then judged, that it ought to be dissolved . . . Every people have a right to be free—to judge of the proper means of securing their freedom—to determine when they ought to become independent of former connections—and to constitute for themselves such a government as they choose.[4]

Contending that the people could make and unmake governments as they so chose, and invoking the Declaration of Independence as evidence, Lathrop reiterated the monarchy-busting logic of the Revolutionary War. By implying that there might be cause for another revolution in 1794, he and others threatened to derail the nation-building project altogether. Lathrop's address, given on the Fourth of July during the heart of violent protests against the government, typified the anti-federalist, pro-democracy attitudes that the new federal government had to confront after the ratification of the Constitution.

From Shays's Rebellion to the Whiskey Rebellion, the enduring democratic spirit of revolution posed problems for nation-builders. Though leaders demanded that citizens acquiesce to laws made by rulers they elected, the right to revolution was not easily expurgated from public memory. Even the authors of *The Federalist,* who hoped to tame revolution, paid lip service to this right—for it was central to the republican tradition as Americans conceived it. James Madison labeled the ability of citizens to "abolish or alter their governments" as enumerated in the Declaration of Independence a "transcendent and precious right of the people" in Federalist 40.[5] The Constitution created an apparatus for punishing those who violated the new post-Revolutionary order, so while America's revolutionary past continued to frustrate politicians in the 1790s, the federal government had new resources at its disposal for dealing with "rebellion" following ratification. The Constitution did not, however, solve the dilemmas of American nationalism. The Constitution's prescription for the state's coercive power had to be realized in practice, and this required both political strategy and rhetorical ingenuity. The first president of the United States, George Washington, and his cabinet faced difficult challenges in the young nation's first years: to monopolize the right to violence, taking it away from potential rebels, while persuading citizens that the state's use of violence against unruly Americans was legitimate. As we will see, the remaking of post-Revolutionary democracy was furthered, though not completed, by the naming of a series of enemies.

In the summer of 1794, as widespread frontier protests against the federal government were reaching their climax, General Anthony Wayne led an army of United States soldiers to victory at the Battle of Fallen Timbers, which in turn opened much of the Ohio Valley for settlement. The promises of expansion, alongside rhetoric demonizing "Indians," helped to redirect the energies of indignant frontiersmen westward away from the government. At the same time, President Washington called on common citizens to form an "Army of the Constitution" that would defend the government from its domestic enemies. The naming of an external enemy helped to ease the rage of an internal enemy; the naming of that internal enemy simultaneously helped redefine the meaning of citizenship for many Americans who might have been lukewarm about ratification. In the abstract, it was easy to berate the federal government. When this government actually protected Americans from danger, it became real, useful, and harder to resist. As Federalists began to think of citizens as allies in governance rather than subjects to be dominated, the reach of government was increased. In this chaotic moment of democratic protest, the founders furthered the Second American Revolution by redefining the meaning of political power and altering what it meant to be a citizen in the United States.

Economic Development
and the Whiskey Rebellion

"The Storm in the west was brewing," St. George Tucker, a prominent
Virginia judge and lawyer, reported ominously to his friend James Madison regarding the event that is now known as the Whiskey Rebellion.
Tucker provided Madison with the perfect metaphor for the events: the
storm. Storms, like the great hurricane that wrecked the Caribbean in
October 1780 and was not far from public memory, represented the con-
tingencies of chance and fortune that made nations tremble. The same
unpredictability characterized the democratic violence that persisted
beyond Shays's Rebellion into the 1790s. All across the United States,
from Tucker's Virginia to Kentucky to western Pennsylvania, citizens took
to the streets, tarring and feathering tax collectors and closing roads,
because they were unhappy with how the new government, especially
Alexander Hamilton's Treasury Department, managed its affairs.[6]

Hamilton was an inspired choice to be the first secretary of the Treasury, and he took on the task of reforming America's pathetic postwar
economy with gusto. Hamilton set out his commercial philosophy in three
reports presented before Congress: the Report on Public Credit (January
1790), the Opinion on the Constitutionality of a National Bank (February
1791), and the Report on the Subject of Manufactures (December 1791).
In these reports, Hamilton demonstrated his understanding that commerce depended on not just physical realities but also symbolic representations. He wrote in his first report that "Opinion is the soul" of credit,
and that credit was influenced "by appearances, as well as realities."[7] In
order to create the appearance that the United States was a safe haven for
foreign and domestic investment, Hamilton argued that the U.S. government should assume the states' remaining debts from the Revolutionary
War. This produced a massive national debt—which in turn necessitated
taxes, banks, and a steadying government hand to manage fiscal policy. In
this way, Hamilton furthered the nation-building project by expanding the
reach of the federal government and cementing the states' dependence
upon Congress. Following assumption of the debts, Hamilton calculated
the nation's debt to foreign governments and private investors at nearly

60 million dollars (including interest). Hamilton's plan for paying back this debt was semiotic brilliance. He championed annuities, investments with hard currency in the government to be paid back with interest rates beginning at 6 percent. Calling on citizens to invest in their own debt, Hamilton assured a steady stream of specie for the U.S. treasury. He also called for an elaborate system of taxes on commodities including whiskey to pay the interest due on annuities.[8]

Hamilton demonstrated a thorough mastery of the rhetorical nature of economics. By altering the economy's appearance and creating, in the words of one skeptic, "imaginary capital," Hamilton's policies had profound effects.[9] Though Hamilton's program for funding the national debt did not immediately change material realities, it significantly altered representations of public finance by simulating financial stability and encouraging investment. Hamilton's plan was a performative gesture: he attempted to bring about the desired state of economic affairs through his words. His policies worked masterfully. From 1790 to 1791, tax revenue amounted to $4.4 million; in 1793, $4.6 million; in 1795, $5.9 million. The tax receipts for 1792 alone superseded all the taxes paid by the states to the federal government from October 30, 1781, to March 31, 1787. Moreover, by creating a stable, funded debt with a proliferating capital market for bonds, Hamilton exponentially increased foreign investment in the U.S. economy.[10] Due to his brilliant manipulation of financial appearance and reality, Hamilton is rightfully remembered as America's economic savior.

Though economics might be at the base of things, they do not a complete picture make. By focusing more on the nation's finances and less on personal liberties, Hamilton's plans were threatening to citizens who did not care about the nation's debts and who traditionally equated taxes with slavery. The memory of America's colonial experiences with taxation, and England's taxation of the colonies "without representation," caused citizens to dread a slippery slope of political treachery. Soon, they feared, tax collectors with arbitrary power would ransack their homes and steal their property. Taught harshly by the king's thugs, frontiersmen feared the economic and political reach of the federal government. For the essayist "A Farmer" in Philadelphia's *National Gazette*, it was "an excise law which renders the house of a citizen no longer sacred and which prevents the farmer from enjoying the just fruits of his industry."[11] In the debates over Hamilton's plan in the House of Representatives, a frontier legislator feared that it would "let loose a swarm of harpies, who, under the denomination of revenue officers, will range through the country, prying into every man's house and affairs, and like a Macedonian phalanx bear down all before them."[12] Referencing mythology (harpies) and history (the mighty Macedonian military), protestors anchored their vision of how the American Republic should operate in the history of Ancient Greece, which was the birthplace of republicanism and democracy. Looking back on the past, protestors labeled Federalism an intolerable perversion of true republican principles.

Hamilton's financial plans threatened the livelihood of poor citizens, and had the unintended consequence of unifying infuriated dissenters into an alliance of both rural and city anti-federalists that would become Thomas Jefferson's Democratic-Republican (hereafter just Republican) party. In this case, many citizens' perceptions that Federalists were their enemies created the first oppositional political party in the United States. The voice of this new proto-party was Philip Freneau's *National Gazette*, a twice-weekly paper published in Philadelphia covertly sponsored by Jefferson, who hoped to use the news to discredit his political rivals. The heart and soul of this popular movement were extralegal associations known as Democratic-Republican Societies, which imitated the Sons of Liberty and the Committees of Correspondence in the 1770s and the Jacobin clubs of the French Revolution. These societies carried the democratic principles of the Revolutionary War into the 1790s; their stated purpose was to monitor the new government and correct its abuses. By creating space for conversations about government, they reopened democratic possibilities that were closed following Shays's Rebellion, providing citizens with a forum for passing judgment upon the government's policies.[13]

According to Kentuckians, the Democratic-Republican Societies recovered the more democratic, egalitarian, critical spirit of the Revolutionary War, gathering "not only to discuss the proceedings of Government, but to examine into the conduct of its officers in every department."[14] Members of Pennsylvania societies claimed that the Constitution did nothing to protect them; they had to protect themselves. "Continued vigilance is best calculated to preserve those principles in their purity," they mused, "and is the best security against the encroachments of unlawful power."[15]

Calling for wider political participation, freedom of assembly and press, reductions in legal fees, the abolition of imprisonment for debt, reformation of criminal codes, the establishment of public libraries, and free public education for all citizens, members of the Democratic-Republican Societies organized a grass-roots social movement for democratic change from the ground up.[16] In response to the apparent avariciousness of their enemies, the Democratic-Republican Societies attempted to dismantle the gospel of moneyed men and upend the culture of deference that characterized the post-Revolutionary United States. Many urban and rural Americans shared a dislike of Federalists—especially Hamilton—and their mutual antagonism with the ruling party unified them into an oppositional coalition stressing more democratic ideals.

In parts of western Pennsylvania, citizens took the principles of vigilance a step further by employing violence to police the government. Two western Pennsylvania societies, one in Washington County and the other at Mingo Creek, helped to radicalize protests into an open democratic revolt now known as the Whiskey Rebellion. There was little attachment to government and virtually no support for the Constitution on the Pennsylvania frontier where these societies were formed. Protests like the Carlisle riots of 1787 were common in western Pennsylvania, which was a hotbed of anti-federalism in the late 1780s and generally rejected centralized government in the early 1790s. In fact, as America was seeking sovereignty from Britain, the western counties sought sovereignty from America.

The border regions of Pennsylvania and Virginia attempted to secede and form the state of Westsylvania during the summer of 1776, claiming that "no country or people can be either rich, flourishing, happy or free" when the seat of government was "four or five hundred miles distant, and separated by a vast, extensive and almost impassible tract of mountains, by nature itself formed and pointed out as a boundary between this country and those below it."[17] The Westsylvanians' petition was a rejection of the nation-building project as citizens of western Pennsylvania imagined an alternative future for themselves premised on self-rule. Their petition for statehood, like those for other proposed states in the 1780s and 1790s, including Fair Play in Pennsylvania, Transylvania and Harrodsburg in Kentucky, Watauga in North Carolina, and Franklin in Virginia, was rejected by the Continental Congress and later governing bodies.[18] Pennsylvania claimed that it owned the western lands of Westsylvania; to take them away would have been "theft." Nonetheless, citizens of this region continued to press for statehood in the 1780s, prompting the Pennsylvania legislature in 1782 to pass a law prescribing a death sentence for anyone attempting to organize a new state within Pennsylvania's boundaries—a cruel fate for potential revolutionaries in this world-historical moment of revolution.[19]

On the surface, protestors' anger focused on Hamilton's whiskey tax. At this time, drinking water was unsafe and milk was not pasteurized, which made whiskey the safest and cheapest drink. Whiskey was a vital commodity and essential bartering tool on the frontier, and thus a tax on whiskey threatened to complicate even the most routine exchanges of frontier life.[20] Furthermore, frontiersmen were outraged that the federal government contemplated taxing them at all, contending that the woes of frontier life excused them from taxation and other such burdens. On a deeper level, however, protestors simply rejected federal control and took up arms to resist modernity, federation, and centralization. As one historian writes, the Whiskey Rebellion is something of a misnomer, because "the stakes were far higher. This protest was about popular beliefs that the state and national governments were undermining equality and democracy to enrich and empower a handful of moneyed men."[21]

Resistance to Hamilton's policies reached its peak in the summer of 1794 in western Pennsylvania, as citizens regulated government by closing roads and tarring and feathering tax collectors.[22] On July 16, approximately fifty settlers gathered at the house of the supervising tax collector for western Pennsylvania, John Neville, demanding that he turn over his tax records and surrender. When he refused, the aggressors exchanged fire with Neville's men. On the next day, between four hundred and eight hundred protestors gathered at Neville's house, and after Neville fled (with his tax records) they burned the house to the ground. Setting the house ablaze was a symbolic act, for an individual's house was a marker of identity in the eighteenth century.[23] Neville's clapboard house, constructed from European materials and immaculately decorated with carpet, wallpaper, two dozen paintings in gilt frames, five feather beds, and a large library, stood in sharp relief to settlers' small hovels and was for many a moral stain on a poverty-stricken frontier. In 1791, as a member of the Pennsylvania Assembly, Neville voted with the majority in passing a resolution condemning the whiskey tax; soon after, he accepted the post of excise inspector. Neville's actions appeared hypocritical, arousing the animus of his poor neighbors, who were particularly incensed by what they interpreted as his brazen opportunism and shameless elitism. Asked whether he cared about "the good opinion of his neighbors," Neville reportedly answered that "he did not regard their good will, he had got an independent salary of 600 a year."[24] Burning his house was a form of moral regulation. By burning Neville's house, protestors also destroyed the symbol of his wealth and punished him by incinerating his many possessions, thereby calling attention to his errors and also the abuses of the Federalist government.

Though protestors targeted Neville, their anger was deeper and would have found expression had Neville's house not been there to be fired. Their resentment of the federal government's financial policies and the demands it made on their conduct needed an outlet, and they would have a victim. On August 1, 1794, protests escalated as between 5,400 and 7,000 protestors marched on Pittsburgh and performed a military demonstration at Braddock's Field, where in July 1755, during the Seven Years War, General Edward Braddock's army—which included a young George Washington—was defeated by French forces. According to the Princeton-trained judge and lawyer who witnessed the events at Braddock's Field, Hugh Henry Brackenridge, protestors labeled Pittsburgh—the town he called home—"Sodom," after the sordid biblical town. In the 1790s, only 60 percent of western Pennsylvanians owned land. Towns like Pittsburgh were dirty, and life there was squalid. Most of the settlers did not own land; instead, they rented or owned only small "town lots," and were as a consequence forced to labor for a wage.[25] Protestors longed to smite this ugly urban blight from the earth, proclaiming "that Sodom had been burnt by fire from heaven; but this second Sodom should be burned with fire from earth."[26]

The second Sodom was not burned. Still, organizing on the spot where President Washington was defeated almost twenty years before was a brazen challenge to the government's authority. Frontiersmen escalated the Whiskey Rebellion into a contest over how best to govern. Whereas

Hamilton pushed a federal financial and political agenda, frontiersmen asked to be left alone. At this point, Brackenridge feared that protests would spiral out of control, observing that the enthusiasm at the Stamp Act protests was "by no means so general, and so vigorous, amongst the common people, as the spirit which now existed in this country." Protesters at Braddock's Field mocked America's thirteen-striped flag by raising their own six-striped flag representing a new frontier nation that would be comprised of four Pennsylvania and two Virginia counties. Amid an exploding frontier stoked by the taxation required to float the modern state, western Pennsylvanians contemplated another revolution to establish a small nation premised upon local control of politics.[27]

Protestors insisted that they were neither criminals nor traitors, but legitimate defenders of the nation's revolutionary legacy. They had a point—using violence to defend their autonomy was a logical and defensible outcome of America's revolutionary history. In the words of one essayist, citizen vigilance leading to coordinated protests against unjust uses of power was a "distinguished trait in our national character."[28] By making grand, sweeping claims about their place in American history, frontier citizens attempted to stall the steady westward march of deference and hierarchy with a more direct democracy. Moreover, participants in both Shays's Rebellion and the Whiskey Rebellion believed success certain. Popular violence had rarely failed to advance their goals, which they interpreted to mean that history was on their side. An essayist in the *National Gazette* reported in 1792 that when "the spirit and regulations of a military corps" was introduced "into civil government" and "arbitrary laws interfere in the private actions of citizens," it demonstrated "shameful ignorance of that knowledge of history," because "the history of civil society does not furnish a single instance of legislators interfering with, and directing the occupations of citizens, but with injury."[29] Looking back on the histories of Greece, Rome, and England, this essayist mocked Hamilton's and other would-be dictators' shameful ignorance of the past. The *telos* of historical force demanded that the government's injurious policies be defeated by common folks, the rightful guardians of political power.

This author's arguments exposed the divergent interpretations of history underlying public address in the early Republic. Whereas antifederalists derived lessons from the long arc and (supposed) direction of history, which saw the world becoming more democratic, federalists were more pragmatic, deriving lessons from the immediate past to solve contemporary problems and build a nation.[30] Federalists possessed a more sophisticated understanding of the production of history than anti-federalists, who clung to a false but comforting teleological model of historical development. In the early United States, federalists criminalized many of the modalities of democratic mobilization common during the Revolutionary War by clamping down on the types of direct action—what was called "Regulation"—championed by protestors. Watching their myths crumble, citizens were shaken by profound and seemingly irreversible changes. As they well knew, if Hamilton had his way, there would be no corner of the nation outside the reach of the modern economy or federal law.

Hamilton was a staunch proponent of standing armies—he was, in fact, along with Pennsylvania's James Wilson, one of the few participants in the Constitutional Congress to speak openly in their favor.[31] Events like Shays's Rebellion proved to Hamilton that state violence was essential to the long-term stability of the nation. State violence, in turn, was justified as essential for the people's security. In Federalist 23, Hamilton argued that "the circumstances that endanger the safety of nations are infinite; and for this reason, no constitutional shackles can wisely be imposed on the power to which the care of it is committed." He concluded: "There can be no limitation of that authority, which is to provide for the defence and protection of the community, in any matter essential to its efficacy."[32] For Hamilton, there could be no constitutional limit placed on the governing authority that provided citizens with safety, security, defense, and protection. When it came to protecting citizens from danger, the government could not be shackled.

The Whiskey Rebellion was a crisis, but like Shays's Rebellion, it was also an opportunity. Hamilton hoped to make an example of the western Pennsylvanians who protested against his whiskey tax—and he did all that he could to provoke them into an open rebellion that the government could justifiably crush.[33] As William Findley, a U.S. congressman from western Pennsylvania, observed in 1792, "The wrongful Secretary wishes to make us examples." "The scene of operation will be Washington County," he rightfully predicted.[34] The state desired a confrontation for two reasons. First, to demonstrate its strength—which, it was hoped, would dissuade democratic dissidents from rising up against the government. Second, to justify its strength to those who believed that the only purpose of a standing army was to mount a defense against monarchal oppression. This is the circular, use-it-or-lose-it logic of domestic repression: use it or it is not necessary, and use it to make it seem as though it is necessary.

Hamilton called for a military response to tax protests as early as 1792, only to be rebuffed by President Washington. As the events grew worse and the rebels more bold in the summer of 1794, Hamilton once again urged President Washington to respond by raising and deploying an army, telling him: "A competent force of Militia should be called forth and employed to suppress the insurrection and support the Civil Authority in effectuating Obedience to the laws and the punishment of Offenders."[35] Using capitals for emphasis, Hamilton illuminated his goal and what, for him, was the purpose of military force: to frighten Americans into obedience to the laws and punish those who refused to obey. Hamilton, here, echoed General William Shepard's plea for the government to use military force to "rivet" a conviction of the government's authority on the minds of dissidents during Shays's Rebellion. Believing that fear would transform protestors into obedient citizens, Hamilton's vision of governance was founded on the rhetorical production of this emotion. His goal was to make citizens fear the power of government so that they would think twice about disobeying the laws.

To justify the use of military force in response to the Whiskey Rebellion, Hamilton had to overcome the jealousy with which Americans guarded their liberties. He did this through a brilliant rhetorical maneuver. In eighteenth-century civic republican discourse, it was customary to posit a distinction between power and liberty.[36] Hamilton, however, made power the ally rather than the enemy of liberty by positing a new binary: anarchy/liberty. To defend a military response to protests in Pennsylvania, Hamilton published a series of essays in *Dunlap and Claypoole's American Daily Advertiser,* in which he told his readers that the United States "can scarcely lose its liberty from any other cause than that of anarchy."[37] By articulating the government's response in the language of anarchy, Hamilton shifted the conversation away from economics to security, arguing

that state power should be embraced as liberty's guarantor against criminal protestors. Protestors argued for equality and local control; Hamilton
attempted to remove the ground on which they stood by getting Americans to focus on the terror of anarchy: on what they might lose, and on
what might happen to them if *anarchia* was unchecked. Talk of anarchy
and danger made power a friend rather than an enemy of liberty, for it was
the government, not rebellious citizens, that would protect law-abiding
Americans from democracy in the streets. Through the principle of dialectical opposition, Hamilton made government the protector, and not
the enemy (as protestors insisted), of liberty.

In 1794, the government stepped into this new role. After sending
out proclamations, contacting Pennsylvania's governor, and otherwise
exhausting all other options, President Washington invoked the Militia
Law of 1792 to call up militia members from Pennsylvania, Virginia, New
Jersey, Maryland, and other states on August 7, 1794. In September,
Washington—accompanied by Hamilton and the Revolutionary War
hero Henry "Light Horse Harry" Lee—marched at the head of an army
of nearly 13,000 militiamen into western Pennsylvania to compel submission to the nation's laws. Earlier, Washington, Hamilton, and Lee
all framed the Constitution as necessary to control flare-ups of popular
violence like Shays's Rebellion. Now, they put the Constitution into action to do just that.

This army was massive by eighteenth-century standards, rivaling
the armies of the Revolutionary War: approximately 1,400 troops at the
Battle of Bunker Hill on June 17, 1775; approximately 11,000 at the decisive victory at Saratoga on October 7, 1777; and approximately 9,000
Americans (and 8,000 French) at the Battle of Yorktown in September/
October, 1781.[38] A domestic army 13,000 strong could serve no practical
purpose; a much smaller army could have handled the malcontents. Yet
the government had decided to make western Pennsylvania the testing
ground of federal authority. By raising an army capable of fighting the
British, President Washington demonstrated to citizens that disobedience to the Constitution would not be tolerated in the United States. The
government's deployment of military force to Pennsylvania was therefore
a rhetorical act: The Constitution, this army said, was sacred. Americans,
this army said, should obey.

"Whether We Shall Submit Ourselves to the Savages, or They to Us?"

When the 1783 Treaty of Paris ended the American Revolution, it ceded many British lands to the United States, including the agriculturally rich farmlands of present-day Ohio, Indiana, Illinois, Michigan, and Wisconsin. Americans solidified their claims to this area with several treaties during the 1780s. Believing these territories rightfully theirs, large portions of the lands were sold by the Land Ordinance of 1785, and a provisional government was established with the Northwest Ordinance of 1787. Politicians and settlers found the Indians already living there unwilling to abide by treaties dictated to them, or to cede their homelands to the proximate colonial power. President Washington, Secretary of War Henry Knox, and Secretary of the Treasury Hamilton all understood the importance of land to America's future. Rowdy frontiersmen could be placated with land; by procuring land and then selling it off, the government could raise the capital needed to govern. A central plank of Hamilton's program to resuscitate the economy was therefore a magnificent auction of America's frontiers to settlers, speculators, and private land companies. Eyeing bountiful profits and imagining domestic tranquillity, politicians gazed west.

When the new government was established in 1789, it confronted potential war with the Creeks on its Georgia frontier, the Cherokees on its North Carolina frontier, and the Wabash on its Pennsylvania and Virginia frontiers. On the rapidly expanding borders of the United States, these nations (and others) blocked American westward movement. Yet the new government also understood that the cash-starved United States did not have the resources to wage a frontier war. Washington therefore succeeded in prolonging war on the Georgia and North Carolina frontiers, but it became apparent to both him and his advisors that war was necessary in the Ohio Valley.[39] Consequently, one of the president's first actions was to deploy the military to secure national expansion in the Northwest Territory.

In 1790 and 1791, armies under Josiah Harmar and Arthur St. Clair battled Miami, Shawnee, Wyandott, Huron, Ottawa, Chippewa,

Pottawatomie, Sauk, Fox, and Wabash warriors who forged a confederacy in response to U.S. aggression. These were the first two wars waged by the United States; the results were devastating as the young nation sputtered in its early attempts at imperial domination. Harmar was defeated, and St. Clair's army was slaughtered: of his 1,400 troops, 630 were killed or unaccounted for, and almost 300 were injured, making this one of the United States' worst military defeats ever. These wars did nothing to advance American interests in the Ohio Valley; they succeeded only in emboldening America's foes. A general council of the victors in 1793 contended that U.S. claims to their land were spurious and that resistance would continue. "The King of England never did, nor never had a right, to give you our Country, by the Treaty of peace," they averred, and "no consideration whatever can induce us to sell the lands on which we get sustenance for our women and children."[40] Clearly, the United States was not yet a world power—and these nations expressed their intention to battle the American enemy to the death.

The defeats were a public-relations crisis for the president. The mounting expenses and accumulating body count of a stalled imperial giant inspired criticism of Washington that would have been unthinkable in the 1780s. The losses shook some citizens' faith in the moral fortitude of their leaders. An outraged essayist in Philadelphia's *Federal Gazette* criticized Washington for waging wars without merit or morals. "Providence has given them a good country," this author observed. "Their title to it is unquestionable. Doubtless they chuse to continue in it, and to exist as a nation, in some sort, at least independent of us." The United States might expand beyond its borders, but it should do so legally, through treaties, as the law of nations demanded. "Righteousness should be the rule of our conduct, nor what we may possibly need in ages to come. If we gain their lands, either by conquest or knavery, we shall," he or she concluded, "lay a foundation for the miseries of posterity."[41] This observer questioned the commonplace belief that American empire would necessarily be a force for good in the world. President Washington had led Americans astray from the path of justice and righteousness, this essayist argued, and if the United States did not turn things around, the judgment of history would be harsh.[42]

Far from piling on criticism, Brackenridge did his best to turn military defeats into rhetorical victories. He counseled Americans to embrace the violence of empire as an antidote to domestic coercion. The Whiskey Rebels terrified Brackenridge. "A revolution, did not suit me, nor any man else that had any thing to lose, or was in a way of making something" he observed. Caught in the middle of frontier protests, Brackenridge's property acted as the foundation for his counter-revolutionary stance—for, he recognized, it was people like him, people who had property to lose, who would likely be the victims of revolutionary violence.[43]

While terrifying, being on the scene in Pittsburgh provided Brackenridge with inside information that he used to formulate a plan for diffusing violence: he attempted to displace protestors' anger onto a more acceptable target, "the Indian," thereby distracting them from thoughts of revolution and economic justice. After the events had died down, he bragged in his history of the Whiskey Rebellion, *Incidents of the Insurrection* (1795), that his efforts were successful and that his conduct "was necessary to bring the public mind . . . to a proper sense of interest and duty."[44] Brackenridge's boast that he alone solved the Whiskey Rebellion was bombast. Still, his response to protests remains significant—not because Brackenridge's rhetoric influenced politicians or protestors, though it might have done so, but because he modeled a strategy of governing that worked in this case, and that would work time and time again in the future for managing revolutionary sentiments. Brackenridge was important because he was one of the first to turn the rhetoric of enemyship to productive ends in the United States.

In many ways, Thomas Paine's task in *Common Sense* was more difficult than Brackenridge's. Paine had to get Americans to "see with other eyes," as he said, making them view the world differently. Americans were not yet united in their fear of Britain; he even had to invent a new word ("enemyship") to signify what such an oppositional unity might look like. Brackenridge's rhetorical situation was completely different. Frontiersmen—and, more generally, "Americans"—were bound in mutual opposition to "the Indian," and the frontiersmen raging against the government already desired a war for control of the Ohio Valley. Brackenridge didn't have to get them to see differently. He only had to get them to open their eyes. He did, however, hope to persuade the federal government—and in particular, politicians like Hamilton—that displacement was a better reaction to protests than suppression. He therefore argued that a war would solve the crisis by protecting the lives, liberties, and property of the moneyed men from the greedy hands of poor frontiersmen while making the rich even richer. Once the United States had gained "control" over the Indians of the Ohio Valley, Brackenridge proclaimed, those lucky enough to have invested in American Empire would make a killing from land speculation and the fur trade.

Brackenridge's opinions on Indians were not out of the mainstream. He was just one of many actors across the political spectrum who wanted the Indians taken care of. Here, Brackenridge found himself in league with the high Federalist wordsmith Fisher Ames, and also with Washington's secretary of state Jefferson, who spoke highly of the great Indian orator Logan in his 1785 *Notes on the State of Virginia* and who repeatedly praised the character of Indians in his letters, but who created the legal mechanisms for disenfranchising Indians of their property well before Brackenridge pondered their destruction. Equally important, Brackenridge found himself in league with his target audience, poor frontiersmen, who tended to despise "the Indian" and believed their removal essential.[45] On the frontier, where violence was a daily reality, frontiersmen commonly complained that the government failed to protect them from Indians as they outstripped, through westward expansion, the government's ability to do this. The fear and hatred of the Indian hence cut across the political and economic spectrum, binding politicians who hated one another in a common cause with frontiersmen who hated the government.[46] It did not matter if Americans lived on the frontier or the eastern seaboard, if they were federalist or anti-federalist, rich or poor, Federalist or Republican. The subjectivity of white Americans was founded upon the contrast between "civilization" and "savagery."[47]

With his warm embrace of empire, Brackenridge waded into a debate at the heart of the American experiment. In the eighteenth century, it was received wisdom that republics had to be small. Baron de Montesquieu was one of the Enlightenment's foremost experts on republicanism, and he argued that if republics became too large, their political virtue would diminish. Retaining many of Montesquieu's insights about the centrality of constitutions to the liberal political order, but drawing on the American colonies' own experience of steady westward expansion in the 1760s and

1770s, Madison refuted this argument in Federalist 10. All nations, Madison insisted, were divided into classes of those who owned property and those who did not; the inequality of property was, for him, the origin of faction and political conflict. Unlike later political theorists—including Marx and Engels, who also recognized that material inequality led to political strife—for Madison there was no point in addressing the causes of faction: the inequality of property relations. There would be no levelling revolution. Instead, Madison argued that relief from factional conflict "is only to be sought in the means of controlling its *effects*."[48]

Maintaining that factions were more dangerous in smaller societies where they might win control of government, Madison claimed that in a large republic, factions would cancel themselves out. His logic opened the door for a counterargument to Montesquieu's very un-American emphasis on smallness, for Madison claimed that if "a common motive" of a faction existed in a large republic, "it will be more difficult for all who feel it to discover their own strength, and to act in unison with each other."[49] For Madison, the cure to domestic faction was found not in a revolution that would promote material equality—as many participants in the Whiskey Rebellion called for—but instead in expansion and diffusion. Continental domination and the indulgence of empire: these were Madison's cures for strife. Though Jefferson felt differently than Madison about democracy, he too understood that the future of the United States was in expansion. He told his friend Francois d'Ivernois in 1795, "The smaller the societies, the more violent and more convulsive their schisms," and thus he speculated that his historical era "will probably be distinguished in history, for its experiments in government on a larger scale than has yet taken place."[50] By checking factions, diffusing conflict, and making it infinitely more difficult to organize a revolutionary movement to change the structure of government, expansion became a politically expedient choice for politicians grappling with the dilemmas of American nationalism.

The westward march of empire was, however, premised on an untenable fiction. Enlightenment philosophers including John Locke and Adam Smith described North America as filled with "vacant places" and "Waste lands."[51] With such descriptions, they voiced the doctrine of *res nullius*, an Enlightenment fiction decreeing that any lands not put to use, especially agricultural use, were up for grabs.[52] *Res nullius* was premised on the assumption that because Indians did not work the land to English (or American) standards, they could not own it. The doctrine of *res nullius* had deep roots in Western culture; even the settlers of Thomas More's island haven *Utopia* (1516) believed it was their right to seize "waste lands" from natives.[53] Emmerich de Vattel made *res nullius* a principle of international law in his popular *The Law of Nations* (1758), which went through at least thirty-two editions in the United States during the eighteenth and nineteenth centuries. Vattel stated the case simply: "The people of Europe, too closely pent up at home, finding land of which the savages stood in no particular need, and of which they made no actual and constant use, were lawfully entitled to take possession of it."[54] The words of Locke, Smith, and Vattel were influential in the United States because they employed the bold authority of nature itself to legitimate the primitive accumulation of "vacant" lands. Brackenridge himself paid no regard "to any right which is not founded in *agricultural occupancy*," and therefore in line with *res nullius* he concluded that "Indians" did not own the lands in the Ohio Valley.[55]

To say that Indian lands not cultivated to European and American standards could justifiably be appropriated by Anglo-Americans was one thing; to say that these "waste" lands were "vacant" was another. Though Locke, Smith, and Vattel claimed that the western lands of North America were "vacant," Americans knew better. Indians resisted white expansion from the beginning. In 1622, for instance, Chief Opechancanough led the Powhatan Confederacy against settlers from the Virginia Company of London, killing almost 350 settlers in a grisly act of resistance to the settlers' seemingly insatiable lust for land. In response, the governor of Virginia, Francis Wyatt, expounded:

> Our first worke is expulsion of the Savages to gaine the free range of the countrey for encrease of Cattle, swine &c which will more then restore us, for it is infinitely better to have no heathen among us, who at best were but thornes in sides, then to be at peace and league with them . . . Adde to these defence against a forrein enemy, and you will find, that extirpating of the Savages, winning of the Forest, encrease of cattle, swine &c building houses convenient for both seasons, planting

gardens and orchards for delight and health setting vines and Mulberry trees for raising those two excellent commodities of wine and Silke, is worke enough for one seven yeares, and will employ our whole forces.[56]

Wyatt's God created the world in seven days; here, Wyatt planned the creation of a new world in North America, including clearing the forest, planting gardens, building houses, breeding livestock, and that other small point, "extirpating of the Savages." Wyatt recognized, however, that this would take longer than seven days. He also recognized that genocide would necessarily precede his civilization's accumulation of land, for the "savages" had to be removed before the land could be cultivated. There were no vacant lands in North America; the lands would have to be vacated before they could be cultivated to European standards. Though the doctrine of res nullius gave some Americans in the early Republic comfort, their colonial past bequeathed to them a rhetorical legacy of justifying imperial violence. In this case, Wyatt argued that violence would be justified by the results, as the earth was cultivated, as hostile, indigent Indians were replaced with beautiful, sweet-smelling vineyards.

Similar resistance to white expansion was mounted during the Pequot War (1637), King Philip's War (1675–1676), the Seven Years War (1756–1763), and Pontiac's Rebellion (1763–1764). Resistance continued once Americans declared their independence from Britain. While some Indian nations, including the Oneidas and Tuscaroras, fought alongside Americans against the redcoats during the Revolutionary War, others— including the remaining members of the mighty Iroquois Confederacy, the Mohawk, Seneca, Onondaga and Cayuga nations—allied themselves with the British and fought for their own security from Americans.[57] And then there were the devastating losses in 1790 and 1791, proving definitely that "vacant" lands were not vacant at all, and that empire would be no walk in the park.

While some easterners called on the president to dismantle the blundering imperial apparatus in response to these defeats, Brackenridge called for more war—because, he argued, war would redirect the anger of frontiersmen at more acceptable targets. Brackenridge made his case in two essays published in Philadelphia's National Gazette in February 1792.[58] His sentences were muddled, and his ideas were strung together in an uneven staccato. Nevertheless, Brackenridge made his purpose clear: to rebut arguments like Hamilton's that the government should respond to frontier protests with force. Coercion might suppress protestors for a moment, Brackenridge reasoned, but it would ultimately solve nothing because it did not address the primary causes of resistance to government in western Pennsylvania. Echoing Jefferson's famous response to Shays's Rebellion, in which he defended popular violence and all the blood it might spill, Brackenridge claimed that the tree of liberty had to be refreshed from time to time. However, instead of calling for the institutionalization of revolution into politics, Brackenridge advocated a full-scale, society-wide embrace of empire and confrontation with the Indians living in the Ohio Valley. Understanding hatred, fear, and rage to be opiates that could overwhelm citizens' emotions and occupy their minds to the point of distraction, Brackenridge attempted to redirect the energies of frontier protestors with the rhetorics of enemyship. While he admitted that the federal government might well be an enemy for frontiersmen, nevertheless he advised citizens to choose the lesser of two evils and support the government in its war against a more nefarious enemy: the Indian.

War would act as a release for frontier anger, Brackenridge believed, but coercion would not. He therefore had a stern warning for eastern politicians, including Washington and Hamilton. "Be careful not to check the spirit of the people," he cautioned in 1792. "It is electrical, and if confined may burst. Let it have an egress in acquisitions to the westward, and you may rest safe."[59] He repeated his warning in 1794. Coercion would only make things worse, he cautioned, by escalating the crisis and provoking citizens to undertake even more brazen acts of defiance. If the government attacked frontiersmen, they would strike back—hard. "Should an attempt be made to suppress these people, I am afraid the question will not be, whether you will march to Pittsburgh, but whether they will march to Philadelphia, accumulating in their course, and swelling over the banks of the Susquehanna like a torrent, irresistible, and devouring in its progress," he advised, concluding ominously, "There can be no equality of contest, between the rage of a forest, and the abundance, indolence, and opulence of a city."[60]

Replying to protests with force was a grave error because the living spirit of revolution was electrifying and any attempt to bottle it up would only prolong the inevitable explosion of democratic violence. Bracken-ridge was convinced that the coercive repression of citizen anger would backfire. Living in Pittsburgh, Brackenridge observed the unbelievable poverty, unconscionable inequality, and violent hostility towards the state generated in the post-Revolutionary years. As increasingly disempowered and frustrated citizens entertained thoughts of insurrection, they needed a release for their rage—the rage of a forest. Rather than the suppression of democratic impulses with coercive force, Brackenridge called on the government to displace violent impulses onto a different target, and to sublimate those violent impulses into more desirable pursuits, including imperialism and property acquisition.

Pennsylvania was founded on a rich and robust tradition of peace and diplomacy between white settlers and Indian nations, a tradition that held for much of the seventeenth and eighteenth centuries. The Seven Years War shifted relations toward war.[61] In the winter of 1763, dozens of western Pennsylvanians calling themselves the Paxton Boys murdered twenty-one unoffending Conestogas, scalping and mutilating the bodies that they had not already blown to bits. Following this politically charged massacre, Benjamin Franklin observed that "the Spirit of killing all In-dians, Friends and Foes, [has] spread amazingly thro' the whole Coun-try."[62] In 1768, Frederick Stump employed the Paxton Boys' techniques to massacre ten Senecas and Mohicans in Carlisle, Pennsylvania. John Sullivan's 1779 raid into Iroquois territory in upstate New York, in which his soldiers indiscriminately massacred their enemies and then burned over forty villages to the ground, was cheered on the Pennsylvania fron-tier. In 1782, the Pittsburgh militia, which consisted of several former Paxton Boys and future Whiskey Rebels, lined up ninety-six unsuspecting Delawares, including women and children, and then used hatchets to bludgeon them to death execution-style, one by one, in an outhouse.[63] In 1791, after the Pittsburgh militia committed four particularly graphic murders, a reporter from Fort Pitt observed: "Although this action ap-pears very much like deliberate murder, yet it is approved of, I believe, by a majority of people on the Ohio."[64] Though frontiersmen shared diverse allegiances, one thing that united many settlers was their shared hatred of "the Indian."

Scholars have argued that nations, as imagined communities, were unthinkable before the print revolution of the eighteenth century.[65] A public sphere of print literature outside the immediate influence of the government created the conditions of possibility for an American identity to develop.[66] Though historians have focused on the immense possibilities this public sphere created for rational discourse, informed citizens, and better public discussion, at the same time the public sphere made enemy-ship possible on a new and unimaginable scale. Brackenridge attempted to produce fear and transmit hatred of "the Indian" across space, using the burgeoning print economy as the vehicle for an imagined American community premised on mutual antagonism with the enemy. Bracken-ridge's rhetoric was mobile in a way that even the Paxton Boys' equally nasty rhetoric was not. The words of the Paxton Boys were printed mainly in Philadelphia, though they were circulated throughout Pennsylvania.[67] Brackenridge's rhetoric, in contrast, simultaneously reached citizens east and west. In fact, his essays, which were originally published in a major Philadelphia paper, were reprinted in at least fifteen more, from Philadel-phia to New York City to Boston to Charleston and many smaller cities in between.[68]

Brackenridge could have published his essays in the paper he helped to establish in 1786, the *Pittsburgh Gazette*, which was the first newspaper in the United States published west of the Allegheny Mountains. Yet by publishing his pieces in the *National Gazette*, a Philadelphia newspaper read widely in the state and closely by Hamiltonians, Jeffersonians, and others in the nation's capital, Brackenridge directed his opinions at two audiences. First, at frontiersmen, whom he hoped to convince that the government was not as bad as Indians, who were the proper target of their rage. Second, at the government and other easterners, whose support for another war in the Ohio Valley he hoped to secure.

Speaking to the diverse audience of the *National Gazette*, and also to the readers of the many newspapers that reprinted his musings, Brack-enridge symbolically united Americans through their mutual antagonism to "the Indian." In the early Republic, there was no such thing as "the Indian," just as there was no such thing as "the American." "Indians" and "Americans" were useful categories for simplifying the complex reality of political life. In the 1790s, the United States government negotiated separately with individual Indian nations. Moreover, not all of these nations were enemies; in fact, St. Clair recruited Chickasaw warriors to accompany him on his expedition into the Ohio Valley in 1791. Thus, to say in blanket terms that "the Indian" was an enemy of Americans was false. Brackenridge himself recognized this fact in earlier writings.

Still, Brackenridge understood the tremendous utility of enemyship on the frontier—especially in this particular rhetorical situation, where he hoped to use all of the available means of persuasion at his disposal to protect his property from rebellious frontiersmen. Brackenridge understood one of the foundational rhetorical prescriptions of governing in the United States: when in a tight spot, name an enemy. Brackenridge's strategy had tremendous potential because many frontiersmen already felt united by their mutual antagonism with Indians, and this was an antagonism that, on at least one important occasion, overrode their anger at the federal government. The protestors who marched on Braddock's Field in 1794 hoped to achieve what the Regulators in Massachusetts failed to do, raiding the federal armory at nearby Fort Pitt and arming themselves for battle with federal troops. Two days before the march, however, the chief planner, David Bradford, canceled the raid when he learned that the munitions housed there were intended for battling Indians in the Northwest Territory. "We have been informed that the ammunition which we were about to seize was destined for General Scott who is just going out against the Indians," Bradford wrote, and "we therefore have concluded not to touch it."[69] These angry protestors would not touch weapons that, we should note, could have greatly furthered their aims but that were intended for fighting Indians. For them, the frontier hierarchy of enemies was clear: while the government was bad, Indians were worse and trumped all others.

In other work, including his deeply sympathetic and courageous 1785 essay "The Trial of Mamachtaga," Brackenridge took the side of the Indians against the white citizens of Pittsburgh.[70] Brackenridge was no genocidal maniac. But he was an astute rhetor who took advantage of the available persuasives to make his case. In his 1792 essays, then, to achieve maximum rhetorical effect, Brackenridge dropped the sympathy and excoriated the character of "the Indian." Brackenridge argued that all Indians were enemies of Americans because of their nature and their savage, aggressive, irrational hearts.

Brackenridge began his case for war by considering objections to his position. His essays hence echoed the appendixes to later drafts of *Common Sense*, where Paine took on his opponents. Neither Paine nor Brackenridge gave their opponents' objections serious consideration; instead, they invoked them to create the appearance of a fair-minded dialogue that never occurred. "I can easily excuse those who, from motives of humanity, call in question the justness of our cause in the war against the Indians," Brackenridge started, only to immediately revoke his pledge to do any excusing—for he proceeded not just to completely undercut his opponents' objection to this war, but to demolish the argumentative ground on which dissenters from any war with Indians stood. He did this by naming an enemy so terrible and ruthless that dialogue was nonsensical and war was imperative. "But could I make my observations their's with respect to the ruthless disposition of the savage, that is not soothed continually by good offices, or kept down by fear . . ." he continued in a dramatic compound sentence of 146 words and eighteen clauses that enumerated the accumulated evils of Indians, which ranged from rejecting American goodwill to slaughtering innocent frontier families in cold blood. "I consider men who are unacquainted with the savages like young women who have read romances, and have as improper idea of the Indian character in the one case, as the female mind has of real life in the other," he concluded, denouncing those who objected to war with the Indian as women—challenging their opinions, their manliness, and consequently their right to participate in public debate at all.[71]

To advance his case that "business with the Indians is war and reduction" and that this business should trump anti-government mobilization on the frontier, Brackenridge shared the following gruesome story with his readers:

> Some years ago, two French gentlemen, a Botanist and Mineralist, Monsieur Sograin and M. Pike, the Botanist, a very learned man, and truly a philosopher—but his brain turned with Jean Jacques Rousseau's, and other rhapsodies—the man of nature was his darling favorite. He had the Indians with him at his chamber every day. Fitting out a small boat on the Ohio, with only three other persons, and without arms, he descended. It was in vain to explain the danger, and dissuade him. He

was conscious to himself of loving Indians, and doubtless, they could wish him no harm. But approaching the Scioto river, a party came out in a canoe, as he thought, to pay their respects to him; but the first circumstance of ceremony when they came on board, was to impress the tomahawk and take off the scalp of the philosopher.[72]

This story invoked familiar tropes associated with natural history as educated philosophers traveled into the natural world to see nature; yet it ended with the naive explorer being scalped and murdered by his erroneous fantasies of a benevolent cosmos. If natural history was one of the first empiricist philosophies, Brackenridge testified that death was the result of bad ideas coming into contact with a hostile world. This story was meant to act as a fable, instructing Americans that all Indians were the same: they were all murderers who deserved to die.

Brackenridge's story defined the proper relations between premodern and modern, between "savagery" and "civilization," for government and citizenship in the United States. The philosopher was modern man: educated, enlightened, all head, no heart. The "savage" was premodern man: uneducated, irrational, and emotional. Premodern man killed and scalped modern man, literally stealing a part of his head and hence the marker of his Enlightenment. By having "the Indian" kill "the philosopher," Brackenridge implied that modern man was deficient. While his theories were elegant, the real world proved them to be nothing more than blabber. Ironically, then, modern man—be he this educated French *philosophe* or an eastern American politician—was unsuited for modern life. The message was that Americans had to balance the premodern and the modern or meet certain doom. The Enlightenment called for universal education to transcend the dogmas and superstitions of premodern life; it also called for disciplining the irrational, fantastic, and violent impulses that underlined the modern subject. Brackenridge cut to the heart of the Enlightenment project by suggesting that it should proceed via displacement, not repression. For Brackenridge, the dark places of the soul—the irrational, uncontrollable premodern impulses—should be preserved because of their invaluable social utility. If politicians could somehow harness the premodern lust for violence manifested by the protestors, they might be fit for life in a republic. Brackenridge argued that premodern citizens could only be made modern if their elemental impulses were indulged, not repressed. To build a nation, then, the hostility of frontiersmen had to be redirected at the Indian. Moreover, Brackenridge claimed, if easterners would indulge their bloody fantasies, they would discover that they were, at bottom, like settlers—united in their love of violence. In violence, they would be redeemed.[73]

In "The Trial of Mamachtaga," Brackenridge emphasized the similarities between Indians and white Americans, suggesting that they could be friends. In his 1792 essays, Brackenridge made it seem as though Indians and Americans were so different that they could not communicate—and the bright lines of incommunicability meant that they could only resolve their disputes through violence. Because they could never be friends, Brackenridge reasoned that either Americans would defeat the Indians, or the Indians would defeat Americans. Either way, war was inevitable in the absence of compromise and diplomacy. According to Brackenridge, the question was not whether the whiskey tax was valid or whether the wars in the Ohio Valley should have been waged. Rather, "the question is, Whether we shall submit ourselves to the savages, or they to us? I say, let us conquer because we cannot depend upon them; for the weaker ever distrusts the mightier, and the unenlightened man, the sensible."[74] Changing the topic from economics to savages, Brackenridge redirected the animus. Though American relationships with Indians were complicated, opinions like Brackenridge's were common on America's frontiers and especially in Pennsylvania, where no topic, not even Hamilton's financial policies, was more discussed than "the Indian war." Thus, Brackenridge called on protestors to forget their anger toward Hamilton and the moneyed men and to preemptively strike their enemies.

While frontiersmen were bound by their hatred and fear of the Indian, in the early 1790s such emotions did not always trump their anger toward the federal government. To ensure the preoccupation with the Indian over the government—to ensure, in short, that the gaze of Americans looked west rather than east—Brackenridge wove together divergent fears, resurrecting revolutionary rhetorics and old resentments. During the Revolutionary era, many colonists believed that King George and his royal cronies had hatched a malevolent plan to take their money, steal their freedoms, and usurp their liberties. Conspiracy theories were common in the eighteenth century, and even after America won her independence, the British continued to play the role of a national enemy—as many leading politicians assumed that another war with England was inevitable. To escalate the situation in the Ohio Valley into a crisis that demanded immediate action, Brackenridge tapped into the extant fears of Great Britain and blamed a scheming king for the defeats in the Ohio Valley. There was something to this, for Great Britain continued to ally itself with the Indian nations there following the Revolutionary War. The British believed that an Indian buffer between the United States and Canada would hem in America's colonial ambitions, continental expansion, and agricultural development. Brackenridge framed these alliances as part of an entrenched, overarching British plot to destroy the United States. This "is not a war, therefore, with Indians merely; it is a war with the British king, under cover," he announced, making it the duty of Americans to fight back. "Have we felt the jaw of the lion, and shall we be still lashed with his tail?" he asked.[75]

Hearkening back to the rhetoric of '76, Brackenridge made the situation in the 1790s dire by arguing that the United States was caught "between two fires": westerners were threatened by "savages," and easterners by the British Navy. Facing a dual threat, it was in the interest of all Americans to rally behind the U.S. government for another war that would finally achieve security from their enemies. A victory over frontier Indians was also a victory over Britain, and thus an essential step towards national prosperity and continued independence. Like protestors of Hamilton's policies, Brackenridge invoked the memory of the Revolutionary War. He did so, however, not to challenge the authority of government, but to bolster it. Accordingly, he called on all veterans to defend the legacy of revolution by uniting to defend themselves from the resurgent British threat that lived on in the Indian menace.

The Joys of Empire

Understanding that many influential easterners might not sympathize with his call for imperial violence, Brackenridge employed a second line of argument for imperialism over coercion. He would rally frontiersmen for war, and gain eastern support, by emphasizing the shared financial benefits of empire. Brackenridge reminded his readers that a successful war would greatly expand the size of the United States and multiply its natural resources. With expansion came profit, for the new states parsed from the Northwest Territory would become suppliers of vital agricultural products, and a greedy market for eastern goods. Moreover, selling this land would create life-saving revenue for the federal government. Just like Hamilton, who focused much of his energy as secretary of the Treasury on winning the support of the wealthy, Brackenridge attempted to ply the moneyed men to his cause. He could do this because while war was costly (in lives and dollars), it was also profitable for a lucky few.

Brackenridge turned against frontier protestors, he noted, because a revolution did not suit him—he had too much to lose. Wealthy easterners were not in as much immediate danger of losing their property as people living in Pittsburgh. So, Brackenridge instead focused on what they had to gain from war, merging the profitability of empire to the rhetorics of enemyship for a potent rhetorical force that politicized war by tying fear and hatred to profit and gain. Though many easterners complained that another war in the Ohio Valley would be too expensive, Brackenridge assured eastern investors that they would make a killing on their imperial investments. "Why dread the expense of an effective and lasting armament" on the frontier, he asked: "The moment we take command of the savages, instead of leaving them to Britain, the fur-trade of the immense world of this west will amply repay us creating a trade to the sea coast parts."[76] The immense west was a wonderworld of profits for the discriminating investor. Thus, if Americans could be brought to see the pecuniary value of war and the profits of empire, they might overlook their short-term differences over domestic policy for a long-term, profitable alliance.

The current federal policy of decentralized Indian war—of establishing a few posts, and mainly letting frontiersmen fight the war with random raids and military excursions—was woefully ineffective, Brackenridge argued. He counseled that "the best defense is *offense*. Instead of wading off blows, give one." And he framed the current ineffective Indian policy in the language of the farmer: "It is but watching beasts of prey, who come against our fields, instead of penetrating the forests where they hunt, and extirpating the race."[77] The Indians had to be reduced, he claimed, like beasts of prey. Though educated elites in the eastern United States might have found Brackenridge's calls for extirpation off-putting, his rhetoric was nevertheless appealing to wealthy land speculators and moneyed men like President Washington, Secretary of the Treasury Hamilton, and Secretary of War Knox. Washington had a financial stake in the management of the frontier as president. In fact, he owned over 58,000 acres of prime farmland west of the Appalachians, including 4,695 acres in southwestern Pennsylvania where the Whiskey Rebels were driving down the value of his land and making it difficult to collect rents. If successful, another war would advance political fortunes and secure personal profits for those involved.

Brackenridge therefore got what he wanted. Following the embarrassing defeats of 1790 and 1791, General Anthony Wayne led a well-trained and rigorously drilled Federal Army of nine hundred soldiers against a fragmented Ohio Confederacy; on August 20, 1794, at the Battle of Fallen Timbers, Wayne's army routed their foes, losing one hundred men but killing twice that many. After this victory, the United States was able to negotiate a peace with the British and the allied Indian nations. Wayne's victory influenced one treaty, the Jay Treaty (1795), by which the British abandoned their forts in the Ohio Valley and also their Indian allies; and it spawned another, the Treaty of Greenville (1795), which opened much of the Ohio Valley to American settlement. Last but certainly not least, victory increased the value of Washington's holdings by about 50 percent, making war a profitable investment for him and other wealthy gentlemen.[78]

Brackenridge got the war he wished for, but the fate of the Jay Treaty was uncertain. Many Federalists saw the Jay Treaty as a necessary step toward the solidification of the future of the United States, but it was perceived by Republicans as a slap in America's face. This treaty allowed the United States to avoid war with the British for a time, yet it answered few of America's grievances—and when the text of the treaty was leaked to the public, it was met with widespread condemnation. To secure the Jay Treaty, Fisher Ames stepped to the floor of the House to great anticipation. There, on April 28, 1796, he gave one of the most famous orations of the early Republic. Ames was widely acclaimed as the best orator of the Federalist Party, and when he died, he was compared to Demosthenes and Cicero. Ames's speech was immediately noteworthy because, as James Farrell notes, in a milieu in which "most enlightened American politicians considered that proper decisions resulted only from the exercise of cool reason," Ames nevertheless appealed to the passions of the representatives, calling on them to delve into their hearts and do what they felt was right.[79] In line with Scottish Enlightenment writings on rhetorical theory, to make his audience feel, Ames deployed vivid language and graphic descriptions that made the dangers of failing to ratify the treaty immediate and real.[80]

Brackenridge attempted to unite frontiersmen with eastern politicians and redirect the anger of protestors away from the government (and his property) and toward the enemy. Ames, too, attempted to unite a deeply divided audience and redirect the anger and hostility of their constituents away from the government and his Federalist Party. Refusal to ratify the Jay Treaty meant, he warned, that the British would hold their forts in the Northwest Territory and continue to encourage "the friends of our enemies," the Indians there, to attack frontier Americans. For Ames, Indians were evil, savage hordes doing the bidding of Machiavellian behind-the-scenes actors fixated on the destruction of the United States. The immediate effect of rejecting the Jay Treaty would be the mass slaughter of western Americans. No logical or empirical "proof" was needed to cement this argument, Ames insisted. Instead, he announced, "From arguments calculated to produce conviction, I will appeal directly to the hearts of those who hear me," for "on this subject, you need not suspect any deception on your feelings; it is a spectacle of horror, which cannot be overdrawn." Ames understood that political action sprung from emotion as much as reason. He therefore warned that to reject the Jay Treaty was to reject the protection and security of Americans, and to "light the savage fires" and "bind the victims." "We are answerable," he demanded, for the "widows and orphans," the "wretches that will be roasted at the stake."[81]

Having put the slaughter of innocent Americans in the hands of his audience, Ames continued to paint a vivid picture of "the cries of our future victims":

> The voice of humanity issues from the shade of the wilderness; it exclaims, that while one hand is held up to reject this treaty, the other

grasps a tomahawk. It summons our imagination to the scenes that will open. It is no great effort of the imagination to conceive that events so near are already begun. I can fancy that I listen to the yells of savage vengeance and the shrieks of torture; already they seem to sigh in the western wind; already they mingle with every echo from the mountains.[82]

Ames understood that his best bet to secure support for the treaty was to produce a snap emotional judgment in his audience; to make them fear an impending onslaught; and, additionally, to make them feel shame that they could have done something to prevent the bloodbath. Just as his rhetoric preyed on the fears of common citizens, it also played on the shame of those in power—who had a solemn duty to provide protection and security to their constituents. Without protection there was no obligation for citizens to obey. By naming the enemy and escalating the crisis into a present danger, Ames was able to paint dissent not just as un-American but also as synonymous with an act of war on America. He made it clear that those who voted against the treaty were really voting for Great Britain and their "Indian auxiliaries." In the place of division, Ames created an imagined American unity through mutual enmity, fear, and shame. And though Americans did not, of course, instantly become united, Ames was successful in securing his ends.

Alongside Wayne's victory, the Jay Treaty and the Treaty of Greenville answered many of the grievances that led frontiersmen to participate in the Whiskey Rebellion. Wayne's victorious march did not void Hamilton's whiskey tax, but it did remove foreign forts from settlers' backyards. Victory provided armed military protection for settlers from external danger and flooded the area with specie that settlers in turn spent on land. By placating protestors with promises of happy futures in the rich farmlands of the Ohio Valley, the Treaty of Greenville funneled dissent away from the government. By making their lives more secure, the treaties further justified the continued existence of the new federal government by making it an agent of security. Many western settlers would soon trade obedience for protection. Alongside the government's deployment of military force into the region, Wayne's victory at the Battle of Fallen Timbers helped to halt the Whiskey Rebellion by redirecting the democratic energies of postwar America westward into the cultivation of land.

The resolution of the Whiskey Rebellion demonstrated that Madison was correct, and that expansion could be coupled with the future of republican government in the United States. One reason that the West occupied an important place in early American mythology was that the seeming boundlessness could absorb tired wrecks and enraged malcontents who, for one reason or another, did not make it in the East. The West was the space of displacement. In the nineteenth century, many prominent politicians believed that western expansion would act as a "safety valve" diffusing hostilities toward government. This theory assumed that unhappy farmers and laborers could journey west into the bountiful lands of the Midwest and toward the golden shores of California for better lives—a notion captured in the pro-labor and anti-slavery activist Horace Greeley's iconic slogan, "Go West, young man." This theory was, of course, both a fiction and a reality: Expansion produced explosive debates, especially over slavery, that would bring the nation to the brink of destruction. Moreover, expansion did placate some groups while enraging others. Nevertheless, the belief in calming expansion was one of the fictions that drove imperialism in the early Republic.

Though the "safety valve" theory characterized American politics in the nineteenth century, it had its genesis in the 1790s, when it became apparent that empire and animosity toward the enemy could displace some hostility toward government.[83] Shays's Rebellion demonstrated the flaws of coercion as a strategy for dealing with the dilemmas of American nationalism. Because nation-building required the constitution of a republican system in which voters took their anger out at the polls and not in the streets, the undisciplined energies and anarchic tendencies of a revolutionary past had to go somewhere. Analogous to displacement, which was a psychological alternative to repression, expansion was a political antidote to coercion. Rather than turning American troops on American citizens, expansion could redirect revolutionary energies westward, away from the government.

In the 1790s, Federalists were preoccupied with reforming the unruly behavior of rowdy citizens. Hamilton was especially invested in producing more docile subjects, for without self-restraint his economic reforms were surefire losers. Nevertheless, Hamilton's economic plans made reform difficult and governing nearly impossible. Hamilton's program favored the wealthy elite, and as such, his policies ran contrary to the democratic legacy of the Revolutionary War. Political problems arose during the Whiskey Rebellion because Americans professed incompatible political economies of upward and downward redistribution. Proponents of upward redistribution attempted to concentrate wealth in the hands of the moneyed elite, whereas proponents of downward redistribution attempted to distribute it equally across class lines. Though frontier democracy required at least rudimentary equality, centralized financial development needed economic stratification—meaning that democracy and capitalism were in tension in the early Republic. These clashing political economies were mirrored in differing visions of government, for Federalists wanted to concentrate power in the hands of the natural aristocracy, whereas protestors called for a more democratic arrangement of power.[84] Hamilton held that upward redistribution was necessary for economic development. Further, Hamilton's vision of governance focused less on liberty and instead on buttressing the strength of the state.[85] He thus reversed the theories of sovereignty advanced during the Revolutionary War, which rejected the king's sovereignty and located political power in "the people." For Hamilton, money, in the form of taxes, and arms, in the form of an army, were the keys to successful governance—so long as they were concentrated in the hands of a wealthy elite.

Protestors, pleading for the downward redistribution of property and political power, lambasted Hamilton's plans. In Philadelphia's *Independent Gazetteer*, the essayist Franklin asked, "Whence are all the clamours and disquietudes among the citizens?" Discounting the counter-revolutionary explanation that the unrest was a plot against the state by deluded maniacs who would be brought to reason, Franklin concluded: "to an extreme inequality of fortune among the citizens bordering upon the distinction of nobility," and to the shameful, selfish actions "a monied aristocracy" who "are the minute men of government, ready to muster at a ministerial tap."[86] During 1776, poor minutemen represented democracy; in 1794, wealthy speculators represented republicanism. These minutemen acted for profit, not freedom. Similar critiques filled the pages of the *National Gazette*. To counter the Treasury's policies that "increase these *natural distinctions* by favoring an inequality of property," the *National Gazette* exhorted the government to "reduce extreme wealth towards a state of mediocrity, and raise extreme indigence towards a state of comfort."[87] Only in this way would unrest cease. For Brutus, the Treasury Department created unjust upward redistribution with financial policies "calculated to aggrandize the few and the wealthy, by oppressing the great body of the people."[88] For this author, the only possible solution was to have another Revolutionary War levelling America's glaring inequalities: "Since the glorious and honorable peace of 1783, artifice and deception has effected one revolution in favour of the *few*—Another revolution must and will be brought about in favour of the PEOPLE."[89] By enacting an economic revolution redistributing private property, it would also be possible to achieve a political revolution that redistributed power.

Frontier Pennsylvanians mistrusted their representatives because they mistrusted how much space the system of representation created between themselves and their representatives. This mistrust made collecting taxes difficult, while stymieing the type of hierarchical reform Federalists hoped would further the Second American Revolution. According to Federalists, the key to negotiating the problems inherent to the founding of an orderly republic was found in the form of representatives and other political elites. Designated the "moneyed men," the privileged played an indispensable role in governing. Hamilton and other Federalists forwarded a top-down vision of governance in which powerful elites reformed citizen conduct. Federalists attempted to turn the emerging bureaucracy of representatives, judges, and tax collectors against rowdy citizens—whose worst fears of an encroaching, unstoppable power were confirmed whenever Hamilton spoke. In wealthy, property-owning elites, Federalists saw a potential response to the problematic aspects of early American democracy, for if these property owners could be persuaded to support the government, they could use their influence on a local scale to put out the lingering fires of revolution. The need to empower representatives hinted at a conundrum at the heart of governing in the early Republic, for if citizens did not identify with their representatives, then they would not listen to them. And if citizens did not respect the decisions of their representatives, then the Republic was doomed.[90]

Following ratification of the Constitution, frontier citizens came to understand how this new form of less-responsive republican government worked. When their representatives attempted to exert distant control over their lives, however, frontier citizens rejected the Constitution. Hamilton noted that the law was still in its "infancy" on the frontier.[91] Moreover, western Pennsylvanians did not yet imagine themselves as part of a national community. For Brackenridge and Ames, this imagined community was constituted by emphasizing what East and West had in common—they were not Indians, and they hated Indians. By opening the Ohio Valley to settlement, the Treaty of Greenville expanded the frontier and made it possible for all frontiersmen to be property owners in a prosperous region relatively free from immediate danger. Facilitated by the rhetorics of enemyship, private property in the form of cheap land became the medium symbolically uniting Americans as a people—for Americans could own land and Indians could not. In the 1790s, then, the meaning of "the people" was redefined; they were no longer a revolutionary brethren, but instead a community of property owners.[92] By giving them property and property rights, the enemy that facilitated ratification just a few years earlier, the restive demos desirous of the moneyed men's property, was reincorporated into the national community.

In the discourses of the late eighteenth century, political power was linked to private property, and Americans were defined as citizens who could own property. This definition of possessive individualism was premised on exclusion, for property rights were defined in contrast to those (like Indians) who could not own land. In the formative years of the United States, poor whites were incorporated into the nation by extending to them the privileges of property ownership and sovereignty. Though rebellious citizens might fret at federal policies like Hamilton's, they could imagine a union with elite politicians who could also own property and vote; they might have little, after all, but at least they were better off than Indians, who were stripped of their lands and often slaughtered.

Conceptions of the Indian furthered the constitution of a stable post-Revolutionary order by establishing a commercial bond between citizens and their representatives. Because Americans owned land, it was in the interest of citizens to respect their representatives, who could maneuver the state's monopolization of violence to defend their property—which their representatives did, signing and then disregarding pacts with Indian nations to placate settlers as they practiced "colonialism by treaty."[93] So long as there was an enemy to steal their property and threaten their lives, citizens needed government. In this formative moment, a proto-capitalist order of property rights became the basis of what it meant to be an American citizen. In practice, this meant that Federalists laid the groundwork for an expansion of demophobia in the middle 1790s. If the fear of democracy was at bottom the fear that someone was going to steal your stuff, then the more people who had stuff to lose, the more people could potentially fear democracy. Not all Americans adopted this fear; many property owners clung to the revolutionary dream of equality and self-rule. But many others turned to the government to protect them and their belongings from the needy grasp of poor criminals and the democratic doctrines they spouted.

In the early Republic, commercial development and the production of enemies hence went hand in hand. Adam Smith, the father of modern economics, understood this. For Smith, capitalism began with a lesson in othering. In the opening pages of *The Wealth of Nations*, published in 1776 as Americans were embarking on their experiment with independence, Smith derided the laboring practices of "savage nations of hunters and fishers," who "are so miserably poor, that from mere want, that they are frequently reduced, or, at least, think themselves reduced, to the necessity sometimes of directly destroying, and sometimes of abandoning their infants, their old people, and those afflicted with lingering diseases, to perish with hunger, or be devoured by wild beasts." By contrast, "civilized and thriving nations" didn't have to abandon anyone. In modern nations, there was so much food that "a workman, even of the lowest and poorest order, if he is frugal and industrious, may enjoy a greater share of the necessaries and conveniences of life than it is possible for any savage to acquire." Free trade propelled societies to search for new markets in a globalizing world, making confrontations between nations fundamental to modernity. As it so happened, Smith conjectured, these confrontations were one of the most productive aspects of capitalism. If poverty was the unintended but inevitable result of modern economics, then confrontations with enemies could ease the plight of the poor. Not only were the "civilized" poor better off than members of "savage nations," Smith attested that class stratification within "civilized" societies was psychologically insignificant when compared with the poverty of "savage" societies: "The accommodation of an European prince does not always so much exceed that of an industrious and frugal peasant, as the accommodation of the latter exceeds that of many an African king, the absolute master of the lives and liberties of ten thousand naked savages." Hence, Smith discovered the persuasive power of sorry comparisons—which comforted the downtrodden by boosting them above the "savage"—as an indispensable technique of modern governance.[94]

Making History

As the first major political uprising following ratification of the Constitution, and the first instance of the United States government using military force against its citizens, the Whiskey Rebellion was immediately historicized. These histories reveal not only what Americans thought of the Whiskey Rebellion but also what they learned from it. Here, the debate between how best to manage the dilemmas of American nationalism came to a fever pitch. Choosing to disregard what happened in the immediate aftermath of Shays's Rebellion, for many Federalists the Whiskey Rebellion proved the efficacy of coercion as the optimal means for achieving post-Revolutionary stability. In November, the *Worcester Intelligencer* printed a letter from Pennsylvania that reassured anxious Massachusetts citizens that the federal government's actions were successful, and that "The insurrection in the western counties of this State is completely suppressed."[95] The government's largely symbolic deployment of a massive army demonstrated to everyone in the world that government in the United States was serious. In America, the *Worcester Intelligencer* concluded: "*Anarchy* trembles, and *order* triumphs."[96]

John Marshall, a Federalist who would become the formidable chief justice of the Supreme Court from 1801 to 1835, offered a similar interpretation in his popular *The Life of George Washington* (1804). He wrote:

> Thus, without shedding a drop of blood, did the prudent vigour of the executive terminate an insurrection which, at one time, threatened to shake the government of the United States to its foundation. That so perverse a spirit should have been excited in the bosom of prosperity, without the pressure of a single grievance, is among those political

phenomena which occurs not unfrequently in the course of human affairs, and which the statesman can never safely disregard. When real ills
are experienced, there is, something positive and perceptible to which
the judgment may be directed, the actual extent of which may be as-
certained, and the cause of which may perhaps be discerned. But when
the mind, inflamed by suppositious dangers, gives a full loose to the
imagination, and fastens upon some object with which to disturb itself,
the belief that the danger exists seems to become a matter of faith, with
which reason combats in vain.[97]

In one fell swoop, Marshall brushed aside any legitimate reasons for the
insurrection, pitted protestors against reason itself, and justified the government's use of force against its own citizens. It was impossible to bring
protestors to reason, so violence was the only remaining option. Marshall
opposed the "perverse spirit" of protesters against the "prudent vigor" of
the government, making the Whiskey Rebellion into an unlawful rebellion, not a legitimate expression of popular discontent. Of course blood
was shed, and the grievances of protestors did represent "real ills," yet as a
powerful judge authorized to write history, Marshall could spin the event
as he chose. He therefore stressed the political efficacy of coercion. The
myth of coercion hence lived on in the days following Shays's Rebellion.

The president offered a different interpretation of events. Describ-
ing the government's accomplishments in his Sixth Annual Address to
Congress of November 19, 1794, Washington observed that the government's attempt to suppress protestors was successful, ensuring the future
of domestic coercion in the United States. However, what Washington
found most encouraging about the Whiskey Rebellion was not the success of coercion, but the willingness of citizens to defend the Constitution. "While there is cause to lament" the events in western Pennsylvania,
he conceded, nevertheless the insurrection "demonstrated that our
prosperity rests on solid foundations, by furnishing an additional proof
that my fellow citizens understand the true principles of government and
liberty," for Americans came to the aid of government and "are now as
ready to maintain the authority of the laws against licentious invasions
as they were to defend their rights against usurpation." The citizens who
marched into Pennsylvania were "the highest advantage of republican

government." Washington expressed his happiness that Americans were willing to serve their Constitution by taking up arms against their fellow citizens and putting down a rebellion. These citizen-soldiers were "the army of the Constitution—undeterred by a march of 300 miles over rugged mountains, by approach of an inclement season, or by any other discouragement."[98] The threats posed to the nation by America's domestic enemies called citizens into action, persuading them to become an Army of the Constitution dedicated to defending the nation.

Politicians in the late 1700s began to theorize methods for making governing more efficient. According to the Italian criminologist Cesare Beccaria, generally recognized as the Enlightenment's foremost penologist, "Within a country's borders there should be no place which is outside the law. Its power should follow every citizen like a shadow."[99] Beccaria posited a revolutionary new goal for counter-revolutionaries: a society in which criminality was impossible because there was no place the law did not reach. This dream could become reality, Beccaria and others believed, because in modern states the law was upheld not simply by a centralized power, but by citizens who policed one another and, like their shadows, themselves. Thinking along these lines, Jeremy Bentham applied his panopticon model of penal incarceration to labor sites like London's shipyards.[100] The panopticon was based on a revolutionary idea: it was a jail in which prisoners were always visible to guards. The genius of the panopticon was that criminals eventually internalized the gaze of authority, making actual guards unnecessary. So long as the criminals believed they were being watched, they behaved properly—whether or not they were actually being watched.[101] Bentham transformed visibility into a trap by making it permanent and all-encompassing.

In the aftermath of the Whiskey Rebellion, Washington and others began to adapt these principles to post-Revolutionary republican government. By making citizens the guards, they reconceptualized political power so that it was consensual, not coercive. In the early Republic, the most successful governments did not rule through military repression or hard power; they ruled through the gentle hand of soft power by teaching citizens to love their nation, and then calling on them to defend that nation from its enemies. They ruled, in short, by calling on Americans to become an Army of the Constitution.

The Whiskey Rebellion found the Army of the Constitution in its formative phases, for citizens from New Jersey, Maryland, Pennsylvania, and
Virginia marched three hundred miles with President Washington across
the Allegheny Mountains to take on the Whiskey Rebels. A letter from
a soldier in the famed New Jersey Artillery published in Philadelphia's
Independent Gazetteer explained why he and other soldiers risked their
lives to repress their fellow citizens:

> Deluded men unconscious of the boon that Heaven accords, with pari-
> cidal hands would plunge a dagger into the bosom of their country, but
> ours is the glorious task to interpose a shield. Though painful the task,
> yet it is ours, my fellow soldiers, united in one common purpose, to
> drive home confusion to their hearts, who, with polluted hands, pro-
> fane the best of constitutions: but let us hope that returning reason will
> heal the breach, and their complete submission slacken the army of
> vengeance![102]

This citizen answered the Constitution's call for defense, and expressed
his willingness to risk his life to defend his nation and compel the "complete submission" of protestors, who were, like the Regulators of Shays's
Rebellion, "deluded" and hence unpredictable. This type of sacrifice
boded well for the government, for if citizens could be persuaded to police
one another—and if they could be persuaded to act as a "shield" defending the nation from harm, as these patriotic New Jersey men said—then
the efficiency of government would increase even as its cost decreased.

Whereas Bowdoin (during Shays's Rebellion) and Hamilton (during
the Whiskey Rebellion) attempted to coerce rebellious citizens into line,
believing that state violence could actually alter the subjectivities of citizens, Washington argued that transforming citizens into an Army of the
Constitution was the best and most efficient way to govern citizens in a
post-Revolutionary age. The genius of this strategy was that it distributed
political power more evenly throughout society while simultaneously
making this power constitutive of federal authority. This was, after all,
what frontiersmen wanted: a greater say in governing themselves. Yet
the nation-building project transformed the desire for self-government
into the governing of the self by reconstituting the subject in line with

the demands of a less-democratic and more-hierarchal republicanism. Americans would be given the freedom to govern themselves, which they greatly desired, only if they first learned to respect the foundational principles of republican government: that the Constitution, the laws, and their representatives were sacred.

CHAPTER FOUR

The Contract of Blood

The date was July 4, 1793, and, as John Adams had hoped in 1776, the anniversary of the signing of the Declaration of Independence was "solemnized with pomp and parade, with shews, games, sports, guns, bells, bonfires, and illuminations, from one end of this continent to the other, from this time forward forevermore."[1] Independence Day was *the* holiday in the early Republic, especially in Boston, the city that launched a young Adams into political prominence. An oil-and-water amalgamation of choreographed pageantry and world-turned-upside-down reverie, Boston's Fourth of July celebrations were not for the faint of heart.[2] This was not the nice but banal world of backyard barbeques, homemade ice cream, and community fireworks; Bostonians sped right past solemnization into joyous, drunken celebration. The fireworks were as likely to follow a strong left to the head as they were a military salute, and as party politics became the accepted vehicle of American politics, Federalists and Republicans staged competing celebrations in a decades-long battle for control of the hearts and minds of Bostonians. This particular day opened and closed with the discharge of cannon; in between, the *Boston Gazette* noted simply, the holiday "was celebrated with the greatest hilarity and good-humour, by every class of citizens."[3] One wonders about the revelry hiding behind this rather parsimonious description, but given Boston's reputation for partying hard, we can be sure that everyone had a good time.

Amidst the pomp and parade, the shows, games, sports, guns, bells, bonfires, and illuminations of the day, the keynote speaker at Boston's Faneuil Hall was Adams's son, John Quincy, a gifted orator who would later become the first Boylston Professor of Rhetoric and Oratory at Harvard University. The younger Adams understood the ins and outs of this genre of speaking as well as anyone alive, and he translated his almost encyclopedic knowledge of rhetorical theory into a speech that was met with the hearty huzzahs of his ebullient audience. According to the *Boston Gazette*, the speech was the best of its kind ever given. This meant something very specific in the early Republic—for this particular rhetorical situation called on the orator to turn the rostrum into a podium, and the town hall into a schoolroom. For John Quincy Adams and many others, the Fourth of July was an excellent reason to celebrate, but an even better opportunity for civic education. In the early Republic, the Fourth of July stage was reserved for educated elites and honored members of the community—in short, for the clergy, educators, and politicians who had the social capital and influence to alter how Americans imagined their relationship to the nation. These speeches are rhetorically interesting, then, not because they reveal how Americans conceptualized patriotism in their day—as one prominent historian has written—but because they reveal how patriotism was prescribed by the powerful.[4] On the Fourth of July, elites taught the masses what it meant to be an American in the post-Revolutionary age.

Rhetoric is an imaginative art, and this is nowhere more apparent in early Fourth of July addresses. Generally, these speeches recounted stories of heroism gone by and articulated a vision of the coming days of milk and honey. Tying the past to the future was the human agent. The future was pure potential that could not be reached but through the present, and unless individuals acted to make it so. The alternative futures dreamed up by the orator demanded that the audience reform their behaviors. In his Harvard lectures on rhetoric, Adams pointed to Fourth of July addresses as the best example of epideictic rhetoric, the rhetoric of praise and blame, telling his students that the goal of epideictic "is to point the finger of admiration or scorn; to deal out the mead of honor and of shame." "Invective is not one of the pleasing functions of oratory; nor is it her amiable aspect. But she is charged with a sting, as well as with honey," he continued. "Her terrors are as potent, as her charms; as the same omnipotent hand is manifested by the blasting volley of thunder, as by the genial radiance of the sun."[5] By providing models for an audience to emulate and eschew, and by delineating the boundaries between appropriate and inappropriate behavior, Adams argued that the "omnipotent hand" of the epideictic orator could improve the conduct of his or her audience. The Fourth of July was thus an opportunity to display the best of America and the worst of America's foes, to point the finger of approval and disapproval, to pass judgment on history and the present, and to transform the Revolutionary War into a viable foundation for the United States.

In his Harvard lectures, Adams made the temporal dimensions of American life explicit: past and future in the United States were connected by the American agent, who was properly "American" only insofar as he or she did what was expected of him or her and acted to move the nation forward. Adams held that "every line of praise upon the fathers should be received, as a line of duty for the children."[6] The Fourth of July was a weighty holiday; before the masses got drunk and beat each other up, they were reminded of their duties as citizens. Foreshadowing his father's famous conclusion that the "real American Revolution" was the "radical change in the principles, opinions, sentiments, and affections of the people," much of Adams's speech was backstory, detailing changes in public opinion before the curtain went down and the fighting began. His goal in 1793 was to recall the "feelings, manners and principles" that drove Americans to revolution, which, he announced, were threefold: "The feelings of injured freedom, the manners of social equality, and the principles of eternal justice."[7] According to Adams, Americans desired revolution for two related but distinct reasons: because their feelings had been injured, and because their manners/principles demanded it.

The Revolutionary War was fought for ideals like life, liberty, happiness, and justice, and thus Adams argued that when Americans honored their fathers, they performed "a sacrifice at the alter of Liberty herself." The Revolutionary War was the product of ideology. At the same time, the Revolution had a less idealistic and more emotional side. Americans were injured; they were attacked. "The enduring ties of consanguinity" were cut, and "instead of returning the sentiments of fraternal affection, which animated the Americans," the British "indulged their vanity with preposterous opinions of insulting superiority." The British people "expected an alleviation of their burden, from the accumulation of ours," and King George III "was inexorable to the remonstrances of violated freedom" because, of course, he was the ultimate cause of the crisis.[8]

To capture the emotions running wild during the revolution, Adams described the conflict in religious language, noting that "a large proportion of the audience, whose benevolence is at this moment listening to the speaker of the day, like him were at that period too little advanced beyond the threshold of life to partake of the divine enthusiasm which inspired the American bosom" during the Revolutionary War.[9] Suggesting that the revolutionaries were filled with "divine enthusiasm" was an odd descriptive choice, for "enthusiasm" was a predominantly negative term at the time, associated with craziness and fanaticism. Both of the great lexicographers of the English language, Samuel Johnson and Noah Webster, defined "enthusiasm" as a crazed belief in the ability to talk with God. During the First Great Awakening of the 1730s and 1740s, critics applied the term "enthusiast" to popular Methodist preachers, including John Wesley and George Whitefield, who encouraged their audiences to be filled with the spirit, and who employed emotional language to spread the gospel far and wide. John Locke went so far as to frame the Enlightenment project as an attack on enthusiasts who shunned the evidence of the empirical world in favor of religious dogma and fantasies of divine communication. He claimed that enthusiasm was "founded neither on reason nor divine revelation" but was the product of "the conceits of a warmed or overweening imagination."[10]

Obviously, Adams did not employ this term to stigmatize the revolutionaries as religious zealots, for while many of the revolutionaries were indeed Christians filled with the spirit, many others were deists—and, of course, the founders created a "godless constitution" and with good reason, remembering the religious wars of their ancestors and pledging, never again.[11] Widespread fear of religious enthusiasm in fact led to the Constitution's wall of separation between church and state (to use Jefferson's pertinent metaphor), and thus the founders wanted to protect the public sphere from religious fanaticism, not the other way around. On the contrary, Adams used religious language and described the revolutionaries as filled with "divine enthusiasm" to highlight the emotional aspects of the Revolutionary War. While other Fourth of July speakers in the 1790s emphasized the calm, cool, collected, and rational nature of revolution, Adams rightly remembered that revolution was the product of warmed imagination, heightened desire, and extreme emotions. Participating in revolution was to lose oneself in something greater. It was to be swept up by the tide of forces inevitable.

Accounting for both the feelings and the principles of revolution was necessary to ensure the future of the United States. On the Fourth of July, orators like Adams taught Americans how to feel. On this holiday, Americans learned to see the subtle machinations of international affairs as insults to the nation's dignity; they also learned that a slight to the United States was a slight to them and their families. Adams was sincere when he argued that Americans should learn from the revolutionaries' manners of equality and principles of justice—and he put these principles into action in the nineteenth century as a vigorous crusader against the evils of slavery and the barbarity of the slave power.[12] Yet in the 1790s, the young, weak nation was encircled by hostile powers. Americans therefore needed to understand the feelings of injured freedom, and like good teachers, Adams and others taught them how to respond to an attack on the United States.

In the 1790s, citizens were told to view a national threat as a personal threat; they were also instructed that it was their duty to come to the nation's defense when called. These lessons were foundational to the Second American Revolution in American politics in the 1780s and 1790s. While Adams expressed his "rational hope . . . that our country will have no occasion to require of us those extraordinary and heroic exertions which it was your fortune to exhibit," the United States might be attacked—and Americans had to be prepared. "Should the prospect hereafter darken, and the clouds of public misfortune thicken to a tempest; should the voice of our country's calamity ever call us to her relief," he argued, "we swear by the precious memory of the sages who toiled, and of the heroes who bled in her defence, that we will prove ourselves not unworthy of the prize, which they so dearly purchased; that we will act as the faithful disciples of those who so magnanimously taught us the instructive lesson of republican virtue."[13] It was not just the Constitution's "We, the People" that interpellated Americans into the national order and called them to attention; it was "our country's calamity." Calamities persuaded Americans to defend the Constitution, and not vice versa. The Revolutionary War was about more than simply besting the British. It was a model for how Americans should act. For Americans to honor the founders, patriotic adulation was not enough. Americans had to act by defending the nation from its enemies. A contract of blood with the past weighed heavy on the present.

In the late 1790s, the once powerful Federalist Party suffered a stunning demise. Putting a new spin on the tumultuous period of John Adams's presidency, in this chapter I argue that the XYZ Affair of 1798, and the subsequent event known as "Fries's Rebellion" in 1799, precipitated a crisis in Federalism as party leaders, especially President Adams and Alexander Hamilton, were divided by differing views on how best to govern. Both Adams and Hamilton agreed on the virtues of naming international enemies, and they happily embraced the political turmoil caused by the XYZ Affair. The XYZ Affair was a significant event, in turn, because it allowed Federalists to rewrite the social contract in the popular imagination as a contract of blood. This reading of the social contract demanded that Americans behave virtuously in the present in order to live up to the example of Revolutionary martyrs in the past. By deploying the rhetoric of enemyship, Federalists offered subsequent politicians a useful precedent for managing the dilemmas of American nationalism. By deploying enemyship, Federalists furthered the counter-revolution in American politics.

For Hamilton, however, the French were not the only enemy to be subdued. Hamilton mistrusted citizens and doubted their capacity for reform. To him, the people were just another enemy of government. He therefore dreamed of creating a massive military force that would forever shackle the possibility of a democratic revolution toppling the moneyed men from power, and he put his military plans into play in response to Fries's Rebellion. Initially a backer of Hamilton's plans, President Adams soon grasped the pitfalls of coercion and pardoned John Fries, but it was too late. As the Federalists named a band of poor Pennsylvanians America's enemies, and set a massive army upon them, the errors of domestic coercion became clear to the voting public. First, Pennsylvanians voted the Federalist governor out of office in 1799; second, in 1800, Americans turned the Federalist Adams out of office as well. From this point forward, politicians would be more careful about whom they named enemies and whom they did not. Federalists were successful to the degree that they nationalized enemies. When this rhetorical project failed, they did, too.

Republican Machines

After a lengthy career, George Washington retired in 1796. For the first time, then, Americans participated in a presidential election with an outcome that was not preordained. Though the Federalist John Adams was eventually elected, his popularity paled in comparison to his predecessor's. Adding to his troubles, Adams inherited a galling political situation when he entered office. This was a low point in the relations between the United States and its former Revolutionary ally, France. Believing the commercial agreement between the United States and Great Britain codified in the Jay Treaty of 1795 to be an act of treachery, France issued decrees in July 1796 and March 1797 giving French privateers free reign to plunder American shipping. Lacking a navy, the United States was helpless to defend itself. Consequently, Americans lost 330 ships to France in 1797, causing insurance rates to rise astronomically and imports/exports to drop precipitously.[14] Through piracy, France waged war on the United States.

Ignoring the more hawkish members of his cabinet, Adams responded to the crisis by seeking concord with the French despite their retributive actions. After much wrangling, a Federalist delegation was deployed to Paris in the summer of 1797 to seek an honorable peace with France. They were, however, quickly entangled in the seedy upside-down world of Parisian diplomacy. Bankrupt from wars with England, France needed money; therefore, three French agents known as X, Y, and Z demanded an extortionate loan and a ridiculous bribe to receive the American diplomats. This was a profound slight to the national pride. It was also a political opportunity. Indeed, the XYZ Affair provided Federalists with the rhetorical ammunition they needed to bolster their authority and push their defense plans through a divided Congress. Adams released the XYZ documents to Congress on April 3, 1798, and within a week they were read in newspapers all over the country, letting loose a torrent of outraged patriotism echoing the high points of the Revolutionary War. On July 7, 1798, the United States rescinded its treaties with France, and the so-called Quasi-War began.

This conflict tempered some of the partisan bitterness of the moment and transformed many Americans into a people willing to receive Federalists as their leaders. Following Adams's inflammatory speeches of March and April 1798, and the publication of the XYZ documents in major newspapers, Americans came together as they had only a few times before. There was dissent, of course, which grew louder as Federalists attempted to consolidate their power with coercive force; but in the early months of the crisis, there was an outpouring of nationalism in parades, speeches, plays, and songs like "Adams and Liberty" and "Hail Columbia," which was a popular Federalist war anthem that became one of America's unofficial national anthems. Citizens also declared their support of the government with short jingoistic letters mailed to the president. Adams relished these affirmations. He took time to personally respond to most of them, and even regaled some of the hardy patriots who hand-delivered their messages to the executive mansion in Philadelphia with impromptu orations in full military regalia. Many of these addresses were published in major U.S. newspapers and then reprinted, along with Adams's responses, as *A Selection of the Patriotic Addresses, to the President of the United States, Together with The President's Answers.* This compendium, which included addresses from fourteen states and the district of Maine, was simultaneously the type of rhetoric that made war productive, and a revealing exposé of how the French enemy affected Americans in 1798.

In Federalist 41, Madison announced that "America united, with a handful of troops, or without a single soldier, exhibits a more forbidding posture to foreign ambition, than America disunited, with a hundred thousand veterans ready for combat."¹⁵ In the 1790s, many Americans came to share the assumption of the authors of *The Federalist*: that war followed from weakness and division, peace from strength and unity. One of the most prominent themes in the *Patriotic Addresses* was consequently the steadfast unity of Americans in the face of their enemies. According to the legislature of New Hampshire: "By union, our independence can be maintained; by division it is lost forever."¹⁶ Similarly, the citizens of Georgetown, Maryland, claimed that "whatever difference of opinion may exist among us" would evaporate in the face of danger: "If the necessity of a solemn appeal to arms should be imposed upon us, America, so far from shewing herself a degraded and divided people, will exhibit to the world an example of unanimity and patriotism not to be exceeded."¹⁷ Public declarations of unity, unanimity, and patriotism were necessary, these citizens claimed, because the XYZ documents represented Americans as a fractured people, and because domestic enemies were attempting to divide Americans from their government on behalf of France.

This moment of enemyship convinced Americans to stand firm behind the government—for it was the government which provided them with protection from their enemies. The grand jurors of Columbia County, New York, suggested that insofar as the "crisis in our relations to the French republic . . . menaces our independence," it "awakens our zeal, and draws closer our affections to the government by which alone our independence can be secured." Similarly, the citizens of Chapel Hill, North Carolina, declared that "we feel an attachment to your person as our chief magistrate, and one who has borne a distinguished part in the defence and establishment of our rights and liberties—and that when those liberties and rights are placed at stake, we are ready to stand by you and our government, to defend both at the expense of our last blood." Of course, Americans were not completely united, and Republicans battled on in the face of such statements. But the important point was that the crisis with France persuaded many Americans that the new nationalism demanded unity rather than dissent, deference rather than rebellion—for Federalists protected the independence, liberties, and rights of Americans from the French. Each of these states, towns, communities, and groups assumed that national unity was both a deterrent to war and a prerequisite for victory; hence they assured the president, their fellow citizens, and America's enemies that they were united and prepared to defend the government.[18]

Residents of Adams's hometown of Quincy, Massachusetts, recorded the sociological effects of the XYZ Affair: it coordinated citizens, who not long ago were engaged in rancorous partisan warfare, behind the government. "The joyous effects are every where visible!" they reported, observing that "the people, who in great numbers before, alarmingly separated in affection and confidence from their government, and rendered jealous of the first characters of their own election, convinced of the snares spread for their country by foreign intrigue, are now crowding to its standard, and consecrating their fortunes and lives for its defence." Though the people of Quincy noted the "joyous effects" of a looming war, it was not just France's actions, but how these actions were framed in public discourse that cultivated unity. The citizens of Philadelphia recognized this and commended Adams on his successful rhetoric. "Permit us to congratulate you," they wrote, "on the prospect of unanimity that now presents itself to the hopes of every American, and on the spirit of independent patriotism that is rapidly rising into active exertion." Understanding that words could foster union, these Philadelphians praised Adams for his words. Adams himself observed, "with infinite satisfaction, that the alarming prospect of a war, which is seen to be just and necessary, has silenced all essential differences of opinions, and that a union of sentiments appears to prevail very generally throughout our land."[19] The best way to cultivate this union of sentiments was to produce alarm and prepare for war. As he told supporters from Jefferson's Virginia, "Although we may view war as particularly injurious to the interests of our country, providence may intend it for our good, and we must submit."[20]

The Constitution was defended as an instrument of peace, yet here the president argued that Americans had to submit to war. How to square the desire for peace with the necessity of war was a central tension in the early Republic, and it has continued to vex politicians since the founding period. By naming a savage enemy, Americans have time and time again been able to frame war as an unfortunate necessity and an exception to the rule.[21] Enemyship helped Americans to reconcile their professed love of peace with the omnipresent reality of war. Yet

Adams said something more. He argued that providence might intend war for the good of Americans. How could war be a force for good? The answer was provided by Adams's friend and interlocutor Benjamin Rush. Dr. Rush hated war; he even proposed an amendment to the Constitution that would establish a Peace Department to counter the influence of the War Department.[22] Yet Rush was repeatedly led back to the utility of war. He thus represented the United States in miniature: for him and his country, war was inescapable.

During the Revolutionary War, Rush found himself wishing not for victory, but for more war. War, he observed, made men into men and taught common people how to behave virtuously. War was a source of temperance, modesty, justice, and godliness. For the deeply religious Rush, then, war made Christian soldiers—and onward, he urged them. "A peace at this time would be the greatest curse that could befall us," he told Adams in 1777, and continued: "I hope the war will last until it introduces among us the same temperance in pleasure, the same modesty in dress, the same justice in business, and the same veneration for the name of the Deity which distinguished our ancestors."[23] War taught moderation and boldness. Rush therefore worried about what would happen after the war was over—for war provided Americans with the enemies that tied them together as a people. "We stand in need of all the follies and vices of our enemies to give us a national character," he concluded in 1782, for "it is a melancholy truth that most of our virtues have sprung from those impure sources. The patriotism of too many is founded only in resentment."[24]

Though war was the path to independence, many Americans mistrusted war as a social good because they believed that it was the surest road to despotism.[25] Americans living in the years following the Revolutionary War were suspicious of military force; they feared a standing army, and there was widespread popular outrage over the Society of the Cincinnati, a group of elite Revolutionary War veterans (headed by General George Washington) who founded a secret, hereditary society to protect their interests and preserve their prestige for all time.[26] Republicanism was, after all, often posed in contradistinction to military government in the eighteenth century. Still, war created a rhetorical situation calling on citizens to unite in the face of danger, and to behave virtuously lest the Republic fall. During wartime, rhetors appealed to unity, virtue, and patriotism, praising those who risked everything to come to the nation's defense. War created the possibility for heroism, for battling the enemy, for standing up for principle, for refusing to step down, and for the ultimate act of republican virtue—dying for the cause.

Following the Revolutionary War, Rush brought his obsessions with medicine and nosology to the problem of how best to create social order. The United States could be made strong, he argued, only by transforming citizens into "republican machines" who worked hard, behaved virtuously, respected their social superiors, and did as they were told.[27] For Rush, building a nation required disciplining citizens to behave virtuously. In the eighteenth century, virtue denoted a willingness to put the public good before the private; and though this moral characteristic was thought to be necessary in all forms of government, it was said to be the glue of republics. "let our pupil be taught that he does not belong to himself, but that he is public property," Rush wrote, and therefore "Let him be taught to love his family, but let him be taught, at the same time, that he must forsake, and even forget them, when *the welfare of his country requires it*."[28] Rush's suggestion that citizens would forsake and forget their families to defend the nation "when the welfare of his country requires it" was significant, because he opposed virtue to liberty and called on citizens to behave virtuously at the expense of their liberties. Indeed, Rush called for the invention of methods of constraint to counter the liberating discourse of the Revolutionary War, thereby transforming unruly citizens into orderly subjects who were lawful and would sacrifice themselves to defend the nation from its enemies. Though Rush and others feared war, he came to understand that confronting the enemy created discipline, and living in fear of the enemy encouraged citizens to submit to authority.

For the state to grow strong, citizens had to act virtuously—that is, in defense of the nation from its many enemies, foreign and domestic. The utility of government and the meaning of citizenship were therefore most pronounced during times of great danger. The model for the patriot-citizen was found in the Revolutionary War and also in 1794, when over 13,000 Americans from New Jersey, Maryland, Pennsylvania, and Virginia marched three hundred miles with President George Washington across the Alleghenies to suppress the Whiskey Rebellion. This "Army of the

Constitution," as the president called it, was constituted by Americans who believed their nation was under attack. To the degree that Americans held opinions like these, and were willing to step up and die for the Constitution, the future of the young nation was secure. But how to ensure that future Americans understood, with crystal clarity, that their bodies were public property? How to ensure that if their nation called, Americans would answer? These questions were confronted by Federalists in 1798–1799.

Public Memory and the Politics of Virtue

Following ratification of the Constitution, elites prescribed many behaviors associated with living in a republic; at the top of the list was the duty to defer to decisions made by one's representatives. Yet also high on this expansive list was the duty to come to the nation's defense in times of crisis. One of the primary rhetorical moves for disciplining revolutionary democracy—and redirecting it so that it would serve the interests of government rather than running counter to them—was to teach citizens to love their nation so dearly that they would die for it. American nationalism hence combined civic and martial virtue. A central requirement of being a United States citizen was contributing to the common good by defending the nation—when it was challenged by its enemies—with force. Following the Revolutionary War, the founders were faced with a series of challenges, including how to convince citizens that defending the nation was their duty, and that it was in the best interest to submit to the Constitution rather than to resist it.

For many thinkers, education was the preferred means for reforming conduct, disciplining democracy, and nurturing obedience to the laws. One scholar went so far as to label "patriotism" a branch of moral philosophy that should be taught in the nation's schools.[29] Education, many concluded, was the highest form of power over citizens. Noah Webster was among those who championed education as an instrument of social control. Before the XYZ Affair, Webster joined a chorus of elites rethinking the meaning of "power." Webster taught Americans how to spell and talk, working to develop a standardized American system of spelling and the first *American Dictionary* because he believed that "a *national lan-guage* is a band of *national union*."³⁰ Webster understood the intimate connection between language and thought, and his pedagogy was based on the assumption that by instructing Americans to think a certain way, it was possible to make them act in certain ways as well. By controlling language, Webster believed he could control thought and, ultimately, be-havior. He therefore concluded that a system of public education should replace the outdated, barbaric pedagogies of punishment and war in the United States.

During the ratification debate, Webster agreed that virtue was the foundation of a republican government, but he concluded that *"Virtue, patriotism, or love of country, never was and never will be, till mens' natures are changed*, a fixed, permanent principle and support of government."³¹ For much of the 1790s, in turn, Webster argued that education and not war was the quickest, surest, and safest way to change the natures of men. In *On the Education of Youth in America* (1790), Webster claimed that how a society educated its citizens was "adapted to its particular stage" and "local circumstances." The main difference between premod-ern "barbarous" states and modern "civilized" states was their evolving relationship to war:

> While nations are in a barbarous state, they have few wants and conse-quently few arts. Their principal objects are defense and subsistence; the education of a savage therefore extends little farther than to enable him to use with dexterity a bow and a tomahawk. But in the progress of manners and of arts, war ceases to be the employment of whole na-tions; it becomes the business of a few who are paid for defending their country . . . Education proceeds therefore by gradual advances, from simplicity to corruption. Its first object, among rude nations, is safety; its next, utility; it afterwards extends to convenience; and among the opulent part of civilized nations it is directed principally to show and amusement.³²

Premodern states educated citizens exclusively in the ways of war; look-ing back to Sparta, for example, Niccolò Machiavelli insisted that military training was the means for teaching citizenship and transforming a soft mass of people into the hard rock of the state.[33] Yet modernity was about more than learning to wield a bow. Modern states, Webster argued, took war out of the hands of citizens, freeing them to engage in more enlightened pursuits. For Webster, then, "civilization" meant transcending war, because war was the quickest road to despotism.

The XYZ Affair, however, demonstrated that enemyship could discipline citizens in ways that peacetime education could not. Politicians expected citizens to put the common good before their personal interests. Though the meaning of the common good was subject to debate, in times of danger, when the enemy was poised to attack, it was clearer. In the early Republic, enemyship created space for virtue, which, it was said, was the essence of republicanism. "That virtue is the true principle of republican government," John Warren observed in one of the first Fourth of July orations in 1783, "has been sufficiently proved by the ablest writers on the subject, and, that whereas other forms of government may be supported without her, yet that in this she is absolutely necessary to her existence."[34] Teaching citizens to behave virtuously was essential to republicanism, and therefore virtue preoccupied many politicians in the formative years of the United States. On the one hand, virtue meant acting as a good citizen, participating in civic life, and acting appropriately in the agora.[35] On the other hand, virtue in the early Republic was intimately tied to the confrontation, and conquest, of the enemy. Warren explained that American virtue denoted the willingness to sacrifice oneself for the nation. "A general prevalence of that love for our country which teaches us to esteem it glorious to die in her defence," he argued, "is the only means of perpetuating the enjoyment of that liberty and security, for the support of which all government was originally intended."[36] In republics, citizens had to be willing to fight and die for their nation.

Significantly, the need to behave virtuously was pronounced during crises when the nation was in peril. In the aftermath of the XYZ Affair, Americans expressed their determination to use any means necessary to defend the nation from both foreign and domestic enemies, thereby quashing pro-France sympathizers and other malcontents at home. Citizens from Hartford pledged their support of government and stated their confidence in victory, because "we humbly trust that the hand of Providence, which has supported us through greater perils, will enable us to withstand the arts or attacks of the foreign or internal enemies of our freedom." Citizens of the towns of Windsor, Montgomery, Princeton, and Kingston, New Jersey, promised the support of the famed New Jersey militia to battle foreign enemies or repress internal enemies, just as they had done during the Whiskey Rebellion in 1794 as a vital part of the Army of the Constitution. They proclaimed that if the president should ask, "the militia of New-Jersey, will, as they have always done, fly at your command, either to repel the invasion of foreign enemies, or to crush the villainy of domestic traitors." These sentiments no doubt pleased Federalists, for the threat of war brought citizens in line with their government and persuaded them to act virtuously, in defense of the nation.[37]

These statements contradicted the French philosopher Charles Louis de Secondat, baron de Montesquieu's influential argument that virtue and fear belonged to different types of government. In *The Spirit of Laws* (1748), he claimed that "the laws of education will be therefore different in each species of government; in monarchies they will have honor for their object; in republics, virtue; in despotic governments, fear."[38] Though monarchies privileged honor and despotisms fear, republics were premised on virtue—which, in the civic republican tradition, meant a type of civic-minded ability to put the interests of the community first, and also a more martial willingness to step up when called and defend the community from its enemies. Obviously, these lines were blurry. Born from a monarchy, the politics of honor continued to play a pivotal role in the United States following the Revolutionary War.[39] The rhetorics of virtue, in turn, were central to the Country and Whig traditions in England.[40] While honor and virtue were important to different forms of government, proving that Montesquieu's lines were not as cut and dry as he suggested, fear was a sticking point—for Americans in the 1770s and 1780s framed their new republican governments in opposition to fear.

In 1776, for example, John Adams used the politics of fear to draw a line between America and England. In his popular *Thoughts on Government*, Adams claimed that the worst governments in the world (like King George III's) were founded on coercion, intimidation, and fear, and he instructed his readers that the new American government, whatever form it might take, would be different. "Fear is the foundation of most governments," he observed, "but it is so sordid and brutal a passion, and renders men, in whose breasts it predominates, so stupid, and miserable, that Americans will not be likely to approve of any political institution which is founded on it."[41] For Adams, the American experiment was a rejection of traditional European government—government by fear and force, government that restrained citizens and bottled up their tremendous political potential. Still, fear had a central place in the republic of virtue, for the presence of the enemy could discipline citizens to behave virtuously. But before citizens could fear properly, they had to be taught to love their nation—and this meant teaching Americans to think historically.

The rhetorics of nationalism, fear, war, history, and enemyship were intimately related in the early Republic, and they all came together in Webster's rhetoric. On July 4, 1798, having observed the effects of the XYZ Affair, Webster changed his mind about the relationship between civilization and war. Understanding war to be a transforming experience, he imagined an orderly United States unified around common dangers and a reverence for the past. At the core of citizenship, he explained, was virtue. By turning to the past, he found a key to persuading Americans to behave virtuously in the present. In this speech, like most of his public address in the 1780s and 1790s, Webster was preoccupied with stability and order. He keenly understood the dangers that revolutionary sentiments posed to the emerging constitutional order of the United States, and his overarching goal was to persuade Americans that it was their duty to defend the Constitution, not to oppose centralized power as they had done in the 1770s. He therefore defined America as a conservative place, mindful of tradition and the past.

According to Webster, the United States was no longer a land of revolution, but a sanctuary from it—a nation destined "for the reception of the wrecks" of European despotism. The French Revolution played a formative role in Webster's thinking, conjuring up disturbing images of guillotines, pitchforks, decapitated bodies, and other signs of democracy run amok. "Even admitting what some enthusiasts affirm"—perhaps he was thinking of Jefferson here—"that the present political storms in Europe are necessary to rouse men from their lethargy," Webster derided the French Revolution as lunacy, and noted that there was "no reason why we should suffer the same revolutionizing frenzy to penetrate into this peaceful Republic." For Webster, revolution was banished from the United

States because "*Our* business is to love our country, and to maintain its independence." In this oration, Webster erased the undesirable parts of the Declaration of Independence from America's public memory and forwarded a new interpretation of America's history. In the past, citizens had the right to alter or abolish governments destructive of life, liberty, and the pursuit of happiness; now, it was their duty to defer and defend. Webster's Fourth of July Address heralded a shift in American politics: where there once was revolution, there would now be consent.[42]

Americans no longer had any business talking about revolution; they were obligated to love their country. Webster's address was partly prescriptive, partly descriptive. Webster was a shrewd cultural critic, and he understood that a profound change had occurred since the Revolutionary War: revolution had lost much of its appeal in the United States. This can be explained, in part, by a society-wide backlash against the French Revolution.[43] However, the evolving status of revolution was also influenced by a shift in how Americans imagined their history and their relationship to war. Though Americans wrote histories of the Revolutionary War almost immediately, by 1798 they had a longer perspective—and it appeared that their earlier boasts of building a lasting nation had been realized.[44] Furthermore, Americans had a new sacred text to replace the Declaration of Independence, and the Constitution recalibrated the meaning of American history by giving the Revolutionary War a *telos*, a meaning—and most importantly, an endpoint. According to America's leaders in the late 1790s, though "the people" still retained the right to alter or abolish governments, such actions were no longer necessary; the American Revolution ended once the Constitution was ratified. Now, Americans lived in post-Revolutionary times.

One of the most popular tropes in early discourse about the Revolutionary War was an elemental human symbol: blood. "Descriptions of blood soaking the American soil to consecrate it as holy ground filled printed materials and commemorations of all kinds," from the battles of Lexington, Concord, and Bunker Hill in 1775 forward. During the Revolutionary War, Americans deployed the rhetorics of martyrdom to great effect, encouraging Americans to battle their enemies by ensuring them that their sacrifices would be remembered, hence giving meaning to the brutality of war and the loneliness of death. During the 1780s, Americans developed rhetorics of gratitude that expressed, in public speeches and rituals, the tremendous debt the living owed to the blood sacrifice of the dead.[45] During the 1790s, the rhetorics of blood, martyrdom, sacrifice, and gratitude were turned into productive principles of governance that altered American behaviors. During this decade, many speakers claimed that when second- and third-generation Americans were born, they entered into a social contract not only with their rulers but also with America's past. This was *the contract of blood*, and once articulated, it revolutionized American identity in a counter-revolutionary direction. The contract of blood, more than anything else in the post-Revolutionary years, forwarded the project of disciplining democracy and producing orderly, patriotic citizens.

The post-Revolutionary moment in the United States was one of great historical weight. The first citizens of the United States measured themselves by their relationship to the American Revolution, praising the brave patriotism of soldiers in public address and struggling to live up to the courageous precedent in their own lives. The Constitution changed how Americans experienced this history, for it was now possible to argue that the establishment of a federal government was the primary motivation for independence, when in fact a federal government was on the minds of few revolutionaries, obsessed as they were with achieving greater autonomy and local control. Webster contended that "our fathers were *men*—they were heroes and patriots—they fought—they conquered—and they bequeathed to us a rich inheritance of liberty and empire, which we have no right to surrender to the all-grasping fangs of the French government."[46] If the point of revolution was to establish the Constitution, which protected liberty and generated empire, then the citizens living under it were bound by the past to honor the present by defending America's government. The past no longer demanded that citizens refresh "the tree of liberty" with "the blood of patriots & tyrants," as Jefferson wrote during Shays's Rebellion.[47] It now compelled citizens to uphold America's independence by fighting America's enemies.

With the contract of blood, Americans secularized religious imagery to further the creation of the Republic. Just like Catholics, who consumed the blood of Christ during communion, Americans consumed the blood of their dead mothers and fathers, who also sacrificed themselves for a better future.[48] Unlike religious acolytes, however, Americans had no choice. The liberal tradition of John Locke taught that the origin of private property was labor: those who worked the land owned it. In the 1790s, American politicians taught citizens that their labor earned them property and something more. When Americans worked the land and took sustenance from the earth, it was said, and when they enjoyed the liberties and freedoms provided by the Constitution, they communed with the martyrs who stained the earth with their blood during the Revolutionary War. In turn, those who drew nourishment from the soil were encouraged to show their gratitude by reforming their behaviors. The heroism of America's past demanded virtuous conduct in the present. Capturing the burden of children trying to live up to their parents' example, Webster insisted that when Americans failed to behave properly, they disappointed their dead mothers and fathers. To misbehave was to spit on the graves of martyrs.

Changing rhetorics of property were central to the counter-revolution of the early Republic. In *Common Sense*, Thomas Paine argued that among other horrors they would prosecute, the British would take Americans' property when they invaded North America. Federalists made a similar argument during the ratification debates, only this time they cultivated fear of common folks like Daniel Shays. Indeed, federalists were remarkably successful at coupling elites' fears of democracy with fears that if given the chance, everyday citizens would steal their stuff. The perception that Shays and his men were levellers intent on a society-wide, downward redistribution of property helped to secure ratification of the Constitution. After ratification, politicians changed their tune, because property was central to securing allegiance to the Constitution and the laws. During the Whiskey Rebellion, orators including Hugh Henry Brackenridge encouraged Americans to lust after the rich agricultural lands in the Ohio Valley, currently occupied by Indians. If only frontiersmen would turn their minds westward, they might forget how much they hated the federal government and its odious whiskey tax. Stolen land could then form the basis of a lawful, obedient people. By giving rowdy citizens land, the government also gave them something that needed to be protected—and with protection came obligation. When bound to rhetorics that named the enemy, land was a potent force for reforming the democratic sentiments nurtured during the Revolutionary War.

Building on these foundations, Webster argued that property was not just a right and a privilege, but also a debt. In the aftermath of the XYZ Affair, many Americans came to understand things similarly. The citizens of Concord reported that "Concord drank the first blood of martyered freemen," and, understanding that the lands of the United States were soaked through with the blood of dead revolutionaries, these citizens recognized their duty to come to the government's aid. Never forgetting "the divine enthusiasm of '75," the citizens of Concord resolved "in holy remembrance of those who bled, that we will defend by our valor, what they won by their blood."[49] For the citizens of Concord, the social contract compelled them to defend the Constitution. Following the XYZ Affair, the social contract was redefined as a contract of blood, tradition, and order.

The contract of blood was impressed on the second generation of Americans, who seized the opportunity created by the XYZ Affair to demonstrate their own understanding of American history, and their deep and abiding commitment to defending the nation.[50] Born after the Revolutionary War, a group of citizens calling themselves "the youth" of Portsmouth, New Hampshire, told the president that they would come to his aid if the nation was threatened by enemies. "These blessings having received as our birth-right, we will never part with but with life," they wrote in the *Patriotic Addresses*, "purchased as they were by the blood and treasure of our gallant ancestors without *our* aid: We will defend them with the last drop and particle of our own, and endeavour to prove ourselves worthy the rich inheritance." Similarly, the students of Harvard University informed President Adams: "Our lives are our only property; and we were not the sons of those who sealed our liberties with their blood, if we would not defend with these lives that soil, which now affords a peaceful grave to the mouldering bones of our forefathers."[51] These statements suggest that Federalists had, by naming a series of internal and external enemies, altered the definition of citizenship and the meaning of revolution in the United States. Rather than fighting for equality or shedding elite blood, revolution now meant sacrifice. What the revolutionary fathers had begun, covenant and precedent demanded that their sons and daughters complete.

As they called on citizens to forget the enduring defense of revolution in the preamble of the Declaration of Independence, and encouraged them to focus instead on the sacrifices of colonial martyrs, politicians in the late 1790s devised a clever and lasting way of managing the dilemmas of American nationalism and propping up the nation-state. By infusing the deaths of soldiers with meaning, rhetors created a binding covenant between living and dead. Webster implored Americans: "Let us then rally around the Independence and Constitution of our country; resolved, to a man, that we will never lose by folly, disunion or cowardice, what has been planned by wisdom, and purchased with blood."[52] A Boston orator echoed Webster:

> *On this our infant Nation's natal day*
> *Our solemn vows this gratitude we pay.*
> *And by the blood of heroes, patriots, shed,*
> *Whose souls of blissful realms have long since fled,*
> *By all that's dear and sacred, just and fair,*
> *By* LIBERTY's *immortal name we swear,*
> *Our country's Independence to defend,*
> *'Gainst any foreign foe our force will bend.*[53]

Like Webster, this speaker argued that America's revolutionary past compelled citizens to defend the nation against "any foreign foe." The contract of blood was discursively linked to the rhetoric of enemyship. In fact, the contract of blood assumed that there was always already an enemy, for a threat was required to actualize the covenant.

The Rhetorical Compulsion of Enemyship

In his lectures on rhetoric at Harvard University, John Quincy Adams emphasized the duties that all citizens possessed insofar as they were born into a nation founded on the blood sacrifice of martyrs. Citizens, he argued, tied the future to the past; without their determination to defend the Constitution from its enemies, the sacrifices of revolutionary mothers and fathers would be in vain. As we have seen, the insistence that there was a contract of blood between generations was—when actualized in moments of danger with the rhetorics of enemyship—a potent force for disciplining revolutionary democracy, and stressing consent to government in its place. While citizenship entailed strong obligations, so did government. The Revolutionary War was not waged to establish another monarchy or anything like it, Adams recollected. The Revolutionary War was waged to provide Americans with security while freeing them from fear and oppression. For Adams, this meant that government had an obligation to choose deliberation over coercion whenever possible, and to engage citizens in the public sphere by giving reasons for its policies. Government, in short, was obliged to open the realm of communicative possibility rather than closing it, as the British did in the years preceding the Revolutionary War.[54]

The obligations of government were foundational to Adams's rhetorical theory, for he hoped to guide future leaders to the true rhetorical republic he took to be the point of the Revolutionary War. With the flourish of a perfect peroration, Adams closed his 1805 inaugural lecture as the first Boylston Professor of Rhetoric and Oratory at Harvard University, later published as the first chapter of *Lectures on Rhetoric and Oratory* (1810), with a lofty vision of political discussion in the United States:

> Under governments purely republican, where every citizen has a deep interest in the affairs of the nation, and, in some form of public assembly or other, has the means and opportunity of delivering his opinions, and of communicating his sentiments by speech; where government itself has no arms but those of persuasion; where prejudice has not acquired an uncontrolled ascendancy, and faction is yet confined within the barriers of peace; the voice of eloquence will not be heard in vain.[55]

For Adams, the beauty of republican government was that it privileged speech over violence and eloquence over force; republican government, in short, made eloquence a form of power.[56] This dream of a rhetorical republic proved that Adams was no sociologist, for this statement could only be said to be true in bounded spaces like the New England town-hall meeting, and then only for fleeting moments. Still, the force of these words came not from their correspondence to reality, but instead from how well they communicated the hopes and dreams associated with republicanism. From Cicero's *De Oratore* to *The Federalist*, Adams's words captured the promise of a republican polity of educated citizens who had embraced the fiction of consensus and traded in the bangs of battle for the gentle repartee of argument. Moreover, Adams's Harvard lectures painted a portrait of the almost boundless power of rhetoric, and the limitless power of the orator to mold and shape public opinion. For him, rhetoric was the republic's salvation. Only the orator could delay the inevitable demise of all empires and advance a fledgling, youthful nation along its path to maturation and glory.

Adams offered a deeply Ciceronian vision of republican discourse.[57] About this Roman orator-statesman and rhetorical theorist, it has been observed that "one could say without much fear of contradiction that he was and remains the most prominent figure in the history of rhetoric."[58] Cicero was a looming figure in the early Republic, where he exercised a profound influence on the politics and rhetorical theories of the founders.[59] In *De Oratore*, Cicero went to great lengths to enumerate the necessary conditions for meaningful deliberation, and they were most burdensome on the individual. The orator had to be capable of arguing and rebutting any line of argument in any rhetorical situation; thus, achromatic erudition was required. The orator had to be versed in *controversia* (or *dissoi logoi*), the practice of arguing both sides of an issue, because politicians who could do this were more likely to see the merits of alternative positions, and hence less likely to liquidate the opposition. And, understanding that no positions were foolproof and no decisions final, the orator had to act as a functional skeptic who adopted a stance of "neo-stoic resignation."[60] The skeptic stepped back, disciplining the urge to react hastily to a stimulus, and instead considered an opponent's arguments coolly and dispassionately. The skeptic was suspicious of any claims to "truth" and submitted all arguments to the most rigorous examination. In addition to these personal attributes, the very experience of reading *De Oratore*, a tedious work full of arcane allusions, provides one final insight: civic deliberation requires a relaxed time frame and a quiet, safe space in which to digest arguments.[61] Good deliberation requires, but rarely receives, freedom from fear.

The founders of the United States prized deliberation, which for them meant "reason, order, information, commonality of interests, and farsightedness."[62] Deliberation meant reason, but it did not preclude passion. David Hume complained that the Enlightenment, framing itself as an age of reason, did not give passion its due; he wrote in *A Treatise of Human Nature* that "Nothing is more usual in philosophy, and even in common life, than to talk of the combat of passion and reason, to give the preference to reason, and to assert that men are only so far virtuous as they conform themselves to its dictates."[63] Hume and other philosophers in Scotland attempted to reorient the attention of theorists on passion, because, they argued, passion was unavoidable. The founders, who were deeply influenced by the rhetorical theorists of the Scottish Enlightenment, recognized that passion was a profound motivational force, and hence that it was always central to persuasion. Adams himself taught that the purely rational deliberation valued by Enlightenment philosophers like Kant—"real deliberation," he dubbed it—was a doubly insidious fiction.[64] To focus on reason alone was to overlook most of the available means of persuasion for public discussion. It was also to leave the orator at a distinct disadvantage during a rough-and-tumble rhetorical battle. When confronted with a barrage from the whole artillery of persuasion, long and learned treatises on validity conditions made a weak rebuttal. By stressing the validity of passion and the centrality of the rhetorics of praise and blame to deliberative politics, rhetorical theorists like Adams opened the door for the inclusion of strategies like enemyship in the deliberative realm.

Enemyship, however, challenged deliberation by escalating the crisis and creating a sense of dialogue under distress. In moments of great danger, there was little time for deliberation about the best course of action. Equally problematic, enemyship narrowed the range of acceptable political positions. As we saw in the later editions of Thomas Paine's *Common Sense*, enemyship made it unacceptable to be a pacifist, for to dissent from war was to side with the enemy—who was hell bent on killing families. I argued in chapter 1 that this was an unintended and not altogether welcome consequence of Paine's rhetoric. In the early Republic, however, political elites wanted to narrow the political playbook by making certain revolutionary and democratic positions unthinkable. What was an unintended consequence of enemyship during the Revolutionary

War became productive of a new order of things in the early Republic. Thus, politicians argued that to invoke the revolutionary preamble of the Declaration of Independence in the 1790s was a criminal action, because revolution no longer meant life, liberty, and the pursuit of happiness. To talk of revolution now was to embolden domestic enemies hoping to kill the wealthy and steal their property; it was to invite foreign enemies to attack the United States.

Enemyship was potentially advantageous for the founders because it compromised the ability of citizens to justify democratic mobilization, constricting the political playing field by making citizens speak the language of friends and enemies. While enemyship was useful, it was also dangerous—for it called on those who deployed it to achieve the impossible. In enemyship, there is a totalizing urge to close the social, hence replicating in reality what is so clear in the realm of symbols. In his wide-ranging history of the rhetorics of populism, *On Populist Reason*, Ernesto Laclau argues that political and rhetorical theorists should understand the social as a heterogeneous force that can never be closed—by which he means that it can never be completely harnessed by the rhetorical prescriptions of the political advocate. One of the lessons of populist movements, Laclau counsels, is that it is impossible for the political advocate to master the social world with his or her representations of inside and outside, us and them, friend and enemy. For Laclau, "the field of representation is a broken and murky mirror, constantly interrupted by a heterogeneous 'Real' which it cannot symbolically master," and thus the "construction of an 'inside' is going to be only a partial attempt to master an 'outside' which will always exceed those attempts."[65] While enemyship attempts to create a perfect antithesis of friend and enemy, it never can. There is always a leftover, a remainder that cannot be captured by symbols and that works constantly and consistently to undermine the stable binaries of discourse.[66]

While Laclau focuses his study on populist movements against the government, his insight remains true for rhetorical strategies deployed by the government to stifle democratic discourses and popular movements. Enemyship can never master the social field, no matter if deployed by anti-government populists or anti-populist governments: by a Thomas Paine or a John Adams. During moments of enemyship, political actors must therefore deal with the limits of their rhetorical choices. What I find most interesting about such situations in the formative years of the United States is that they reveal the coercive tendencies that underline enemyship, as those who deploy this rhetorical strategy attempt to close the social with stifling legislation and state violence. This, then, was the problem with deploying enemyship in a republic that was founded on deliberative ideals enumerated by John Quincy Adams—for Americans would prove their differences from the British by choosing deliberation over violence as the preferred means of domestic conflict resolution. Enemyship narrowed the realm of political possibility by shuttering the rhetorical openness Cicero and Adams prized; but enemyship also set political actors down the road to coercion and violence as they named enemies and then acted in a way that made them so.

While enemyship quickly monopolized the discursive field, it could never monopolize the public sphere. When the rhetorics of enemyship met the obdurate world, those who deployed this rhetorical strategy were therefore forced to make a series of choices. What would they do when the antithesis of friend and enemy was not replicated in the political realm? How would they deal with "enemies" who acted like "friends," and "friends" who acted like "enemies"? How would they deal with subjects who did not easily fit into either category? And how would they deal with dissent—from both those "enemies" who rejected this label, and those "friends" who did not believe that their "enemies" were really "enemies"?[67]

These problems were readily apparent in the aftermath of the XYZ Affair of 1798. Following the publication of the XYZ dispatches in America's newspapers, popular rags like Philadelphia's *Gazette of the United States* proclaimed that "He is but a luke-warm friend who wavers in the cause of his country," and *"He that is not for us, is against us."*[68] Such statements were indicative of the narrowed range of political possibilities in the post-Revolutionary world—for while past revolutionaries were canonized in public memory, present revolutionaries were named enemies. In turn, Federalists attempted to silence debate and criminalize dissent with the Alien and Sedition Acts, which were deployed to prosecute and jail many influential Republicans, including Vermont congressman Matthew Lyon, prominent editors William Duane (Philadelphia's *Aurora*) and Thomas

Cooper (Northumberland, Pennsylvania's *Gazette*), and journalist James Callender, and to otherwise intimidate those who had the courage to stand up to the Federalist government.[69] And when a group of Pennsylvania Germans protested Federalist policies by dumping hot water on tax collectors and springing several of their neighbors from a county jail, the Federalist press labeled the events the "Northampton Insurrection." President Adams marked it "treason," and the president deployed a massive military force to break up the "rebellion."[70] With its response to the so-called Fries's Rebellion, Federalists tried to close the social and make their rhetorical prescriptions real by crushing dissent. After these events, a prominent Republican paper complained that Federalists had become despots who employed "the logic of the bayonets" to govern.[71] Federalists, this paper charged, had chosen coercion over civic deliberation as the modus operandi of government.

Here, we can begin to penetrate the circular logic of enemyship in the early Republic. Coercion was a choice of politicians like Hamilton, but it was also entailed by their rhetoric. Once they had deployed the either/or grammar of enemyship, suggesting (as the *Gazette of the United States* did) that Americans were either for or against government, any protest—no matter how local—became intolerable. And once protestors like John Fries and his men were viewed through the lens of an either/or lens of friend/enemy, their military repression was logically entailed. But many Republicans questioned the premise of the Federalist argument that there were only two possibilities—that citizens could only be for or against government—and, having countered this logic, they suggested that Fries was not an enemy at all. Here, we see that the naming of enemies was not the end of enemyship but the beginning, for who was and who was not an enemy was always up for discussion. Thus, politicians who named enemies during 1798–1799 got caught up in *the rhetorical compulsion of enemyship*. For while Federalist violence was entailed by the conclusion that Fries was an enemy, this violence was also rhetorical in nature—it was intended to prove that Fries was an enemy, for why would the government respond so forcefully if he was not an enemy? Thus, enemyship became the means to power, but also an end in itself. Enemyship is a rhetoric that serves the demands of the rhetor, but it has demands of its own as well—raising the question of who is really in charge, the rhetor or the rhetoric?

Fries's Rebellion

In the repressive environment of the Quasi-War and the Alien and Sedition Acts, effective congressional opposition to Federalist policies was eviscerated. Consequently, Adams was able to sponsor a series of laws that created America's first national security state and its first war machine, including the New Army: a domestic standing army of over 12,000 soldiers—and later a 30,000-troop auxiliary: the Eventual Army.[72] Though most of Adams's wishes were granted following the XYZ Affair, in this case he got more than he desired. As he recognized, these armies were the work of Alexander Hamilton, who was retired but would simply not go away. Adams contested Hamilton's appointment as a military leader, but was trumped by George Washington's wishes. The de facto leader of the New Army, Hamilton found the door opened for a return to power. Adams joined many Republicans in fearing that Hamilton desired to stage a military coup; though there was little evidence for this, Hamilton's role in the New Army made him a potential despot.[73] After Adams discovered that he could not directly control Hamilton or Hamilton's Army, he countered Hamilton's military influence by promoting peace with France. In February 1799, he nominated William Vans Murray to negotiate peace, and the diplomat's efforts proved successful. The prospects for peace crippled the effort to establish the New Army, and the effects of enemyship waned. Jefferson reported: "The X.Y.Z. delusion is wearing off."[74]

The XYZ Affair allowed Federalists to dramatically increase defense spending. In fact, the defense appropriations of Congress in 1798 totaled over $10 million, making the costs of national defense $4 million more than the entire congressional budget in 1797. To raise the necessary revenue, the federal government passed a direct tax on slaves, lands, and dwelling houses. The rapidly ballooning expenses of the Federalist national security state produced a mounting backlash in Republican circles, with the most prominent examples being the Kentucky and Virginia

Resolutions—authored by Jefferson and Madison to contest the Alien and Sedition Acts with a resurgent rhetoric of states' rights. Dissent was also prominent in Pennsylvania, where over 18,000 people signed petitions protesting Federalist policies, and this was a state in which only 20,000 citizens voted in the 1796 presidential election. Arguing that Federalist legislation was "contrary not only to the spirit but to the letter of the Constitution," over 1,100 citizens from Northampton County in the southeastern part of the state alone petitioned the government to repeal the Alien and Sedition Acts and disband the New Army. Refusing to buy into Federalist fear-mongering, and finding their petitions ignored, German Americans in Northampton and Bucks counties took their protests a step further, gathering in meeting halls and taverns, raising liberty poles, and barring tax collectors from surveying their land in the late months of 1798. Unlike the Regulators or the Whiskey Rebels, however, these protestors positioned their acts as properly republican. They did not want to overturn the current regime or cancel the laws. Expressing their reverence for the Constitution, one liberty pole tempered an old revolutionary credo with a new message: "The Constitution Sacred, No Gagg Laws, Liberty or Death."[75]

During the early months of 1799, protestors in these counties dumped hot water on government officials. In early March, seventeen protestors were jailed and locked in the Sun Inn Tavern in Bethlehem. News traveled quickly that these citizens would be transported to Philadelphia and tried in front of strangers. Accordingly, a troop of 150 uniformed militia and 250 unarmed men from Northampton and Bucks counties marched to the Sun Inn on the afternoon of March 7, 1799, to spring their incarcerated neighbors. Many of these men had marched together during the Revolutionary War and now donned their militia uniforms once again, framing their actions as an extension of America's proud democratic history. Exercising a calculated reserve, the militia did not overrun the tavern. Instead, their leader, an auctioneer named John Fries, attempted to negotiate the release of twelve prisoners, arrested for defying tax assessors, who were confined there. Arguing that the Sixth Amendment right of the prisoners to a jury of their peers had been violated, Fries offered to post bail for his neighbors so they could be tried near their homes by their peers. U.S. Marshal William Nichols rebuffed Fries's offers, and only released the prisoners as the crowd grew increasingly hostile. The militia then disbanded and Fries returned to his job, not knowing he would soon be arrested and sentenced to hang.[76]

The event known today as Fries's Rebellion was not a "rebellion" at all. Though the government worked hard to make the connection, this was definitely no Shays's Rebellion or Whiskey Rebellion. It certainly did not qualify as an armed "insurrection" in the eighteenth-century argot. It was more accurately called a "protest." The First Amendment protected the right of assembly, so protestors gathered to discuss the government's policies; they then petitioned Congress to repeal the tax laws. When their petitions failed, they marched on the Sun Inn. Understanding the need to demonstrate that his goals were limited, each time Fries entered the tavern he left his weapons outside, thereby conducting negotiations as nonviolently as possible. John Fries and his militia were not nation-destroyers. This was not the first blow in a transnational conspiracy to topple the United States government. Fries's actions may have been illegal, but they did not constitute treason. Moreover, Fries was a Revolutionary War veteran and a proud member of the Army of the Constitution who had declared his support for the government in 1794 by marching with President Washington into western Pennsylvania to suppress the Whiskey Rebellion. While many of his fellow protestors wore tricolored cockades in the style of the French Revolution when they marched on the Sun Inn, in a further symbol of his allegiance to the Constitution, Fries donned the same black cockade that Federalists wore to show their support for government following the XYZ Affair.[77]

Four days after the march on the Sun Inn, the news reached Philadelphia. On March 11, 1799, John Fenno's arch-Federalist *Gazette of the United States* broke the news that "ANOTHER INSURRECTION Has broken out in the Western part of this State." Though Bethlehem was clearly in the eastern part of the state, Fenno located it in the western part of Pennsylvania in order to link it to the Whiskey Rebellion. Fenno's *Gazette* claimed that this was dangerous business—more dangerous, in fact, than the Whiskey Rebellion, bearing "a more serious and formidable aspect, than that of Gallatin and the other patriots in the mountains." Fenno here seized the opportunity to smear the outspoken Republican senator Albert Gallatin, who had opposed the whiskey tax in the early 1790s and who often represented the Whiskey Rebels in Federalist discourse. In a year when Federalists and Republicans were engaged in vicious polemical warfare, Pennsylvania protests provided yet another opportunity for Federalists to blast Republicans. Though it announced that Pennsylvanians were in open rebellion against the state government, the *Gazette* reassured its readers that hope was not lost. "One pleasant circumstance has grown out of this alarming intelligence," the *Gazette* observed, which was "an immediate stir amongst the volunteers, who are, we learn, to be immediately paraded for review, in order to be perfectly prepared for the defence of their government and country at a moment's warning."[78] Finding a silver lining in these events, the *Gazette* reported that good citizens recognized their enemies and were coming together to defend their nation.

The *Gazette of the United States*'s pronouncements caused William Duane's *Aurora General Advertiser* to fear a Federalist conspiracy against Republicans and republicanism itself. The next day, March 12, this staunch Republican periodical reported that "The public attention has been engaged for two or three days by some occurrences that have taken place in Northampton county in this state," and "Efforts are making to magnify these occurrences into a terrible and bloody conspiracy against the government, &c." Outbursts like the *Gazette*'s were part of a plot to amplify these "occurrences" into mass protests like Shays's Rebellion or the Whiskey Rebellion when they were nothing of the sort. Though the *Gazette* announced that serious violence had occurred, the *Aurora* objected that violence was minimal: "In Northampton county while a person was in the act of measuring the windows of a house, a woman poured a shower of *hot water* over his head, in other places they were hooted at, and every expression of odium made use of, but no other violence done than the *hot water war* carried on by the female." The *Aurora* was clever to redescribe Fries's Rebellion as the "Hot Water War." It was correct to note that it was not "another insurrection," but wrong to argue that it was not illegal. It was right to be afraid, for protests quickly became a rationale for Federalist politicking. Thus, the *Aurora* set in motion a newspaper war by condemning Federalists and suggesting that there were better ways "to bring them to justice, than by the odious means of an armed military force." Further, the *Aurora* questioned the government's motives for raising an army, suggesting that there might be some "unfledged, Alexander desirous of burning some of the flourishing towns, in the course of such an expedition, in order to give spirit and energy to the military movements."[79] By comparing Alexander Hamilton to the infamous Macedonian conqueror Alexander the Great, the *Aurora* made its primary fear apparent: it was concerned that the Hot Water War was escalated into an "insurrection" in order to excuse the hidden Federalist plot to transform the United States into a military despotism.

Stephen Hartnett and Jennifer Mercieca note that by the summer of 1798, the United States had finally launched a fleet—including the *Constellation*, the *United States*, and the *Constitution*—capable of deterring French piracy in the Caribbean. Moreover, they recall that Bonaparte's French fleet had been destroyed by British Admiral Nelson at the Battle of the Nile. Given these historical facts, they argue that "much of the war talk that summer was less about defending national security than about projecting politically useful fear—that is, hyperbolic war rhetoric rallying the nation around the Federalists served local political purposes rather than national security purposes."[80] Similarly, Craig Smith argues that "the American public had been softened by loyalists, alienated by revolutionaries, and persuaded by British leaders that the French were pure evil," and while there were real dangers during the XYZ Affair, ultimately Federalist rhetoric during this period was partisan: "Thus, an ulterior motive emerged that put the spur to the Federalist propaganda horse: They wanted to keep their party in power."[81] For these rhetorical scholars, the purpose of Federalist rhetoric was not to further natural security, but instead to consolidate political power in a moment of Republican ascendance by manipulating the emotions of Americans. Premising their rule on international crises and hyperbolic rhetoric denouncing America's foes, Federalists needed enemies. Following the XYZ Affair, and due in part to Adams's rhetoric, they had France. But as Adams worked to secure peace as a way of countering Hamilton's influence over the military, the localized resistance in Pennsylvania became doubly useful to Federalists. By labeling protests an "insurrection," Federalists legitimized the instruments of domestic coercion created after the XYZ Affair. They also furthered the counter-revolutionary aims of both Federalists and Republicans by calling on citizens to trade obedience for protection, and to participate in the suppression of national enemies.

On March 12, 1799, Adams issued a proclamation denouncing the actions of Fries and his militia. This document was constitutive of how many Federalists viewed the "Northampton Insurrection," and many of its details were repeated in future Federalist discourse. As Adams told the story, "persons exceeding one hundred in number" who were "armed and arrayed in a warlike manner" marched on the Sun Inn and "there compelled William Nichols, Marshall of the United States, in and for the District of Pennsylvania, to desist from the execution of certain legal process in his hands to be executed," and also "compelled him to discharge and set at liberty certain persons, whom he had arrested by virtue of criminal process." The protestors did this, Adams reported, "by threats of personal injury" and a determination "to withstand by open violence the lawful authority of the Government of the United States." Fries's actions, Adams noted, "amount to treason, being overt acts of levying war against the United States."[82] Adams thus portrayed Fries as a dangerous criminal determined to subvert and destroy the laws of the United States.

When discussing Fries's Rebellion, we would do well to remember that Fries and his men did not believe they had committed a crime at the Sun Inn. As such, they had no reason to turn themselves in. Moreover, Pennsylvania was at peace in the days following the conflagration at the Sun Inn. There was no further violence; there was no rebellion. Nevertheless, on March 26 the *Philadelphia Gazette* escalated the crisis by circulating rumors that Fries had not submitted to the law, making him a fugitive from justice. This paper also announced ominously but incorrectly that "Fries, and his adherents" were "undismayed by the prospect of military force," and that resistance "appears from day to day to assume symptoms of greater malignance and force." Rising violence and fleeing criminals made federal intervention inevitable. Fries's actions proved "the propriety and NECESSITY of strong and active measures." "The mild voice of conciliation can never be successful amongst a horde of unprincipled Jacobins, whose submission to *law*, is a constant warfare with their natures, and whose sudden, resentful, and treacherous submission, is scarcely to be trusted but at the point of the bayonet," this paper concluded.[83] This paper was representative of Federalism in that it posed

an inherent conflict between the people and law: the people were naturally lawless, and could only be contained "at the point of the bayonet."
Government, in this schema, was hemmed in, and had to respond to
protests strongly because it was the bayonet. Here we can see that the
language of response remained remarkably consistent across the three
major democratic uprisings of the early Republic—Shays's Rebellion, the
Whiskey Rebellion, and Fries's Rebellion. Proponents of coercion talked
about the need for strong and active measures because they feared the
people and dreaded democracy's potential to lead to another revolution.

Federalists overreacted to Fries's Rebellion because it was a
confirmation of their worst fears: it proved that the people were not obedient, that the final authority of government was not established, and
that at least some citizens were willing to fight for liberty and self-de-
termination even if that meant running afoul of the law. In the relatively
mild Fries's Rebellion, Federalists couldn't help but see Shays's Rebellion
and the Whiskey Rebellion and the French Revolution and their worst
nightmares. This overreaction was, in turn, politically motivated. Fries
would continue the "delusion" (to use Jefferson's word) that the crisis
with France began—a delusion that we can now see as one of the consequences of enemyship. Fries was the F to the XYZ in a whole new
affair that would shock Americans and bind them to government. And to
undermine anyone (i.e., Republicans) who might suggest that the danger
posed by Fries was nothing like the danger posed by a France or a Great
Britain, Federalists connected the dots, making Fries a stooge of outside
forces conspiring to bring down the government. According to Federalists, little enemies were in league with big enemies.

During the 1790s, France, Haiti, and Ireland erupted into revolt, and
thousands of French, Haitian, and Irish refugees streamed into the United
States to flee oppression and revolution. On April 26, the *Gazette of the
United States* tied Fries's Rebellion, which it argued was "commenced
in deceit and wickedness, and ended in a complete display of madness,
dissolution and folly," to these events. It reported that "Such is the nature
of the age in which our lot is cast, that no event that emerges, however
apparently simple in its aspect, ought to be viewed in an unconnected
light." Rather, the world was "driven from outrage to outrage, and from
insurrection to insurrection." Understanding that eighteenth-century

revolutions were transatlantic phenomena, and that revolutionary ideologies flowed freely between Europe, the Caribbean, and North America, Federalists argued that "a band of French mercenaries" were "preparing an Insurrection of the whole state," which, when leagued with France and "the moody Rebellion of the Land of Slaves" (Haiti), would continue their "holy work of dismembering the Union."[84] The disobedient slave was the model Southern enemy, so this Federalist periodical linked events in the North to Southern fears of a slave uprising modeled on the Haitian Revolution. With the 3/5ths clause of the Constitution, Southern states were more important than Northern states in national elections.[85] Without a Southern base and its additional electoral votes, it would be difficult for Adams to prevail in the coming presidential battle. By linking events in Pennsylvania with a potential revolution in the South, Federalists perhaps hoped that they could pull enough support away from Jefferson to win enough states to keep a Federalist in power.

To bolster their authority and make Federalism a truly national party, Federalists turned the gaze of Americans abroad, suggesting that the United States was particularly vulnerable to invasion because of the democratic instability of the revolutionary past. In the early Republic, it was external enemies, like the British during the Revolutionary War, that threatened to invade the United States. Internal enemies like Daniel Shays or the Whiskey Rebels, on the other hand, were threats to law and order and property rights. But the *Gazette* broke down the lines between internal and external enemies. It warned that the enemies who would invade the United States would do so with the assistance of enemies who were already inside the gates. For this paper, there was little difference between internal and external enemies. Fries's daring rebellion had created the impression that Americans, in the North and in the South alike, were divided—encouraging the United States' many international enemies to strike.

In the years following the Revolutionary War, politicians were gripped by demophobia and struggled to ensure that there would be no further democratic revolutions in the United States. Robert L. Ivie argues that this fear of democracy produced conflicts like the Quasi-War and the War of 1812 because the founders were terrified that foreign demagogues would lead the demos into rebellion, and they hoped, through international conflict, to control democratic distemper by eliminating the world's corrupting influences. Through war and empire, the United States would make the world safe for democracy.[86] The fear of democracy led to the articulation of internal and external enemies. Here, I give a different spin on the story Ivie tells. The founders of the United States named enemies not only to make the world safe for democracy but also to control, tame, and discipline democracy, transforming it into something safer. Americans were urged, during the Whiskey Rebellion, to confront internal enemies and form an Army of the Constitution dedicated to upholding the Constitution. And during the XYZ Affair, Americans were urged to repay the blood sacrifice of their ancestors by defending the Constitution from revolutionary enemies abroad.

The naming of enemies at home and abroad was central to the founders' counter-revolutionary project of taming democracy. In the early Republic, however, it was easier to name external enemies than internal enemies, for there were definite political risks in naming American citizens enemies. Sometimes, internal enemies—like Daniel Shays or the Whiskey Rebels—frightened Americans sufficiently to augment the authority of government as the defender of the people's safety. There was, however, a danger that by naming citizens enemies, the government would be perceived as a bully. The battle to defeat external enemies generally happened somewhere else, and it was much easier to defend the government's motives when innocents were dying over there: in Tripoli or Canada or Mexico, for example, far from the public eye. But when people at home were named enemies, and then deprived of their rights or even killed, the rhetorical stakes increased astronomically. The fight against domestic enemies happened on American soil. Any collateral damage from the war consequently affected the families and property of American civilians, not some dark-skinned "other" whose rights and humanity were easily dismissed with othering rhetorics.[87] The process of naming internal enemies was more demanding rhetorically than naming international enemies, for domestic enemyship was fraught with potentially disastrous political consequences. Initially, President Adams chose to walk this path.

According to Adams, Fries and his men "proceeded in a manner subversive of the just authority of the Government, by misrepresentations to render the laws odious, by deterring the public officers of the United States to forbear the execution of their functions, and by openly threatening their lives."[88] This Pennsylvania auctioneer got the full workup. Fries was a potential revolutionary, a subversive akin to Daniel Shays. He was a traitor who refused to abide by American laws. And he was a pawn of foreign aggressors bent on invasion, subjugation, and the destruction of the Constitution. Sitting at the nexus of American fears, Fries was public enemy number one. Having named Fries an enemy, the president activated the Eventual Army to suppress the treasonous rebels, once again turning the military might of the United States against its own citizens. The army marched into Northampton and Bucks counties on April 4 and had no trouble repressing a minor uprising. Just as citizens in eastern Pennsylvania voted not to oppose the federal army marching into their territory in 1794, so too protestors in the western part of the state voted in 1799. Fries was captured on April 6, and by April 7 most of the "rebels" had been rounded up or had surrendered. The "Northampton Insurrection" ended without a single burned building, military display by protestors, or soldier's death—demonstrating that it was not a "rebellion" like Shays's Rebellion or the Whiskey Rebellion, but protests that Federalists labeled a "rebellion" because they needed enemies to stay in power.

While Adams almost certainly saw the political benefits of a strong response to Fries's Rebellion, there is evidence from his personal correspondence suggesting that he genuinely believed it was a threat to the nation.[89] Unlike Adams, Hamilton had no illusions about the danger posed by Fries's Rebellion. In fact, Hamilton's private letters reveal that he knew that this was no "rebellion" at all. On the contrary, he talked of "rebellion" because he believed that there was political utility in naming domestic enemies. With such enemies afoot, the government's power as the protector of the people would be increased. Moreover, by putting down a transnational conspiracy to topple the United States government, his Federalist Party would become the champions of security and order—making it much easier to paint Jefferson's ascendant Republican Party as the advocates of confusion and anarchy as they headed into the important elections of 1799 and 1800. But, most importantly, domestic enemies justified the amassing of a standing army during peacetime to suppress citizens who believed too deeply in the promises of revolution and democracy.

On March 18, Hamilton drafted instructions for how the military should present itself to Pennsylvanians to ensure the maxim rhetorical effect. "Beware, my Dear Sir, of magnifying a riot into an insurrection, by employing in the first instance an inadequate force," he told Secretary of War James McHenry; "Tis better far to err on the other side." Hamilton clearly understood that the "Northampton Insurrection" was not a "rebellion," but a common "riot"—yet he argued that it should be treated as though it was an "insurrection." Without the proper display of force, a "riot" could become a "rebellion"; Hamilton therefore argued that all unrest, no matter how civil, should be treated as if it was a rebellion. If the army marched into Pennsylvania without sufficient force to rout the rioters, Hamilton prophesied that this would create an impression of weakness that would, in turn, encourage an actual rebellion against the government. He counseled McHenry, "Whenever the Government appears in arms it ought to appear like a *Hercules*, and inspire respect by the display of strength."⁹⁰ For Hamilton, the situation required contradictory exertions. On the one hand, the army had to suppress a "riot" before it became an "insurrection." On the other, the government had to demonstrate to citizens that there was an "insurrection" to justify deploying the army—it had, in short, to demonstrate that the enemies it named were really enemies. It would do this by deploying a mighty force to Pennsylvania, the type of force that would only be deployed to confront real enemies. This was the rhetorical compulsion of enemyship: enemies were named, and then treated like enemies to prove that they were in fact enemies. This was also a dangerous cycle. Though caution was required when deploying enemyship in a republic, this was not a rhetorical strategy that lent itself to delicacy.

Hamilton intended the army to be an engine for civic education, teaching citizens what it meant to be a good citizen in the post-Revolutionary moment. Upon arrival in Pennsylvania, General William MacPherson therefore distributed a manifesto warning citizens of the dire consequences of resisting government. He then proceeded to offer the malcontents a civics lesson in "how just it is to submit to the laws." The battlefield became a classroom as MacPherson explained that the

essence of republican government was obedience to the laws, no matter
how unjust they might seem:

> It cannot be unknown to you, my fellow citizens, nor to any part of the
> people of the United States that submission to the laws, constitution-
> ally made, is absolutely necessary for the support of the government;
> and that in a republic, where laws are made by general consent, this
> consent must be manifested by the majority of such persons as have
> been appointed for that purpose by the people in general, according to
> the constitution.[91]

MacPherson's manifesto spoke directly to one of the central paradoxes of
republican government, the paradox of consent. According to MacPherson, law-breaking was illogical in a republic because all laws flowed from
the people (via their representatives). To break the law was therefore to
transgress one's own will, which was illogical.

Though MacPherson intended this pamphlet to be educative, Pennsylvanians were wrestling with similar issues only to come to a very different conclusion. The Pennsylvanians who rose up in the early 1790s
and in 1799 felt alienated from government. They understood just how
precarious the synecdochal relationship between representative and
represented was, and they were crushed when the government did not
represent their wishes. While the Constitution created a beautiful form
of government—and unlike the Whiskey Rebels, for Fries and his men it
was indeed beautiful—they understood that there was no guarantee that
their representatives would represent their wishes. Theoretically, laws
were expressions of the people's will. But only theoretically. John Fries
and his men had not assented to paying taxes for the military establishment, nor had they assented to the Alien and Sedition Acts. For them,
legislation building armies and gagging dissent was contradictory to the
spirit of the Constitution and, even more galling, their wishes. Accordingly, they resisted the compulsion to consent.

Following his capture, Fries was twice tried for treason (the first was
ruled a mistrial), convicted twice by a Federalist Supreme Court (on
May 7, 1799, and April 24, 1800), and sentenced twice to die. Executing
Fries, it was proclaimed, would act as an example, deterring citizens from

misbehaving.⁹² "The end of all *punishment* is *example*," Supreme Court Justice Samuel Chase told Fries and those present at Fries's trial, "and the enormity of your crime requires that a severe example should be made to deter others from the commission of *like* crimes in the future."⁹³ Chase understood that the constitution of republican subjects works through example, and thus he hoped that citizens would internalize Fries's punishment and thereby learn how not to behave. Executions would also prove, beyond a doubt, that America's enemies were real and not illusory, as Republicans claimed. For Federalists, executions would demonstrate that Fries's Rebellion was authentic, would position their party as strong leaders tough on crime, and would work by example to constitute law-abiding, deferential subjects. Fries was therefore sentenced to hang along with his friends and accomplices, John Gettman and Frederick Heaney, on May 23 at the intersection of Bethlehem and Norristown Roads in Quakertown, near his home in Lower Milford. As their lifeless bodies swayed in the wind, the dead traitors would stand as an example of the damnation that would befall all of America's enemies—rebels, levellers, traitors alike.

On the day he was sentenced to death, Fries had to withstand the punishment of Justice Chase's acid tongue as he harangued the condemned for his unconscionable behavior. Chase reminded Fries that "You live under a constitution (or form of government) framed by the people themselves; and under laws made by your representatives, faithfully executed by independent and impartial judges. Your government secures to every member of the community *equal liberty* and *equal rights* . . . You enjoyed, in common with your fellow-citizens, *all those rights*." With rights come responsibilities, including the duty to submit to the laws of the United States, which were, Federalists repeatedly said, made by representatives elected by "the people." Citizens invested their political power in their representatives, and when they violated the laws that purportedly originated with them, they deserved to die. The tone of Chase's speech was consistently indignant, revealing his continued frustration with common folks who simply did not understand the post-Revolutionary order of things. Reading his words, it seems that Chase could not understand why anyone would violate the laws—this was not monarchy, he insisted. "It is almost incredible, that a people living under the best and mildest government in the whole world, should not only be dissatisfied and discontented, but should break out into open resistance and opposition to its laws," he claimed, implying that Fries's actions were naive, yet worthy of punishment nevertheless because of their baleful consequences. To justify sentencing Fries to death, Chase detailed the likely consequences of his protests, which included violence, oppression, rapine, destruction, waste, murder, fratricide, and the eventual death of the state. For Federalists, the state had to step in with full force to correct citizens who simply could not behave as they were told.[94]

To perpetuate the enemyship of the XYZ Affair into 1799, and to further the constitution of a post-Revolutionary republican government, Federalists labeled a group of poor German Americans enemies. Enemies had to be subjugated, and the government deployed an army to Pennsylvania. The Federalist press, in turn, proclaimed the military expedition a success. On April 19, 1799, the *Gazette of the United States* reported that the "deluded people" in Northampton were "completely subdued, and many of them begin to be sensible of their error."[95] Similarly, *Kline's Carlisle Weekly Gazette* of Carlisle, Pennsylvania, reported on April 24, 1799, that the military expedition in rebel territory was "hourly producing the most salutary effects upon the minds of the people." "Many, who were led away by misrepresentation, have become sensible of the artifices practiced upon them; while others, more determined in their hatred to government, sullenly submit to its operation," this paper noted.[96] Yet it, and the *Gazette of the United States* as well, was shortsighted, for while the military contained protests, it also wreaked havoc on Pennsylvanians. Most arrests were conducted after midnight, reminding citizens of the dark days of the 1770s when British troops terrorized families in their homes. The application of military force is rarely precise, and when it spills over, the innocent victims become enraged. This is one of the most sobering consequences of enemyship.

Federalists named enemies and then acted as though they were indeed enemies. Republicans battled back by arguing that Fries and his men were not enemies, and by suggesting that the military expedition in Pennsylvania proved Federalists despots, not effective leaders. Of course, the two complaints were linked; Federalists became despots in order to prove that Fries was an enemy. And though Federalists attempted to shut down the Republican press with the Sedition Act, Americans around the country nevertheless read several damning letters from Americans on the scene that framed the military "success" in a different light. On April 11, the same day that MacPherson ordered his army to stage an elaborate military demonstration in order to create the appearance of the army's military strength and cement the seriousness of his manifesto to misbehaving citizens, the *Aurora* printed a letter from a witness to the army's actions, who attested: "The system of terror here I am sorry to say is carried far beyond what in my opinion the public good requires." "The scenes of distress I have witnessed among these poor people, I cannot describe," this writer noted, but asked his or her readers to put them- selves in the victims' shoes: "Conceive your house entered at dead of night by a body of armed men, and yourself dragged from your wife and screaming children." "These poor people are extremely ignorant but they have feelings, and they always consider that death awaits any one who is seized, be he culpable or not," this observer concluded, chastising the army, and the government, for "an inhuman disposition exhibited" with these simple words: "They have feelings."[97] The Pennsylvania Germans were not traitors intent on subverting the Constitution, as Federalists like Justice Chase said. They were people, too, with the same feelings, the same fears, and the same rights as other citizens. By appealing to the shame and pity of the audience, and to their basic human decency, this writer worked to undo the government's enemyship. The army's actions did not nurture respect. Instead, the army's actions cultivated anger at governing elites desperately seeking to bolster their legitimacy.

The disturbing consequences of domestic enemyship became ap- parent in the diaries of two volunteers in the Eventual Army. These soldiers embodied the republican emphasis on virtuous self-sacrifice by risking their lives to defend the Constitution. However, they soon found themselves questioning the government's motives and its rhetoric. The first soldier reported that "Had I conceived that some things, which I have witnessed here could have taken place, I should have never given my assent to march a mile on the expedition." The second echoed these sentiments, questioning the efficacy, and the morality, of coercion. He wrote: "I can scarcely persuade myself that I tread on the soil of Penn- sylvania when I witness the sufferings of these poor, well-meaning, but ignorant, Germans. They are treated in no respect like citizens of the same country."⁹⁸ These soldiers gained first-hand experience of their "enemies," and as they did, they learned that protestors were not enemies, but misguided, though well-intentioned, fellow citizens. The consistent theme of ignorance in reports made the army's laborious march unwarranted. The spectacle of state terror got them and others thinking that there had to be better ways of governing, and as they did, they and others turned their backs on Federalists.

During Shays's Rebellion, militia in Massachusetts refused the government's call for help, instead siding with protestors. Protest lost none of its virulence in the early Republic, but more and more Americans were willing to heed the government's call for aid—making insurrection easier to control. While many Americans answered President Washington's call and volunteered to march into Pennsylvania following the Whiskey Rebellion, becoming part of the Army of the Constitution, and while citizens expressed their willingness to come to the nation's call after the XYZ Affair, soldiers in 1799 came to believe that Adams's government violated the republican spirit of the Constitution. Republicanism called for deference to the decisions of governing elites, but it also called for these elites to respect the dignity and rights of citizens. For republicanism to work, the government had to treat citizens as friends to be engaged in dialogue, rather than as enemies to be repressed. During the XYZ Affair and Fries's Rebellion, Adams's government attempted to establish its authority by naming enemies and then providing Americans with protection from those enemies. There were limits to enemyship, however—especially when the enemies named were American citizens, and especially when what the government called protection looked dangerously like politically motivated repression. Understanding that Federalists had gone too far, a disgruntled but prescient officer writing from Millarstown, Pennsylvania, on April 10 correctly predicted: "One effect produced by the distress is that every individual, whom I meet, is disgusted, and a sentiment generally prevails, which, contrary to expectation, will, I apprehend, completely destroy the federal influence at the next election."⁹⁹ He was right, for the suppression of democratic protests turned popular sentiment against the government in Pennsylvania—just as history suggested it would.

Following the Massachusetts government's decision to forcefully suppress the popular protests of Shays's Rebellion with an army four thousand strong, popular opinion turned against Governor James Bowdoin's government. That government went too far as well, reminding many citizens of what it was like to live in the 1770s under the imperial British forces. In the April 1787 state elections, Massachusetts citizens went to the poles an angry and restless bunch. The lopsided election produced a 74 percent turnover in the House of Representatives, and a new governor, John Hancock. In Massachusetts, the violent suppression of domestic enemies backfired. During the 1799 election in Pennsylvania, Republicans lambasted Federalists for turning common citizens into enemies, publishing a newspaper called *Cannibal's Progress* that was devoted to the singular purpose of publicizing the army's abuses.[100] Essayists in Republican newspapers like the *Aurora* reiterated that Fries was not an enemy, and that the crisis was contrived for partisan purposes. "It is said that ALEXANDER HAMILTON has once more arrived in this city—For what purpose? can it be to foment another insurrection, and thereby to encrease the energies of the government?" the *Aurora* asked, poking fun at a political enemy but also proving that it understood what Hamilton and other Federalists were doing, and had been doing since the 1780s—fomenting insurrections in order to prove the necessity of a stronger government.[101]

Having labeled Fries's Rebellion a hoax, a fabrication on the part of a government seeking to manufacture consent, the *Aurora* treated the government's response with contempt. "Whence this precipitation on the part of the government of the United States, to march a body of troops against the people of Northampton and Bucks?" this paper asked, continuing: "Are these people in arms against the government? No one will dare to say that they are. Whence then, it may be asked again, such precipitation?" The *Aurora* contrasted President Adams's response to Fries's Rebellion with President Washington's response to the Whiskey Rebellion, for at least Washington tried proclamations and other actions before deploying military force to Pennsylvania. Demonstrating that Washington had already ceased to be a real political actor and instead had achieved the status of a mythical superhero above politics, this paper argued that Washington, unlike Adams, "was not of the opinion that men like himself were first to be tossed upon the bayonet, and afterwards instructed in their duty." Whether or not Washington actually believed this was unimportant, for the *Aurora* hoped to decouple Washington from his vice president and then to use the former president's memory against Adams in the upcoming election. This was classic partisan warfare. Yet at the heart of the *Aurora*'s cant was a grain of political truth, a lesson from the rough-and-tumble political world of the late 1790s as important as the tried-and-true efficacy of enemyship:

> It is true that in despotic government, where there are no citizens, but where all are slaves, and where *force* and not reason is the alphabet of instruction; in such government indeed, it would be incongruous to argue the people into obedience. The logic of bayonets is there the only one employed, and it is employed with *promptitude*. Is there any analogy between such a government and ours? If not, why such a similarity of measures?[102]

The promise of republicanism is one of rhetoric replacing violence as a means of conflict resolution. This is one of the chief reasons that the Revolutionary War was waged: in order to establish a government of laws where disagreements were settled with deliberation, not force. In republics, politicians are supposed to govern with language, not force. The sin of the Federalists was not naming enemies. The art of enemyship was, even at this early point, central to politics and public culture. All politicians named enemies. Future politicians would continue to name enemies. The sin of Federalists was how they treated the enemies they named. The mere presence of enemies—real or fabricated—need not lead to enemyship. Political actors need not employ the rhetorical maneuvers of estrangement and escalation. Instead, they might employ the contrasting rhetorical maneuvers of reconciliation and deflation to keep the relationship between enemies within the bounds of comity. Republican government creates space for enemies to coexist, but only if a commitment to deliberation is maintained—which is, we should note, no small thing in itself. Federalists violated norms of civil deliberation by conceiving a republic in which there was no offering of opinions, no exchanging of perspectives, and no public debate. In this republic, where there was no middle ground, where everyone was either a friend or enemy, and where all dissent was treated like rebellion, critics rightfully charged

Federalists with transgressing the limits of republicanism and moving the United States toward despotism.

Many Americans came to believe that Federalist authority rested on the logic of bayonets, and in a nation that still remembered the Revolutionary War, the rhetoric of bayonets misfired—just as they had done for the British in the 1770s and the Massachusetts government in 1787. The Republican campaign to turn public opinion against Federalists was successful. Widespread dissent in Pennsylvania led to the landslide victory of a Republican, Thomas McKean, in the fall 1799 gubernatorial election.[103] And this electoral defeat, Adams understood, was a harbinger of things to come.

Beyond Enemyship

Curiously, after the XYZ Affair, Adams left America's seat of government in Philadelphia and returned to his hometown of Quincy, Massachusetts, acting as president from afar. Having returned to the state where Shays's Rebellion was born, Adams watched his fellow Federalists react to protests in Pennsylvania with rising alarm. He understood that McKean's election was a referendum on Federalism. To salvage his presidency and soothe the wounds created by his rhetorical leadership, Adams pardoned Fries and everyone else involved in the brouhaha. With his enemyship, Adams closed the space for dialogue and dissent. With his pardon, Adams reopened this space by arguing that protestors were not enemies but "miserable Germans" who were "as ignorant of our language as they were of our laws."[104] Labeling protestors ignorant, not enemies, Adams reiterated vernacular discourse about Fries's Rebellion that paved the way for Fries and his men to be reincorporated into the body politic and the community of friends. During this moment, Adams came to understand that when carried too far, enemyship destabilized society by making citizens resentful of state power.

To say that Hamilton disagreed with Adams about how best to govern would be a grave understatement. The president's decision to pardon Fries infuriated him; he interpreted it as a conspiracy, an anti-Hamiltonian, pro-Jeffersonian plot. Ten years earlier, Hamilton had collaborated with

Madison to create *The Federalist*, one of the most significant statements of American political philosophy ever penned. Yet in 1799, an enraged Hamilton wrote something much dumber: a scandalous tract denouncing the president's behavior. This pamphlet, titled *A Letter from Alexander Hamilton, Concerning the Conduct and Character of John Adams, Esq, President of the United States,* detailed Adams's many failings and injustices and implied that Adams was a deranged lunatic. To defuse the danger of another Adams administration, Hamilton called on his fellow Federalists to endorse Charles Cotesworth Pinckney instead of the incumbent for president. Though this heated rant was intended as a private communiqué between Hamilton and his friends, Aaron Burr obtained a copy and leaked it to the *Aurora*, which gleefully published excerpts on October 25, 1799. To avoid misrepresentation, Hamilton soon published the diatribe in its entirety, to almost universal shock and scorn. Needless to say, Burr's actions contributed to Hamilton's downfall in more ways than one, for this was one provocation for their fatal duel.[105]

In May 1800, Adams took aim at two of Hamilton's foremost allies, forcing Secretary of War James McHenry to resign, and firing Secretary of State Timothy Pickering. Adams's audacity outraged Hamilton—but his greatest vitriol was reserved for the president's response to Fries's Rebellion. Though Hamilton knew that the "Northampton Insurrection" was a rhetorical construction on the part of a government hoping to augment its powers over the lives and deaths of Americans, he defended deploying the New Army to Pennsylvania "to destroy this dangerous spirit" of rebellion. A consistent champion of coercion because he doubted the moral constitution of citizens and feared that they were easily manipulated, Hamilton decried Adams's decision to pardon Fries. Not only did Adams miss an opportunity to portray the state as powerful and to strike yet another blow in the now decades' long war against democracy, Hamilton maintained, his actions sent the wrong message to domestic enemies and their Jacobin buddies. Fries's dead body would have deterred potential traitors, and therefore Adams's clemency was "disavowed by every page of our law books." He wrote:

> No wonder that the public was thunderstruck at such a result—that
> the friends of Government regarded it as a virtual dereliction—it was

impossible to commit a greater error. The particular situation in Pennsylvania, the singular posture of human affairs, in which there is so strong a tendency to the disorganization of Government—the turbulent and malignant humors which exist, and are so industriously nourished throughout the Untied States; every thing loudly demanded that the Executive should have acted with exemplary vigor, and should have given a striking demonstration, that condign punishment would be the lot of the violent oppressors of the laws.[106]

For Hamilton, humans naturally shunned government and tended towards anarchy; only formidable state violence could hold things together. Believing that punishment was the best deterrent of wrongdoing and the best incentive for correct behavior, Hamilton called on the state to execute Fries to prevent citizens from realizing their malevolent designs—especially in Pennsylvania, which was, as far as he and many other Federalists were concerned, a toxic breeding ground for anarchy. According to Hamilton, Adams's weakness gave heart to the unruly demos. "It is by temporisings like these," Hamilton concluded, "that in times of fermentation and commotion, Governments are prostrated, which might easily have been upheld by an erect and imposing attitude."[107] Taunting Adams as a flaccid leader too weak to do what the nation-building project demanded he do, Hamilton destroyed his own political career to defend the repression of internal enemies who were not really enemies at all.

Adams broke from Hamilton and the negative consequences of enemyship—but it was too late to stop his party's precipitous fall. To fend off popular and political disapproval, Federalists voted to end enlistments in the New Army in January 1800. They then voted to disband the army altogether in May. Nevertheless, Hamilton's public disagreement with Adams over how best to govern made the divisions that had been developing within Federalism manifest to voters, splintering the party into supporters of Adams and supporters of Hamilton's candidate, Pinckney. Hamilton hence assisted Jefferson's election by breaking up tried and true Federalist political alliances. Adams learned from the events of the late 1790s, but it was too late to save his political career. While the enemy made his presidency, ultimately Adams was one of the first politicians in American history done in by the negative consequences of enemyship.

CONCLUSION

Hobbes's Gamble
and Franklin's Warning

In *Examination into the Leading Principles of the Federal Constitution* (1787), Noah Webster asked a question that was on the minds of all the founders—a question that if adequately answered would solve all of the problems posed by the nation-building project: "In what consists the power of a nation or of an order of men?"[1] Significantly, he returned to the English philosopher Thomas Hobbes to answer this question. "The present situation of our American states is very little better than a state of nature," Webster reported. In a state of nature, there was no government, and "Suppose every man to act without control or fear of punishment—every man would be free, but no man would be sure of his freedom one moment. Each would have the power of taking his neighbor's life, liberty or property; and no man would command more than his own strength to repel the invasion." "From such liberty, O Lord, deliver us!" Webster concluded.[2] Webster was a brilliant lexicographer, and we know him today because of his inescapable red-white-and-blue-covered *American*

Dictionary. His *Examination into the Leading Principles of the Federal Constitution* revealed that he was also an astute student of power. In 1787, Webster discovered a philosophical foundation for political power in Hobbes.

A land of fascinating contradictions, the United States is founded on multiple ironies. The most obvious is that the Declaration of Independence, written by a slave owner, proclaimed life, liberty, and the pursuit of happiness inalienable rights. While not as glaring, two further ironies were central to the post-Revolutionary moment. The first was that while the founders publicly claimed that sovereignty rested with "the people," common citizens neither authored America's Constitution nor ran the first governments. Sovereignty in the early Republic was delegated to representatives, and thus, Dr. Benjamin Rush observed in 1787, "all power is derived from the people, they possess it only on the days of their elections. After this it is the property of their rulers."[3] This statement was misleading; many elite politicians hoped that citizens would exercise sovereignty only on election days. In actuality, the idea of popular sovereignty in the early United States had little to do with voting and everything to do with the ultimate threat. The people possessed sovereignty because of the precedent of 1776: if things got bad, they could legitimately stage a revolution and start over. Only this never happened, for the American political system was designed to prevent this possibility. The second irony, then, had to do with how the founders managed to tell the people they had the right to scrap the whole system, while ensuring that this right would never be exercised. This was paradoxical, because as the founders pragmatically tested their ideas about governing against reality, they—like Noah Webster—were led back to the philosophy of Thomas Hobbes. Born from a revolution against monarchy, the republican founders of the United States returned to the playbook of kings.

Given his philosophical doctrines, Hobbes had an auspicious birthday: April 5, 1588, the eve of the Spanish Armada's invasion of England. "My mother was filled with such fear," he later joked, "that she bore twins, me and together with me fear."[4] Hobbes was a tutor in Paris during the English Civil War from 1642 to 1651, and as the royalists fled to the continent, Hobbes befriended many refugees and tutored the young Prince of Wales. His philosophy was molded in response to a civil war that claimed over 180,000 lives, including King Charles I. His two major treatises were published in 1651: *Leviathan* and an English translation of *De Cive*, "On the Citizen," which had originally been published in Latin in 1642. Both works were driven by the desire to theorize how the acquisitive individual—the modern subject—could be persuaded to submit to a sovereign power. Grasping the transforming power of fear better than any thinker of his generation, Hobbes premised his answer on a nightmare.[5] To convince self-interested individuals, desirous of power above all else, to band together into nations, Hobbes contrasted the security and prosperity of nations with the "perpetual fear of death" in the state of nature, before nations, laws, or government.[6]

In Hobbes's state of nature, humans lived in perpetual terror because they were equal to their foes. The strong did not have a monopoly on survival in this state; weapons and mobs evened everything out. In the state of nature, "every man is Enemy to every man," and therefore there could be no rest, reprieve, or respite.[7] There was no morality other than kill or be killed. Kicking, biting, scratching: it was all fair game in the fight for one's life. In the state of nature, "nothing can be Unjust. The notions of Right and Wrong, Justice and Injustice have there no place." The resulting panic caused even the most basic social exchanges to break down. Hobbes's state of nature was a picture of everything good steadily grinding to a halt. In the war of all against all, there was no industry; no harvest; no travel; no communication; "no account of Time; no Arts; no Letters; no Society." In one of the most famous passages in western literature, Hobbes pronounced "the life of man" in this degraded state "solitary, poore, nasty, brutish, and short."[8]

Hobbes's state of nature was an allegory for the primal human fear of death. For him, humans were tormented by the fact that they would die. The first rule of human nature was therefore self-preservation; for Hobbes, humans desired safety above all else.[9] Yet in the absence of a coercive power, life was fragile. The state of nature was a state of war because everyone was equal and there were no consequences. The state of nature Hobbes described was so terrible because the most basic social binary, friend or foe, collapsed. Everyone in the state of nature was potentially an enemy all the time. There was no trust. A life in the state of nature was a life perpetually on the edge of disaster. A century earlier,

Niccolò Machiavelli instructed leaders to treat everyone as enemies, and every gesture, no matter how benevolent, as the sign of a conspiracy.[10] While Machiavelli counseled leaders not to trust anyone, Hobbes understood that perpetual suspicion was too taxing for most people. Obsessed with death, and constantly looking over our shoulders: this was a state too awful to last. To ease humanity's fears, Hobbes argued for the creation of the Leviathan: a monarchal state ruled by the sovereign's iron fist. In the Leviathan, subjects traded their natural rights for protection from danger.

Hobbes positioned monarchy as the cure for humanity's existential fears. Even if we grant his picture of the state of nature, his philosophy seemed poorly equipped to achieve its aim. How could his sovereign rule? Early liberal philosophers, including John Locke, argued for obedience, because laws were contractual negotiations between ruler and ruled that, when violated by the sovereign, could be renegotiated. Hobbes made no such claim. Moreover, he was emphatic that citizens did not possess the right of revolution, a cornerstone of Lockean social-contract theory. For Locke, the end of government was "the good of mankind." When rulers abused this good, citizens were permitted to remove them with revolutions like the Glorious Revolution of 1688 and the American Revolution.[11] For Hobbes, the end of government was not the public good or social happiness, but peace. In Hobbes's world, the sovereign need not forbid revolution, because it was banned by natural right.[12] For Hobbes, humans did not bargain with their rulers; rather, they made a free gift of their rights to the sovereign in the hope that he would provide protection. Hobbes's subjects entered society without the ability to make demands on a sovereign. So long as the sovereign did not violate the fundamental law of nature, to pursue peace at all costs and war only if peace was impossible, citizens were bound to obey. *Protego ergo obligo*, Hobbes claimed—protection therefore obligation, or, to put it slightly differently, the sovereign's ability to provide protection created the obligation to obey.[13]

People formed governments to achieve protection in the sanctuary of the state, where human frailty was offset by the strength of the body politic. Hobbes's thought experiment about the state of nature revealed the nature of the state: at bottom, it was the protector of bodies and the guarantor of self-preservation, organizing "the repelling of a foreign enemy."[14] Though Hobbes framed the Leviathan as an antidote to war, it nevertheless depended upon the fear of the enemy characteristic of wartime for its existence. If the state existed to repel foreign enemies, there had to be foreign enemies to repel. The sovereign's power was premised on its ability to protect, yet protection required danger. The Leviathan functioned only in the presence of a threat—which meant that politicians had to court enemies even while they talked of peace, or else the fragile bonds between individuals would break and the state would cease to exist.[15] Hobbes's Leviathan walked a performative tightrope, professing peace while courting war. It was an imperial machine, seeking out dangers and threats to national security when there were none to justify its continued existence.

Like many other Enlightenment philosophers, Hobbes was deeply mistrustful of rhetoric.[16] For him, the dangers of rhetoric were symbolized by the preaching orators of the English Civil War and the Christian rhetoric of "conscience," which precluded compromise and discussion between political adversaries. Hobbes's solution was to divest citizens of their power to judge the world, and give this power to the sovereign. When people had to talk in public in Hobbes's world, they would be guided by reason. In fact, Hobbes was the first modern philosopher to use the term "public reason," which in *Leviathan* signified a set of discursive conditions for guiding public discussion in spite of private or personal disagreements.[17] By providing citizens with a set of rules for judgment, reason altered the meaning of civic judgment. Hobbes was not the only philosopher to place his faith in reason. Equally distrustful of rhetoric, Immanuel Kant did as well. Yet Hobbes's conception of reason was very different from Kant's, and Hobbes's philosophy created a space for rhetoric in a way that Kant's did not.

While Hobbes favored a polity guided by public reason, this was not an anti-rhetorical polity—for Hobbes meant something very specific and deeply rhetorical by reason: namely, the desire to secure peace at any cost.[18] Hobbes's understanding of peace unfolded against the backdrop of the state of nature: a state of pure, unadulterated, existential terror. In such a state, humans spent all their time looking over their shoulders, waiting for a knife in the back. Hobbes understood that people could not live for long in such a state, and he therefore predicted that the desire to be free from war would result in the free gift of citizens' natural rights

to a sovereign promising safety. The flight from fear was the beginning of
the social. He reasoned: "All men as soon as they arrive to understanding
of this hateful condition, do desire, even nature itself compelling them,
to be freed from this misery."[19] Hobbes awakened his audience (in a very
different way than René Descartes) to the true meaning of the *cogito*. I
think, therefore I pursue peace. Reason was not the slave of the passions,
as David Hume argued; reason was a slave of self-preservation, which
called on humans to submit to state power.

For Hobbes, humans were frightened, lonely, anxious beings in
search of peace. "Anxiety for the future time, disposeth men to enquire
into the causes of things," he wrote. Anxiety was the engine of civilization,
compromise, and scientific inquiry. Politics for Hobbes was the process of
transforming anxiety into stability, obedience, and political truth. Hobbes
therefore distinguished between "Feare," which for him signified "*Aversion*, with opinion of *Hurt* from the object," and "Panique Terror," which
was "*Feare*, without the apprehension of why, or what."[20] Fear for Hobbes
was a natural reaction to a concrete, specific danger; panic, however, was
fear without a cause. Panic was an ambiguous, vague fear in reaction to a
nebulous threat. While the state of nature was a state of fear, specifically
it was a state of panic: for there were no friends, and one was constantly
in danger of being killed.

Peace had to be understood in relationship to this distinction. For
Hobbes, "The nature of War, consisteth not in actuall fighting; but in
the known disposition thereto, during all the time there is no assurance
to the contrary. All other time is Peace."[21] Peace was a state in between
wars and the preparation for war. Peace was a stillness characterized by
the absence of worry and fear. Peace was a mental state of calm in which
anxiety just ebbed away. The fact that peace was a physical state (the absence of war) and also a mental state (the feeling of calm in the absence
of worry) had profound implications for Hobbes's political and rhetorical
theory. Because peace existed on a mental level, it was subject to symbolic manipulation. While humans naturally existed in a state of panic,
the sovereign ruled by naming enemies and thereby mitigating panic so
that humans could live in peace by stepping in and naming enemies—
helping people cope with their anxieties by giving them a cause, a name,
and a face. Naming enemies was a way to cultivate politically useful fear,

and at the same time to name enemies was to point toward a cure for anxiety by concretizing worry. Reason, or the drive to achieve peace at any cost, therefore enabled symbolic manipulation of the masses by a clever sovereign. Reason—or the drive for peace at any and all costs—allowed the sovereign to rule.

Clearly, the Revolutionary War was a rebellion against Hobbes's vision of the state. Sovereignty was one of the most significant issues that divided Americans from the British during the 1760s and 1770s. Hobbes articulated a theory of indivisible and unlimited sovereignty residing in the king, yet the American theory of sovereignty was born out of a set of material conditions that allowed for precisely the opposite: in the colonies, power was divided, local, and popular.[22] There was no way that Americans could establish a government like Hobbes's, nor did they desire to. Unlike the machinations of Hobbes's Leviathan, the techniques of governing in the United States had to be subtle and indulge citizens' democratic longings. But the founders still faced many of the problems that Hobbes addressed. While the Constitution divided sovereignty between the judicial, legislative, and executive branches; between the federal, state, and local governments; and, presumably, between government and the people, it had to compel assent to the laws, persuade citizens to work together for the common good, and temper the democratic impulses that exploded in revolution in the 1770s. It had, in short, to make Americans obedient to government, rather than the other way around. Though they sought to establish a republic and not a monarchy, Hobbes's philosophy of sovereignty and techniques of governing were extremely useful for the founders.

Hobbes's genius was to conceptualize sovereignty and political power as the products of pageantry and theater. Hobbes's sovereign manipulated the people's fears and exaggerated dangers in order to justify his rule as necessary for their protection. Hobbes the monarchist hence taught the founders of the United States two essential lessons about governance. First, that the point of government was to provide protection. And second, that political authority could be achieved by harnessing fear. While it was undoubtedly true that genuine threats to individual liberty and national security did exist, Hobbes imagined a world in which politicians exploited their constituents' fears to bolster their authority and manufacture consent by naming the enemy.

"A Little Temporary Safety"

Benjamin Franklin was prescient. In preparation for the Albany Confer-
ence of June 1754, Franklin published his famous sketch "JOIN, or DIE" in
the *Pennsylvania Gazette*—an image of a segmented snake representing
colonial union in the face of its enemies that was reprinted up and down
the seaboard that year. Later, during the Stamp Act Crisis of 1765–66, the
image took on a life of its own as a representation of united colonial resistance to Parliamentary sovereignty in America. Lester Olson notes that
"this was the earliest known pictorial representation of colonial union
produced by a British colonist in America."[23] Drawing on both secular
and biblical images and beliefs common at the time, Franklin compared
the fate of the colonies to that of the snake. Olson observes: "As a rhetorical technique, the illustration was a figurative analogy or proportional
metaphor: the colonies were to their fate what a segmented snake was
to its fate. The caption stated the conclusion: the colonies could join,
or die."[24] In offering up the earliest known representation of American
unity, Franklin also offered up one of the first—if not the first—visions
of enemyship in the American context. Concerned to cement the loyalty
of the Iroquois Confederacy on the New York and Pennsylvania colonial
borders in the ongoing struggle with the French and their Indian allies
during the Seven Years War, confident that the colonies united could better defend themselves from incursions and invasions, and certain that a
united colonial front would prevent attacks by causing enemies to think
twice about attacking, Franklin promoted unity in the divided colonies by
threatening them with death. Do this or else, he argued, forecasting the
catastrophic consequences of division for the future.

 Franklin foreshadowed the type of enemyship Paine employed in
Common Sense, calling on Americans to unite in the face of danger.
The call for unity is one of the most basic modalities of enemyship. It
has probably existed since the beginning of human history, and it is in
no way unique to the American story. There was nothing revolutionary
about how Franklin hoped to engender unity. And, when it comes down
to it, there was nothing particularly revolutionary about Paine's rhetoric,
either. He simply arranged and articulated a rhetorical strategy that was

uniquely adapted to the rhetorical situation of the American colonies in 1776. What was revolutionary was what politicians did with enemyship in the post-Revolutionary moment.

Just as colonists redeployed Franklin's snake image during the Stamp Act crisis in ways that he did not intend and that, in fact, he actively reproached, so too politicians redeployed Paine's enemyship during the early Republic in ways that were counter to Paine's purpose in *Common Sense*. Paine hoped to create a more democratic world through enemyship; governing elites in the 1780s and 1790s used enemyship to make the United States less democratic. While the enemyship of Franklin and Paine was designed to promote American unity in the face of danger, politicians in the early Republic deployed enemyship to alter citizens' behaviors and subjectivities. By talking of danger, by calling on Americans to trade obedience for protection, and by stressing that Americans had a contract of blood with past martyrs that demanded their support of government, politicians transformed enemyship from a type of war rhetoric into a technique of governing. Here, again, Franklin was prescient—for he had foreseen this possibility well before the other founders of the United States.

In November 1755, in the midst of fighting in the Susquehanna Valley during the Seven Years War, a controversy broke out in the Pennsylvania Assembly.[25] In response to colonial governor Robert Hunter Morris's charge, the Assembly passed a militia law and funding for defense; they also inquired into why the Shawnees and Delawares, who had been British allies, had defected to the French. They asked the governor if it had to do with the Indians' "grievances," and then called on him to do everything in his power to regain their friendship. Governor Morris did not respond kindly. He denounced the Assembly's message of friendship, taking particular umbrage at the Assembly's focus on the grievances "of the Indians so engaged in laying waste the Country, and butchering the Inhabitants."[26] He also rejected the Assembly's plan for taxing estates to raise funds for defense, arguing that it was not in his power to pass such legislation. Hearing the governor's angry words, the Assembly designated a committee to draft a reply. Franklin was a member of this committee, and while we have long since forgotten the context, the immortal words of his reply live on in public memory even today.

After expressing frustration with the system by which colonial funding decisions were made, this committee bristled at the governor's harsh
words about Indians. "As this Colony had been founded on Maxims of
Peace, and had hitherto maintained an uninterrupted Friendship with
the Natives, by a strict Observation of Treaties, conferring Benefits on
them from Time to Time, as well as doing them Justice on all Occasions,
it could not but surprise us to hear, that our old Friends were on a sudden
become our cruel Enemies," they reasoned, positioning this particular
moment in the context of Pennsylvania's well-founded traditions of peace
and diplomacy with neighboring Indian nations. In such a case, when
who was and was not an enemy was indeterminate, "it seemed natural and
proper for us to enquire . . . whether the Indians complained of any Injury
from this Providence, either in regard to their Lands, or on any other
Account; and to express our Readiness to do them Justice (in case such
Complaints were well founded) before Hostilities were returned, and the
Mischief grew more extensive."[27] Pennsylvania had enough enemies; it
did not need more—if these enemies could be made friends again.

The rejoinder ended with a plea for solidarity between Pennsylvanians living in Philadelphia and on the distant western frontier, and an
assurance that the Assembly was doing all it could, given the bureaucratic
shackles imposed from without, to offer these western colonists protection from danger. "In fine, we have the most sensible Concern for the
poor distressed Inhabitants of the Frontiers. We have taken every Step
in our Power, consistent with the just Rights of the Freemen of Pennsylvania, for their Relief, and we have Reason to believe, that in the Midst
of their Distresses they themselves do not wish us to go farther," the
committee reported—announcing that while safety was important, there
were nevertheless limits to what a governing body should do in order to
secure protection for its constituents. The committee did not enumerate
what "Reason" it had to assume that frontier colonists believed, even in
the midst of their distress, that the Assembly should not take any further
steps to provide protection. It even left tantalizingly vague what such
steps might look like. But it did announce in the next sentence, which
seems jarring given the lack of transition: "Those who would give up
essential Liberty, to purchase a little temporary Safety, deserve neither
Liberty nor Safety."[28] What colonists on the frontier feared—a fear that

was seconded by Franklin's committee—was that Pennsylvanians might abdicate their essential liberties to a colonial government promising them safety from their enemies.

With an almost intuitive grasp of the power dynamics of government and subjection, Franklin warned against what we might call Hobbes's gamble. Hobbes bet that citizens would trade their liberties for protection, and thus he called on the king to frighten citizens into obedience to the laws. Fear was at the heart of Hobbes's government: fear of punishment, and fear of the enemy. Recognizing that liberty was fragile and easily trampled by government, Franklin attempted to prescribe the boundaries of what government should, and should not, do. Good government protected citizens, but it did not ask them to trade liberty for protection. A government that protected citizens by taking their liberties was as bad as a government that did not protect citizens. There had to be a balance, Franklin insisted, between liberty and safety. Moreover, he recognized that safety was necessarily "temporary." There would always be new dangers to the safety of Pennsylvanians, meaning that a government that took away liberties in 1755 would have very little reason to return them in 1756 or 1757 or later. Safety was fleeting. So, too, was liberty—for once abdicated, it would not be easily returned.

Franklin's rhetoric reveals a tension at the heart of the American experiment. Franklin threatened colonists with destruction in 1754 if they did not unite to meet their enemies: "JOIN, or DIE." In 1755, he then warned Pennsylvanians never to trade their liberties for "a little temporary safety." But more than that: he chastised those who engaged in Hobbes's gamble, suggesting that they did not "deserve" the liberty they abdicated or the safety they may or may not have achieved. The threatening rhetorics of enemyship, of JOIN or DIE, however, encouraged Americans to do just this—to trade what rights they had for protection, or face certain death at the hands of enemies who were wicked and savage, who would not listen to reason, and who were plotting disaster. Franklin was right to caution Americans not to trade liberty for security. But he did not tell them how to balance these competing demands. This was a tension that subsequent generations of Americans had to negotiate for themselves.

Like those who lived through the Seven Years War, Americans who lived through the Revolutionary War were forced to ponder the proper balance of liberty and security. The rhetorics of security were central to the justifications for the Revolutionary War. In *Common Sense*, Paine argued that Americans were no longer obligated to obey the king, because he no longer kept them safe. Jefferson similarly denounced the king for declaring "us out of his Protection" in the Declaration of Independence, arguing that Americans now had to protect themselves. The Declaration made safety central to its vision of independence. The most famous phrase in the Declaration was and undoubtedly remains "life, liberty and the pursuit of happiness." Generations of beguiled Americans have attempted to understand what Jefferson meant by this phrase, and as they unraveled its strategic ambiguity they almost always reinterpreted its meaning in light of what happiness meant to them and during their time. Most did not realize that this phrase was common in the eighteenth century, and one of the things it entailed was safety. Alluding to Micah 4:4, Pauline Maier notes that "for Jefferson and his contemporaries, happiness no doubt demanded safety or security, which would have been in keeping with the biblical phrase one colonist after another used to describe the good life—to be at peace under their vine and fig tree with none to make them afraid."[29] Safety was foundational to the logic of the Declaration. Obviously, life required safety. So did liberty, as Montesquieu insisted in his profoundly influential *The Spirit of Laws* (1748).[30] To the extent that life, liberty, and the pursuit of happiness is an American mantra, so too is the sanctity of safety.

The Revolutionary War was justified as essential for securing the safety of Americans and their families. So, too, was the Constitution. Both the Constitution's defenders and its opponents agreed that the point of government was to provide citizens with security. In his list of the "principle purposes to be answered by union," Hamilton placed "the common defense of the members" first—a sentiment echoed by the anti-federalist Cato, who claimed that "Government, to an American, is the science of his political safety."[31] While anti-federalists fought tooth-and-nail against a form of government they believed was designed to promote financial inequality and military despotism, such statements played right into the hands of the counter-revolutionaries, who first justified the Constitution as an agent of safety, and then called on citizens to reform their behaviors by trading protection for the obligation to obey.

The founders of the United States asked Americans to take Hobbes's gamble, and many did.

The Constitution is a flawed document in many ways, especially about slavery, but it has nevertheless proven to be a viable foundation for the United States. As historians and legal scholars have observed, its success is related to its elasticity.[32] A novel document, the Constitution's built-in mechanism for change made complete overhaul or another revolution unnecessary. Once the Bill of Rights was included, the Constitution became a document capable of protecting the interests of wealthy gentlemen and common folks alike. But it was not just the Constitution's structure that brought stability. It was also how the Constitution was discussed, framed, and deployed in public discourse. Though anti-federalists fought eloquently against what they saw as the Constitution's despotic potential, and though resistance continued well into the nineteenth century, nevertheless the Constitution helped the founders of the United States to redefine the meaning of citizenship.

Enemyship was central to the counter-revolutionary rhetorics of the post-Revolutionary period. In the first place, enemies were a tool of distraction, keeping the minds of citizens occupied so they did not think about prosecuting another revolution. Hard work was equated with virtue and idleness with vice in the early Republic.[33] Hard-working Americans were good Americans; the idle poor were trouble—because, it was believed, potentially dangerous, disobedient, unmanageable thoughts arose when the imagination was left to wander. Good politicians therefore engaged in a poetics of distraction by providing citizens with a steady diet of stimuli to disturb their minds and distract them from the violence within. Enemies occupied the minds of citizens, keeping them too busy with worry about their safety and the safety of their friends, families, and loved ones to think about revolution. Enemies helped to sublimate thoughts of revolution into concerns about national defense, keeping citizens too distracted to think of rebelling against a government that was committed to protecting them from danger.

While enemies were instruments of distraction, at the same time, naming enemies was a strategy for reforming revolutionary sentiments and disciplining democracy. Enemyship coordinated a top-down bond between representatives and citizens by persuading citizens that they had to obey the authorities or else they would endanger themselves and their families. Citizens were bound to obey their representatives, because they had citizens' best interests at heart, they had information that common folks did not, they had calmly deliberated and decided on the best course of action, and, most importantly, they offered protection from America's enemies.

Hamilton observed in Federalist 8 that "Safety from external danger, is the most powerful director of national conduct. Even the ardent love of liberty will, after a time, give way to its dictates." He continued to predict that "the continual effort and alarm attendant on a state of continual danger, will compel nations the most attached to liberty, to resort for repose and security to institutions which have a tendency to destroy their civil and political rights. To be more safe, they, at length, become willing to run the risk of being less free."[34] Hamilton used this argument, premised on an understanding of both Hobbes's gamble and Franklin's warning, to defend the Constitution—for, he argued, the Constitution would create a stable political foundation for protecting the security of Americans, hence removing the dangers of a state of nature that might encourage Americans to trade liberty for security. This was an admirable sentiment, and one of the best defenses of the Constitution. The problem was that federalists devoted much of their energy to frightening Americans, proving that dangers would not be removed after ratification. The Constitution might have created a structure for managing dangers, but it would not remove them.

In the years following ratification, politicians demanded not so much that Americans trade liberty for protection, but that they alter what liberty meant in order to fit it into a new political schema: one that stressed obedience, equated democracy with anarchy, and demanded unity in the face of danger. Danger, announced and made productive through the rhetorics of enemyship, became the means to disciplining the fires of revolution and cultivating a new political subjectivity. Hamilton reminded Americans in Federalist 25 that "the territories of Britain, Spain, and of the Indian nations in our neighbourhood, do not border on particular states; but encircle the union from MAINE to GEORGIA." "The danger, though in different degrees, is therefore common," he proclaimed, "and the means of guarding against it, ought, in like manner, to be the objects of common councils, and of a common treasury."³⁵ The authors of *The Federalist* all reiterated this point, which was central to demonstrating the necessity of the Constitution and the utility of a federal government. Americans could no longer resist their enemies disunited; their enemies were nationalized, and they had to be confronted as a nation.

Democratic fear in the early Republic was tied to the dilemmas of American nationalism—to the fact that America's defense of revolution as codified in the Declaration of Independence lived on in the postwar years, terrifying elites that they would be democracy's next victims. Enemyship was not just a coping mechanism but also a rhetorical strategy for reforming behaviors and promoting an ideal of citizenship that was orderly, deferential, and virtuous. Because the government protected citizens, it was in their interest to obey. Moreover, when filtered though the contract of blood, which seized on the tremendous debts Americans owed to revolutionary martyrs, the naming of enemies helped to confirm the commitment of citizens to the Constitution. The contract of blood was soaked in the emotions of pride and guilt. In the 1790s, Federalists argued that to resist government, to fail to defend the United States from its enemies, was to let down all the mothers and fathers who died in order to give their children the gift of independence. In this moment, many Americans began to rethink what it meant to be a citizen.

During Shays's Rebellion and the Whiskey Rebellion, protestors justified resistance to government as a characteristic of American identity as codified in the Declaration of Independence and other revolutionary documents. During Fries's Rebellion, protestors attempted to demonstrate that they were not resisting the Constitution, but in fact protesting what they took to be unjust, unconstitutional, and anti-republican legislation. These protestors fought for the Constitution rather than against it. By the time Jefferson was elected president in 1800, after the Federalist Party's rhetoric of naming internal enemies backfired, the counter-revolution was secure. Jefferson was therefore able to declare in his First Inaugural Address that the United States was blessed with "the strongest Government on earth" because "it is the only one where every man, at the call of the law, would fly to the standard of the law, and would meet invasions of the public order as his own personal concern."³⁶ According to Jefferson, the strength of the United States came from its citizens, who now, rather than disrupting the machinery of government, were committed to defending their nation and its laws from "invasions of the public order." Perhaps this is why Jefferson trusted common folks so much. From revolution to virtue, from democracy to hierarchy—this was the path Americans traveled in the early Republic as they laid the groundwork for national stability. The founders of the United States developed successful techniques for managing the dilemmas of American nationalism and completing the Second American Revolution in the early Republic through enemyship. The continued success of government in the United States therefore had much to do with the ability of politicians to convince Americans that they shared enemies, and that the government would protect them from their foes—*if*, and it was a big if, Americans were committed to defending the government rather than overturning it.

Notes

INTRODUCTION. THE SECOND AMERICAN REVOLUTION

1. "Address by Roosevelt," *New York Times*, April 14, 1943, 16. For a contemporary description that sets the scene, see Sidney Shalett, "Roosevelt, Hailing Jefferson, Looks to Gain Liberty," *New York Times*, April 14, 1943, 1.

2. Patrick J. Deneen, *Democratic Faith* (Princeton, NJ: Princeton University Press, 2005).

3. "Address by Roosevelt," 16.

4. Though the Jefferson Memorial's slavery passage is presented as one long quotation, it is in fact a collage of five different sources, the first published in 1774 and the last in 1821; it is therefore a questionable and deliberately misleading collection of writings spread across forty-seven years that creates the illusion that Jefferson was opposed to slavery. As historian James Loewen summarizes and critiques the sly prevarications of this panel: "The effect of this medley is to create the impression that Thomas Jefferson was very nearly an abolitionist. In their original contexts, the same quotations reveal quite a different Jefferson conflicted about

slavery—at times its harsh critic, often its apologist." James W. Loewen, *Lies across America: What Our Historic Sites Get Wrong* (New York: Touchstone, 2000), 308.

5. The best study of the rhetorical challenges of the Declaration, and, in my opinion, one of the finest works of rhetorical criticism ever penned, remains Stephen E. Lucas, "Justifying America: The Declaration of Independence as a Rhetorical Document," in *American Rhetoric: Context and Criticism*, ed. Thomas W. Benson (Carbondale: Southern Illinois University Press, 1989), 67–130. For other helpful works, see Carl L. Becker, *The Declaration of Independence: A Study in the History of Political Ideas* (1922; New York: Vintage, 1958); Garry Wills, *Inventing America: Jefferson's Declaration of Independence* (Garden City, NY: Doubleday, 1978), 49–64; and David Armitage, "The Declaration of Independence and International Law," *William and Mary Quarterly* 59 (2002): 39–64.

6. John Locke, *Second Treatise of Government*, ed. Richard H. Cox (1689; Wheeling, IL: Harlan Davidson, 1982), 140.

7. Jeremy Bentham, *Short Review of the Declaration*, published as an appendix to John Lind, *An Answer to the Declaration of the American Congress* (London: T. Cadell, J. Walter, and T. Sewell, 1776), 131. Bentham's authorship is not noted in the Lind edition, so many have attributed the *Short Review* to Lind; yet, as David Armitage notes in "The Declaration of Independence and International Law," 53, "Its author was not Lind but his friend Jeremy Bentham. Though American historians in general remain unaware of this fact, it has been known since 1968 and has received ample commentary by Bentham scholars." David Ramsay came to the same conclusion as Bentham: "To overset an established government unhinges many of those principles, which bind individuals to each other. A long time, and much prudence, will be necessary to reproduce a spirit of union and that reverence for government, without which society is a rope of sand. The right of the people to resist their rulers, when invading their liberties, forms the corner stone of the American republics. This principle, though just in itself, is not favourable to the tranquility of present establishments. The maxims and measures, which in the years 1774 and 1775 were successfully inculcated and adopted by American patriots, for overturning established government, will answer a similar purpose when recurrence is had to them by factious demagogues, for disturbing the freest governments that were ever devised." David Ramsay, *The History of the American Revolution* (Philadelphia: R. Aitken & Son, 1789), 2:323.

8. Paul Gilje, *The Road to Mobocracy: Popular Disorder in New York City, 1763–1834* (Chapel Hill: University of North Carolina Press, 1987).

9. Peter Shaw, *American Patriots and the Rituals of Revolution* (Cambridge, MA: Harvard University Press, 1981), 185–86.

10. David Walker, *Appeal to the Coloured Citizens of the World*, ed. Peter P. Hinks (1829; University Park: Penn State University Press, 2003), 79.

11. For examples of alternative Declarations of Independence modeled on the original, see Philip S. Foner, ed., *We, the Other People: Alternative Declarations of Independence by Labor Groups, Farmers, Woman's Rights Advocates, Socialists, and Blacks, 1829–1975* (Urbana: University of Illinois Press, 1976).

12. Frank Whitson Fetter, "The Revision of the Declaration of Independence in 1941," *William and Mary Quarterly* 31 (1974): 137–38. Here, I think it is provocative to remember Dean MacCannell's suggestion, just two years after Fetter's harangue, that the "two poles of modern consciousness" are *tourism* and *revolution*: "a willingness to accept, even to venerate, things as they are on the one hand, a desire to transform things on the other." Thinking along with MacCannell, we can argue that tourist attractions, like the Jefferson Memorial, encourage complacent viewing, which is the opposite of the questioning of authority and the desire for change involved in revolution. Thus, the Jefferson Memorial attempts to rewrite the Declaration of Independence not only by altering its content, but also by making it something to be consumed and not employed in radical actions against the state. Dean MacCannell, *The Tourist: A New Theory of the Leisure Class* (1976; Berkeley: University of California Press, 1999), 3.

13. Though Loewen writes that "I know no problem with the words on the fourth panel," it is problematic if studied carefully and in the context of the rhetorical reconstruction of the Declaration. Loewen, *Lies across America*, 308.

14. Thomas Jefferson to Samuel Kercheval, July 12, 1816, in Thomas Jefferson, *Writings*, ed. Merrill D. Peterson, Library of America Series (New York: Literary Classics of the U.S., 1984), 1401–3.

15. Jefferson to Madison, September 6, 1789, in *Writings*, ed. Peterson, 963–64. For discussions of Jefferson's plan for "permanent revolution," see Richard K. Matthews, *The Radical Politics of Thomas Jefferson: A Revisionist View* (Lawrence: University of Kansas Press, 1984), 19–29; and Herbert Sloan, "'The Earth Belongs in Usufruct to the Living,'" in *Jeffersonian Legacies*, ed. Peter S. Onuf (Charlottesville: University of Virginia Press, 1993), 281–315.

16. Madison to Jefferson, February 4, 1790, in *The Papers of Thomas Jefferson*, edited by J. P Boyd, C. T. Cullen, J. Catanzariti, and B. B. Oberg, 32 vols. (Princeton, N.J.: Princeton University Press, 1950–present), 16:147–49. Madison's deconstruction

of Jefferson's plan is equaled only by Garry Wills's; see Wills, *Inventing America*, 123–29.

17. John Dewey, "Presenting Thomas Jefferson" (1940), in John Dewey, *The Later Works, 1925–1953*, ed. Jo Ann Boydston (Carbondale: Southern Illinois University Press, 1988), 14:202; John Dewey, *Freedom and Culture* (1939), in *The Later Works*, 13:173.

18. Philosophically, in addition to Arendt's *On Revolution*, and Dewey's *Liberalism and Social Action* and *Freedom and Culture*, see Richard Rorty, "The Priority of Democracy to Philosophy," in *Objectivity, Relativism, and Truth: Philosophical Papers* (Cambridge: Cambridge University Press, 1991), 1:175–96; Benjamin R. Barber, *Strong Democracy: Participatory Politics for a New Age* (1984; Berkeley: University of California Press, 2003); and Matthews, *The Radical Politics of Thomas Jefferson*. One of the best studies of Jefferson's rhetoric, which is also a model of the art of rhetorical criticism, is Stephen Howard Browne, *Jefferson's Call for Nationhood: The First Inaugural Address* (College Station: Texas A&M University Press, 2003).

19. Jefferson to Kercheval, July 12, 1816, *in Writings*, ed. Peterson, 1400.

20. Thomas Jefferson to Edward Carrington, January 16, 1787, in *Writings*, ed. Peterson, 880.

21. Dewey, "Presenting Thomas Jefferson," 203.

22. Thomas Jefferson to William Stephens Smith, November 13, 1787, in *Writings*, ed. Peterson, 911.

23. On Jefferson in public memory, see Merrill D. Peterson, *The Jefferson Image in the American Mind* (Charlottesville: Thomas Jefferson Memorial Foundation and the University Press of Virginia, 1998).

24. James Madison, "Federalist 10," in *The Federalist*, intro. and notes by Robert A. Ferguson (New York: Barnes & Noble Classics, 2006), 56.

25. John Adams to John Taylor, April 15, 1814, in *The Political Writings of John Adams*, ed. George W. Carey (Washington, DC: Regnery, 2000), 406.

26. James Arnt Aune, "Tales of the Text: Originalism, Theism, and the History of the U.S. Constitution," *Rhetoric & Public Affairs* 1 (1998): 267; and Sandra M. Gustafson, *Eloquence Is Power: Oratory and Performance in Early America* (Chapel Hill: University of North Carolina Press, 2000), 237. On fears of rhetorical abuse and stupid people in the early Republic more generally, see Joseph M. Bessette, *The Mild Voice of Reason: Deliberative Democracy and American National Government* (Chicago: University of Chicago Press, 1994).

27. Gerry quoted in Max Farrand, ed., *The Records of the Federal Convention of 1787*

(New Haven, CT: Yale University Press, 1911), 1:48, 2:57.

28. Gerry, Mason, and Randolph quoted in Farrand, *Records of the Federal Convention*, 1:48, 51.

29. Gordon S. Wood, *The Creation of the American Republic, 1776–1787* (1969; Chapel Hill: University of North Carolina Press, 1998).

30. Peter Linebaugh and Marcus Rediker, *The Many-Headed Hydra: Sailors, Slaves, Commoners, and the Hidden History of the Revolutionary Atlantic* (Boston: Beacon Press, 2000), 238.

31. Terry Bouton, *Taming Democracy: "The People," the Founders, and the Troubled Ending of the American Revolution* (New York: Oxford University Press, 2007), 5, 7, 177.

32. Lucas, "Justifying America," 81; Pauline Maier, *American Scripture: Making the Declaration of Independence* (New York: Alfred A. Knopf, 1997), 130, 155–60.

33. Worthington Chauncey Ford, ed., *Journals of the Continental Congress, 1774–1789* (Washington: Government Printing Office, 1906), 5:516.

34. Jay Fliegelman, *Declaring Independence: Jefferson, Natural Language, and the Culture of Performance* (Stanford, CA: Stanford University Press, 1993); and for a brief discussion of how it was proclaimed, see David Hackett Fisher, *Liberty and Freedom: A Visual History of America's Founding Ideals* (Oxford: Oxford University Press, 2005), 121–26.

35. See Winthrop D. Jordan, "Familial Politics: Thomas Paine and the Killing of the King, 1776," *Journal of American History* 60 (1973): 306–8; David Waldstreicher, *In the Midst of Perpetual Fetes: The Making of American Nationalism, 1776–1820* (Chapel Hill: University of North Carolina Press, 1997), 31.

36. Michael Warner, *The Letters of the Republic: Publication and the Public Sphere in Eighteenth-Century America* (Cambridge, MA: Harvard University Press, 1990), 111–12.

37. "A Citizen of America" [Noah Webster], *An Examination Into the Leading Principles of the Federal Constitution* (1787), in *The Debate on the Constitution: Federalist and Antifederalist Speeches, Articles, and Letters during the Struggle over Ratification*, ed. Bernard Bailyn, Library of America Series (New York: Literary Classics of the U.S., 1993), 1:150.

38. Brutus No. 1, *New York Journal*, October 18, 1787, in *Debate on the Constitution*, 1:165, 168.

39. "A Citizen of Philadelphia" [Pelatiah Webster], Philadelphia, November 8, 1787, in *Debate on the Constitution*, 1:179.

40. Aristotle, *The Rhetoric of Aristotle*, trans. Lane Cooper (Englewood Cliffs, NJ: Prentice-Hall, 1932), 1358b.

41. Quintilian, *De Institutione Oratoria*, reprinted as *Quintilian's Institutes of Oratory: Or, Education of an Orator*, trans. John Selby Watson (London: George Bell & Sons, 1892), book 3, ch. 7, p. 218.

42. Jeffrey Walker, for one, suggests that epideictic rhetoric came first, before deliberative or forensic forms, arguing that pragmatic political rhetoric that aims to emphasize reason in deliberation is always secondary to the constitutive power of epideictic to shape opinions. See *Rhetoric and Poetics in Antiquity* (Oxford: Oxford University Press, 2000).

43. On invective in the early Republic, see Jeremy Engels, "Uncivil Speech: Invective and the Rhetorics of Democracy in the Early Republic," *Quarterly Journal of Speech* 95 (2009): 311-34.

44. Witherspoon, *Lectures on Moral Philosophy, and Eloquence* (Philadelphia: William W. Woodward, 1810), 202–3. On the Enlightenment's hope for a purely rational deliberation that would replace the vagaries of rhetoric in public discussion, see Bryan Garsten, *Saving Persuasion: A Defense of Rhetoric and Judgment* (Cambridge, MA: Harvard University Press, 2006).

45. On the divergent rhetorics of the head and the heart in the early Republic, see Jeremy Engels, "Disciplining Jefferson: The Man within the Breast and the Rhetorical Norms of Producing Order," *Rhetoric & Public Affairs* 9 (2006): 411–36.

46. The inclination to talk about the world as though it was divided into friends and enemies was bolstered by aspects of American Protestantism—which encouraged Americans to think in the Manichean terms of "God's creatures" and "God's enemies" (to use Jonathan Edward's terms from his famous 1741 sermon "Sinners in the Hands of an Angry God"); to see their adversaries as Satan's minions; and to speak in languages of fear, hellfire and brimstone, millennialism, mission, prophecy, and jeremiad. On these themes, see Perry Miller, *Errand into the Wilderness* (1956; Cambridge, MA: Belknap Press of Harvard University Press, 1984); and Sacvan Bercovitch, *The Rites of Assent: Transformations in the Symbolic Construction of America* (New York: Routledge, 1993). For discussions of how Protestant religious views fueled wars, see Jill Lepore, *In the Name of War: King Philip's War and the Origins of American Identity* (New York: Alfred A. Knopf, 1998); and Ronald F. Reid, "New England Rhetoric and the French War, 1754–1760: A Case Study in the Rhetoric of War," *Communication Monographs* 43 (1976): 259–86. On prophetic rhetoric, see James Darsey, *The Prophetic Tradition and Radical Rhetoric in America*

(New York: NYU Press, 1997). On the Protestant jeremiad, see Sacvan Bercovitch, *The American Jeremiad* (Madison: University of Wisconsin Press, 1978).

47. In *Democracy in America,* Tocqueville concluded that the most severe danger to democratic societies is war. He cautioned that "there is no long war that does not put freedom at great risk in a democratic country," specifically by tipping the precious balance between liberty and power toward despotism. And thus he wrote somewhat wryly: "All those who seek to destroy freedom within a democratic nation ought to know that the surest and shortest means of succeeding at this is war." Tocqueville's conclusions are reiterated by Michael Hardt and Antonio Negri, who write: "War has always been incompatible with democracy. Traditionally, democracy has been suspended during wartime and power entrusted temporarily to a strong central authority to confront the crisis . . . War takes on a generalized character, strangling all social life and posing its own political order." Alexis de Tocqueville, *Democracy in America*, trans. Harvey C. Mansfield and Delba Winthrop (1835; Chicago: University of Chicago Press, 2000), 621; Michael Hardt and Antonio Negri, *Multitude: War and Democracy in the Age of Empire* (New York: Penguin, 2004), xi–xii.

48. Robert L. Ivie, *Democracy and America's War on Terror* (Tuscaloosa: University of Alabama Press, 2005), 5, 10, 30–31.

49. Thomas Paine, *The American Crisis*, No. 1, in *The Thomas Paine Reader*, ed. Michael Foot and Isaac Kramnick (New York: Penguin, 1987), 122.

50. John Jay, "Federalist 2," 14.

51. John Quincy Adams, *An Oration, Pronounced July 4th, 1793, at the Request of the Inhabitants of the Town of Boston, in Commemoration of the Anniversary of American Independence* (Boston: Benjamin Edes & Son, 1793), 18; George Clinton, *An Oration, Delivered on the Fourth of July, 1798, Before the General Society of Mechanics and Tradesmen, the Democratic Society, the Tammany Society or Columbian Order, the New York Cooper's Society, and a Numerous Concourse of Other Citizens* (New York: M.L. & W.A. Davis, 1798), 8.

52. Thomas Jefferson, *Autobiography* (1821), in *Writings*, ed. Peterson, 70–71.

53. Thomas Paine, *The American Crisis*, no. 3, April 19, 1777, in *The Complete Writings of Thomas Paine*, ed. Philip S. Foner (New York: The Citadel Press, 1945), 1:87.

54. Thomas Jefferson, *Notes on the State of Virginia* (1785), ed. William Peden (1954; Chapel Hill: University of North Carolina Press, 1982), 121–22.

55. Estimates of 120,000 were given by Paine himself and are repeated in Eric Foner, *Tom Paine and Revolutionary America* (1976; Oxford: Oxford University Press,

2005), 79, and John Keane, *Tom Paine: A Political Life* (New York: Little, Brown & Co., 1995), 108–11. A much more conservative estimate of at most 75,000 copies is given in Trish Loughran, "Disseminating *Common Sense*: Thomas Paine and the Problem of the Early National Bestseller," *American Literature* 78 (2006): 17. A "highly implausible" (according to Loughran) estimate of 500,000 is given by Philip Foner in *The Complete Writings of Thomas Paine*, 1:xiv, and repeated in Merrill Jensen, ed., *Tracts of the American Revolution, 1763–1776* (1963; Indianapolis: Hackett, 2003), lxvi–lxvii, and Scott Liell, *46 Pages: Thomas Paine, Common Sense, and the Turning Point to Independence* (Philadelphia: Running Press, 2003), 95.

56. John Keegan, *The Face of Battle* (New York: Penguin, 1978), 320–31, lists *impersonalization*, along with *deliberate cruelty* and *coercion* as the three facets of "the inhuman face of war."

57. John Adams to Thomas Jefferson, June 30, 1813, in *The Adams-Jefferson Letters: The Complete Correspondence between Thomas Jefferson and Abigail & John Adams*, ed. Lester J. Cappon (1959; Chapel Hill: University of North Carolina Press, 1987), 346.

58. Bouton, *Taming Democracy*, 61, 70.

59. For a discussion of the government's response to Shays's Rebellion, and a much earlier attempt to wrap my head around the rhetorical foundations of the counter-revolutionary tradition in the United States, see Jeremy Engels, "Reading the Riot Act: Rhetoric, Psychology, and Counter-Revolutionary Discourse in Shays's Rebellion, 1786–1787," *Quarterly Journal of Speech* 91 (2005): 63–88.

60. Gustafson, *Eloquence is Power*, 205.

61. Wood writes that for the anti-federalists "it was unbelievable that [the Constitution] could have even been proposed"; *Creation of the American Republic*, 499.

62. Benjamin Rush, "An Account of the Influence of the Military and Political Events of the American Revolution Upon the Human Body" (1787), in *Medical Inquiries and Other Observations*, 2nd American edition (Philadelphia: Thomas Dobson, 1794), 1:277.

63. Even Immanuel Kant, who hoped that the Enlightenment project would extend to "the great unthinking masses," suggested in 1784 that even the most liberal ruler required "a numerous and well-disciplined army to assure public peace." Immanuel Kant, "Answer to the Question: What is Enlightenment?" (1784), in *Basic Writings of Kant*, ed. Allen W. Wood (New York: The Modern Library, 2001), 141.

64. Leonard Richards, *Shays's Rebellion: The American Revolution's Final Battle* (Philadelphia: University of Pennsylvania Press, 2002), 23–24.

65. *A Selection of the Patriotic Addresses, to the President of the United States. Together with The President's Answers* (Boston: John W. Folsom, 1798), 144.

66. The idea of legitimation crises is explored in Jürgen Habermas, *Legitimation Crisis* (1973; Cambridge: Polity Press, 1997).

67. Here, I draw on Hannah Arendt's argument in *On Violence* (San Diego: Harcourt Brace Jovanovich, 1969). Arendt distinguishes between violence and power, arguing that violence can never produce power, only more violence. A similar point is made in Paul Virilio and Sylvere Lotringer, *Pure War*, trans. Mark Polizzotti (1982; New York: Semiotext(e), 1997), 56, where Virilio argues: "One cannot use violence against what is already violence, one can only reinforce it, take it to extremes—in other words, to the State's maximum power."

68. Webster, *An Examination into the Leading Principles of the Federal Constitution*, 155.

69. Here, see Steven Watts, *The Republic Reborn: War and the Making of Liberal America, 1790–1820* (Baltimore: Johns Hopkins University Press, 1987); and on the rhetoric surrounding the War of 1812, see Ronald L. Hatzenbuehler and Robert L. Ivie, *Congress Declares War: Rhetoric, Leadership, and Partisanship in the Early Republic* (Kent, OH: Kent State University Press, 1983).

70. Tocqueville, *Democracy in America*, 620. The military and the civic are bound in Machiavelli's term *virtù*, which means the ability to act decisively to combat *fortuna* and is a civic virtue best learned through military training; see Niccolò Machiavelli, *The Art of War*, ed. Neal Wood (1521; Cambridge, MA: Da Capo Press, 2001), 76–81. Building on Machiavelli's 1521 *Art of War*, Carl von Clausewitz observed in his 1832 *On War* that "Today practically no means other than war will educate a people in this spirit of boldness . . . Nothing else will counteract the softness and the desire for ease which debase the people in times of growing prosperity and increasing trade. A people and nation can hope for a strong position in the world only if national character and familiarity with war fortify each other by continual interaction"; Carl von Clausewitz, *On War*, ed. and trans. Michael Howard and Peter Paret (1832; Princeton, NJ: Princeton University Press, 1972), 192.

71. The "antithesis" was in fact a popular rhetorical technique in eighteenth-century rhetorical practice: see Hugh Blair, *Lectures on Rhetoric and Belles Lettres* (Dublin: Whitestone, Colles et al., 1783), 1:417–20.

CHAPTER ONE. HOW ENEMYSHIP BECAME COMMON SENSE

1. On William Wirt's invention of the Patrick Henry myth in 1816, see Ray Raphael, *Founding Myths: Stories That Hide Our Patriotic Past* (New York: W.W. Norton, 2004), 145–56.

2. Thomas Jefferson, *Autobiography* (1821), in Thomas Jefferson, *Writings*, ed. Merrill D. Peterson, Library of America Series (New York: Literary Classics of the U.S., 1984), 70–71.

3. Bernard Bailyn, *Faces of Revolution: Personalities and Themes in the Struggle for American Independence* (1990; New York: Vintage, 1992), 67—and this is saying something, for as Bailyn writes in *The Ideological Origins of the American Revolution* (1967; Cambridge, MA: Harvard University Press, 1992), it was in pamphlets that "the best thought of the day expressed itself" (3). The various cases for Paine's influence, specifically his rhetorical influence, are reviewed in David C. Hoffman, "Paine and Prejudice: Rhetorical Leadership through Perceptual Framing in *Common Sense*," *Rhetoric & Public Affairs* 9 (2006): 373–410.

4. Dixon Wecter, "Hero in Reverse," *Virginia Quarterly Review* 18 (1942): 243.

5. The best study of Paine's early writings is Edward Larkin, "Inventing an American Public: Thomas Paine, the *Pennsylvania Magazine*, and American Revolutionary Political Discourse," *Early American Literature* 33 (1998): 250–76, which is expanded in Larkin's wonderful *Thomas Paine and the Literature of Revolution* (Cambridge: Cambridge University Press, 2005). In Robert Ferguson's able judgment, *Common Sense* is rivaled in importance only by Jefferson's Declaration of Independence, Harriet Beecher Stowe's *Uncle Tom's Cabin*, and Lincoln's Gettysburg Address; Robert A. Ferguson, "The Commonalities of *Common Sense*," *William and Mary Quarterly* 57 (2000): 466. For Scott Liell, *Common Sense* was "the single most influential political work in American history, rivaled perhaps only by the Communist Manifesto in the history of the world"; Scott Liell, *46 Pages: Thomas Paine, Common Sense, and the Turning Point to Independence* (Philadelphia: Running Press, 2003), 16.

6. Philadelphia's *Port Folio* and Boston's *Mercury and New-England Palladium*, quoted in John Keane, *Tom Paine: A Political Life* (New York: Grove/Atlantic, 1995), 457.

7. John Adams, *The Diary and Autobiography of John Adams*, ed. L. H. Butterfield (Cambridge, MA: Harvard University Press, 1961): 3:333; John Adams quoted in Worthington Chauncey Ford, ed., *Statesman and Friend: Correspondence of John Adams with Benjamin Waterhouse, 1784–1822* (Boston: Little, Brown & Company,

1927), 31.

8. Justice and Humanity [Thomas Paine], "African Slavery in America" (1775), in *The Thomas Paine Reader*, ed. Michael Foot and Isaac Kramnick (New York: Penguin, 1987), 52–56.

9. These are the characteristics of early American democratic discourse as identified in Kenneth Cmiel, *Democratic Eloquence: The Fight over Popular Speech in Nineteenth-Century America* (New York: W. Morrow, 1990), 62–64.

10. According to Lucas, Paine "clarifies the direction of the essay early, the mood develops swiftly and forcefully, the ideas unfold easily and spontaneously . . . Thus he brings his readers step by step to the conclusion that independence is necessary, beneficial, and practical." Stephen E. Lucas, *Portents of Rebellion: Rhetoric and Revolution in Philadelphia, 1765–76* (Philadelphia: Temple University Press, 1976), 170.

11. Thomas Paine, *The American Crisis*, no. 1, December 23, 1776, in *The Complete Writings of Thomas Paine*, 1:50.

12. Thomas Paine, *Common Sense* (1776), in *The Thomas Paine Reader*, 65, 93.

13. Paine, *Common Sense*, 65; Thomas Paine, *Letter to the Abbé Raynal* (1782), in *The Thomas Paine Reader*, 163.

14. For a discussion of how social-contract theory functioned in the rhetoric of the period, see Robert A. Ferguson, *The American Enlightenment, 1750–1820* (Cambridge, MA: Harvard University Press, 1997), 80–123.

15. For Paine, "Society in every state is a blessing, but government even in its best state is but a necessary evil; in its worst state an intolerable one." Paine, *Common Sense*, 66.

16. Paine, *Common Sense*, 67–68.

17. Lucas, *Portents of Rebellion*, 177.

18. "Philadelphia, December 14," *Pennsylvania Evening Post*, December 14, 1775, 576.

19. Paine, *The American Crisis*, no. 1, *Complete Writings*, 1:51.

20. For the numbers of slaves in colonial North America in 1774, see Ray Raphael, *A People's History of the American Revolution: How Common People Shaped the Fight for Independence* (New York: Perennial, 2002), 311. On Lord Dunmore's War, see Woody Holton, "'Rebel against Rebel': Enslaved Virginians and the Coming of the American Revolution," *Virginia Magazine of History and Biography* 105 (1997): 157–92, and *Forced Founders: Indians, Debtors, Slaves, and the Making of the American Revolution in Virginia* (Chapel Hill: University of North Carolina Press, 1999), 133–63; and Sylvia R. Frey, *Water from the Rock: Black Resistance in a Revolutionary Age*

(Princeton, NJ: Princeton University Press, 1991), 45–80. The story is discussed in Gary B. Nash and Jean R. Soderlund, *Freedom by Degrees: Emancipation in Pennsylvania and Its Aftermath* (New York: Oxford University Press, 1991), 77; and Peter H. Wood, "'The Dream Deferred': Black Struggles on the Eve of White Independence," in *In Resistance: Studies in African, Caribbean, and Afro-American History*, ed. Gary Y. Okihiro (Amherst: University of Massachusetts Press, 1986), 177–78. Its authenticity is questioned in Benjamin Quarles, *The Negro in the American Revolution* (Chapel Hill: University of North Carolina Press, 1961), 31.

21. Lee and Rutledge quoted in Holton, "'Rebel against Rebel,'" 185, 187.
22. Paine, *Common Sense*, 81.
23. For discussions of the Seven Years War and its effects on colonial relations with the Crown, see Francis Jennings, *Empire of Fortune: Crowns, Colonies, and Tribes in the Seven Years War in America* (New York: W.W. Norton & Company, 1988); Richard White, *The Middle Ground: Indians, Empires, and Republics in the Great Lakes Region, 1650–1815* (Cambridge: Cambridge University Press, 1991), 240–56; Fred Anderson, *Crucible of War: The Seven Years' War and the Fate of Empire in British North America, 1754–1766* (2000; New York: Vintage, 2001); and Colin G. Calloway, *The Scratch of a Pen: 1763 and the Transformation of North America* (Oxford: Oxford University Press, 2006).
24. Paine, *Common Sense*, 81.
25. Ibid., 83.
26. On the birth of the American Navy, which corrected the flaw in Paine's analysis and protected American free trade, see William M. Fowler, *Jack Tars and Commodores: The American Navy, 1783–1815* (Boston: Houghton Mifflin, 1984); A. B. C. Whipple, *To the Shores of Tripoli: The Birth of the U.S. Navy and Marines* (New York: William Morrow and Company, 1991); and Kenneth J. Hagan, *This People's Navy: The Making of American Sea Power* (New York: The Free Press, 1991).
27. "Our plan is commerce, and that, well attended to, will secure us the peace and friendship of all Europe; because it is the interest of all Europe to have a *free port*. Her trade will always be a protection, and her barrenness of gold and silver secure her from invaders"; Paine, *Common Sense*, 83. For a discussion of Paine's commercial philosophy, see Eric Foner, *Tom Paine and Revolutionary America* (1976; Oxford: Oxford University Press, 2005), 144–82.
28. Paine, *Common Sense*, 81.
29. The publication history of *Common Sense* was complicated and confusing, and there were 1776 editions floating around—not the first edition, but later editions

published by Robert Bell—that altered the enemyship passage slightly, reading "a very roundabout way of proving relationship, but it is the nearest and only true way of proving enmity (or enemyship, if I may so call it)." This is the version reprinted by Philip Foner in *The Complete Writings of Thomas Paine*, ed. Philip S. Foner (New York: The Citadel Press, 1945), 1:19. Why this change was made escapes me, though this passage has the advantage of offering a definition of the neologism "enemyship." On the complicated publication history of *Common Sense*, see Richard Gimbel, *Thomas Paine: A Bibliographic Check List of Common Sense, with an Account of Its Publication* (New Haven, CT: Yale University Press, 1956); and A. Owen Aldridge, *Thomas Paine's American Ideology* (Newark: University of Delaware Press, 1984), 40–46.

30. Paine, *Common Sense*, 80.

31. Lucas, *Portents of Rebellion*, 201–24. On the colonies' reluctance to revolt and their strong British identities, see also Bailyn, *The Ideological Origins of the American Revolution*; Michael Zuckerman, "Identity in British America: Unease in Eden," in *Colonial Identity in the Atlantic World, 1500–1800*, ed. Nicholas Canny and Anthony Pagden (Princeton, NJ: Princeton University Press, 1987), 115–57; Jack P. Greene, *Peripheries and Center: Constitutional Development in the Extended Polities of the British Empire and the United States, 1607–1788* (1986; New York: W.W. Norton & Company, 1990), 79–150; and Linda Colley, *Captives: Britain, Empire, and the World, 1600–1850* (New York: Anchor Books, 2002), 137–67.

32. Benjamin Franklin, "An Infallible Method to Restore Peace and Harmony," *The Public Advertiser* (London), September 8, 1773, in Benjamin Franklin, *Writings*, ed. J. A. Leo Lemay, Library of America Series (New York: Literary Classics of the U.S., 1987), 689.

33. See Anthony Pagden, *Lords of All the World: Ideologies of Empire in Spain, Britain, and France c. 1500–1800* (New Haven, CT: Yale University Press, 1995).

34. Jay Fliegelman, *Prodigals and Pilgrims: The American Revolution against Patriarchal Authority, 1750–1800* (Cambridge: Cambridge University Press, 1982).

35. Peter Shaw, *American Patriots and the Rituals of Revolution* (Cambridge, MA: Harvard University Press, 1981), 41.

36. T. H. Breen, *The Marketplace of Revolution: How Consumer Politics Shaped American Independence* (Oxford: Oxford University Press, 2004); Robert Kagan, *Dangerous Nation: America's Place in the World from Its Earliest Days to the Dawn of the Twentieth Century* (New York: Alfred A. Knopf, 2006), 7–70.

37. Gordon S. Wood, *The Creation of the American Republic, 1776–1787* (1969; Chapel

Hill: University of North Carolina Press, 1998), 46–90; Bailyn, *Ideological Origins of the American Revolution*, 94–159.

38. Paine, *Common Sense*, 70, 72.

39. Paine, *Common Sense*, 71–72, 75–79. The most celebratory manifestation of anti-Catholicism in colonial America was the Pope's Day holiday, which took place every November 5 in Boston, New York, and many other cities in New England. This festival commemorated the failed Gunpowder Plot of 1605, when Guy Fawkes attempted to blow up the Houses of Parliament. On this day, lower-class colonists turned the city upside down and ruled it for a day, drinking heavily, causing mayhem, and bumming change off of the rich. The highlight of the day was a contest of rival parades, as colonists from the North End and the South End paraded elaborate effigies of the Pope and the Devil to a designated point, and then brawled to determine who would seize their rival's Pope. The victors then got the privilege of burning the other side's Pope (along with their own) at their end of town. Though this holiday was disorderly and inspired much fear in the more well-to-do, elites allowed it to continue until the 1760s, for they "appreciated the stabilizing impact of anti-papal rhetoric, which unified and bound a socially disparate people together," as Francis D. Cogliano writes in *No King, No Popery: Anti-Catholicism in Revolutionary New England* (Westport, CT: Greenwood Press, 1995), 23.

40. Thomas Paine, "Epistle to Quakers" (1776), in *Complete Writings of Thomas Paine*, 2:56.

41. Thomas Paine, *The American Crisis*, no. 3, April 19, 1777, in *Complete Writings of Thomas Paine*, 1:82.

42. Paine, *Common Sense*, 76.

43. On the conflicted cultural responses to Islam in Anglo-American culture, see Edward Said, *Orientalism* (New York: Pantheon, 1978). For discussions of images of Muslims in America, see James Lewis, "Savages of the Seas: Barbary Captivity Tales and Images of Muslims in the Early Republic," *Journal of American Culture* 13 (1990): 75–84; Fuad Sha'ban, *Islam and Arabs in Early American Thought: The Roots of Orientalism in America* (Durham, NC: Acorn Press, 1991); Robert J. Allison, *The Crescent Obscured: The United States and the Muslim World, 1776–1815* (Chicago: University of Chicago Press, 1995); and Kevin J. Hayes, "How Thomas Jefferson Read the Qur'ân," *Early American Literature* 39 (2004): 247–62. For a discussion of images of Muslims in British culture, see Colley, *Captives*, 23–134.

44. *The Life of Mahomet; or, the History of that Imposture, which was Begun, Carried on, and Finally Established by Him in Arabia; and Which has Subjugated a Larger*

Portion of the Globe, Than the Religion of Jesus Has Yet Set at Liberty. To Which is Added, an Account of Egypt (London: Printed for the Booksellers, 1799), 61, 147. The first American edition of this work was published in May 1802 in Worcester, Massachusetts, by Isaiah Thomas, Jr., under the same title.

45. "Character of Mohamet," *Massachusetts Magazine*, September 1790.

46. Plato, *Gorgias*, trans. Walter Hamilton (New York: Penguin, 1960), 46. Though Socrates was Plato's puppet for preaching the perks of reason, Friedrich Nietzsche argues that "Socrates should appear as the first and supreme *Sophist*, as the mirror and epitome of all sophistical tendencies" because of his skill at bending logic and abusing language. Friedrich Nietzsche, *The Birth of Tragedy, Or: Hellenism and Pessimism* (1872), in *Basic Writings of Nietzsche*, ed. Walter Kaufmann (1966; New York: Modern Library, 1992), 86–87.

47. I take the term "rhetrickery" from Wayne C. Booth, *The Rhetoric of Rhetoric: The Quest for Effective Communication* (Malden, MA: Blackwell, 2004), 107–47.

48. Nabil Matar, "Turning Turk: Conversion to Islam in English Renaissance Thought," *Durham University Journal* 86 (1994): 33–41. This trope was drawn from captivity narratives—see Paul Baepler, "The Barbary Captive Narrative in Early America," *Early American Literature* 30 (1995): 95–120; and Paul Baepler, "The Barbary Captivity Narrative in American Culture," *Early American Literature* 39 (2004): 217–46. For a collection of these early American captivity narratives, see *White Slaves, African Masters: An Anthology of American Barbary Captivity Narratives*, ed. Paul Baepler (Chicago: University of Chicago Press, 1999).

49. *The Life of Mahomet*, 94.

50. Paine, *Common Sense*, 89.

51. Richard Hofstadter argues that Americans as a people are uniquely prone to paranoia, a tendency that manifested itself in the pre-Revolutionary period as a belief that all-powerful enemies were engaged in a conspiracy against the American colonies. Wood tempers many of Hofstadter's conclusions. He grounds conspiratorial thinking in the epistemology of the late eighteenth century, demonstrating that conspiracy theories were not uniquely American, but instead arose from a contradiction inherent to the Enlightenment: "At this very moment when the world was outrunning man's capacity to explain it in personal terms, in terms of the passions and schemes of individuals, the most enlightened of the age were priding themselves on their ability to do just that." The mechanistic laws of the Enlightenment advanced a science of cause and effect that replaced premodern talk of miracles, chance, and divine will. In this new, modern world, the motives and designs of

humans were identified as the causes of human events, and because it was believed
that nothing occurred without someone first willing it, the Enlightenment compelled individuals to search for the hidden causes behind unhappiness, hardship,
distress, and death. Conspiratorial thinking made sense out of the complexities of
modernity, and enemies played a vital role in revolutionary thought because they
were the originators of evil designs. If Wood is right that eighteenth-century Americans assumed that all plots had a mastermind, then positing a plot was a brilliant
way to name an enemy. The ultimate enemy acting behind the scenes with shrewd
designs on the souls of humans was Satan, a devious character in Milton's *Paradise
Lost* who appeared in the Enlightenment in Descartes's *Discourse on Method* as
the "evil genius" and other such fictions. Paine framed the plot against America
not in biblical terms, but as the king's design. Richard Hofstadter, "The Paranoid
Style in American Politics," in *The Paranoid Style in American Politics and Other
Essays* (London: Jonathan Cape, 1965), 3–40; Gordon S. Wood, "Conspiracy and
the Paranoid Style: Causality and Deceit in the Eighteenth Century," *William and
Mary Quarterly* 39 (1982): 411. For further discussions of conspiracy theories and
the Revolutionary War, see Bailyn, *Ideological Origins of the American Revolution*,
85–93, 95–102, 119–43; and Wood, *Creation of the American Republic*, 16, 22–23,
30–36, 40–43.

52. Paine, *Common Sense*, 82, 87.

53. For two helpful histories of the meaning of communication, see Armand Mattel-
art, *The Invention of Communication*, trans. Susan Emanuel (1994; Minneapolis:
University of Minnesota Press, 1996); and John Durham Peters, *Speaking into the
Air: A History of the Idea of Communication* (Chicago: University of Chicago Press,
1999).

54. Jay Fliegelman, *Declaring Independence: Jefferson, Natural Language, and the Culture of Performance* (Stanford, CA: Stanford University Press, 1993), 24, 190–91.

55. Fliegelman, *Declaring Independence*, 38.

56. Adam Smith, *The Theory of Moral Sentiments*, ed. D. D. Raphael and A. L. Macfie
(1759; Indianapolis: Liberty Fund, 1976), 337.

57. David Hume, *A Treatise of Human Nature* (1739–40), ed. L. A. Selby-Bigge (1888;
Oxford: Clarendon Press, 1978), 581.

58. William B. Warner, "Communicating Liberty: The Newspapers of the British Empire as a Matrix for the American Revolution," *ELH* 72 (2005): 345.

59. Paine, *Common Sense*, 86.

60. On the battle for public opinion following the battles of Lexington and Concord,

see Fisher, *Paul Revere's Ride*, 261–80; and Raphael, *Founding Myths*, 66–83. For a study of how these early battles were framed in public memory during the Revolutionary War, see Sarah J. Purcell, *Sealed with Blood: War, Sacrifice, and Memory in Revolutionary America* (Philadelphia: University of Pennsylvania Press, 2002), 11–48.

61. Paine, *Common Sense*, 79, 86–87.
62. Smith enumerates this principle in *Theory of Moral Sentiments*, 82–83, and note that he follows Mandeville and makes self-interest the basis of modern economics and capitalist societies in Adam Smith, *The Wealth of Nations*, ed. Edwin Cannan (1776; New York: The Modern Library, 2000), 15, writing, "It is not from the benevolence of the butcher, the brewer, or the baker, that we expect our dinner, but from their regard to their own interest. We address ourselves, not to their humanity but to their self-love, and never talk to them of our own necessities but of their advantages. Nobody but a beggar chuses to depend chiefly upon the benevolence of his fellow-citizens."
63. Paine, *Common Sense*, 84. The variability of sympathy was a major concern in the late eighteenth century, and is explored in the first novel published in the United States: William Hill Brown, *The Power of Sympathy, or, The Triumph of Nature. Founded in Truth* (Boston: Isaiah Thomas and Company, 1789). For a discussion of eighteenth-century understandings of sympathy, see Fliegelman, *Prodigals and Pilgrims*.
64. Paine, *Common Sense*, 85.
65. Thomas Paine, "Liberty Tree" (1775), in *Thomas Paine Reader*, 63–64.
66. Paine, *Common Sense*, 111.
67. G. W. F. Hegel, *Phenomenology of Spirit* (1807), trans. A. V. Miller (1807; Oxford: Oxford University Press, 1997), 111–19.
68. Paine, *Common Sense*, 99.
69. H. Larry Ingle, *First among Friends: George Fox and the Creation of Quakerism* (New York: Oxford University Press, 1994), 172.
70. Thomas Paine, "Thoughts on Defensive War" (1775), in *Complete Writings of Thomas Paine*, 2:53.
71. J. Michael Hogan and Glen Williams, "Defining 'the Enemy' in Revolutionary America: From the Rhetoric of Protest to the Rhetoric of War," *Southern Communication Journal* 61 (1996): 277–88.
72. Paine, *Common Sense*, 111–13.
73. Ibid., 99–100.

74. Ibid., 78, 92.

75. Ibid., 110.

76. "To the extent there is always an enemy lurking about, or at least a rhetorical incentive to construct such an enemy, there can never be a sufficiently secure time for democratic adversaries to engage and persuade one another"—Robert L. Ivie, "Evil Enemy versus Agonistic Other: Rhetorical Constructions of Terrorism," *Review of Education, Pedagogy and Cultural Studies* 25 (2003): 182.

77. Robert A. Dahl, *On Democracy* (New Haven, CT: Yale University Press, 1998), 38.

78. Liell, *46 Pages*, 83–83, 147–48.

79. Paine, *Common Sense*, 85, 104.

80. Ibid., 85.

81. Elizabeth A. Perkins, *Border Life: Experience and Memory in the Revolutionary Ohio Valley* (Chapel Hill: University of North Carolina Press, 1998), 155. Indeed, to take just one example, John Quincy Adams berated Aristotle's rhetorical theory because it praised revenge as a virtue; see John Quincy Adams, *Lectures on Rhetoric and Oratory, Delivered to the Class of Senior and Junior Sophisters in Harvard University* (Cambridge: Hilliard and Metcalf, 1810), 1:244–45. For a theorization of the relationship between the rhetorics of revenge and the nation-building project, and a discussion of how revenge remains integral to American subjectivity, see Jeremy Engels and Gregory Goodale, "'Our Battle Cry Will Be: Remember Jenny Mc-Crea!': A Précis on the Rhetoric of Revenge," *American Quarterly* 61 (2009): 93–112.

82. Paine, *Common Sense*, 103.

83. Ibid., 86.

84. Ibid., 92–93; Ferguson points out the biblical allusion in "The Commonalities of *Common Sense*," 486.

85. Paine, *Common Sense*, 91.

86. Susan Jacoby, *Freethinkers: A History of American Secularism* (New York: Metropolitan Books, 2004), 35–65.

87. Paine, *Common Sense*, 93.

CHAPTER TWO. THE DILEMMAS OF AMERICAN NATIONALISM

1. "America" [Noah Webster], "To the Dissenting Members of the late Convention of Pennsylvania," *Daily Advertiser* (New York), December 31, 1787, in *The Debate on the Constitution: Federalist and Antifederalist Speeches, Articles, and Letters during the Struggle over Ratification*, ed. Bernard Bailyn, Library of America Series

(New York: Literary Classics of the U.S., 1993), 1:553.

2. On the culture of deference, see Gordon S. Wood, *The Radicalism of the American Revolution* (New York: Vintage, 1991), 57–77, 179–80, 271–86; and Michael Schudson, *The Good Citizen: A History of American Civic Life* (Cambridge, MA: Harvard University Press, 1998), 11–89.

3. For discussions of the democratic ideals that propelled the Revolutionary War, see Elisha P. Douglass, *Rebels and Democrats: The Struggle for Equal Political Rights during the American Revolution* (Chapel Hill: University of North Carolina Press, 1955); Peter Linebaugh and Marcus Rediker, *The Many-Headed Hydra: Sailors, Slaves, Commoners, and the Hidden History of the Revolutionary Atlantic* (Boston: Beacon Press, 2000), 211–47; Ray Raphael, *A People's History of the American Revolution: How Common People Shaped the Fight for Independence* (New York: Perennial, 2002); Gary B. Nash, *The Unknown American Revolution: The Unruly Birth of Democracy and the Struggle to Create America* (New York: Viking, 2005); and Terry Bouton, *Taming Democracy: "The People," the Founders, and the Troubled Ending of the American Revolution* (New York: Oxford University Press, 2007).

4. Mercy Otis Warren, *History of the Rise, Progress and Termination of the American Revolution. Interspersed with Biographical, Political and Moral Observations* (Boston: Manning and Loring, 1805), 1:146.

5. Thomas Paine, *Common Sense* (1776), in *The Thomas Paine Reader*, ed. Michael Foot and Isaac Kramnick (New York: Penguin, 1987), 92.

6. Thus, Christopher Looby has read the Revolutionary War in Freudian terms as the expression of an Oedipus complex, and both Peter Shaw and Len Travers have read it in anthropological terms as a coming-of-age rite through which the colonists achieved adulthood by killing the father. Christopher Looby, *Voicing America: Language, Literary Form, and the Origins of the United States* (Chicago: University of Chicago Press, 1996), 99–144; Peter Shaw, *American Patriots and the Rituals of Revolution* (Cambridge, MA: Harvard University Press, 1981), 194–96; Len Travers, *Celebrating the Fourth: Independence Day and the Rites of Nationalism in the Early Republic* (Amherst: University of Massachusetts Press, 1997), 22–23.

7. Shaw, *American Patriots and the Rituals of Revolution*, 14.

8. These events are recounted in Winthrop D. Jordan, "Familial Politics: Thomas Paine and the Killing of the King, 1776," *Journal of American History* 60 (1973): 306–8.

9. David Waldstreicher, *In the Midst of Perpetual Fetes: The Making of American Nationalism, 1776–1820* (Chapel Hill: University of North Carolina Press, 1997), 31.

10. Spartanus, "The Interest of America, Letter 1," *New-York Journal, or the General Advertiser*, May 30, 1776, 1; Spartanus, "The Interest of America, Letter 2," *New-York Journal*, June 13, 1776, 1; Spartanus, "The Interest of America, Letter 3," *New-York Journal*, June 20, 1776, 1–2.

11. *The People the Best Governors: or a Plan of Government Founded on the just Principles of Natural Freedom* (n.p., 1776), preface.

12. "Extract from a Charge delivered by the Hon. Judge Rush, to the Grand Jury of the county of Berks, at August Term, 1794—and now published at their request," *Gazette of the United States and Daily Evening Advertiser*, August 25, 1794, 2. For a similar argument against Regulation during Shays's Rebellion that forecast the changing terms of post-Revolutionary citizenship, see A Republican, "*To the* PUB-LICK," *Massachusetts Gazette*, October 10, 1786, 2.

13. James Madison, "Federalist 51," in *The Federalist*, intro. and notes by Robert A. Ferguson (New York: Barnes & Noble Classics, 2006), 288; and on Madison's reading of democracy, see Richard K. Matthews, *If Men Were Angels: James Madison and the Heartless Empire of Reason* (Lawrence: University Press of Kansas, 1995).

14. Hannah Arendt explains, "If foundation was the aim and the end of revolution, then the revolutionary spirit was not merely the spirit of beginning something new but of starting something permanent and enduring; a lasting institution, embodying this spirit and encouraging it to new achievements, would be self-defeating. From which it unfortunately seems to follow that nothing threatens the very achievements of revolution more dangerously and more acutely than the spirit which has brought them about." Hannah Arendt, *On Revolution* (New York: Viking, 1963), 235. Though she does not reference Arendt, another historian of the Declaration of Independence, Pauline Maier, makes essentially the same point, writing: "Revolutionary documents are always uncomfortable for established governments. Even nations founded in revolutions quickly become conservative, if only to preserve the advances that revolution has brought." Pauline Maier, *American Scripture: Making the Declaration of Independence* (New York: Alfred A. Knopf, 1998), 211.

15. Thomas Paine, *Dissertations on Government, the Affairs of the Bank, and Paper Money* (1786), in *The Thomas Paine Reader*, 168, 175–76, 182. Like many other rhetoricians in the early Republic, Paine employed what Emma Rothschild calls the eighteenth century's "conflict of political thermometers" to describe reality. See Emma Rothschild, *Economic Sentiments: Adam Smith, Condorcet, and the Enlightenment* (Cambridge, MA: Harvard University Press, 2001), 26, 168.

16. Michael Hardt and Antonio Negri, *Multitude: War and Democracy in the Age of*

Empire (New York: Penguin, 2004), 241–47.

17. For two helpful discussions of the dynamics of representation, which is dependent upon the rhetorical maneuver of synecdoche, see Kenneth Burke, *A Grammar of Motives* (1945; Berkeley: University of California Press, 1962), 507–11; and Stephen John Hartnett, *Democratic Dissent and the Cultural Fictions of Antebellum America* (Urbana: University of Illinois Press, 2002), 132–72.

18. Leonard Richards, *Shays's Rebellion: The American Revolution's Final Battle* (Philadelphia: University of Pennsylvania Press, 2002), 1–3.

19. The best discussion of Regulation is E. P. Thompson, "The Moral Economy of the English Crowd in the Eighteenth Century," *Past & Present* 50 (1971): 76–136. On the Regulations in the Carolinas, see Richard Maxwell Brown, *The South Carolina Regulators* (Cambridge, MA: Harvard University Press, 1963); Rachel N. Klein, *Unification of a Slave State: The Rise of the Planter Class in the South Carolina Backcountry, 1760–1808* (Chapel Hill: University of North Carolina Press, 1990), 47–108; Marjoleine Kars, *Breaking Loose Together: The Regulator Rebellion in Pre-Revolutionary North Carolina* (Chapel Hill: University of North Carolina Press, 2002); and Nash, *The Unknown American Revolution*, 72–87, 103–14.

20. Adam Wheeler, "For the WORCESTER MAGAZINE. To the PUBLIC," *Worcester Magazine*, November 1786, 414.

21. Richards, *Shays's Rebellion*.

22. Christopher Clark, *The Roots of Rural Capitalism: Western Massachusetts, 1780–1860* (Ithaca, NY: Cornell University Press, 1990), 44; and on the clashing global and local economies, see also his "Economics and Culture: Opening Up the Rural History of the Early American Northeast," *American Quarterly* 43 (1991): 279–301, and "Rural America and the Transition to Capitalism," in *Wages of Independence: Capitalism in the Early American Republic*, ed. Paul A. Gilje (Madison, WI: Madison House, 1997), 65–79. For further discussions of rural economies in Massachusetts, see Robert Mutch, "Yeoman and Merchant in Pre-Industrial America: Eighteenth Century Massachusetts as a Case Study," *Societas* 7 (1977): 279–302; and David P. Szatmary, *Shays' Rebellion: The Making of an Agrarian Insurrection* (Amherst: University of Massachusetts Press, 1980), 1–36.

23. On the Massachusetts Constitution, see Douglass, *Rebels and Democrats*, 136–213; and Robert J. Taylor, ed., *Massachusetts: Colony to Commonwealth: Documents on the Formation of Its Constitution, 1775–1780* (Chapel Hill: University of North Carolina Press, 1961).

24. On the war bonds controversy and the funding of Massachusetts' debt, see Richard

Buel, Jr., "The Public Creditor Interest in Massachusetts Politics, 1780–86," in *In Debt to Shays: The Bicentennial of an Agrarian Rebellion*, ed. Robert A. Gross (Charlottesville: University Press of Virginia, 1993), 47–56; and Woody Holton, "'From the Labours of Others': The War Bonds Controversy and the Origins of the Federal Constitution in New England," *William and Mary Quarterly* 61 (2004): 271–316.

25. Edwin J. Perkins, *American Public Finance and Financial Services, 1700–1815* (Columbus: Ohio State University Press, 1994), 173–86 (stats, 180).

26. On resistance to financial policies in the period leading up to Shays's Rebellion, see Roger H. Brown, *Redeeming the Republic: Federalists, Taxation, and the Origins of the Constitution* (Baltimore: Johns Hopkins University Press, 1993), 32–138; Perkins, *American Public Finance and Financial Services*, 137–96; Robert A. Becker, *Revolution, Reform, and the Politics of American Taxation, 1763–1783* (Baton Rouge: Louisiana State University Press, 1980), 219–29; Robert J. Taylor, *Western Massachusetts in the Revolution* (Providence, RI: Brown University Press, 1954), 112–21; and John L. Brooke, "To the Quiet of the People: Revolutionary Settlements and Civil Unrest in Western Massachusetts, 1774–1789," *William and Mary Quarterly* 46 (1989): 425–62.

27. Petition from the Town of Greenwich to the Massachusetts Assembly, January 16, 1786, reprinted in *The Radical Reader: A Documentary History of the American Radical Tradition*, ed. Timothy Patrick McCarthy and John McMillian (New York: The New Press, 2003), 52.

28. Alexander Hamilton, "Federalist 6," 31.

29. Stephen T. Riley, "Dr. William Whiting and Shays' Rebellion," *Proceedings of the American Antiquarian Society* 66 (1956): 133.

30. See *Worcester Magazine*, April 1787, 51, where we find "a list of persons convicted by the Supreme Judicial Court at their late session in the county of Berkshire," which includes "*William Whiting*, of Great Barrington, Esq; for uttering divers seditions and inflammatory speeches, and for making and publishing a seditious libel, was sentenced to pay a fine of £.100, suffer 7 months imprisonment, and to be bound to good behaviour for 5 years."

31. Plain Truth, "*For the* CENTINEL," *Massachusetts Centinel*, February 18, 1786, 1.

32. Richards, *Shays's Rebellion*, 10.

33. Samuel Adams quoted in William V. Wells, *The Life and Public Services of Samuel Adams, Being a Narrative of his Acts and Opinions, and of His Agency in Producing and Forwarding the American Revolution* (Boston: Little, Brown and Company,

1865), 3:246.

34. Jeremy Belknap quoted in John H. Lockwood, *Westfield and its Historic Influences 1669–1919: The Life of an Early Town, With a Survey of Events in New England and Bordering Regions to which it was Related in Colonial and Revolutionary Times* (Springfield, MA: Springfield Binding Co., 1922), 2:112.

35. William Shepard to James Bowdoin, December 17, 1786, in *The Bowdoin and Temple Papers*, in *Collections of the Massachusetts Historical Society*, Seventh Series (Boston: Massachusetts Historical Society, 1907), 6:119.

36. Shepard to James Bowdoin, February 18, 1787, in *The Bowdoin and Temple Papers*, 142.

37. As the episteme shifted, it brought about the possibility of "new epistemologies of emotion," to use Dana Rabin's words, and "a whole new order of concepts," to use Michel Foucault's. Dana Rabin, "Bodies of Evidence, States of Mind: Infanticide, Emotion and Sensibility in Eighteenth-Century England," in *Infanticide: Historical Perspectives on Child Murder and Concealment, 1550–2000*, ed. Mark Jackson (Burlington, VT: Ashgate, 2002), 78; Michel Foucault, *Madness and Civilization: A History of Insanity in the Age of Reason*, trans. Richard Howard (1961; New York: Vintage, 1988), 219. For a helpful overview of changes that Enlightenment philosophy brought to how the self and its relationship to the world was conceptualized, see Charles Taylor, *Sources of the Self: The Making of Modern Identity* (Cambridge, MA: Harvard University Press, 1989).

38. John Locke, *An Essay Concerning Human Understanding*, ed. Alexander Campbell Fraser (1690; New York: Dover Publications, 1959), 1:121–22, 157; 2:146.

39. Bernard Lamy, *The Art of Speaking* (1676), reprinted in *The Rhetorics of Thomas Hobbes and Bernard Lamy*, ed. John Harwood (Carbondale: Southern Illinois University Press, 1986), 230, 247, 361, 374.

40. Thomas Hobbes, *De Cive* (1642), in Thomas Hobbes, *Man and Citizen*, ed. Bernard Gert (Indianapolis: Hackett Publishing Co., 1998), 231.

41. Lamy, *Art of Speaking*, 241.

42. "COMMONWEALTH of MASSACHUSETTS. In SENATE, February 23, 1787," *Worcester Magazine*, March 1787, 608.

43. The perception that citizens might mimic criminals was rooted in eighteenth-century epistemology, which created the problem of "mimetic corruption" discussed in Michael Meranze, *Laboratories of Virtue: Punishment, Revolution, and Authority in Philadelphia, 1760–1835* (Chapel Hill: University of North Carolina Press, 1996), 87–127.

44. "COMMONWEALTH *of* MASSACHUSETTS. In the Year of Our Lord One Thousand Seven Hundred and Eighty-Six. *An* ACT *for suspending the privilege of the Writ of* HABEAS CORPUS," *Worcester Magazine*, December 1786, 435.

45. Richards, *Shays's Rebellion*, 21.

46. Ibid.

47. One of the more telling warnings came from General Benjamin Lincoln. In a February 20, 1787, letter to Bowdoin, he voiced reservations about the government's strategy and urged clemency: "People who have been in arms are hourly coming in. Their flight into the bosom of their country will I doubt not be in some proportion to the mild terms held out by government as the conditions on which they may expect its favours." Lincoln argued that if the government became tyrannical, its citizens would take up arms against it out of desperation and the inability to enact political change any other way. For Lincoln, then, who was one of the state's leading military figures, Massachusetts citizens did not need to be controlled, but appeased. On February 22, Lincoln stressed cautious terms to Bowdoin, noting that "our goals [jails] are now full" and that "The Sheriff will not apprehend any others, unless he should meet some who are the most aggravatedly guilty." He recommended complete and universal clemency: "I am fully in opinion that we might now liberate, under bonds, all who have been apprehended on State warrants in this county." The irony is thick: the Massachusetts government accused dissenters of madness, but refused to listen to reasonable advice like Lincoln's, choosing instead to follow a self-destructive policy of full-scale rhetorical warfare. Lincoln to James Bowdoin, February 20, 1787, and February 22, 1787, in *The Bowdoin and Temple Papers*, 145, 157.

48. See, for instance, King George III, Proclamation, August 23, 1775, reprinted in *The Spirit of '76: The Story of the American Revolution as Told by Participants*, ed. Henry Steele Commager and Richard B. Morris (New York: Da Capo Press, 1995), 281.

49. Richard D. Brown, "Shays's Rebellion and Its Aftermath: A View from Springfield, Massachusetts, 1787," *William and Mary Quarterly* 40 (1983): 610.

50. Ibid., 603. The crime wave that shook post-Revolutionary America is described in Daniel Cohen, *Pillars of Salt, Monuments of Grace: New England Crime Literature and the Origins of American Popular Culture, 1674–1860* (Oxford: Oxford University Press, 1993), 119–20. The conservative turn against Regulation is discussed in Gilje, *The Road to Mobocracy*, 71–92.

51. Brown, "Shays's Rebellion and Its Aftermath," 609.

52. For a contemporary portrayal of the election results, see "General Election, at

Boston, 1787," *Worcester Magazine*, June 1, 1787. As Richard Brown describes the election: "Although hundreds of men in the western counties were disqualified from voting because of pro-Shays activities, the mobilization of voters set a record for a statewide election. In the absence of other variables, it is clear that the rebellion and the actions of the government had generated a wave of interest in politics that had not been seen since the early years of the Revolution." Richard Brown, "Shays's Rebellion and the Ratification of the Federal Constitution in Massachusetts," in *Beyond Confederation: Origins of the Constitution and American National Identity*, ed. Richard Beeman, Stephen Botein, and Edward Carter (Chapel Hill: University of North Carolina Press, 1987), 120.

53. Woody Holton writes, "The Constitutional Convention was largely a response to the farmers' rebellions of the 1780s and the state assemblies' subsequent adoption of legislation that allegedly violated public and private contracts." Woody Holton, *Unruly Americans and the Origins of the Constitution* (New York: Hill and Wang, 2007), 227.

54. James Madison to J. G. Jackson, December 27, 1821, in *The Records of the Federal Convention of 1787*, ed. Max Farrand (New Haven, CT: Yale University Press, 1911), 3:449. For discussions of the events that led to the writing and ratification of the Constitution, see Jack N. Rakove, *Original Meanings: Politics and Ideas in the Making of the Constitution* (New York: Vintage, 1997); David C. Hendrickson, *Peace Pact: The Lost World of the American Founding* (Lawrence: University of Kansas Press, 2003); Max M. Edling, *A Revolution in Favor of Government: Origins of the U.S. Constitution and the Making of the American State* (Oxford: Oxford University Press, 2003); and Akhil Reed Amar, *America's Constitution: A Biography* (New York: Random House, 2005). For the most forceful arguments that Shays's Rebellion assisted in justifying the revision of the Articles of Confederation into the Constitution, see Richards, *Shays's Rebellion*, 117–64; Szatmary, *Shays' Rebellion*, 120–34; Brown, "Shays's Rebellion and the Ratification of the Federal Constitution in Massachusetts," 113–27; and Holton, *Unruly Americans*. Madison lent support to this thesis. He expounded: "As the pub. mind had been ripened for a salutary Reform of the pol. System, in the interval between the proposal & the meeting, of Comrs. at Annapolis, the interval between the last event, and the meeting of Deps. at Phila. had continued to develop more & more the necessity & the extent of a Systematic provision for the preservation and Govt. of the Union; among the ripening incidents was the Insurrection of Shays in Massts. against her Govt; which was with difficulty suppressed, notwithstanding the influence of the insurgents of

an apprehended interposition of the Fedl. troops." Shays's Rebellion was the only event Madison listed as "ripening" the Constitutional movement. James Madison, "Preface to Debates in the Convention of 1787," in Farrand, *Records of the Federal Convention*, 3:547.

55. John Adams to Thomas Jefferson, November 30, 1786, in *The Adams-Jefferson Letters: The Complete Correspondence between Thomas Jefferson and Abigail & John Adams*, ed. Lester J. Cappon (1959; Chapel Hill: University of North Carolina Press, 1987), 156.

56. Thomas Jefferson to Abigail Adams, February 22, 1787, in *Adams-Jefferson Letters*, 173.

57. Thomas Jefferson to William Stephens Smith, November 13, 1787, in Thomas Jefferson, *Writings*, ed. Merrill D. Peterson, Library of America Series (New York: Literary Classics of the U.S., 1984), 911.

58. Jefferson to Madison, September 6, 1789, in *Writings*, ed. Peterson, 963.

59. Madison to Jefferson, February 4, 1790, in *The Papers of Thomas Jefferson*, ed. Julian Boyd (Princeton, NJ: Princeton University Press, 1961), 16:147.

60. Jefferson's interlocutor Abigail Adams, for one, completely disagreed with his interpretation. "With regard to the Tumults in my Native state," she wrote in January 1787, "Ignorant, wrestless desperadoes, without conscience or principals, have led a deluded multitude to follow their standard, under pretence of grievances which have no existence but in their imaginations." Here, she found herself directly opposed to Jefferson, and was not bashful in telling him so: "Instead of that laudible spirit which you approve, which makes a people watchfull over their Liberties and alert in the defence of them, these mobish insurgents are for sapping the foundation, and distroying the whole fabrick at once." Shays's Rebellion had no value for her. It was nothing more than an ignorant attack on the very idea of government. She announced her verdict in September 1787: "The ferment and commotions in Massachusetts has brought upon the surface abundance of Rubbish." Adams offered the antithesis of Jefferson's view, disparaging the methods through which common folks in Massachusetts participated in politics. Abigail Adams to Jefferson, January 29, 1787, and September 10, 1787, in *Adams-Jefferson Letters*, 168, 198.

61. William Manning, *The Key of Libberty: Shewing the Causes Why a Free Government Has Always Failed and a Remedy against It. Addressed to the Republicans, Farmers, Mechanics, and Labourers in America by a Labourer* (1799), in *The Key of Liberty: The Life and Democratic Writings of William Manning, "A Laborer," 1747–1814*, ed. Michael Merrill and Sean Wilentz (Cambridge, MA: Harvard University Press,

1993), 165. On Manning's rhetoric, see Jennifer R. Mercieca and James Arnt Aune, "A Vernacular Republican Rhetoric: William Manning's *Key of Libberty*," *Quarterly Journal of Speech* 91 (2005): 119–43.

62. George Richards Minot, *The History of the Insurrections, in Massachusetts, In the Year MDCCLXXXVI, and the Rebellion Consequent Thereon* (Worcester, MA: Isaiah Thomas, 1788), 170. Minot's influence was profound. As historian Robert Gross notes in "White Hats and Hemlocks: Daniel Shays and the Legacy of the Revolution," in *The Transforming Hand of Revolution: Reconsidering the American Revolution as a Social Movement*, ed. Ronald Hoffman and Peter J. Albert (Charlottesville: University Press of Virginia, 1996), 297: "Minot did not simply frame discussion in print of Shays's Rebellion; he monopolized it."

63. Bernard Bailyn argues that the Constitution "is the final and climactic expression of the ideology of the American Revolution," but Gordon Wood argues that by creating a strong central government with the power to coerce dissent and squash democracy, the Constitution completely reneged on the spirit of the Revolution. For Wood, "the Americans of 1787 shattered the classical Whig world of 1776." How one reads this formative period in U.S. history depends, in large part, upon whether one agrees with Bailyn or Wood on the nature of the Constitution. Bernard Bailyn, *The Ideological Origins of the American Revolution* (1967; Cambridge, MA: Harvard University Press, 1992), 321; Wood, *The Creation of the American Republic*, 606.

64. Delaware, December 7, 1787 (30 to 0); Pennsylvania, December 12, 1787 (46 to 23); New Jersey, December 18, 1787 (38 to 0); Georgia, December 31, 1787 (26 to 0); Connecticut, January 9, 1788 (128 to 40); Massachusetts, February 6, 1788 (187 to 168); Maryland, April 26, 1788 (63 to 11); South Carolina, May 23, 1788 (149 to 73); New Hampshire, June 21, 1788 (57 to 47); Virginia, June 25, 1788 (89 to 79); New York, July 26, 1788 (30 to 27); North Carolina, November 21, 1789 (194 to 77); Rhode Island, May 29, 1790 (34 to 32)—see *Debate on the Constitution*, 2:1064–74.

65. George Washington to Henry Lee, Jr., October 31, 1786, in *The Papers of George Washington: Confederation Series*, ed. W. W. Abbott (Charlottesville: University Press of Virginia, 1995), 4:318.

66. Ibid., 4:320.

67. On Americans' desire for the cultural distinction that owning china would provide, see John Kuo Wei Tchen, *New York before Chinatown: Orientalism and the Shaping of American Culture, 1776–1882* (Baltimore: Johns Hopkins University Press, 1999), 3–24.

68. Thomas Jefferson to John Adams, October 28, 1813, in *Adams-Jefferson Letters*, 388.

On the natural aristocracy's demands for deference, see Gordon S. Wood, *The Radicalism of the American Revolution* (New York: Vintage, 1991), 57–77, 179–80, 271–86.

69. Alexander Hamilton, "Federalist 1," 9; Centinel, Letter 1, in *Complete Anti-Federalist*, 2:137.

70. Jürgen Habermas, *The Structural Transformation of the Public Sphere: An Inquiry into a Category of Bourgeois Society*, trans. Thomas Burger (1962; Cambridge, MA: MIT Press, 1999).

71. Jürgen Habermas, *The Theory of Communicative Action*, trans. Thomas McCarthy (Boston: Beacon Press, 1984), 1:10.

72. Jürgen Habermas, *Communication and the Evolution of Society*, trans. Thomas McCarthy (1976; Boston: Beacon Press, 1979), 3.

73. On Habermas's theory of universal pragmatics, see Maeve Cooke, *Language and Reason: A Study of Habermas's Pragmatics* (Cambridge, MA: MIT Press, 1994). For critiques of Habermas's philosophy because it ignores perlocutionary speech acts, the primacy of antagonism, and persuasion more generally, see Chantal Mouffe, *The Democratic Paradox* (London: Verso, 2000), 48, 83–90; and Daniele S. Allen, *Talking to Strangers: Anxieties of Citizenship since* Brown v. Board of Education (Chicago: University of Chicago Press, 2004), 54–64.

74. Kenneth Burke, *Language as Symbolic Action: Essays on Life, Literature, and Method* (Berkeley: University of California Press, 1966), 5.

75. Kenneth Burke, *A Rhetoric of Motives* (1950; Berkeley: University of California Press, 1969), 19–20.

76. James Jasinski, "Rhetoric and Judgment in the Constitutional Ratification Debate of 1787–1788: An Exploration in the Relationship between Theory and Critical Practice," *Quarterly Journal of Speech* 78 (1992): 197–218.

77. "A Countryman" [Roger Sherman?], Letter 2, *New Haven Gazette* (Connecticut), November 22, 1787, in *Debate on the Constitution*, 1:412; "The Address and Reasons of Dissent of the Minority of the Convention of the State of Pennsylvania to their Constituents," *Pennsylvania Packet* (Philadelphia), December 18, 1787, in *Debate on the Constitution*, 1:528.

78. "Alexander Hamilton's Conjectures about the New Constitution," September 1787, in *Debate on the Constitution*, 1:9.

79. Federal Farmer, Letter 5, October 13, 1787, in *The Complete Anti-Federalist*, ed. Herbert J. Storing (Chicago: University of Chicago Press, 1981), 2:253.

80. David Humphreys to George Washington, November 1, 1786, in *The Papers of*

George Washington, 4:351.

81. On the Levellers, see Linebaugh and Rediker, *Many-Headed Hydra*, 104–42.

82. John Locke, *Second Treatise of Government*, ed. Richard H. Cox (1689; Wheeling, IL: Harlan Davidson, 1982), 75.

83. Michel Foucault, *Discipline and Punish: The Birth of the Prison*, trans. Alan Sheridan (1975; New York: Vintage, 1995), 257–92; Peter Linebaugh, *The London Hanged: Crime and Civil Society in the Eighteenth Century* (Cambridge: Cambridge University Press, 1991), 371–441.

84. Paine, *Common Sense*, 99.

85. Philadelphus, "To the Printer of the Pennsylvania Herald," *Pennsylvania Herald, and General Advertiser* (Philadelphia), April 18, 1787, 2.

86. Cato, "For the Centinel," *Massachusetts Centinel* (Boston), August 22, 1787, 177.

87. "Philadelphia, August 6," *City Gazette and Daily Advertiser* (Charleston, SC), September 20, 1788, 2; "Daniel Shays," "To the *Antifederal Junto* in Philadelphia," *American Herald* (Philadelphia), October 8, 1787, 2.

88. *Daily Advertiser* (New York City), December 4, 1787, 2.

89. *Massachusetts Gazette* (Boston), October 19, 1787, 2. Shays was similarly pitted against Washington and Franklin in the *Independent Gazetteer*, October 13, 1787, 2.

90. Hamilton, "Federalist 84," 474.

91. Holton, *Unruly Americans*, 253, 278.

92. Ibid., 273.

93. Benjamin Rush to Jeremy Belknap, May 6, 1788, in *Letters of Benjamin Rush*, ed. L. H. Butterfield (Princeton, NJ: Princeton University Press, 1951), 1:460–61. Rush's reaction was similar to Adams's, in that he assured his interlocutors that everything would turn out for the best. "All will be well," he continued. "The last thing that I can believe is that providence has brought us over the Red Sea of the late war to perish in the present wilderness of anarchy and vice. What has been, will be, and there is nothing new under the sun. We are advancing through suffering (the usual road) to peace and happiness. Night preceded day, and chaos, order, in the creation of the world."

94. William Shepard to James Bowdoin, February 18, 1787, in *The Bowdoin and Temple Papers*, 142; Fisher Ames, "Camillus, No. II," in *Works of Fisher Ames. With a Selection from His Speeches and Correspondence*, ed. Seth Ames (Boston: Little, Brown and Company, 1854), 2:103; Samuel Lyman to Samuel Breck, December 27, 1786, *Bowdoin and Temple Papers*, 122; "Important Intelligence. COPY of a Letter from General LINCOLN to Captain SHAYS," *Worcester Magazine*, February 1787, 534; *Worcester*

Magazine, January 8, 1787; Benjamin Rush, "An Account of the Influence of the Military and Political Events of the American Revolution Upon the Human Body" (1787), in *Medical Inquiries and Other Observations*, 2nd American edition (Philadelphia: Thomas Dobson, 1794), 1:277.

95. Henry Knox to George Washington, October 23, 1786, *Papers of George Washington*, 300.

96. *Worcester Magazine*, November 1786, 414. After reading Wheeler's letter "To *the* PUBLIC," the reader then read an article titled *"The following is said to be a* CURE *for the* BITE *of a* MAD DOG."

97. For a discussion of how rhetorics of madness helped to define "the civilized" and "the rational" through antithesis, see Foucault, *Madness and Civilization*.

98. Benjamin Rush, "An Account of the Influence of the Military and Political Events of the American Revolution Upon the Human Body," 277.

99. Philolaos, "To the People of Massachusetts," *Worcester Magazine*, April 1, 1787; Minot, *The History of the Insurrections*, 41.

100. Hamilton, Speech of June 18, 1787, in *Records of the Federal Convention*, 1:289.

101. Camillus [Fisher Ames], *Worcester Magazine*, April 1, 1787.

102. Fisher Ames, Speech at the Massachusetts Ratifying Convention, January 15, 1788, in *The Debate on the Constitution*, 1:894.

103. According to Szatmary, at Springfield there were 300 men from Berkshire, 1,000 men from Hampshire, 1,000 men from Worcester and Middlesex. Shepard's army had 1,000 militiamen, and nearly 4,400 men were in the government army under Lincoln that was marching to Springfield but arrived too late for the battle. See Szatmary, *Shays' Rebellion*, 100–101.

104. Minot, *The History of the Insurrections*, 111; and Marion Starkey, *A Little Rebellion* (New York: Alfred A. Knopf, 1955), 132–33.

105. Daniel Shays's proclamation to Benjamin Lincoln, dated Pelham, January 30, 1787, reprinted in Minot, *History of the Insurrections*, 120.

106. Alexander Hamilton, "Federalist 21," 112.

107. Washington and Adams quoted in Wood, *Radicalism of the American Revolution*, 27.

108. "A Landholder" [Oliver Ellsworth], Letter 5, *Connecticut Courant* (Hartford), December 3, 1787, in *Debate on the Constitution*, 1:241. Similarly, Pennsylvania's *Newport Herald* asked, "What would have been the fate of Massachusetts had not Shays aped a Massinelio, and arrayed himself in all the pomp of military prowess to overturn the fair fabric of order and justice, before he had counted his strength?"

Newport Herald (Newport, PA), January 17, 1788, 2.

109. Henry Lee, Address of June 9, 1788, at the Virginia Ratifying Convention, in *Debate on the Constitution*, 2:640.

110. David Humphreys, Joel Barlow, John Trumbull, and Lemuel Hopkins, *The Anarchiad: A New England Poem, 1786–87*, ed. Luther G. Riggs and Thomas H. Pease (New Haven, CT: T.H. Pease, 1861), 20.

111. Humphreys, Barlow, Trumbull, and Hopkins, *The Anarchiad*, 61.

112. Centinel, Letter 9, in *Complete Anti-Federalist*, 2:182.

113. *The Address and Reasons of Dissent of the Minority of the Convention of Pennsylvania To Their Constituents*, originally published in the *Pennsylvania Packet and Daily Advertiser*, December 18, 1787, in *Complete Anti-Federalist*, 3:163–64.

114. Philadelphus, "To the Printer of the Pennsylvania Herald."

115. Hamilton, "Federalist 28," 149–50.

116. Ibid., 153.

117. Benjamin Lincoln to George Washington, February 3, 1788, in *Documentary History of the Ratification of the Constitution*, ed. Merrill Jensen (Madison: State Historical Society of Wisconsin, 1976), 7:1573.

118. Here, I rely on Gregory S. Goodale, "America's Rhetorical Revolution: Defining Citizens in Benjamin Rush's Philadelphia, 1783–1813," Ph.D. diss., University of Illinois, Urbana-Champaign, 2007.

119. Benjamin Rush, "Address to the People of the United States," *The American Museum* (Philadelphia), January 1787. For discussions of the perceived moral decay of the masses following the Revolutionary War, see Wood, *Creation of the American Republic*, 107–24, 393–467; Bailyn, *The Ideological Origins of the American Revolution*, 230–319; Ronald Takaki, *Iron Cages: Race and Culture in 19th-Century America* (1979; Oxford: Oxford University Press, 2000), 1–65; Bouton, *Taming Democracy*; and Holton, *Unruly Americans*.

120. Article 4, Section 4 authorized the federal government to protect states against "domestic Violence"; Article 1, Section 8 allowed the Militia to "suppress Insurrections"; and Article 1, Section 9 permitted the suspension of the writ of habeas corpus "in cases of Rebellion or Invasion." In one fell swoop, the Constitution hence discredited many of the actions that helped colonists win the Revolutionary War, and created an apparatus for punishing those who violated the new order of things.

121. Foucault, *Discipline and Punish*, 135–228. For an example of discipline as punishment, see John Clarke, *An Essay Upon the Education of Youth in Grammar-Schools. In Which the Vulgar Method of Teaching Is Examined, and a New One Proposed,*

for the More Easy and Speedy Training Up of Youth to the Knowledge of the Learned Languages (1720), reprinted in Wilson Smith, *Theories of Education in Early America, 1655–1819* (Indianapolis, IN: Bobbs-Merrill, 1973), 89–90. For a more modern discussion of education as the means of correct training, see Amable-Louis-Rose de Lafitte du Courteil, *Proposal To Demonstrate the Necessity of a National Institution in the United States of America, for the Education of Children of Both Sexes. To Which is Joined, a Project of Organization, etc.* (1797), in *Essays on Education in the Early Republic*, ed. Frederick Rudolph (Cambridge, MA: Harvard University Press, 1965), 227–70. In fact, Lafitte, a teacher at an academy for boys in Bordentown, New Jersey, modeled his proposal for American education on military training in France.

122. Foucault, *Discipline and Punish*, 149–51.

CHAPTER THREE. THE ARMY OF THE CONSTITUTION

1. Centinel, Letter 7, in *The Complete Anti-Federalist*, ed. Herbert J. Storing (Chicago: University of Chicago Press, 1981), 2:175. For discussions of the Carlisle riots of 1787, see Saul Cornell, "Aristocracy Assailed," *Journal of American History* 76 (1989–1990): 1148–72; and *The Other Founders: Anti-Federalism and the Dissenting Tradition in America, 1788–1828* (Chapel Hill: University of North Carolina Press, 1999), 109–20. For recaps of the ratification debates in Pennsylvania, see Michael Gillespie and Michael Lienesch, *Ratifying the Constitution* (Lawrence: University of Kansas Press, 1989); and Jack N. Rakove, *Original Meanings: Politics and Ideas in the Making of the Constitution* (New York: Vintage, 1997), 116–18.

2. The 1776 Constitution is discussed in J. Paul Selsam, *The Pennsylvania Constitution of 1776: A Study in Revolutionary Democracy* (New York: Octagon Books, 1971).

3. Gordon S. Wood, *The Radicalism of the American Revolution* (New York: Vintage, 1991), 336.

4. Joseph Lathrop, *The Happiness of a Free Government, and the Means of Preserving it: Illustrated in a Sermon, Delivered in West-Springfield, On July 4th, 1794, in Commemoration of American Independence!* (Springfield, MA: James R. Hutchins, 1794), 12–13.

5. James Madison, "Federalist 40," in *The Federalist*, intro. and notes by Robert A. Ferguson (New York: Barnes & Noble Classics, 2006), 221.

6. St. George Tucker to James Madison, March 8, 1795, quoted in Richard A. Ifft, "Treason in the Early Republic: The Federal Courts, Popular Protest, and Federalism

during the Whiskey Insurrection," in *The Whiskey Rebellion: Past and Present Perspectives*, ed. Steven R. Boyd (Westport, CT: Greenwood Press, 1985), 165. On the 1780 hurricane, see Trevor Burnard, *Mastery, Tyranny, and Desire: Thomas Thistlewood and his Slaves in the Anglo-Jamaican World* (Chapel Hill: University of North Carolina Press, 2004), 5–6, 65–66. On the role of *fortuna* in Renaissance humanist conceptions of state formation, see J. G. A. Pocock, *The Machiavellian Moment: Florentine Political Thought and the Atlantic Republican Tradition* (1975; Princeton, NJ: Princeton University Press, 2003), 31–48.

7. Alexander Hamilton, "Report on Public Credit," January 9, 1790, in Alexander Hamilton, *Writings*, ed. Joanne B. Freeman, Library of America Series (New York: Literary Classics of the U.S., 2001), 560, and see also 532, 534, 552, 578, 655 for similar sentiments.

8. For overviews of Hamilton's economic policies, see Drew McCoy, *The Elusive Republic: Political Economy in Jeffersonian America* (Chapel Hill: University of North Carolina Press, 1980), 136–65; Stanley Elkins and Eric McKitrick, *The Age of Federalism: The Early American Republic, 1788–1800* (New York: Oxford University Press, 1993), 92–131; and Edwin J. Perkins, *American Public Finance and Financial Services, 1700–1815* (Columbus: Ohio State University Press, 1994), 199–265.

9. Brutus, "Brutus, No. 2. On the Funding System," *National Gazette* (Philadelphia), March 19, 1792, 162.

10. Max M. Edling, *A Revolution in Favor of Government: Origins of the U.S. Constitution and the Making of the American State* (Oxford: Oxford University Press, 2003), 208–10. For discussions of the effectiveness of Hamilton's financial policies, see E. James Ferguson, *The Power of the Purse: A History of American Public Finance, 1776–1790* (Chapel Hill: University of North Carolina Press, 1961), 289–329; Elkins and McKitrick, *The Age of Federalism*, 114–23; Perkins, *American Public Finance*, 199–234; and Max M. Edling and Mark D. Kaplanoff, "Alexander Hamilton's Fiscal Reform: Transforming the Structure of Taxation in the Early Republic," *William and Mary Quarterly* 61 (2004): 713–44.

11. A Farmer, "For the National Gazette. No. III," *National Gazette*, March 15, 1792, 158. On frontier fears of taxation, see Thomas P. Slaughter, *The Whiskey Rebellion: Frontier Epilogue to the American Revolution* (Oxford: Oxford University Press, 1986), 11–27; and "The Tax Man Cometh: Ideological Opposition to Internal Taxes, 1760–1790," *William and Mary Quarterly* 41 (1984): 566–91.

12. *Annals of Congress*, 1st Cong., 3rd Sess., 1891–92.

13. For discussions of the Democratic-Republican Societies, see Eugene P. Link,

The Democratic-Republican Societies, 1790–1800 (New York: Columbia University Press, 1942); Philip S. Foner, ed., *The Democratic-Republican Societies, 1790–1800: A Documentary Sourcebook of Constitutions, Declarations, Addresses, Resolutions, and Toasts* (Westport, CT: Greenwood Press, 1976), 3–51; and Robert M. Chesney, "Democratic-Republican Societies, Subversion, and the Limits of Legitimate Political Dissent in the Early Republic," *North Carolina Law Review* 82 (2004): 1525–79. For discussions of the Democratic-Republican Societies in Pennsylvania, see Jeffrey A. Davis, "Guarding the Republican Interest: The Western Pennsylvania Democratic Societies and the Excise Tax," *Pennsylvania History* 67 (2000): 43–62; and Albrecht Koschnik, "The Democratic Societies of Philadelphia and the Limits of the American Public Sphere, circa 1793–1795," *William and Mary Quarterly* 58 (2001): 615–36.

14. Foner, ed., *Democratic-Republican Societies*, 359.

15. Ibid., 85.

16. Sean Wilentz, *The Rise of American Democracy: Jefferson to Lincoln* (New York: W.W. Norton & Co., 2005), 57–58.

17. Westsylvanians quoted in Slaughter, *The Whiskey Rebellion*, 33.

18. The literature on the snags of U.S. nation-building is vast. For a general treatment, see Peter Onuf, *The Origins of the Federal Republic: Jurisdictional Controversies in the United States, 1775–1787* (Philadelphia: University of Pennsylvania Press, 1983), 21–46. On Fair Play, see George D. Wolf, *The Fair Play Settlers of the West Branch Valley, 1769–1784: A Study in Frontier Ethnography* (Harrisburg, PA: Pennsylvania Historical and Museum Commission, 1969). On Transylvania, see William Steward Lester, *The Transylvania Colony* (Spencer, IN: S.R. Guard & Co., 1935); and Eric Hinderaker, *Elusive Empires: Constructing Colonialism in the Ohio Valley, 1673–1800* (Cambridge: Cambridge University Press, 1997), 195–201. On Watuga and Franklin, see Malcolm J. Rohrbough, *The Trans-Appalachian Frontier: People, Societies, and Institutions, 1775–1850* (New York: Oxford University Press, 1978), 21–63.

19. Solon J. Buck and Elizabeth Hawthorne Buck, *The Planting of Civilization in Western Pennsylvania* (Pittsburgh, PA: University of Pittsburgh Press, 1939), 171.

20. W. J. Rorabaugh, *The Alcoholic Republic: An American Tradition* (New York: Oxford University Press, 1979), 25–57, 95–122.

21. Terry Bouton, *Taming Democracy: "The People," the Founders, and the Troubled Ending of the American Revolution* (New York: Oxford University Press, 2007), 219–20.

22. On closing roads as protest, see Bouton, *Taming Democracy*, 197–215.

23. For an insightful reading of the symbolism of burning houses in early America, see Robert Blair St. George, *Conversing by Signs: Poetics of Implication in Colonial New England Culture* (Chapel Hill: University of North Carolina Press, 1998), 206–95. These actions reveal the confused rhetorical economy of frontier life. Though many frontier communities united in opposition to the Indian, nevertheless frontiersmen freely adopted the techniques of their enemies to protest the encroaching federal government. During the eighteenth century, self-identity was correlated with property ownership; hence, when Indians burned colonial settlers' houses, they obliterated the possessions that marked colonists as civilized Europeans in a premodern world of "savagery." Such actions represented the symbolic destruction of settlers themselves. For a discussion of what it meant when Indians burned colonists' houses, see Jill Lepore, *In the Name of War: King Philip's War and the Origins of American Identity* (New York: Alfred A. Knopf, 1998), 71–96.

24. William Findley, *History of the Insurrection in the Four Western Counties of Pennsylvania in the Year MDCCXCIV. With a Recital of the Circumstances Specially Connected Therewith* (Philadelphia: Samuel Harrison Smith, 1796), 79, 80.

25. E. Eugene Harper, *The Transformation of Western Pennsylvania, 1770–1800* (Pittsburgh, PA: University of Pittsburgh Press, 1991), 17–39, 81–106.

26. Hugh Henry Brackenridge, *Incidents of the Insurrection in the Western Parts of Pennsylvania, In the Year 1794* (Philadelphia: John McCulloch, 1795), 1:43–44.

27. Ibid., 1:41, 99, 102.

28. Frankliniensis, "For the National Gazette," *National Gazette*, January 23, 1792, 99.

29. A Farmer, "To the Yeomanry of the UNITED STATES," *National Gazette*, March 26, 1792, 172.

30. On the clashing visions of history offered by federalists and anti-federalists, see Michael Lienesch, *New Order for the Ages: Time, the Constitution, and the Making of Modern American Political Thought* (Princeton, NJ: Princeton University Press, 1988).

31. James Wilson, speech of October 6, 1787, in *The Debate on the Constitution: Federalist and Antifederalist Speeches, Articles, and Letters during the Struggle over Ratification*, ed. Bernard Bailyn, Library of America Series (New York: Literary Classics of the U.S., 1993), 1:65–66; Alexander Hamilton to the Continental Congress, June 18, 1787, reprinted in *The Records of the Federal Convention of 1787*, ed. Max Farrand (New Haven, CT: Yale University Press, 1911), 1:297–98.

32. Alexander Hamilton, "Federalist 23," 125–26.

33. On Hamilton's machinations, see Bouton, *Taming Democracy*, 229–30.

34. Findley quoted in Bouton, *Taming Democracy*, 230.

35. Hamilton to Washington, August 2, 1794, in *Writings*, 825.

36. Bernard Bailyn, *The Ideological Origins of the American Revolution* (1967; Cambridge, MA: Harvard University Press, 1992), 55–93.

37. Alexander Hamilton, *Tully* No. 3, *Dunlap and Claypoole's American Daily Advertiser*, August 28, 1794, in *Writings*, 830.

38. On Bunker Hill, see W. J. Wood, *Battles of the Revolutionary War, 1775–1781* (Chapel Hill: Algonquin Books, 1990), 3–34; and Richard M. Ketchum, *Decisive Day: The Battle for Bunker Hill* (New York: Doubleday, 1991). On Saratoga, see Wood, *Battles of the Revolutionary War*, 132–71; and Richard M. Ketchum, *Saratoga: Turning Point of America's Revolutionary War* (New York: H. Holt, 1997).

39. For an overview of the difficult political situation the new United States government inherited when it assumed power in 1789, see Reginald Horsman, *Expansion and American Indian Policy, 1783–1812* (1967; Norman: University of Oklahoma Press, 1992), 53–103.

40. Representatives of the Wyandots, Seven Nations of Canada, Delawares, Shawnees, Miamis, Ottawas, Chippewas, Senecas, Potawatomis, Conoys, Munsees, Nanticokes, Mahicans, Mississaugas, Creeks, and Cherokees, "Proposal to Maintain Indian Lands, 1793," in *The World Turned Upside Down: Indian Voices from Early America*, ed. Colin Calloway (Boston: Bedford, 1994), 181–82.

41. "Observations on the Present Indian War," *Federal Gazette and Philadelphia Daily Advertiser* (Philadelphia), May 12, 1792, 2. For similar sentiments, see *Boston County Gazette, and the Country Journal* (Boston), March 5, 1792, 1; and *Federal Gazette* (Philadelphia), November 19, 1792, 2.

42. On early American visions of a benevolent empire, see Peter S. Onuf, *Jefferson's Empire: The Language of American Nationhood* (Charlottesville: University of Virginia Press, 2000).

43. Brackenridge, *Incidents of the Insurrection*, 1:41.

44. Ibid., 1:106.

45. As historian Eric Hinderaker argues, though Americans "remained divided on a wide range of social and political questions, the Euroamerican residents of the Ohio Valley could unify in support of aggressive national expansion." And, in the words of Terry Bouton, "for most Westerners, removing Indians was just as fundamental a part of their vision of Independence as their notions of good governance." Hinderaker, *Elusive Empires*, 226; Bouton, *Taming Democracy*, 235.

46. Bernard Sheehan writes about the early Republic: "In the sense that the Indian

represented a completely foreign culture, or, perhaps more pertinent, because he stood for savagery, the antithesis of civilization, white men found it easy to bury their own differences in dealing with him." Bernard W. Sheehan, *Seeds of Extinction: Jeffersonian Philanthropy and the American Indian* (Chapel Hill: University of North Carolina Press, 1973), 6.

47. This point is developed in Roy Harvey Pearce, *Savagism and Civilization: A Study of the Indian in the American Mind* (1953; Baltimore: The Johns Hopkins Press, 1967).

48. James Madison, "Federalist 10," 55.

49. Ibid., 58.

50. Thomas Jefferson to Monsieur d'Ivernois, February 6, 1795, in *The Writings of Thomas Jefferson*, ed. Albert Ellery Bergh (Washington, DC: Thomas Jefferson Memorial Association, 1803–4), 9:300.

51. John Locke, *Second Treatise of Government*, ed. Richard Cox (1689; Wheeling, IL: Harlan Davidson, 1982), 23–4; Adam Smith, *The Wealth of Nations*, ed. Edwin Cannan (1776; New York: The Modern Library, 2000), 610.

52. Ellen Meiksins Wood, *Empire of Capital* (London: Verso, 2003), 89–109.

53. "If the natives won't do what they're told, they're expelled from the area marked out for annexation," More wrote, and "If they try to resist, the Utopians declare war—for they consider war perfectly justifiable, when one country denies another its natural right to derive nourishment from any soil which the original owners are not using themselves, but are merely holding on to as a worthless piece of property." Thomas More, *Utopia*, trans. Paul Turner (1516; New York: Vintage, 1986), 80.

54. Emerich de Vattel, *The Law of Nations; or, Principles of the Law of Nature, Applied to the Conduct and Affairs of Nations and Sovereigns* (1758), trans. Joseph Chitty (Philadelphia: T. & J.W. Johnson & Co., 1867), 100. From my research, I found that Vattel's *Law of Nations* was published in New York in 1787, 1796, and 1848; in Northampton, MA, in 1805, 1820; in Philadelphia in 1807, 1817, 1829, 1834, 1835, 1839, 1844, 1849, 1852, 1853, 1854, 1855, 1856, 1857, 1858, 1859, 1861, 1863, 1865, 1867, 1869, 1870, 1872, 1876, 1879, and 1883; and in Charlottesville, VA, in 1891. This is probably not the complete publication history, however.

55. Brackenridge, "Thoughts," 1.

56. "Letter of Sir Francis Wyatt, Governor of Virginia, 1621–1626," *William and Mary Quarterly* 6 (1926): 118–19. On the "Virginia Massacre," see Alden T. Vaughan, "'Expulsion of the Savages': English Policy and the Virginia Massacre of 1622," *William and Mary Quarterly* 35 (1978): 57–84.

57. On the Indian participation in the Revolutionary War, see Barbara Graymont, *The*

Iroquois in the American Revolution (Syracuse, NY: Syracuse University Press, 1972); and Colin G. Calloway, *The American Revolution in Indian Country: Crisis and Diversity in North American Communities* (Cambridge: Cambridge University Press, 1995).

58. Hugh Henry Brackenridge, "For the NATIONAL GAZETTE. THOUGHTS on the present Indian War," *National Gazette*, February 2, 1792, 1; "For the NATIONAL GAZETTE. Farther and concluding THOUGHTS on the Indian War," *National Gazette*, February 6, 1792, 1–2.

59. Brackenridge, "Farther and concluding THOUGHTS," 2.

60. Hugh Henry Brackenridge to Tench Coxe, August 8, 1794, in Brackenridge, *Incidents of the Insurrection*, 3:131.

61. Francis Jennings, *Empire of Fortune: Crowns, Colonies, and Tribes in the Seven Years War in America* (New York: W.W. Norton & Company, 1988); Richard White, *The Middle Ground: Indians, Empires, and Republics in the Great Lakes Region, 1650–1815* (Cambridge: Cambridge University Press, 1991), 240–56; Fred Anderson, *Crucible of War: The Seven Years' War and the Fate of Empire in British North America, 1754–1766* (New York: Vintage, 2001); and Colin Calloway, *The Scratch of a Pen: 1763 and the Transformation of North America* (New York: Oxford University Press, 2006).

62. Benjamin Franklin to Richard Jackson, February 11, 1764, in *The Papers of Benjamin Franklin*, ed. Leonard L. Labaree (New Haven, CT: Yale University Press, 1959–1999), 11:77. I offer a more detailed discussion of the Paxton Boys and the rhetorical foundations of colonial violence in Jeremy Engels, "'Equipped for Murder': The Paxton Boys and 'the Spirit of Killing all Indians' in Pennsylvania, 1763–1764," *Rhetoric & Public Affairs* 8 (2005): 355–82.

63. On the Paxton Boys' legacy, see James Kirby Martin, "The Return of the Paxton Boys and the Historical State of the Pennsylvania Frontier, 1764–1774," *Pennsylvania History* 38 (1971): 117–33; and Alden T. Vaughan, "Frontier Banditti and the Indians: The Paxton Boys' Legacy, 1763–1775," *Pennsylvania History* 51 (1984): 1–29.

64. Major Isaac Craig to General Knox, March 6, 1791, in *The St. Clair Papers. The Life and Public Services of Arthur St. Clair Soldier of the Revolutionary War; President of the Continental Congress; and Governor of the North-Western Territory*, ed. William Henry Smith (Cincinnati: Robert Clark & Co., 1882), 2:202.

65. See Benedict Anderson, *Imagined Communities: Reflections on the Origin and Spread of Nationalism* (1983; London: Verso, 1991).

66. Michael Warner, *The Letters of the Republic: Publication and the Public Sphere in*

Eighteenth-Century America (Cambridge, MA: Harvard University Press, 1990).

67. Alison Olson, "The Pamphlet War over the Paxton Boys," *Pennsylvania Magazine of History and Biography* 123 (1999): 31–55.

68. I found his essays reprinted in *Daily Advertiser* (New York City), February 7, 1792, 2; *Dunlap's American Daily Advertiser* (Philadelphia), February 7, 1792, 2; *The Mail, or Claypoole's Daily Advertiser* (Philadelphia), February 7, 1792, 2; *New-York Daily Gazette* (New York City), February 7, 1792, 2; *Daily Advertiser*, February 10, 1792, 2; *Columbian Centinel* (Boston), February 15, 1792, 177; *Independent Chronicle and the Universal Advertiser* (Boston), February 16, 1792, 2; *Connecticut Courant* (Hartford), February 20, 1792, 2; *Columbian Centinel*, February 22, 1792, 185; *Norwich Packet* (Norwich, CT), February 23, 1792, 1; *Connecticut Courant*, February 27, 1792, 1; *Litchfield Monitor* (Litchfield, CT), February 28, 1792, 1; *Norwich Packet*, March 1, 1792, 1; *Windham Herald* (Windham, CT), March 3, 1792, 1; *Litchfield Monitor*, March 7, 1792, 1; *City Gazette and Daily Advertiser* (Charleston, SC), March 8, 1792, 2; *Middlesex Gazette* (Middletown, CT), March 10, 1792, 1; *Middlesex Gazette*, March 17, 1792, 1; *Concord Herald* (Concord, NH), March 21, 1792, 1; *Concord Herald*, March 28, 1792, 1. Summaries and criticisms were reprinted in *General Advertiser* (Philadelphia), February 7, 1792, 2; *Boston Gazette, and the Country Journal* (Boston), March 5, 1792, 1; and *Independent Chronicle*, April 12, 1792, 1.

69. David Bradford quoted in Bouton, *Taming Democracy*, 235.

70. "The Trial of Mamachtaga" (1785) is reprinted as preface material to an updated version of Brackenridge's *Incidents*: Hugh Henry Brackenridge, *Incidents of the Insurrection*, ed. Daniel Marder (New Haven, CT: College and University Press, 1972), 25–35.

71. "Farther and concluding THOUGHTS," 1.

72. "Farther and concluding THOUGHTS," 2.

73. Richard Slotkin, *Regeneration through Violence: The Mythology of the American Frontier, 1600–1860* (Middletown, CT: Wesleyan University Press, 1973).

74. Brackenridge, "Farther and concluding THOUGHTS," 2.

75. Brackenridge, "THOUGHTS," 1; "Farther and concluding THOUGHTS," 2.

76. Brackenridge, "THOUGHTS," 1.

77. Ibid., 1.

78. On Washington's landholdings and his war profits, see Slaughter, *The Whiskey Rebellion*, 88, 224. On the Battle of Fallen Timbers, see Wiley Sword, *President Washington's Indian War: The Struggle for the Old Northwest, 1790–1795* (Norman:

University of Oklahoma Press, 1985), 272–322. Here we see Washington not as the idyllic hero of the Cherry Tree myth, but as a shrewd ruler interested in turning a profit. One of the most enduring—and most problematic—facets of American politics is this blending of political stature and private profit.

79. James M. Farrell, "Fisher Ames and Political Judgment: Reason, Passion, and Vehement Style in the Jay Treaty Speech," *Quarterly Journal of Speech* 76 (1990): 420; and for another insightful analysis of this speech that delves deeply into its stylistic architecture, see Beth Innocenti Manolescu, "Style and Spectator Judgment in Fisher Ames's Jay Treaty Speech," *Quarterly Journal of Speech* 84 (1998): 62–79.

80. Ames could thus be said to have participated in the "culture of the performance" described by Jay Fliegelman in *Declaring Independence: Jefferson, Natural Language, and the Culture of Performance* (Stanford, CA: Stanford University Press, 1993). On the disciplining of emotion and the elevation of reasoned debate to the status of desideratum in the United States, see Kimberly Smith, *The Dominion of Voice: Riot, Reason, and Romance in American Politics* (Lawrence: University of Kansas Press, 1999).

81. Fisher Ames, "Speech in the House of Representatives," April 28, 1796, in *Works of Fisher Ames. With a Selection from His Speeches and Correspondence*, ed. Seth Ames (Boston: Little, Brown and Company, 1854), 2:64, 65.

82. Ames, "Speech in the House of Representatives," 2:66.

83. Henry Nash Smith, *Virgin Land: The American West as Symbol and Myth* (New York: Random House, 1950), 234–45; Frederick Merk, *Manifest Destiny and Mission in American History: A Reinterpretation* (New York: Alfred A. Knopf, 1963), 24–88; and Stephen John Hartnett, *Democratic Dissent and the Cultural Fictions of Antebellum America* (Urbana: University of Illinois Press, 2002), 93–101.

84. John Nelson argues that Hamilton's policies were "aimed at a relatively small group of rich and powerful men," and John Murrin suggests that Hamilton's policies produced "some of the grosser windfall profits in American history." John R. Nelson, Jr., *Liberty and Property: Political Economy and Policymaking in the New Nation, 1789–1812* (Baltimore: Johns Hopkins University Press, 1987), 31; John M. Murrin, "The Great Inversion, or Court versus Country: A Comparison of the Revolutionary Settlements in England (1688–1721) and America (1776–1816)," in *Three British Revolutions: 1641, 1688, 1776*, ed. J. G. A. Pocock (Princeton, NJ: Princeton University Press, 1980), 407.

85. Isaac Kramnick describes Hamilton's "state centered" theory of sovereignty in "The Great National Discussion: The Discourse of Politics in 1787," *William and Mary*

Quarterly, 45 (1988): 23–31.

86. Franklin, "To the People of the United States," *Independent Gazetteer* (Philadelphia), August 30, 1794, 2.

87. "Parties," *National Gazette*, January 23, 1792, 99.

88. Brutus, "For the National Gazette. Brutus, No. I. On the FUNDING SYSTEM," *National Gazette*, March 15, 1792, 158.

89. Brutus, "For the National Gazette. Excise Law," *National Gazette*, July 4, 1792, 282.

90. Historian E. Eugene Harper, *Transformation of Western Pennsylvania*, 141, notes: "Western Pennsylvania in the late eighteenth century was governed by men drawn from the highest levels of the class structure. By the mid 1790s, a distinctive governing elite dominated the political life of the region."

91. Alexander Hamilton to George Washington, August 5, 1794, in *The Papers of Alexander Hamilton*, ed. Harold C. Syrett (New York: Columbia University Press, 1961–1987), 17:34.

92. Commerce certainly played an essential role in the building of the United States. In fact, the joys of producing, buying, and selling commodities were coupled in the United States with the Protestant Ethic, which inculcated the belief that hard work demonstrated heavenly salvation in the eyes of God, to make for a situation in which the ties of interstate capitalism would hold the states and bind the American people together. By the 1830s, when he visited the United States for the first time, Alexis de Tocqueville observed in *Democracy in America* (1835) that Americans were united in commerce: in working the soil, in producing commodities, in buying and selling. Here we should note T. H. Breen's argument in *The Marketplace of Revolution: How Consumer Politics Shaped American Independence* (Oxford: Oxford University Press, 2004) that commerce provided the foundation for the shared bonds of revolution in America. For a brilliant analysis of how the discursive spaces of capitalism and consumption made democracy possible in the United States (and how slavery damaged that space), see Philip Fisher, "Democratic Social Space: Whitman, Melville, and the Promise of American Transparency," *Representations* 24 (1988): 60–101.

93. Dorothy V. Jones, *License for Empire: Colonialism by Treaty in Early America* (Chicago: University of Chicago Press, 1982). See also Robert A. Williams, Jr., *Linking Arms Together: American Indian Treaty Visions of Law and Peace, 1600–1800* (New York: Oxford University Press, 1997); and Lindsay Gordon Robertson, *Conquest by Law: How the Discovery of America Dispossessed Indigenous Peoples of Their Lands* (Oxford: Oxford University Press, 2005).

94. Smith, *Wealth of Nations*, xxiv, 13.

95. "Brookfield, November 25. Extract of a letter from a gentleman in Philadelphia, to his friend in this town," *Worcester Intelligencer: Or, Brookfield Advertiser* (Worcester, MA), November 25, 1794, 3.

96. "Extract of a letter dated Bedford, October 21," *Worcester Intelligencer: Or, Brookfield Advertiser*, November 11, 1794, 3.

97. John Marshall, *The Life of George Washington, Commander in Chief of the American Forces, During the War Which Established the Independence of his Country, and First President of the United States* (Philadelphia: G. P. Wayne, 1804), 5:590.

98. George Washington, Sixth Annual Address to Congress, November 19, 1794, in George Washington, *Writings*, ed. Joel Rhodehamel, Library of America Series (New York: Literary Classics of the U.S., 1997), 892–93.

99. Cesare Beccaria, *On Crimes and Punishments* (1763–64), in *On Crimes and Punishments and Other Writings*, ed. Richard Bellamy, trans. Richard Davies (Cambridge: Cambridge University Press, 2000), 92.

100. On Bentham's experiments with criminality and capitalism, see Peter Linebaugh, *The London Hanged: Crime and Civil Society in the Eighteenth Century* (Cambridge: Cambridge University Press, 1991), 396–401.

101. Michel Foucault, *Discipline and Punish: The Birth of the Prison*, trans. Alan Sheridan (1975; New York: Vintage, 1995), 200–201.

102. R. Howell, "Answer. To the Address of Brigadier General Bloomfield and the Infantry and Artillery of Jersey," *Independent Gazetteer*, September 20, 1794, 3. Other articles by militia members printed on this page expressed similar sentiments.

CHAPTER FOUR. THE CONTRACT OF BLOOD

1. John Adams to Abigail Adams, July 3, 1776, in Charles Francis Adams, ed., *Familiar Letters of John Adams and His Wife Abigail Adams, During the Revolution, With a Memoir of Mrs. Adams* (Boston: Houghton, Mifflin and Co., 1875), 194. In this letter, Adams located independence on July 2, 1776, for the Continental Congress formally broke with Great Britain on that day when they voted for Richard Henry Lee's resolution for independence. Thus, as Stephen Lucas points out, Adams was right about the spirit but wrong about the day. On July 4, 1776, Congress approved the Declaration, and the anniversary of the Declaration's signing was marked by such displays in the first years of the United States, and still is (although with

increasing perfunctoriness). Stephen E. Lucas, "Justifying America: The Declaration of Independence as a Rhetorical Document," *American Rhetoric: Context and Criticism*, ed. Thomas W. Benson (Carbondale: Southern Illinois University Press, 1989), 67–68; and see also Charles Warren, "Fourth of July Myths," *William and Mary Quarterly* 2 (1945): 237–72.

2. More precisely, these celebrations combined elements of King's Birthday/Accession Day celebrations and Pope's Day. On Pope's Day in early eighteenth-century Boston, see Peter Shaw, *American Patriots and the Rituals of Revolution* (Cambridge, MA: Harvard University Press, 1981), 15–18; and for a history of the Fourth of July in Boston, see Len Travers, *Celebrating the Fourth: Independence Day and the Rites of Nationalism in the Early Republic* (Amherst: University of Massachusetts Press, 1997), esp. 88–106 on the 1790s.

3. *Boston Gazette, and the Country Journal,* July 8, 1793, 2.

4. Merle Curti, *The Roots of American Loyalty* (1946; New York: Russell & Russell, 1967), 140.

5. John Quincy Adams, *Lectures on Rhetoric and Oratory, Delivered to the Class of Senior and Junior Sophisters in Harvard University* (Cambridge, MA: Hilliard and Metcalf, 1810), 1:238.

6. Adams, *Lectures on Rhetoric and Oratory*, 1:237.

7. John Quincy Adams, *An Oration, Pronounced July 4th, 1793, at the Request of the Inhabitants of the Town of Boston, in Commemoration of the Anniversary of American Independence* (Boston: Benjamin Edes & Son, 1793), 7.

8. Ibid., 6, 9, 10.

9. Ibid., 12.

10. John Locke, *An Essay Concerning Human Understanding*, ed. Alexander Campbell Fraser (1690; New York: Dover Publications, 1959), 2:432.

11. On the reasons that freedom of religion was protected by the Constitution, see Isaac Kramnick and R. Lawrence Moore, *The Godless Constitution: A Moral Defense of the Secular State* (1996; New York: W.W. Norton & Co., 2005); and for a collection of primary writings on the subject, see Forrest Church, ed., *The Separation of Church and State: Writings on a Fundamental Freedom by America's Founders* (Boston: Beacon Press, 2004). On the religious beliefs common to the founding period, see James Turner, *Without God, Without Creed: The Origins of Unbelief in America* (Baltimore: Johns Hopkins University Press, 1985), 35–72.

12. Alexander Saxton, *The Rise and Fall of the White Republic: Class Politics and Mass Culture in Nineteenth-Century America* (1990; London: Verso, 2003), 84–90.

13. Adams, *An Oration, Pronounced July 4th, 1793*, 14–15.

14. Stanly Elkins and Eric McKitrick, *The Age of Federalism: The Early American Republic, 1788–1800* (New York: Oxford University Press, 1993), 645.

15. James Madison, "Federalist 41," in *The Federalist*, intro. and notes by Robert A. Ferguson (New York: Barnes & Noble Classics, 2006), 226.

16. *A Selection of the Patriotic Addresses, to the President of the United States, Together with The President's Answers* (Boston: John W. Folsom, 1798), 17.

17. Ibid., 279, 280.

18. Ibid., 149, 338.

19. Ibid., 73, 191–92, 316.

20. John Adams, "To the Inhabitants of the county of Accomack in the State of Virginia," *Gazette of the United States*, June 20, 1798, 1.

21. Robert L. Ivie, "Images of Savagery in American Justifications for War," *Communication Monographs* 47 (1980): 279–94.

22. Benjamin Rush, "A Plan of a Peace-Office for the United States," in *Essays, Literary, Moral & Philosophical* (Philadelphia: Thomas and Samuel F. Bradford, 1798), 185–88.

23. Benjamin Rush to John Adams, August 8, 1777, in *Letters of Benjamin Rush*, ed. L. H. Butterfield (Princeton, NJ: Princeton University Press, 1951), 1:152.

24. Benjamin Rush to Nathanial Greene, April 15, 1782, in *Letters of Benjamin Rush*, 2:268–69.

25. Thus, a New Hampshire anti-federalist, Thomas Cogswell, had the following things to say about war. War "is at best a curse to any people; it is comprehensive of most, if not all the mischiefs that do or can afflict mankind; it depopulates nations; lays waste the finest countries; destroys arts and sciences, it many times ruins the best men, and advances the worst, it effaces every trace of virtue, piety and compassion, and introduces all kind of corruption in public affairs; and in short, is pregnant with so many evils, that it ought ever to be avoided if possible; nothing but self-defence can justify it. An army, either in peace or war, is like the locust and caterpillars of Egypt; they bear down all before them—and many times, by designing men, have been used as an engine to destroy the liberties of a people, and reduce them to the most abject slavery." A Farmer [Thomas Cogswell], Letter 1, *Freeman's Oracle and New Hampshire Advertiser*, January 11, 1788, in *The Complete Anti-Federalist*, ed. Herbert J. Storing (Chicago: University of Chicago Press, 1981), 4:207.

26. Sarah J. Purcell, *Sealed with Blood: War, Sacrifice, and Memory in Revolutionary America* (Philadelphia: University of Pennsylvania Press, 2002), 87–91.

27. Benjamin Rush, "Of the Mode of Education Proper in a Republic," in *Essays, Literary, Moral & Philosophical*, 14.

28. Rush, "Of the Mode of Education Proper in a Republic," 10–11 (italics added).

29. Samuel Harrison Smith, *Remarks on Education: Illustrating the Close Connection Between Virtue and Wisdom* (1798), in *Essays on Education in the Early Republic*, ed. Frederick Rudolph (Cambridge, MA: Harvard University Press, 1965), 180–81.

30. Noah Webster, *Dissertations on the English Language: with Notes, Historical and Critical, To Which is added, by way of Appendix, an Essay on a Reformed Mode of Spelling, with Dr. Franklin's Arguments on that Subject* (Boston: Isaiah Thomas and Company, 1789), 397. On Webster's efforts to create a national language, see Richard M. Rollins, "Words as Social Control: Noah Webster and the Creation of the American Dictionary," *American Quarterly* 28 (1976): 415–30; and Jill Lepore, *A is for American: Letters and Other Characters in the Newly United States* (New York: Alfred A. Knopf, 2002), 15–41.

31. "A Citizen of America" [Noah Webster], *An Examination Into the Leading Principles of the Federal Constitution* (1787), in *The Debate on the Constitution: Federalist and Antifederalist Speeches, Articles, and Letters during the Struggle over Ratification*, ed. Bernard Bailyn, Library of America Series (New York: Literary Classics of the U.S., 1993), 1:158.

32. Noah Webster, *On the Education of Youth in America* (1790), in *Essays on Education in the Early Republic*, 43–44.

33. J. G. A. Pocock, *The Machiavellian Moment: Florentine Political Thought and the Atlantic Republican Tradition* (Princeton, NJ: Princeton University Press, 1975), 197–202.

34. John Warren, *An Oration, Delivered July 4th, 1783, at the Request of the Inhabitants of the Town of Boston; in Celebration of the Anniversary of American Independence* (Boston: John Gill, 1783), 6.

35. Thus, Robert Hariman argues that the "republican community understands heroism not as the conquest of an alien warrior, but as the individual triumphing over personal limitations to become the exemplar of civic virtue." Robert Hariman, *Political Style: The Artistry of Power* (Chicago: University of Chicago Press, 1995), 121.

36. Warren, *An Oration*, 7.

37. *Patriotic Addresses*, 131, 174.

38. Baron de Montesquieu, *The Spirit of Laws* (1748; London: J. Nourse and P. Vaillant, 1752), 1:42.

39. Here, see Joanne B. Freeman, *Affairs of Honor: National Politics in the New*

Republic (New Haven, CT: Yale University Press, 2001); Andrew S. Trees, *The Founding Fathers and the Politics of Character* (Princeton, NJ: Princeton University Press, 2004); and Jennifer R. Mercieca, "The Culture of Honor: How Slaveholders Responded to the Abolitionist Mail Crisis of 1835," *Rhetoric & Public Affairs* 10 (2007): 51–76.

40. On the Whig tradition, see Basil Williams, *The Whig Supremacy, 1714–1760* (1939; Oxford: Oxford University Press, 1962).

41. John Adams, *Thoughts on Government: Applicable to the Present State of the American Colonies, In a Letter from a Gentleman to His Friend* (Boston: John Gill, 1776), 4–5; and for a similar argument, see *The People the Best Governors: or a Plan of Government Founded on the just Principles of Natural Freedom* (n.p., 1776), 9.

42. Noah Webster, *An Oration Pronounced Before the Citizens of New Haven on the Anniversary of the Independence of the United States, July 4th, 1798; and Published at Their Request* (New Haven, CT: T. and S. Green, 1798), 10, 11, 15.

43. For a discussion of the reaction to the French Revolution in the United States, see Elkins and McKitrick, *The Age of Federalism*, 303–73.

44. On these early histories, see Lester Cohen, *The Revolutionary Histories: Contemporary Narratives of the American Revolution* (Ithaca, NY: Cornell University Press, 1980).

45. Purcell, *Sealed with Blood*, 19, 49–91.

46. Webster, *An Oration Pronounced Before the Citizens of New Haven on the Anniversary of the Independence of the United States*, 16.

47. Thomas Jefferson to William Stephens Smith, November 13, 1787, in Thomas Jefferson, *Writings*, ed. Merrill D. Peterson, Library of America Series (New York: Literary Classics of the U.S., 1984), 911.

48. For a discussion of how nation-builders in the United States secularized religious imagery to assist in the nation-building project, see Sacvan Bercovitch, *The American Jeremiad* (Madison: University of Wisconsin Press, 1978); and *The Rites of Assent: Transformations in the Symbolic Construction of America* (New York: Routledge, 1993). For a similar discussion of the nation-building project in France, see David Bell, *The Cult of the Nation in France: Inventing Nationalism, 1680–1800* (Cambridge, MA: Harvard University Press, 2001).

49. *Patriotic Addresses*, 48, 50, and see also pp. 17, 30, 32, 35, 37, 90, 102, 120–21, 123, 127, 129, 161–62, 232, 236, 306 for similar sentiments.

50. "The remilitarization of patriotism meant that young men finally had the chance to show they had been listening to all those orations: they were indeed faithful sons of

the Revolutionary fathers," David Waldstreicher writes in *In the Midst of Perpetual Fetes: The Making of American Nationalism, 1776–1820* (Chapel Hill: University of North Carolina Press, 1997), 159.

51. *Patriotic Addresses*, 23, 103.

52. Webster, *An Oration Pronounced Before the Citizens of New Haven on the Anniversary of the Independence of the United States*, 16.

53. John Miller Russell, *A Poem, on the Fourth of July, 1798, Being the Anniversary of the Independence of the United States of America* (Boston: Manning & Loring, 1798), 8; and see also *Gazette of the United States*, July 7, 1798, 2, which reprints a Philadelphia Fourth of July speech and dinner toasts that explicitly tie the XYZ Affair to the contract of blood.

54. "The enduring ties of consanguinity, which had connected their ancestors, with those of the Americans, had been gradually loosened to the verge of dissolution," John Quincy Adams argued, for "instead of returning the sentiments of fraternal affection," the British "indulged their vanity with preposterous opinions of insulting superiority." Thomas Jefferson made a similar report in his original draft of the Declaration of Independence, suggesting that "We might have been a free and a great people together; but a communication of grandeur & of freedom it seems is below their dignity." For both Adams and Jefferson, revolution was the outcome of a mounting series of insults, as the British refused to communicate with the Americans as equals, instead imagining themselves as superiors for whom their lowly inferiors were but slaves. Adams, *An Oration, Pronounced July 4th*, 1793, 9; Thomas Jefferson, *Autobiography* (1821), in *Writings*, ed. Peterson, 23.

55. Adams, *Lectures on Rhetoric and Oratory*, 1:30–31.

56. This point is stressed in Sandra M. Gustafson, *Eloquence is Power: Oratory and Performance in Early America* (Chapel Hill: University of North Carolina Press, 2000).

57. Lyon Rathbun, "The Ciceronian Rhetoric of John Quincy Adams," *Rhetorica* 18 (2000): 175–215.

58. Thomas M. Conley, *Rhetoric in the European Tradition* (Chicago: University of Chicago Press, 1994), 34.

59. This Roman orator and rhetorical theorist profoundly influenced the founders, who "found their ideal selves, and to some extent their voices, in Brutus, in Cassius, and in Cicero, whose Catilinarian orations the enraptured John Adams, aged 23, declaimed aloud, alone at night in his room." Bernard Bailyn, *The Ideological Origins of the American Revolution* (1967; Cambridge, MA: Harvard University Press,

1992), 26. For discussions of how the founders returned to Greek and Roman history to find inspiration for the nation-building project, see Richard Gummere, *The American Colonial Mind and the Classical Tradition* (Cambridge, MA: Harvard University Press, 1963); Meyer Reinhold, ed., *The Classick Pages: Classical Reading of Eighteenth-Century Americans* (University Park: Pennsylvania State University Press, 1975); Meyer Reinhold, *Classica Americana: The Greek and Roman Heritage in the United States* (Detroit: Wayne State University Press, 1984); and Carl J. Richards, *The Founders and the Classics: Greece, Rome, and the American Enlightenment* (Cambridge, MA: Harvard University Press, 1994).

60. Kenneth Burke, *A Grammar of Motives* (1945; Berkeley: University of California Press, 1969), 442.

61. Cicero, *De Oratore*, in *Cicero on Oratory and Orators*, ed. and trans. J. S. Watson (Carbondale: Southern Illinois University Press, 1970).

62. Joseph M. Bessette, *The Mild Voice of Reason: Deliberative Democracy and American National Government* (Chicago: University of Chicago Press, 1994), 21, 26.

63. David Hume, *A Treatise of Human Nature* (1739–40), ed. L. A. Selby-Bigge (1888; Oxford: Clarendon Press, 1978), 413.

64. Adams, *Lectures on Rhetoric and Oratory*, 22. On the Enlightenment's elevation of reason in place of rhetoric, see Bryan Garsten, *Saving Persuasion: A Defense of Rhetoric and Judgment* (Cambridge, MA: Harvard University Press, 2006). For a discussion of how the demands for rational discourse infiltrated American conceptions of public discourse in the early Republic, see Kimberly Smith, *The Dominion of Voice: Riot, Reason, and Romance in American Politics* (Lawrence: University of Kansas Press, 1999).

65. Ernesto Laclau, *On Populist Reason* (London: Verso, 2005), 141, 147–48. Jacques Derrida makes a similar point in *The Politics of Friendship*, trans. George Collins (1994; London: Verso, 2005), 114.

66. Or, in Derridian terminology, "the supplement"; see Jacques Derrida, *Of Grammatology*, trans. Gayatri Chakrovorty Spivak (1967; Baltimore: Johns Hopkins University Press, 1997), 145.

67. And thus we see how easily undone are the rhetorics of enemyship; see Jeremy Engels, "Friend or Foe? Naming the Enemy," *Rhetoric & Public Affairs* 12 (2009): 37–64.

68. *Gazette of the United States* (Philadelphia), June 20, 1798, 3. An article printed on this same page and signed by "An Enemy to Traitors" made a similar point and offered advice to Americans on how to spot French agents in their midst. These

articles are indicative of the quality of public discourse at the time.

69. On the Alien and Sedition Acts, see James Morton Smith, *Freedom's Fetters: The Alien and Sedition Laws and American Civil Liberties* (Ithaca, NY: Cornell University Press, 1956); Elkins and McKitrick, *The Age of Federalism*, 582–99; Geoffrey R. Stone, *Perilous Times: Free Speech in Wartime from the Sedition Act of 1798 to the War on Terrorism* (New York: W.W. Norton & Co., 2004), 15–78; and Stephen John Hartnett and Jennifer Rose Mercieca, "'Has Your Courage Rusted?': National Security and the Contested Rhetorical Norms of Republicanism in Post-Revolutionary America, 1798–1801," *Rhetoric & Public Affairs* 9 (2006), 90–102.

70. Paul Douglas Newman, *Fries's Rebellion: The Enduring Struggle for the American Revolution* (Philadelphia: University of Pennsylvania Press, 2004).

71. *Aurora General Advertiser*, March 22, 1799, 3.

72. For a history of the New Army, see Richard H. Kohn, *Eagle and Sword: The Federalists and the Creation of the Military Establishment in America, 1783–1802* (New York: The Free Press, 1975), 193–255. On the Eventual Army, see Paul Douglas Newman, *Fries's Rebellion: The Enduring Struggle for the American Revolution* (Philadelphia: University of Pennsylvania Press, 2004), 144–64.

73. See Kohn, *Eagle and Sword*, 250–55, for the evidence both for and against Hamilton's plans for a coup.

74. Thomas Jefferson to James Monroe, January 23, 1799, in *The Papers of Thomas Jefferson*, ed. Julian Boyd (Princeton, NJ: Princeton University Press, 1950–1990), 30:635.

75. Newman, *Fries's Rebellion*, 39, 72–73, 93.

76. For the witnesses' reports, see Thomas Carpenter, *The Two Trials of John Fries, on an Indictment for Treason; together with a brief report of the trials of several other persons, for Treason and Insurrection, In the Counties of Bucks, Northampton and Montgomery, in the Circuit Court of the United States* (Philadelphia: William W. Woodward, 1800), 27, 31, 33–34.

77. Newman, *Fries's Rebellion*, 44, 133.

78. "ANOTHER INSURRECTION," *Gazette of the United States* (Philadelphia), March 11, 1799, 3.

79. *Aurora General Advertiser* (Philadelphia), March 12, 1799, 3.

80. Hartnett and Mercieca, "'Has Your Courage Rusted?'" 89.

81. Craig R. Smith, "The Aliens Are Coming: The Federalist Attack on the First Amendment," in *Who Belongs in America? Presidents, Rhetoric, and Immigration*, ed. Vanessa B. Beasley (College Station: Texas A&M University Press, 2006), 42, 43.

82. "BY THE PRESIDENT OF THE UNITED STATES OF AMERICA, A PROCLAMATION," *Philadelphia Gazette & Universal Daily Advertiser* (Philadelphia), March 13, 1799, 3.

83. *Philadelphia Gazette,* March 26, 1799, 3.

84. *Gazette of the United States,* April 26, 1799, 3.

85. Indeed, Garry Wills demonstrates that the electoral bump that Jefferson received due to the Constitution's 3/5ths Clause ensured his election. Without the twelve additional votes afforded to slave owners in the Electoral College, Adams would have been elected instead. The enemyship of master and slave led to Jefferson's questionable election, as slave-owning Republicans bonded together to back one of their own. As Boston's admittedly Federalist but nevertheless discerning *Mercury and New-England Palladium* complained, Jefferson made his "ride into the temple of Liberty on the shoulders of slaves." Garry Wills, *"Negro President": Jefferson and the Slave Power* (2003; Boston: Mariner Books, 2005); see p. 2 for the quotation from the *Mercury and New-England Palladium,* January 20, 1801. This point about the 3/5ths Clause and the 1800 election is also made in Akhil Reed Amar, *America's Constitution: A Biography* (New York: Random House, 2005), 61; and for a discussion of legal complexities of this election, see Bruce Ackerman, *The Failure of the Founding Fathers: Jefferson, Marshall, and the Rise of Presidential Democracy* (Cambridge, MA: Harvard University Press, 2005), 55–76.

86. Robert L. Ivie, *Democracy and America's War on Terror* (Tuscaloosa: University of Alabama Press, 2005).

87. Ivie, "Images of Savagery"; Edward Said, *Orientalism* (New York: Pantheon, 1978).

88. Proclamation by John Adams, March 12, 1799.

89. As he would later claim, the three most frightening moments in the early Republic were "the Terrorism of Chaises Rebellion in Massachusetts," "the Terrorism of Gallatins Insurrection in Pensilvania," and "the Terrorism of Fries's, most outrageous Riot and Rescue." The three events about which he spoke were Shays's Rebellion in Massachusetts in 1786–1787, the Whiskey Rebellion in Pennsylvania in 1794, and Fries's Rebellion in Pennsylvania in 1799. John Adams to Thomas Jefferson, June 30, 1813, in *The Adams-Jefferson Letters: The Complete Correspondence between Thomas Jefferson and Abigail & John Adams,* ed. Lester J. Cappon (1959; Chapel Hill: University of North Carolina Press, 1987), 346.

90. Alexander Hamilton to James McHenry, March 18, 1799, in *The Papers of Alexander Hamilton,* ed. Harold C. Syrett (New York: Columbia University Press, 1961–1987), 22:552–53.

91. Proclamation by William Macpherson, April 5, 1799, reprinted in W. W. H. Davis,

The Fries Rebellion 1798–99: An Armed Resistance to the House Tax Law, Passed by Congress, July 9, 1798, in Bucks and Northampton Counties, Pennsylvania (Doylestown, PA: Doylestown Publishing Company, 1899), 83. This proclamation was widely printed in American newspapers; see, for instance, *Aurora General Advertiser* (Philadelphia), April 8, 1799, 2; *Commercial Advertiser* (New York City), April 9, 1799, 2; *City Gazette* (Charleston, SC), April 24, 1799, 2; and *Kline's Carlisle Weekly Gazette* (Carlisle, PA), April 24, 1799, 2.

92. For the thought about capital punishment at this moment, see Louis P. Masur, *Rites of Execution: Capital Punishment and the Transformation of American Culture, 1776–1865* (New York: Oxford University Press, 1989).

93. Chase quoted in Carpenter, *The Two Trials of John Fries*, 203.

94. *The Two Trials of John Fries*, 1, 200, 201, 203.

95. "From Northampton," *Gazette of the United States*, April 19, 1799, 3.

96. *Kline's Carlisle Weekly Gazette*, April 24, 1799, 3.

97. "Extract of a letter dated Quaker-town April 8, 1799," *Aurora General Advertiser*, April 11, 1799, 3.

98. Davis, *Fries Rebellion*, 109–11.

99. Ibid., 110.

100. Kohn, *Eagle and Sword*, 260.

101. *Aurora General Advertiser*, March 22, 1799, 3.

102. Ibid.

103. On McKean's election, see Newman, *Fries's Rebellion*, 189–202.

104. Adams quoted in Jane Shaffer Elsmere, "Trials of John Fries," *Pennsylvania Magazine of History and Biography* 103 (1979): 442–43.

105. Alexander Hamilton, *Letter from Alexander Hamilton, Concerning the Public Conduct and Character of John Adams, Esq, President of the United States*, October 24, 1800, in *Papers of Alexander Hamilton*, 25:186–234, and for a history of the pamphlet, see the editor's overview on 169–85. On the duel, see Thomas Fleming, *Duel: Alexander Hamilton, Aaron Burr, and the Future of America* (New York: Basic Books, 2000); and Joseph J. Ellis, *Founding Brothers: The Revolutionary Generation* (New York: Vintage, 2000), 20–47.

106. Hamilton, *Letter from Alexander Hamilton*, 226, 227.

107. Ibid., 227–28.

CONCLUSION. HOBBES'S GAMBLE AND FRANKLIN'S WARNING

1. A Citizen of America [Noah Webster], *An Examination into the Leading Principles of the Federal Constitution* (1787), in *The Debate on the Constitution: Federalist and Antifederalist Speeches, Articles, and Letters during the Struggle over Ratification*, ed. Bernard Bailyn (Washington: Library of America, 1993), 1:154.

2. Webster, *An Examination into the Leading Principles of the Federal Constitution*, 154.

3. Benjamin Rush, "Address to the people of the united states," *The American Museum* (Philadelphia), January 1787.

4. A. P. Martinich, *Hobbes: A Biography* (New York: Cambridge University Press, 1999), 1–2.

5. Corey Robin argues that while Hobbes "understood fear to be a reaction to real danger in the world, he also appreciated its theatrical qualities. Political fear depended upon illusion, where danger was magnified, even exaggerated, by the state"; *Fear: The History of a Political Idea* (Oxford: Oxford University Press, 2004), 33.

6. Thomas Hobbes, *De Cive* (1642), in Thomas Hobbes, *Man and Citizen*, ed. Bernard Gert (Indianapolis, IN: Hackett, 1998), 226.

7. Thomas Hobbes, *Leviathan*, ed. C. B. Macpherson (1651; New York: Penguin, 1985), 186. He continued to state that the war raged on without end, for "as the nature of Foule weather, lyeth not in a showre or two of rain; but in an inclination thereto of many dayes together: So the nature of War, consisteth not in actuall fighting; but in the known disposition thereto, during all the time there is no assurance to the contrary. All other time is PEACE."

8. Hobbes, *Leviathan*, 186, 188.

9. Hobbes, *De Cive*, 115, 145; Hobbes, *Leviathan*, 190.

10. Niccolò Machiavelli, *Discourses of Livy*, trans. Ninian Hill Thomson (1531; New York: Barnes & Noble, 2005), 264–86; and note that this point is woven throughout *The Prince* (1513) and *The Art of War* (1521) as well.

11. John Locke, *Second Treatise of Government*, ed. Richard H. Cox (1689; Wheeling, IL: Harlan Davidson, 1982), 140.

12. Hobbes, *De Cive*, 287.

13. Hobbes concluded *Leviathan* with the following words: "And thus I have brought to an end my Discourse of Civill and Ecclesiastical Government . . . without other designe, than to set before mens eyes the mutuall Relation between Protection and Obedience" (728).

14. Hobbes, *De Cive*, 187.

15. For Hannah Arendt, "Hobbes's Commonwealth is a vacillating structure and must always provide itself with new props from the outside; otherwise it would collapse overnight into the aimless, senseless chaos of private interests from which it sprang." Michel Foucault reads Hobbes similarly, noting: "Sovereignty . . . is established not by the fact of warlike domination but, on the contrary, by a calculation that makes it possible to avoid war. For Hobbes, it is a nonwar that founds the State and gives it its form." Hannah Arendt, *The Origins of Totalitarianism* (1950; San Diego: Harvest, 1994), 142; Michel Foucault, *"Society Must be Defended": Lectures at the Collège de France, 1975–1976*, trans. David Macey (New York: Picador, 2003), 270.

16. On the Enlightenment fear of rhetoric, see Bryan Garsten, *Saving Persuasion: A Defense of Rhetoric and Judgment* (Cambridge, MA: Harvard University Press, 2006).

17. Garsten, *Saving Persuasion*, 27.

18. He wrote in *De Cive*, 145: "The first dictate of reason is peace; all the rest are means to obtain it, and without which peace cannot be had." And in *Leviathan*, 190: "It is a precept, or generall rule of Reason, *That every man, ought to endeavour Peace, as farre as he has hope of obtaining it; and when he cannot obtain it, that he may seek, and use, all helps, and advantages of Warre.*"

19. Hobbes, *De Cive*, 101.

20. Hobbes, *Leviathan*, 123–24, 167.

21. Ibid., 186.

22. Bernard Bailyn, *The Ideological Origins of the American Revolution* (1967; Cambridge, MA: Harvard University Press, 1992), 202–3, 205, 209, 216. Hobbes was, in fact, the theoretical enemy of American sovereignty. Bailyn notes, "It was, nevertheless, in Hobbes who, in a series of writings in the mid-seventeenth century, first went beyond the immediate claims of monarchy to argue systematically that the only essential quality of sovereignty as such—whoever or whatever its possessor might be—was the capacity to compel obedience; and it was with his name, and with Filmer's, that the colonists came to associate the conception of the *Machtstaat* in its most blatant form" (199). Gordon Wood concludes similarly: "In the development of the idea of sovereignty its representational basis was always in danger of being forgotten and falling away, leaving the sovereign authority simply as the stark power to command—a frightening notion made famous by Hobbes in the seventeenth century and denounced but never really repudiated by almost all

eighteenth-century thinkers." Wood, *Creation of the American Republic, 1776–1787*, 348.

23. Lester C. Olson, *Benjamin Franklin's Vision of American Community: A Study in Rhetorical Iconology* (Columbia: University of South Carolina Press, 2004), 27.

24. Olson, *Benjamin Franklin's Vision*, 38.

25. For discussions of the Seven Years War, see Francis Jennings, *Empire of Fortune: Crowns, Colonies, and Tribes in the Seven Years War in America* (New York: W.W. Norton & Co., 1988); Richard White, *The Middle Ground: Indians, Empires, and Republics in the Great Lakes Region, 1650–1815* (Cambridge: Cambridge University Press, 1991), 240–56; Fred Anderson, *Crucible of War: The Seven Years' War and the Fate of Empire in British North America, 1754–1766* (New York: Vintage, 2001); and Colin Calloway, *The Scratch of a Pen: 1763 and the Transformation of North America* (New York: Oxford University Press, 2006). On the rhetoric of the Seven Years War, see Ronald F. Reid, "New England Rhetoric and the French War, 1754–1760: A Case Study in the Rhetoric of War," *Communication Monographs* 43, no. 4 (1976), 259–86.

26. Pennsylvania Assembly, "Reply to the Governor," November 11, 1755, in *The Papers of Benjamin Franklin*, ed. Leonard W. Labaree (New Haven: Yale University Press, 1963): 6:238.

27. Ibid., 6:239.

28. Ibid., 6:242.

29. Pauline Maier, *American Scripture: Making the Declaration of Independence* (New York: Alfred A. Knopf, 1998), 134. For another attempt to unpack what happiness meant in light of the Scottish Enlightenment, see Garry Wills, *Inventing America: Jefferson's Declaration of Independence* (Garden City, NY: Doubleday, 1978), 248–55. On the commonness of the phrase in Jefferson's world, see Herbert Lawrence Ganter, "Jefferson's 'Pursuit of Happiness' and Some Forgotten Men," *William and Mary Quarterly* 16 (1936): 422–34, 558–85.

30. Baron de Montesquieu, *The Spirit of Laws* (1748; London: J. Nourse and P. Vaillant, 1752), 1:216.

31. Alexander Hamilton, "Federalist 23," in *The Federalist*, intro. and notes by Robert A. Ferguson (New York: Barnes & Noble Classics, 2006), 125, and see also 117, 126, 140, 153, 158, and 165 for similar sentiments; Cato, Letter 1, *New York Journal*, September 27, 1787, in Herbert J. Storing, ed., *The Complete Anti-Federalist* (Chicago: University of Chicago Press, 1981), 2:104.

32. For discussions of the living and breathing Constitution that grows with history, so

that the clothing continues to fit the body politic (to use Jefferson's pertinent metaphor), see Michael Kammen, *A Machine That Would Go of Itself: The Constitution in American Culture* (New York: Alfred A. Knopf, 1986); Jack N. Rakove, *Original Meanings: Politics and Ideas in the Making of the Constitution* (New York: Vintage, 1997); Akhil Reed Amar and Alan Hirsch, *For the People: What the Constitution Really Says about Your Rights* (New York: The Free Press, 1999); Richard H. Fallon, Jr., *The Dynamic Constitution: An Introduction to American Constitutional Law* (Cambridge: Cambridge University Press, 2004); and Akhil Reed Amar, *America's Constitution: A Biography* (New York: Random House, 2005).

33. Drew McCoy, *The Elusive Republic: Political Economy in Jeffersonian America* (Chapel Hill: University of North Carolina Press, 1980), 77–85.

34. Hamilton, "Federalist 8," 42.

35. Hamilton, "Federalist 25," 135.

36. Thomas Jefferson, First Inaugural Address, in Thomas Jefferson, *Writings*, ed. Merrill D. Peterson, Library of America Series (New York: Literary Classics of the U.S., 1984), 493; and for a masterful study of Jefferson's First Inaugural, see Stephen Howard Browne, *Jefferson's Call for Nationhood: The First Inaugural Address* (College Station: Texas A&M University Press, 2003).

Selected Bibliography

Ackerman, Bruce. *The Failure of the Founding Fathers: Jefferson, Marshall, and the Rise of Presidential Democracy.* Cambridge, MA: Harvard University Press, 2005.

Adams, Charles Francis, editor. *Familiar Letters of John Adams and His Wife Abigail Adams, During the Revolution. With a Memoir of Mrs. Adams.* Boston: Houghton, Mifflin and Co., 1875.

Adams, John. *The Political Writings of John Adams.* Edited by George W. Carey. Washington, DC: Regnery, 2000.

———. *Thoughts on Government: Applicable to the Present State of the American Colonies. In a Letter from a Gentleman to His Friend.* Boston: John Gill, 1776.

Adams, John Quincy. *Lectures on Rhetoric and Oratory, Delivered to the Class of Senior and Junior Sophisters in Harvard University.* 2 vols. Cambridge: Hilliard and Metcalf, 1810.

———. *An Oration, Pronounced July 4th, 1793, at the Request of the Inhabitants of the Town of Boston, in Commemoration of the Anniversary of American Independence.* Boston: Benjamin Edes & Son, 1793.

Aldridge, A. Owen. *Thomas Paine's American Ideology.* Newark: University of Delaware Press, 1984.

Allison, Robert J. *The Crescent Obscured: The United States and the Muslim World, 1776–1815.* Chicago: University of Chicago Press, 1995.

Amar, Akhil Reed. *America's Constitution: A Biography.* New York: Random House, 2005.

Amar, Akhil Reed, and Alan Hirsch. *For the People: What the Constitution Really Says about Your Rights.* New York: The Free Press, 1999.

Anderson, Benedict. *Imagined Communities: Reflections on the Origin and Spread of Nationalism.* London: Verso, 1983/1991.

Anderson, Fred. *Crucible of War: The Seven Years' War and the Fate of Empire in British North America, 1754–1766.* New York: Vintage, 2000/2001.

Arendt, Hannah. *On Revolution.* New York: Viking, 1963.

———. *On Violence.* San Diego: Harcourt Brace Jovanovich, 1969.

Aristotle. *The Rhetoric of Aristotle.* Translated by Lane Cooper. Englewood Cliffs, NJ: Prentice-Hall, 1932.

Armitage, David. "The Declaration of Independence and International Law." *William and Mary Quarterly* 59 (2002): 39–64.

Aune, James Arnt. "Tales of the Text: Originalism, Theism, and the History of the U.S. Constitution." *Rhetoric & Public Affairs* 1 (1998): 257–79.

Bailyn, Bernard. *Faces of Revolution: Personalities and Themes in the Struggle for American Independence.* New York: Vintage, 1990/1992.

———. *The Ideological Origins of the American Revolution.* Cambridge, MA: Harvard University Press, 1967/1992.

———, editor. *The Debate on the Constitution: Federalist and Antifederalist Speeches, Articles, and Letters during the Struggle over Ratification.* Library of America Series, 2 vols. New York: Literary Classics of the U.S., 1993.

Beccaria, Cesare. *On Crimes and Punishments.* In *On Crimes and Punishments and Other Writings,* edited by Richard Bellamy, translated by Richard Davies. Cambridge: Cambridge University Press, 1763–64/2000.

Becker, Carl L. *The Declaration of Independence: A Study in the History of Political Ideas.* New York: Vintage, 1922/1958.

Becker, Robert A. *Revolution, Reform, and the Politics of American Taxation, 1763–1783.* Baton Rouge: Louisiana State University Press, 1980.

Bell, David. *The Cult of the Nation in France: Inventing Nationalism, 1680–1800.* Cambridge, MA: Harvard University Press, 2001.

Bentham, Jeremy. *Short Review of the Declaration.* Appendix to *An Answer to the*

Declaration of the American Congress, by John Lind. London: T. Cadell, J. Walter, and T. Sewell, 1776.

Bercovitch, Sacvan. *The American Jeremiad*. Madison: University of Wisconsin Press, 1978.

———. *The Rites of Assent: Transformations in the Symbolic Construction of America*. New York: Routledge, 1993.

Bessette, Joseph M. *The Mild Voice of Reason: Deliberative Democracy and American National Government*. Chicago: University of Chicago Press, 1994.

Blair, Hugh. *Lectures on Rhetoric and Belles Lettres*. 3 vols. Dublin: Whitestone, Colles et al., 1783.

Bouton, Terry. *Taming Democracy: "The People," the Founders, and the Troubled Ending of the American Revolution*. New York: Oxford University Press, 2007.

Boyd, Steven R., editor. *The Whiskey Rebellion: Past and Present Perspectives*. Westport, CT: Greenwood Press, 1985.

Brackenridge, Hugh Henry. "For the NATIONAL GAZETTE. Farther and concluding THOUGHTS on the Indian War." *National Gazette*, February 6, 1792, 1–2.

———. "For the NATIONAL GAZETTE. THOUGHTS on the present Indian War," *National Gazette*, February 2, 1792, 1.

———. *Incidents of the Insurrection in the Western Parts of Pennsylvania, In the Year 1794*. Philadelphia: John McCulloch, 1795.

Breen, T. H. *The Marketplace of Revolution: How Consumer Politics Shaped American Independence*. Oxford: Oxford University Press, 2004.

Brooke, John L. "To the Quiet of the People: Revolutionary Settlements and Civil Unrest in Western Massachusetts, 1774–1789." *William and Mary Quarterly* 46 (1989): 425–62.

Brown, Richard D. "Shays's Rebellion and Its Aftermath: A View from Springfield, Massachusetts, 1787." *William and Mary Quarterly* 40 (1983): 598–615.

———. "Shays's Rebellion and the Ratification of the Federal Constitution in Massachusetts." In *Beyond Confederation: Origins of the Constitution and American National Identity*, edited by Richard Beeman, Stephen Botein, and Edward Carter, 113–27. Chapel Hill: University of North Carolina Press, 1987.

Brown, Richard Maxwell. *The South Carolina Regulators*. Cambridge, MA: Harvard University Press, 1963.

Brown, Roger H. *Redeeming the Republic: Federalists, Taxation, and the Origins of the Constitution*. Baltimore: Johns Hopkins University Press, 1993.

Browne, Stephen Howard. *Jefferson's Call for Nationhood: The First Inaugural Address*.

College Station: Texas A&M University Press, 2003.

Buck, Solon J., and Elizabeth Hawthorne Buck. *The Planting of Civilization in Western Pennsylvania*. Pittsburgh, PA: University of Pittsburgh Press, 1939.

Buel, Richard, Jr. "The Public Creditor Interest in Massachusetts Politics, 1780–86." In *In Debt to Shays: The Bicentennial of an Agrarian Rebellion*, edited by Robert A. Gross, 47–56. Charlottesville: University Press of Virginia, 1993.

Burke, Kenneth. *A Grammar of Motives*. Berkeley: University of California Press, 1945/1962.

———. *Language as Symbolic Action: Essays on Life, Literature, and Method*. Berkeley: University of California Press, 1966.

———. *A Rhetoric of Motives*. Berkeley: University of California Press, 1950/1969.

Burnard, Trevor. *Mastery, Tyranny, and Desire: Thomas Thistlewood and His Slaves in the Anglo-Jamaican World*. Chapel Hill: University of North Carolina Press, 2004.

Calloway, Colin, editor. *The American Revolution in Indian Country: Crisis and Diversity in North American Communities*. Cambridge: Cambridge University Press, 1995.

———. *The Scratch of a Pen: 1763 and the Transformation of North America*. Oxford: Oxford University Press, 2006.

———. *The World Turned Upside Down: Indian Voices from Early America*. Boston: Bedford, 1994.

Cappon, Lester J., editor. *The Adams-Jefferson Letters: The Complete Correspondence between Thomas Jefferson and Abigail & John Adams*. Chapel Hill: University of North Carolina Press, 1959/1987.

Carpenter, Thomas. *The Two Trials of John Fries, on an Indictment for Treason; together with a brief report of the trials of several other persons, for Treason and Insurrection, In the Counties of Bucks, Northampton and Montgomery, in the Circuit Court of the United States*. Philadelphia: William W. Woodward, 1800.

Chesney, Robert M. "Democratic-Republican Societies, Subversion, and the Limits of Legitimate Political Dissent in the Early Republic." *North Carolina Law Review* 82 (2004): 1525–79.

Cicero, *De Oratore*. In *Cicero on Oratory and Orators*, edited and translated by S. Watson. Carbondale: Southern Illinois University Press, 1970.

Clark, Christopher. "Economics and Culture: Opening Up the Rural History of the Early American Northeast." *American Quarterly* 43 (1991): 279–301.

———. *The Roots of Rural Capitalism: Western Massachusetts, 1780–1860*. Ithaca, NY: Cornell University Press, 1990.

———. "Rural America and the Transition to Capitalism." In *Wages of Independence:*

Capitalism in the Early American Republic, edited by Paul A. Gilje, 65–79. Madison, WI: Madison House, 1997.

Cmiel, Kenneth. *Democratic Eloquence: The Fight over Popular Speech in Nineteenth-Century America*. New York: W. Morrow, 1990.

Cogliano, Francis D. *No King, No Popery: Anti-Catholicism in Revolutionary New-England*. Westport, CT: Greenwood Press, 1995.

Cohen, Daniel. *Pillars of Salt, Monuments of Grace: New England Crime Literature and the Origins of American Popular Culture, 1674–1860*. Oxford: Oxford University Press, 1993.

Cohen, Lester. *The Revolutionary Histories: Contemporary Narratives of the American Revolution*. Ithaca, NY: Cornell University Press, 1980.

Colley, Linda. *Captives: Britain, Empire, and the World, 1600–1850*. New York: Anchor Books, 2002.

Commager, Henry Steele, and Richard B. Morris, editors. *The Spirit of '76: The Story of the American Revolution as Told by Participants*. New York: Da Capo Press, 1995.

Conley, Thomas M. *Rhetoric in the European Tradition*. Chicago: University of Chicago Press, 1994.

Cornell, Saul. "Aristocracy Assailed." *Journal of American History* 76 (1989–1990): 1148–72.

———. *The Other Founders: Anti-Federalism and the Dissenting Tradition in America, 1788–1828*. Chapel Hill: University of North Carolina Press, 1999.

Curti, Merle. *The Roots of American Loyalty*. New York: Russell & Russell, 1946/1967.

Darsey, James. *The Prophetic Tradition and Radical Rhetoric in America*. New York: NYU Press, 1997.

Davis, Jeffrey A. "Guarding the Republican Interest: The Western Pennsylvania Democratic Societies and the Excise Tax." *Pennsylvania History* 67 (2000): 43–62.

Davis, W. W. H. *The Fries Rebellion 1798–99: An Armed Resistance to the House Tax Law, Passed by Congress, July 9, 1798, in Bucks and Northampton Counties, Pennsylvania*. Doylestown, PA: Doylestown Publishing Company, 1899.

Deneen, Patrick J. *Democratic Faith*. Princeton, NJ: Princeton University Press, 2005.

Douglass, Elisha P. *Rebels and Democrats: The Struggle for Equal Political Rights during the American Revolution*. Chapel Hill: University of North Carolina Press, 1955.

Edling, Max M. *A Revolution in Favor of Government: Origins of the U.S. Constitution and the Making of the American State*. Oxford: Oxford University Press, 2003.

Edling, Max M., and Mark D. Kaplanoff. "Alexander Hamilton's Fiscal Reform: Transforming the Structure of Taxation in the Early Republic." *William and Mary Quarterly* 61 (2004): 713–44.

Elkins, Stanley, and Eric McKitrick. *The Age of Federalism: The Early American Republic, 1788–1800*. New York: Oxford University Press, 1993.

Ellis, Joseph J. *Founding Brothers: The Revolutionary Generation*. New York: Vintage, 2000.

Elsmere, Jane Shaffer. "Trials of John Fries." *Pennsylvania Magazine of History and Biography* 103 (1979): 432–45.

Engels, Jeremy. "Disciplining Jefferson: The Man within the Breast and the Rhetorical Norms of Producing Order." *Rhetoric & Public Affairs* 9 (2006): 411–36.

———. "'Equipped for Murder': The Paxton Boys and 'the Spirit of Killing all Indians' in Pennsylvania, 1763–1764." *Rhetoric & Public Affairs* 8 (2005): 355–82.

———. "Friend or Foe? Naming the Enemy." *Rhetoric & Public Affairs* 12 (2009): 37–64.

———. "Reading the Riot Act: Rhetoric, Psychology, and Counter-Revolutionary Discourse in Shays's Rebellion, 1786–1787." *Quarterly Journal of Speech* 91 (2005): 63–88.

———. "Uncivil Speech: Invective and the Rhetorics of Democracy in the Early Republic," *Quarterly Journal of Speech* 95 (2009): 311–334.

Fallon, Richard H., Jr. *The Dynamic Constitution: An Introduction to American Constitutional Law*. Cambridge: Cambridge University Press, 2004.

Farrand, Max, editor. *The Records of the Federal Convention of 1787*. 4 vols. New Haven, CT: Yale University Press, 1911.

Farrell, James M. "Fisher Ames and Political Judgment: Reason, Passion, and Vehement Style in the Jay Treaty Speech." *Quarterly Journal of Speech* 76 (1990): 415–34.

Ferguson, E. James. *The Power of the Purse: A History of American Public Finance, 1776–1790*. Chapel Hill: University of North Carolina Press, 1961.

Ferguson, Robert A. *The American Enlightenment, 1750–1820*. Cambridge, MA: Harvard University Press, 1997.

———. "The Commonalities of *Common Sense*." *William and Mary Quarterly* 57 (2000): 465–504.

Fetter, Frank Whitson. "The Revision of the Declaration of Independence in 1941." *William and Mary Quarterly* 31 (1974): 133–38.

Findley, William. *History of the Insurrection in the Four Western Counties of Pennsylvania in the Year* MDCCXCIV. *With a Recital of the Circumstances Specially Connected Therewith*. Philadelphia: Samuel Harrison Smith, 1796.

Fisher, David Hackett. *Liberty and Freedom: A Visual History of America's Founding Ideals*. Oxford: Oxford University Press, 2005.

Fisher, Philip. "Democratic Social Space: Whitman, Melville, and the Promise of American Transparency." *Representations* 24 (1988): 60–101.

Fleming, Thomas. *Duel: Alexander Hamilton, Aaron Burr, and the Future of America.* New York: Basic Books, 2000.

Fliegelman, Jay. *Declaring Independence: Jefferson, Natural Language, and the Culture of Performance.* Stanford, CA: Stanford University Press, 1993.

———. *Prodigals and Pilgrims: The American Revolution against Patriarchal Authority, 1750–1800.* Cambridge: Cambridge University Press, 1982.

Foner, Eric. *Tom Paine and Revolutionary America.* Oxford: Oxford University Press, 1976/2005.

Foner, Philip S., editor. *The Democratic-Republican Societies, 1790–1800: A Documentary Sourcebook of Constitutions, Declarations, Addresses, Resolutions, and Toasts.* Westport, CT: Greenwood Press, 1976.

———, editor. *We, the Other People: Alternative Declarations of Independence by Labor Groups, Farmers, Woman's Rights Advocates, Socialists, and Blacks, 1829–1975.* Urbana: University of Illinois Press, 1976.

Ford, Worthington Chauncey, editor. *Journals of the Continental Congress, 1774–1789.* 34 vols. Washington: Government Printing Office, 1906.

———, editor. *Statesman and Friend: Correspondence of John Adams with Benjamin Waterhouse, 1784–1822.* Boston: Little, Brown & Co., 1927.

Foucault, Michel. *Discipline and Punish: The Birth of the Prison.* Translated by Alan Sheridan. New York: Vintage, 1975/1995.

———. *Madness and Civilization: A History of Insanity in the Age of Reason.* Translated by Richard Howard. New York: Vintage, 1961/1988.

———. *"Society Must Be Defended": Lectures at the Collège de France, 1975–1976.* Translated by David Macey. New York: Picador, 2003.

Fowler, William M. *Jack Tars and Commodores: The American Navy, 1783–1815.* Boston: Houghton Mifflin, 1984.

Franklin, Benjamin. *Writings.* Edited by J. A. Leo Lemay, Library of America Series. New York: Literary Classics of the U.S., 1987.

Freeman, Joanne B. *Affairs of Honor: National Politics in the New Republic.* New Haven, CT: Yale University Press, 2001.

Frey, Sylvia R. *Water from the Rock: Black Resistance in a Revolutionary Age.* Princeton, NJ: Princeton University Press, 1991.

Garsten, Bryan. *Saving Persuasion: A Defense of Rhetoric and Judgment.* Cambridge, MA: Harvard University Press, 2006.

Gilje, Paul. *The Road to Mobocracy: Popular Disorder in New York City, 1763–1834.* Chapel Hill: University of North Carolina Press, 1987.

Gillespie, Michael, and Michael Lienesch. *Ratifying the Constitution*. Lawrence: University of Kansas Press, 1989.

Gimbel, Richard. *Thomas Paine: A Bibliographic Check List of Common Sense, with an Account of Its Publication*. New Haven, CT: Yale University Press, 1956.

Goodale, Gregory S. "America's Rhetorical Revolution: Defining Citizens in Benjamin Rush's Philadelphia, 1783–1813." Ph.D. dissertation, University of Illinois, Urbana-Champaign, 2007.

Graymont, Barbara. *The Iroquois in the American Revolution*. Syracuse, NY: Syracuse University Press, 1972.

Greene, Jack P. *Peripheries and Center: Constitutional Development in the Extended Polities of the British Empire and the United States, 1607–1788*. New York: W.W. Norton & Co., 1986/1990.

Gross, Robert. "White Hats and Hemlocks: Daniel Shays and the Legacy of the Revolution." In *The Transforming Hand of Revolution: Reconsidering the American Revolution as a Social Movement*, edited by Ronald Hoffman and Peter J. Albert, 286–345. Charlottesville: University Press of Virginia, 1996.

Gummere, Richard. *The American Colonial Mind and the Classical Tradition*. Cambridge, MA: Harvard University Press, 1963.

Gustafson, Sandra M. *Eloquence Is Power: Oratory and Performance in Early America*. Chapel Hill: University of North Carolina Press, 2000.

Hagan, Kenneth J. *This People's Navy: The Making of American Sea Power*. New York: The Free Press, 1991.

Hamilton, Alexander. *The Papers of Alexander Hamilton*. Edited by Harold C. Syrett. New York: Columbia University Press, 1961–1987.

———. *Writings*. Edited by Joanne B. Freeman. Library of America Series. New York: Literary Classics of the U.S., 2001.

Hariman, Robert. *Political Style: The Artistry of Power*. Chicago: University of Chicago Press, 1995.

Harper, E. Eugene. *The Transformation of Western Pennsylvania, 1770–1800*. Pittsburgh, PA: University of Pittsburgh Press, 1991.

Hartnett, Stephen John. *Democratic Dissent and the Cultural Fictions of Antebellum America*. Urbana: University of Illinois Press, 2002.

Hartnett, Stephen John, and Jennifer Rose Mercieca. "'Has Your Courage Rusted?' National Security and the Contested Rhetorical Norms of Republicanism in Post-Revolutionary America, 1798–1801." *Rhetoric & Public Affairs* 9 (2006): 79–112.

Hatzenbuehler, Ronald L., and Robert L. Ivie. *Congress Declares War: Rhetoric, Leadership, and Partisanship in the Early Republic.* Kent, OH: Kent State University Press, 1983.

Hayes, Kevin J. "How Thomas Jefferson Read the Qur'ân." *Early American Literature* 39 (2004): 247–62.

Hendrickson, David C. *Peace Pact: The Lost World of the American Founding.* Lawrence: University of Kansas Press, 2003.

Hinderaker, Eric. *Elusive Empires: Constructing Colonialism in the Ohio Valley, 1673–1800.* Cambridge: Cambridge University Press, 1997.

Hobbes, Thomas. *Leviathan.* Edited by C. B. Macpherson. New York: Penguin, 1651/1985.

———. *Man and Citizen.* Edited by Bernard Gert. Indianapolis, IN: Hackett Publishing Co., 1998.

Hoffman, David C. "Paine and Prejudice: Rhetorical Leadership through Perceptual Framing in *Common Sense*." *Rhetoric & Public Affairs* 9 (2006): 373–410.

Hogan, J. Michael, and Glen Williams. "Defining 'the Enemy' in Revolutionary America: From the Rhetoric of Protest to the Rhetoric of War," *Southern Communication Journal* 61 (1996): 277–288.

Holton, Woody. *Forced Founders: Indians, Debtors, Slaves, and the Making of the American Revolution in Virginia.* Chapel Hill: University of North Carolina Press, 1999.

———. "'From the Labours of Others': The War Bonds Controversy and the Origins of the Federal Constitution in New England." *William and Mary Quarterly* 61 (2004): 271–316.

———. "'Rebel against Rebel': Enslaved Virginians and the Coming of the American Revolution." *Virginia Magazine of History and Biography* 105 (1997): 157–92.

———. *Unruly Americans and the Origins of the Constitution.* New York: Hill and Wang, 2007.

Horsman, Reginald. *Expansion and American Indian Policy, 1783–1812.* Norman: University of Oklahoma Press, 1967/1992.

Hume, David. *A Treatise of Human Nature.* Edited by L. A. Selby-Bigge. Oxford: Clarendon Press, 1739–40/1978.

Humphreys, David, Joel Barlow, John Trumbull, and Lemuel Hopkins. *The Anarchiad: A New England Poem, 1786–87.* Edited by Luther G. Riggs and Thomas H. Pease. New Haven, CT: T.H. Pease, 1861.

Ivie, Robert. L. *Democracy and America's War on Terror.* Tuscaloosa: University of Alabama Press, 2005.

———. "Images of Savagery in American Justifications for War." *Communication Monographs* 47 (1980): 279–94.

Jasinski, James. "Rhetoric and Judgment in the Constitutional Ratification Debate of

1787–1788: An Exploration in the Relationship between Theory and Critical Practice." *Quarterly Journal of Speech* 78 (1992): 197–218.

Jefferson, Thomas. *Notes on the State of Virginia*. Edited by William Peden. Chapel Hill: University of North Carolina Press, 1785/1982.

———. *The Papers of Thomas Jefferson*. Edited by J. P Boyd, C. T. Cullen, J. Catanzariti, and B. B. Oberg. 32 vols. Princeton, N.J.: Princeton University Press, 1950–present.

———. *Writings*. Edited by Merrill D. Peterson. Library of America Series. New York: Literary Classics of the U.S., 1984.

Jennings, Francis. *Empire of Fortune: Crowns, Colonies, and Tribes in the Seven Years War in America*. New York: W.W. Norton & Co., 1988.

Jensen, Merrill, editor. *Documentary History of the Ratification of the Constitution*. Madison: State Historical Society of Wisconsin, 1976.

Jones, Dorothy V. *License for Empire: Colonialism by Treaty in Early America*. Chicago: University of Chicago Press, 1982.

Jordan, Winthrop D. "Familial Politics: Thomas Paine and the Killing of the King, 1776." *Journal of American History* 60 (1973): 294–308.

Jürgen Habermas. *Communication and the Evolution of Society*. Translated by Thomas McCarthy. Boston: Beacon Press, 1976/1979.

———. *Legitimation Crisis*. Cambridge: Polity Press, 1973/1997.

———. *The Structural Transformation of the Public Sphere: An Inquiry into a Category of Bourgeois Society*. Translated by Thomas Burger. Cambridge, MA: MIT Press, 1962/1999.

———. *The Theory of Communicative Action*. Translated by Thomas McCarthy. 2 vols. Boston: Beacon Press, 1984.

Kagan, Robert. *Dangerous Nation: America's Place in the World from Its Earliest Days to the Dawn of the Twentieth Century*. New York: Alfred A. Knopf, 2006.

Kammen, Michael. *A Machine That Would Go of Itself: The Constitution in American Culture*. New York: Alfred A. Knopf, 1986.

Kant, Immanuel. "Answer to the Question: What is Enlightenment?" (1784). In *Basic Writings of Kant*, edited by Allen W. Wood, 133–41. New York: The Modern Library, 2001.

Kars, Marjoleine. *Breaking Loose Together: The Regulator Rebellion in Pre-Revolutionary North Carolina*. Chapel Hill: University of North Carolina Press, 2002.

Keane, John. *Tom Paine: A Political Life*. New York: Little, Brown & Co., 1995.

Keegan, John. *The Face of Battle*. New York: Penguin, 1978.

Ketchum, Richard M. *Decisive Day: The Battle for Bunker Hill*. New York: Doubleday,

1991.

———. *Saratoga: Turning Point of America's Revolutionary War.* New York: H. Holt, 1997.

Klein, Rachel N. *Unification of a Slave State: The Rise of the Planter Class in the South Carolina Backcountry, 1760–1808.* Chapel Hill: University of North Carolina Press, 1990.

Kohn, Richard H. *Eagle and Sword: The Federalists and the Creation of the Military Establishment in America, 1783–1802.* New York: The Free Press, 1975.

Koschnik, Albrecht. "The Democratic Societies of Philadelphia and the Limits of the American Public Sphere, circa 1793–1795." *William and Mary Quarterly* 58 (2001): 615–36.

Kramnick, Isaac. "The Great National Discussion: The Discourse of Politics in 1787." *William and Mary Quarterly* 45 (1988): 1–32.

Kramnick, Isaac, and R. Lawrence Moore. *The Godless Constitution: A Moral Defense of the Secular State.* New York: W.W. Norton & Co., 1996/2005.

Laclau, Ernesto. *On Populist Reason.* London: Verso, 2005.

Lamy, Bernard. *The Art of Speaking* (1676). In *The Rhetorics of Thomas Hobbes and Bernard Lamy,* edited by John Harwood. Carbondale: Southern Illinois University Press, 1676/1986.

Larkin, Edward. "Inventing an American Public: Thomas Paine, the *Pennsylvania Magazine,* and American Revolutionary Political Discourse." *Early American Literature* 33 (1998): 250–76.

———. *Thomas Paine and the Literature of Revolution* (Cambridge: Cambridge University Press, 2005).

Lepore, Jill. *A is for American: Letters and Other Characters in the Newly United States.* New York: Alfred A. Knopf, 2002.

———. *In the Name of War: King Philip's War and the Origins of American Identity.* New York: Alfred A. Knopf, 1998.

Lewis, James. "Savages of the Seas: Barbary Captivity Tales and Images of Muslims in the Early Republic." *Journal of American Culture* 13 (1990): 75–84.

Liell, Scott. *46 Pages: Thomas Paine, Common Sense, and the Turning Point to Independence.* Philadelphia: Running Press, 2003.

Lienesch, Michael. *New Order for the Ages: Time, the Constitution, and the Making of Modern American Political Thought.* Princeton, NJ: Princeton University Press, 1988.

The Life of Mahomet; or, the History of that Imposture, which was Begun, Carried on, and Finally Established by Him in Arabia; and Which has Subjugated a Larger Portion of the Globe, Than the Religion of Jesus Has Yet Set at Liberty. To Which is Added, an Account of Egypt. London: Printed for the Booksellers, 1799.

Linebaugh, Peter. *The London Hanged: Crime and Civil Society in the Eighteenth Century.* Cambridge: Cambridge University Press, 1991.

Linebaugh, Peter, and Marcus Rediker. *The Many-Headed Hydra: Sailors, Slaves, Commoners, and the Hidden History of the Revolutionary Atlantic.* Boston: Beacon Press, 2000.

Link, Eugene P. *The Democratic-Republican Societies, 1790–1800.* New York: Columbia University Press, 1942.

Locke, John. *An Essay Concerning Human Understanding.* Edited by Alexander Campbell Fraser. 2 vols. New York: Dover Publications, 1690/1959.

———. *Second Treatise of Government.* Edited by Richard H. Cox. Wheeling, IL: Harlan Davidson, 1689/1982.

Lockwood, John H. *Westfield and Its Historic Influences, 1669–1919: The Life of an Early Town, with a Survey of Events in New England and Bordering Regions to Which It Was Related in Colonial and Revolutionary Times.* Springfield, MA: Springfield Binding Co., 1922.

Loewen, James W. *Lies across America: What Our Historic Sites Get Wrong.* New York: Touchstone, 2000.

Looby, Christopher. *Voicing America: Language, Literary Form, and the Origins of the United States.* Chicago: University of Chicago Press, 1996.

Loughran, Trish. "Disseminating *Common Sense*: Thomas Paine and the Problem of the Early National Bestseller." *American Literature* 78 (2006): 1–28.

Lucas, Stephen E. "Justifying America: The Declaration of Independence as a Rhetorical Document." In *American Rhetoric: Context and Criticism*, edited by Thomas W. Benson, 67–130. Carbondale: Southern Illinois University Press, 1989.

———. *Portents of Rebellion: Rhetoric and Revolution in Philadelphia, 1765–76.* Philadelphia: Temple University Press, 1976.

MacCannell, Dean. *The Tourist: A New Theory of the Leisure Class.* Berkeley: University of California Press, 1976/1999.

Machiavelli, Niccolò. *The Art of War.* Edited by Neal Wood. Cambridge, MA: Da Capo Press, 1521/2001.

———. *Discourses of Livy.* Translated by Ninian Hill Thomson. New York: Barnes & Noble, 1531/2005.

Madison, James, Alexander Hamilton, and John Jay. *The Federalist.* Introduction and notes by Robert A. Ferguson. New York: Barnes & Noble Classics, 2006.

Maier, Pauline. *American Scripture: Making the Declaration of Independence.* New York: Alfred A. Knopf, 1997.

Manning, William. *The Key of Libberty: Shewing the Causes Why a Free Government Has Always Failed and a Remedy against It. Addressed to the Republicans, Farmers, Mechanics, and Labourers in America by a Labourer.* In *The Key of Liberty: The Life and Democratic Writings of William Manning, "A Laborer," 1747–1814,* edited by Michael Merrill and Sean Wilentz. Cambridge, MA: Harvard University Press, 1799/1993.

Manolescu, Beth Innocenti. "Style and Spectator Judgment in Fisher Ames's Jay Treaty Speech." *Quarterly Journal of Speech* 84 (1998): 62–79.

Marshall, John. *The Life of George Washington, Commander in Chief of the American Forces, During the War Which Established the Independence of his Country, and First President of the United States.* 5 vols. Philadelphia: G. P. Wayne, 1804.

Martin, James Kirby. "The Return of the Paxton Boys and the Historical State of the Pennsylvania Frontier, 1764–1774." *Pennsylvania History* 38 (1971): 117–33.

Martinich, A. P. *Hobbes: A Biography.* New York: Cambridge University Press, 1999.

Masur, Louis P. *Rites of Execution: Capital Punishment and the Transformation of American Culture, 1776–1865.* New York: Oxford University Press, 1989.

Matthews, Richard K. *If Men Were Angels: James Madison and the Heartless Empire of Reason.* Lawrence: University Press of Kansas, 1995.

———. *The Radical Politics of Thomas Jefferson: A Revisionist View.* Lawrence: University of Kansas Press, 1984.

McCarthy, Timothy Patrick, and John McMillian, editors. *The Radical Reader: A Documentary History of the American Radical Tradition.* New York: The New Press, 2003.

McCoy, Drew. *The Elusive Republic: Political Economy in Jeffersonian America.* Chapel Hill: University of North Carolina Press, 1980.

Meranze, Michael. *Laboratories of Virtue: Punishment, Revolution, and Authority in Philadelphia, 1760–1835.* Chapel Hill: University of North Carolina Press, 1996.

Mercieca, Jennifer R. "The Culture of Honor: How Slaveholders Responded to the Abolitionist Mail Crisis of 1835." *Rhetoric & Public Affairs* 10 (2007): 51–76.

Mercieca, Jennifer R., and James Arnt Aune. "A Vernacular Republican Rhetoric: William Manning's *Key of Libberty.*" *Quarterly Journal of Speech* 91 (2005): 119–43.

Merk, Frederick. *Manifest Destiny and Mission in American History: A Reinterpretation.* New York: Alfred A. Knopf, 1963.

Miller, Perry. *Errand into the Wilderness.* Cambridge, MA: Belknap Press of Harvard University Press, 1956/1984.

Minot, George Richards. *The History of the Insurrections, in Massachusetts, In the Year* MDCCLXXXVI, *and the Rebellion Consequent Thereon.* Worcester, MA: Isaiah Thomas, 1788.

Montesquieu, baron de. *The Spirit of Laws.* 2 vols. London: J. Nourse and P. Vaillant, 1748/1752.

More, Thomas. *Utopia.* Translated by Paul Turner. New York: Vintage, 1516/1986.

Mutch, Robert. "Yeoman and Merchant in Pre-Industrial America: Eighteenth Century Massachusetts as a Case Study." *Societas* 7 (1977): 279–302.

Nash, Gary B. *The Unknown American Revolution: The Unruly Birth of Democracy and the Struggle to Create America.* New York: Viking, 2005.

Nash, Gary B., and Jean R. Soderlund. *Freedom by Degrees: Emancipation in Pennsylvania and Its Aftermath.* New York: Oxford University Press, 1991.

Newman, Paul Douglas. *Fries's Rebellion: The Enduring Struggle for the American Revolution.* Philadelphia: University of Pennsylvania Press, 2004.

Olson, Alison. "The Pamphlet War over the Paxton Boys." *Pennsylvania Magazine of History and Biography* 123 (1999): 31–55.

Olson, Lester C. *Benjamin Franklin's Vision of American Community: A Study in Rhetorical Iconology.* Columbia: University of South Carolina Press, 2004.

Onuf, Peter S. *Jefferson's Empire: The Language of American Nationhood.* Charlottesville: University of Virginia Press, 2000.

———. *The Origins of the Federal Republic: Jurisdictional Controversies in the United States, 1775–1787.* Philadelphia: University of Pennsylvania Press, 1983.

Pagden, Anthony. *Lords of All the World: Ideologies of Empire in Spain, Britain, and France c. 1500–1800.* New Haven, CT: Yale University Press, 1995.

Paine, Thomas. *The Complete Writings of Thomas Paine.* Edited by Philip S. Foner. 2 vols. New York: The Citadel Press, 1945.

———. *The Thomas Paine Reader.* Edited by Michael Foot and Isaac Kramnick. New York: Penguin, 1987.

Pearce, Roy Harvey. *Savagism and Civilization: A Study of the Indian in the American Mind.* Baltimore: The Johns Hopkins Press, 1953/1967.

The People the Best Governors: or a Plan of Government Founded on the just Principles of Natural Freedom. No publisher, 1776.

Perkins, Edwin J. *American Public Finance and Financial Services, 1700–1815.* Columbus: Ohio State University Press, 1994.

Peterson, Merrill D. *The Jefferson Image in the American Mind.* Charlottesville: Thomas Jefferson Memorial Foundation and the University Press of Virginia, 1998.

Plato. *Gorgias.* Translated by Walter Hamilton. New York: Penguin, 1960.

Pocock, J. G. A. *The Machiavellian Moment: Florentine Political Thought and the Atlantic Republican Tradition.* Princeton, NJ: Princeton University Press, 1975/2003.

Quarles, Benjamin. *The Negro in the American Revolution.* Chapel Hill: University of North Carolina Press, 1961.

Quintilian. *De Institutione Oratoria.* Reprinted as *Quintilian's Institutes of Oratory: Or, Education of an Orator,* translated by John Selby Watson. London: George Bell & Sons, 1892.

Rakove, Jack. N. *Original Meanings: Politics and Ideas in the Making of the Constitution.* New York: Vintage, 1997.

Ramsay, David. *The History of the American Revolution.* Philadelphia: R. Aitken & Son, 1789.

Raphael, Ray. *Founding Myths: Stories That Hide Our Patriotic Past.* New York: W.W. Norton & Co., 2004.

———. *A People's History of the American Revolution: How Common People Shaped the Fight for Independence.* New York: Perennial, 2002.

Rathbun, Lyon. "The Ciceronian Rhetoric of John Quincy Adams." *Rhetorica* 18 (2000): 175–215.

Reid, Ronald F. "New England Rhetoric and the French War, 1754–1760: A Case Study in the Rhetoric of War." *Communication Monographs* 43 (1976): 259–86.

Reinhold, Meyer. *Classica Americana: The Greek and Roman Heritage in the United States.* Detroit: Wayne State University Press, 1984.

———, editor. *The Classick Pages: Classical Reading of Eighteenth-Century Americans.* University Park: Pennsylvania State University Press, 1975.

Richards, Carl J. *The Founders and the Classics: Greece, Rome, and the American Enlightenment.* Cambridge, MA: Harvard University Press, 1994.

Richards, Leonard. *Shays's Rebellion: The American Revolution's Final Battle.* Philadelphia: University of Pennsylvania Press, 2002.

Riley, Stephen T. "Dr. William Whiting and Shays' Rebellion." *Proceedings of the American Antiquarian Society* 66 (1956): 119–66.

Robertson, Lindsay Gordon. *Conquest by Law: How the Discovery of America Dispossessed Indigenous Peoples of Their Lands.* Oxford: Oxford University Press, 2005.

Robin, Corey. *Fear: The History of a Political Idea.* Oxford: Oxford University Press, 2004.

Rohrbough, Malcolm J. *The Trans-Appalachian Frontier: People, Societies, and Institutions, 1775–1850.* New York: Oxford University Press, 1978.

Rollins, Richard M. "Words as Social Control: Noah Webster and the Creation of the

American Dictionary." *American Quarterly* 28 (1976): 415–30.

Rorabaugh, W. J. *The Alcoholic Republic: An American Tradition.* New York: Oxford University Press, 1979.

Rothschild, Emma. *Economic Sentiments: Adam Smith, Condorcet, and the Enlightenment.* Cambridge, MA: Harvard University Press, 2001.

Rudolph, Frederick, editor. *Essays on Education in the Early Republic.* Cambridge, MA: Harvard University Press, 1965.

Rush, Benjamin. "Address to the people of the united states." *The American Museum,* January 1787.

———. *Essays, Literary, Moral & Philosophical.* Philadelphia: Thomas and Samuel F. Bradford, 1798.

———. *Letters of Benjamin Rush.* Edited by L. H. Butterfield. 2 vols. Princeton, NJ: Princeton University Press, 1951.

———. *Medical Inquiries and Other Observations.* 2nd American edition, 2 vols. Philadelphia: Thomas Dobson, 1794.

Said, Edward. *Orientalism.* New York: Pantheon, 1978.

Saxton, Alexander. *The Rise and Fall of the White Republic: Class Politics and Mass Culture in Nineteenth-Century America.* London: Verso, 1990/2003.

Schudson, Michael. *The Good Citizen: A History of American Civic Life.* Cambridge, MA: Harvard University Press, 1998.

A Selection of the Patriotic Addresses, to the President of the United States. Together with The President's Answers. Boston: John W. Folsom, 1798.

Selsam, J. Paul. *The Pennsylvania Constitution of 1776: A Study in Revolutionary Democracy.* New York: Octagon Books, 1971.

Sha'ban, Fuad. *Islam and Arabs in Early American Thought: The Roots of Orientalism in America.* Durham, NC: Acorn Press, 1991.

Shaw, Peter. *American Patriots and the Rituals of Revolution.* Cambridge, MA: Harvard University Press, 1981.

Sheehan, Bernard W. *Seeds of Extinction: Jeffersonian Philanthropy and the American Indian.* Chapel Hill: University of North Carolina Press, 1973.

Slaughter, Thomas P. *The Whiskey Rebellion: Frontier Epilogue to the American Revolution.* Oxford: Oxford University Press, 1986.

Sloan, Herbert. "'The Earth Belongs in Usufruct to the Living.'" In *Jeffersonian Legacies,* edited by Peter S. Onuf, 281–315. Charlottesville: University of Virginia Press, 1993.

Slotkin, Richard. *Regeneration through Violence: The Mythology of the American Frontier, 1600–1860.* Middletown, CT: Wesleyan University Press, 1973.

Smith, Adam. *The Wealth of Nations*. Edited by Edwin Cannan. New York: The Modern Library, 1776/2000.

Smith, Craig R. "The Aliens Are Coming: The Federalist Attack on the First Amendment." In *Who Belongs in America? Presidents, Rhetoric, and Immigration*, edited by Vanessa B. Beasley, 37–60. College Station: Texas A&M University Press, 2006.

Smith, Henry Nash. *Virgin Land: The American West as Symbol and Myth*. New York: Random House, 1950.

Smith, James Morton. *Freedom's Fetters: The Alien and Sedition Laws and American Civil Liberties*. Ithaca, NY: Cornell University Press, 1956.

Smith, Kimberly. *The Dominion of Voice: Riot, Reason, and Romance in American Politics*. Lawrence: University of Kansas Press, 1999.

Smith, Wilson. *Theories of Education in Early America, 1655–1819*. Indianapolis, IN: Bobbs-Merrill, 1973.

St. George, Robert Blair. *Conversing by Signs: Poetics of Implication in Colonial New England Culture*. Chapel Hill: University of North Carolina Press, 1998.

Starkey, Marion. *A Little Rebellion*. New York: Alfred A. Knopf, 1955.

Stone, Geoffrey R. *Perilous Times: Free Speech in Wartime from the Sedition Act of 1798 to the War on Terrorism*. New York: W.W. Norton & Co., 2004.

Storing, Herbert J., editor. *The Complete Anti-Federalist*. 7 vols. Chicago: University of Chicago Press, 1981.

Sword, Wiley. *President Washington's Indian War: The Struggle for the Old Northwest, 1790–1795*. Norman: University of Oklahoma Press, 1985.

Szatmary, David P. *Shays' Rebellion: The Making of an Agrarian Insurrection*. Amherst: University of Massachusetts Press, 1980.

Takaki, Ronald. *Iron Cages: Race and Culture in 19th-Century America*. Oxford: Oxford University Press, 1979/2000.

Taylor, Charles. *Sources of the Self: The Making of Modern Identity*. Cambridge, MA: Harvard University Press, 1989.

Taylor, Robert J. *Western Massachusetts in the Revolution*. Providence: Brown University Press, 1954.

———, editor. *Massachusetts: Colony to Commonwealth: Documents on the Formation of Its Constitution, 1775–1780*. Chapel Hill: University of North Carolina Press, 1961.

Tchen, John Kuo Wei. *New York before Chinatown: Orientalism and the Shaping of American Culture, 1776–1882*. Baltimore: Johns Hopkins University Press, 1999.

Thompson, E. P. "The Moral Economy of the English Crowd in the Eighteenth Century." *Past & Present* 50 (1971): 76–136.

Tocqueville, Alexis de. *Democracy in America*. Translated by Harvey C. Mansfield and
    Delba Winthrop. Chicago: University of Chicago Press, 1835/2000.
Travers, Len. *Celebrating the Fourth: Independence Day and the Rites of Nationalism in the
    Early Republic*. Amherst: University of Massachusetts Press, 1997.
Trees, Andrew S. *The Founding Fathers and the Politics of Character*. Princeton, NJ: Princ-
    eton University Press, 2004.
Turner, James. *Without God, without Creed: The Origins of Unbelief in America*. Balti-
    more: Johns Hopkins University Press, 1985.
Vattel, Emerich de. *The Law of Nations; or, Principles of the Law of Nature, Applied to the
    Conduct and Affairs of Nations and Sovereigns*. Translated by Joseph Chitty. Phila-
    delphia: T. & J.W. Johnson & Co., 1758/1867.
Vaughan, Alden T. "'Expulsion of the Savages': English Policy and the Virginia Massacre
    of 1622." *William and Mary Quarterly* 35 (1978): 57–84.
———. "Frontier Banditti and the Indians: The Paxton Boys' Legacy, 1763–1775." *Pennsyl-
    vania History* 51 (1984): 1–29.
Waldstreicher, David. *In the Midst of Perpetual Fetes: The Making of American National-
    ism, 1776–1820*. Chapel Hill: University of North Carolina Press, 1997.
Walker, David. *Appeal to the Coloured Citizens of the World*. Edited by Peter P. Hinks.
    University Park, PA: Penn State University Press, 1829/2003.
Walker, Jeffrey. *Rhetoric and Poetics in Antiquity*. Oxford: Oxford University Press, 2000.
Warner, Michael. *The Letters of the Republic: Publication and the Public Sphere in Eigh-
    teenth-Century America*. Cambridge, MA: Harvard University Press, 1990.
Warren, Charles. "Fourth of July Myths." *William and Mary Quarterly* 2 (1945): 237–72.
Warren, John. *An Oration, Delivered July 4th, 1783, at the Request of the Inhabitants of
    the Town of Boston; in Celebration of the Anniversary of American Independence*.
    Boston: John Gill, 1783.
Warren, Marcy Otis. *History of the Rise, Progress and Termination of the American Revolu-
    tion. Interspersed with Biographical, Political and Moral Observations*. 2 vols. Boston:
    Manning and Loring, 1805.
Washington, George. *The Papers of George Washington: Confederation Series*. Edited by W.
    W. Abbott. 6 vols. Charlottesville: University Press of Virginia, 1995.
Watts, Steven. *The Republic Reborn: War and the Making of Liberal America, 1790–1820*.
    Baltimore: Johns Hopkins University Press, 1987.
Webster, Noah. *Dissertations on the English Language: with Notes, Historical and Criti-
    cal, To Which is added, by way of Appendix, an Essay on a Reformed Mode of Spell-
    ing, with Dr. Franklin's Arguments on that Subject*. Boston: Isaiah Thomas and

Company, 1789.

———. *An Oration Pronounced Before the Citizens of New Haven on the Anniversary of the Independence of the United States, July 4th, 1798; and Published at Their Request.* New Haven, CT: T. and S. Green, 1798.

Whipple, A. B. C. *To the Shores of Tripoli: The Birth of the U.S. Navy and Marines.* New York: William Morrow and Company, 1991.

White, Richard. *The Middle Ground: Indians, Empires, and Republics in the Great Lakes Region, 1650–1815.* Cambridge: Cambridge University Press, 1991.

Wilentz, Sean. *The Rise of American Democracy: Jefferson to Lincoln.* New York: W.W. Norton & Co., 2005.

Williams, Basil. *The Whig Supremacy, 1714–1760.* Oxford: Oxford University Press, 1939/1962.

Williams, Robert A., Jr. *Linking Arms Together: American Indian Treaty Visions of Law and Peace, 1600–1800.* New York: Oxford University Press, 1997.

Wills, Garry. *Inventing America: Jefferson's Declaration of Independence.* Garden City, NY: Doubleday, 1978.

———. *"Negro President": Jefferson and the Slave Power.* Boston: Mariner Books, 2003/2005.

Witherspoon, John. *Lectures on Moral Philosophy, and Eloquence.* Philadelphia: William W. Woodward, 1810.

Wood, Ellen Meiksins. *Empire of Capital.* London: Verso, 2003.

Wood, Gordon S. *The Creation of the American Republic, 1776–1787.* Chapel Hill: University of North Carolina Press, 1969/1998.

———. *The Radicalism of the American Revolution.* New York: Vintage, 1991.

Wood, Peter H. "'The Dream Deferred': Black Struggles on the Eve of White Independence." In *In Resistance: Studies in African, Caribbean, and Afro-American History*, edited by Gary Y. Okihiro, 166–87. Amherst: University of Massachusetts Press, 1986.

Wood, W. J. *Battles of the Revolutionary War, 1775–1781.* Chapel Hill, NC: Algonquin Books, 1990.

Zuckerman, Michael. "Identity in British America: Unease in Eden." In *Colonial Identity in the Atlantic World, 1500–1800*, edited by Nicholas Canny and Anthony Pagden, 115–57. Princeton, NJ: Princeton University Press, 1987.

Index

disease metaphors, 100, 104

"disjunctive synthesis," 72

displacement or distraction, 26–29, 31, 129–30, 133–35, 139–40, 146, 219

Disqualification Act (Massachusetts, 1787), 79

dissent: Alien and Sedition Acts and, 183–84, 196, 202–3; American identity and opposition to, 26; Bill of Rights and, 98; coercion vs. dialogue to deal with, 28; denunciation of, 138; displacement of, 145; equated with anarchy, 97–98; Hamilton and suppression of, 107, 119, 125; military and suppression of, 82–83, 105–6, 110; Paine vs., 23, 62–65; punishing, as civic pedagogy, 106; siding with enemy, 181; state violence vs., 25; synonymous with act of war, 145; XYZ Affair and, 164–67. *See also* protest; *specific events by name*

Dissertations on Government (Paine), 72

distance, as problem for communication, 51–53

domestic or internal enemies, 96, 116, 171–72, 165, 182, 192–97, 200–202, 205, 204–5

drunkenness, democracy linked with, 108–109

Duane, William, 183, 188

Dunlap and Claypoole's American Daily Advertiser, 125–26

Dunmore, Lord, 40–42, 53, 59

E

economic conditions, 24–27, 46, 86, 97–98, 106, 117–27, 147–48, 150

education, 110, 180; army as engine for, 195–96; fear vs. virtue and, 172; national unity furthered by, 169–71; to transcend premodern life, 139

effigies, 5, 69, 113

elections, 72, 79, 98, 105, 208; of 1787, 200–201, 246–7 (n. 52); of 1796, 163, 186; of 1799, 194; of 1800, 163, 192, 194, 272 (n. 85)

emotion, 18, 139, 144–45, 159–61. *See also* passion

empire and imperialism, 18, 26, 46, 56, 129–35, 141–51, 192

enemyship, 3–4, 13–14, 48; Adams and, 166–67, 203–5; authority vs. equality and, 28; balance of liberty and safety and, 215–18; Brackenridge uses, vs. "the Indian," 129–30, 134–37; citizen resentment of state power and, 203; citizenship redefined by, 30, 171, 219–22; coercion and, 28–29, 183; in *Common Sense*, 21–23, 35, 45, 59–65; contract of blood and, 178–84; danger of domestic, 184, 191, 193–94, 198–203; democratic discourse shaped by, 62–63; desire for peace and, 166–67; dialectical aspect of, 19–20; as distraction, 28–29; elites and, 17, 28–29; and escalation, 81, 21–22, 25, 45, 59, 62, 94, 95–96, 98–99, 101–2, 104–5, 141, 145, 181, 188–90, 202; and estrangement,